CRIMSON STORM
SURGE

CRIMSON STORM
SURGE

Alabama Football Then and Now

CHRISTOPHER J. WALSH

TAYLOR TRADE PUBLISHING
Lanham • New York • Dallas • Boulder • Toronto • Oxford

To my family for putting up with me and being supportive even when
I pursued dreams that took me away from them

Published by Taylor Trade Publishing
An imprint of The Rowman & Littlefield Publishing Group, Inc.
4501 Forbes Boulevard, Suite 200, Lanham, Maryland 20706

Distributed by NATIONAL BOOK NETWORK

Library of Congress Cataloging-in-Publication Data

Walsh, Christopher J., 1968–
  Crimson storm surge : Alabama football then and now / Christopher J. Walsh.—1st
Taylor Trade Pub. ed.
    p. cm.
  Includes bibliographical references and index.
  ISBN 1-58979-279-3 (cloth : alk. paper)
  1. Alabama Crimson Tide (Football team)—History.   2. University of Alabama—
Football—History.   I. Title.
  GV958.A4W35   2005
  796.332'63'0976184—dc22   2005012417

⊗ ™ The paper used in this publication meets the minimum requirements of American
National Standard for Information Sciences—Permanence of Paper for Printed Library
Materials, ANSI/NISO Z39.48-1992.

Manufactured in the United States of America.

Contents

Introduction

*T*o try and sum up more than 100 years of University of Alabama football in a few words wouldn't begin do it justice. Nevertheless, some do stand out.

Championships. Alabama has won 12 national titles, making it the envy of nearly every other college program in the country.

Dignity. In addition to the 12 "recognized" national championships, the Official NCAA Football Records Book credits Alabama with producing national champions in 1945, 1962, 1966, 1975 and 1977, yet the Crimson Tide doesn't claim them because there is another recognized champion those years.

Domination. Despite playing in what many believe to be the toughest league in college football, the Crimson Tide has won 21 Southeastern Conference championships, far and away the most.

Tradition. Alabama has 19 former players or coaches in the College Football Hall of Fame, 91 first-team All-Americans and made a record 52 bowl appearances with 29 victories.

Excellence. Paul W. "Bear" Bryant is regarded as the best to ever coach college football. He won six national championships, 14 SEC titles and broke Alonzo Stagg's career record for victories, finishing 323-85-17, for a staggering winning percentage of .780.

Commitment, sacrifice, passion, dedication, loyalty, winning, trust, family, desire, fortitude and the three hs of honor, heart and history.

But above all else, Alabama football is about one thing: *pride.*

As they say before every home game, "This is Alabama Football . . ."

Part I

CRIMSON

Humble Beginnings

1892–1918

*I*t will probably surprise many people to discover that the University of Alabama existed for decades without football. When the federal government authorized Alabama Territory to set aside a township for the establishment of a "seminary of learning" in 1818, with inaugural ceremonies held in 1831, the game hadn't even been invented yet.

Initially, the university consisted of seven buildings and 52 students. Within six years, it would be one of the first five schools in the country to offer classes in engineering, the first of many important academic achievements.

With the specter of war looming in 1860, the university became a military school with martial departmental and disciplinary systems established. However, in the later stages of the Civil War, General Ulysses S. Grant was looking for ways to both increase his stranglehold on the South and accelerate surrender. In 1865, he dispatched General James H. Wilson to lead a cavalry raid through Alabama, with one of the first stops virtually undefended Tuscaloosa. Wilson ordered the school burned to the ground.

University cadets and local militia were unable to stop the torching but made their stand at the president's mansion, which had just been built in 1841. It was one of only seven structures to survive the attack.

Left with little more than its brief heritage during the Reconstruction Era, the university wasn't able to resume operations until 1871 with 107 students. Within a year, it would open a law school.

It wasn't until 1892—one year before the first two women enrolled at the university—that football came to Tuscaloosa.

William G. Little had been introduced to the game as a high school student at prestigious Phillips Exeter Academy in New England, but the death of his brother brought him back to Alabama to help with the family. Once enrolled, he collected a group of students to form a team that included a future Speaker of the U.S.

3

House of Representatives, state governor, state senator, judge, doctor and prominent businessmen and lawyers.

Among many items Little kept in a scrapbook was an 1892 article titled "Varsity Veteran," which included the following passage: "These games and the direction of them give young men a taste of what self-respect and manliness really are; they educate them to decide calmly under pressure, to keep a cool head in emergency. They are one of the strongest influences towards temperance in college where the 'training man' sets the standard of morals for his classmates."

The hybrid of soccer and rugby—with heavy emphasis on rugby—bore little resemblance to the game today, drawing only slightly-better comparisons to an organized riot. The first game played was on Nov. 6, 1869, between then-fierce rivals Rutgers University and Princeton. Each side had 25 players with more than 100 fans in attendance. Rutgers won 6-4 despite one of its professors pointing his umbrella at participants and yelling "you will come to no Christian end." However, it did help lead to calls for rule changes, which evolved over time.

In 1876, the first attempts at putting together a set of standard rules were made at the Massasoit convention. Walter Camp, player and coach at Yale University and considered the father of modern football, edited every rulebook until his death in 1925. Among his numerous innovations were the idea of one side potentially having undisputed possession of the ball until it gave it up or scored, the number of players on the field for each team decreased from 15 to 11, and he created the quarterback and center positions in addition to the forward pass.

Camp also standardized scoring. In 1892, the equivalent of a field goal was five points, one more than a touchdown. A goal following a touchdown was two points, as was a safety. It wasn't until 1912, eight years before the creation of the professional National Football League that a touchdown increased to six points and a field goal three.

In many ways, the game was also incredibly brutal. There was no neutral zone between teams at the line of scrimmage and few limits to what linemen could do to opposing players. Ball carriers could be picked up and thrown over the line. Gang tackling was the norm and, though extremely dangerous, most teams utilized the "Flying Wedge" formation in which teammates would link together—sometimes using a special belt equipped with handles—to form a "v" and charge into the opposition.

In 1905 alone, college football was credited with 18 deaths and 149 serious injuries. With the game at a crossroad and close to being banned, President Theodore Roosevelt, himself a fan of the sport, stepped in and during two White House conferences with collegiate athletic leaders made it clear that the game would either be reformed or abolished.

In December of that year, chancellor Henry M. MacCracken of New York University headed a meeting of 13 schools to initiate changes in football. It also led to the Intercollegiate Athletic Association of the United States (IAAUS), founded by 62 members. Within four years, it morphed into both a much stronger organization and different name, and thus the National Collegiate Athletic Association (NCAA) was born.

Alabama's uniforms that first season bore little padding, the equivalent of wearing a thick lamb's wool sweater costing $6 ($7 for a specific color) and padded pants. During the first season, Alabama either wore white with crimson stockings, with a large "U of A" on the sweater, or crimson sweaters with a white "A." No one wore shoulder pads or helmets of any kind.

With a team organized, Little was named team captain and E.B. Beaumont, who became somewhat familiar with the sport at the University of Pennsylvania, coach. Still, with football virtually unknown in the South, opponents were scarce. The "Cadets of Alabama" (the university used the military system of organization until 1903, when the Alabama Legislature finally conceded to thirty years of student protest) scheduled the Birmingham Athletic Club, a team made up of former college players from the East, but the day before essentially had a practice game against a collection of high school players from the Birmingham area. Thus, on Nov. 11, 1892, Alabama won its first game 56-0 against the self-proclaimed Birmingham High School team. It then lost 5-4 to the Birmingham Athletic Club.

Here's how a local newspaper described the winning play, a drop-kick by J.P. Ross, who had played rugby in Ireland: "Just as the Birmingham enthusiasts were beginning to despair of a victory, Ross made a clean kick of sixty-five yards which was the most brilliant feat ever witnessed in a match game. The crowd set up cheer after cheer and his admirers gathered him on their shoulders and paraded him around the grounds."

A month later, much-improved Alabama, which unlike the much-burlier club team could practice daily, came back and won the rematch 14-0. It was described as a "battle royal" and "Waterloo for Birmingham," with Beaumont called "One of the best football coaches in America."

In February of the same school year, Alabama scheduled one final game to the inaugural season, Auburn. Like the first three contests, it would be played in Birmingham, but in front of approximately 4,000 fans who were probably far more curious about the sport than any potential rivalry between the teams, though Alabama fans covered the Caldwell Hotel with red and white banners. Auburn won 32-22.

Auburn won the second meeting as well, 40-16 in Montgomery. Without many of its best players from the inaugural season lost to graduation, Alabama finished 1893 winless (0-4), including a loss to its first out-of-state opponent, Sewanee, 20-0.

The season also saw fullback and tackle Eli Abbott take over coaching responsibilities. As for Beaumont, according to the Corolla in its first year as Alabama's official yearbook: "We were unfortunate in securing a coach. After keeping him for a short time, we found that his knowledge of the game was very limited. We therefore got rid of him." It was the first of numerous coaching changes during the first two decades.

Alabama lost its 1894 opener to Mississippi 6-0, but with Abbott scoring four touchdowns at fullback came back to beat Tulane in New Orleans 18-6 in its first trip across a state line. He helped lead a 24-6 victory against Sewanee in Birmingham and scored two touchdowns as Alabama recorded its first victory against

Auburn, 18-0 in Montgomery. It also led to the school's first coaching controversy as Abbott was accused of being paid a salary, thus the equivalent of being a professional.

Abbott's final season as coach was 1895, when Alabama (0-4) lost to Georgia, Tulane, LSU and finally Auburn 48-0 in the first meeting at Tuscaloosa, and was outscored 112-12. The first three games were all played on the road, of which the two in Louisiana were just two days apart.

With Abbott continuing to play for the team, Otto Wagonhurst took over as coach in 1896 and in three games, all played in Tuscaloosa, guided Alabama to a 2-1 record, including a season-ending 20-0 victory against Mississippi A&M (now known as Mississippi State). But with the Board of Trustees concluding it was undignified for teams to play games off campus, scheduling became all but impossible. Only one game was played in 1897, 6-0 victory against the Tuscaloosa Athletic Club, and there was no team in 1898—the year of discontent.

"In reviewing our past athletic season, we find very little to be proud of," read the Corolla in 1897. In the spring of 1899, it said, "We have seen that it is useless to attempt to put out a football team so long as we are compelled to play all of our games on the campus. Doubtless there will be an effort made to induce the Board of Trustees to allow our teams to travel when they meet in June. We believe that our prospects for obtaining their consent are much brighter than they have been heretofore for several of the faculty are with us."

That fall, football returned under the direction of coach W.A. Martin, with Alabama playing three athletic clubs along with Mississippi and finishing 3-1. Again the team had to play on subsequent days, only this time on the road going 185 miles from Jackson, Mississippi to New Orleans. Noted the Corolla: "Athletics have made a greater advance than in any preceding year. For the past four years, our teams have been kept at home like children, but this year the guardians of the University have allowed them to visit twice a year in charge of a nurse to keep them from harm. Our football team was very light but nevertheless reflected great credit on our splendid coach, Mr. Martin."

The new century brought a 2-3 season including a 53-5 loss to Auburn in Montgomery in which an upset Alabama fan threw his hat into the air only to see Auburn tackle Michael Harvey kick it for an imaginary field goal. It caused a row that day, but following a 35-0 season-ending loss to Clemson on Thanksgiving Day, Harvey was hired as Alabama's new head coach.

He lasted only one season, going 2-1-2 with the loss coming to Auburn 17-0 in Tuscaloosa, thus firmly establishing the cause-and-effect relationship of beating the state rival in relation to job security. However, a new rivalry started that year with the first meeting against Tennessee. When the game was called due to darkness with the score tied 6-6, spectators rushed the Birmingham field in protest. Some would argue that the disputes between the football teams and schools have only grown since.

For the next four years, Alabama, which had picked up the nickname "The Thin Red Line" (which Winston Groom speculated in his book "The Crimson Tide: An Illustrated History of Football at the University of Alabama" was borrowed from Rudyard Kipling's poem "Tommy" about a British soldier), was in a state of flux.

With volunteer coaches James Heyworth and Abbott, Alabama went 4-4 in 1902 and didn't score a point in the four losses. W.B. Blount took over the following season and finished 3-4, but beat both LSU and Tennessee and managed an upset victory against Auburn to keep his job. The rivalry also took another step when an Auburn player apparently kicked Alabama's W.C. Gates in the head, rendering him unconscious.

During the first season Alabama played a 10-game schedule, with victories on three successive days against LSU in Baton Rouge (11-0), Tulane in New Orleans (6-0) and the Pensacola Athletic Club (10-0) in Florida. Bount's team finished 7-3, but a 29-5 loss to Auburn sealed the coaches' fate.

During his only season coaching Alabama, Jack Leavenworth was able to beat Auburn 30-0 with 5,000 fans in attendance in Birmingham, but went 5-4 against everyone else including a 42-6 loss to Sewanee. But 1905 also saw the emergence of one of the school's first star players, team captain Auxford Burks, whose 95-yard return against Maryville was believed to be the first kickoff return for a touchdown in school history.

In 1906, Alabama hired the first of many coaches who would be feared by his players, J.W.H "Doc" Pollard, who led wins against Auburn (10-0) and Tennessee (51-0) en route to a 5-1 record. The lone loss was 78-0 to Vanderbilt after Pollard tried to re-schedule or cancel the game because seven of the 11 starters were injured and the coach knew his backups didn't match up. Of course, Vanderbilt balked.

It was in part due to Pollard's tactics that the Alabama-Auburn rivalry would take a four-decade break. During the 1906 game, Pollard unveiled the "Military Shift," a maneuver he learned at Dartmouth, but had never been seen in the South. Pollard held secret practices to work on the formation, which was described as every player except the center lining up on the line of scrimmage and joining hands, but then turning right or left to form an unbalanced line.

Bucks scored a touchdown and kicked a field goal for a 10-0 victory, but afterward Auburn coach Mike Donahue was so upset that he threatened to cancel the series. A year later, with the teams also in dispute over expense money and referees, it essentially happened after Pollard came up with another unique scheme, the "Varsity Two-Step," which was a variation of the Military Shift only much more confusing. Alabama used it to score the touchdown it needed for a 6-6 tie in the last meeting until 1948.

The 1907 team was known as "Pollard's Pets," but also marked a change in the nickname when sports writer Hugh Roberts of the Birmingham Age-Herald called the team the "Crimson Tide," in part from all the red mud it kicked up during games in Birmingham, following the Auburn tie. With a 5-0 victory against Tennessee on Thanksgiving Day, in which the only touchdown was off a blocked punt returned for a touchdown by Derrill Pratt, Alabama finished the season 5-1-2.

As was the case with his first two seasons, Pollard lost only one game in each of his last two seasons at Alabama. In 1908, it was an 11-6 decision to Georgia

Tech in Atlanta—just before the game some consider the best ever played in Tuscaloosa, against the Haskell Indian Institution, coached by Island Eagle.

Though the Indians had a significant size advantage, the game was decided by one play when Alabama's Herschel Arant batted a pass to teammate Bryant Edwards, who returned the interception 65 yards and sidestepped Island Eagle for the touchdown and 9-8 victory.

Undefeated and unscored on through the first six games of the 1909 season, Alabama was without its best player and captain, Pratt, for the season finale, a 12-6 Thanksgiving loss to LSU in Birmingham. Pollard concluded his Alabama career with a record of 21-4-5, by far the best mark in the team's brief history. The following year he returned leading Washington & Lee, which Alabama defeated 9-0 in Birmingham to conclude to 1910 season. Still, it was an uninspiring 4-4 season, and Guy Lowman, the team's 12th coach in 18 years, quietly retired.

The coaching carousel turned to Missouri alum D.V. Graves, who during his first season reportedly noted: "In September the squad looked light and of poor physical development. Everything was discouraging. I had not yet become familiar with the Alabama spirit—that indescribable something which made the efforts of a light team bring seemingly impossible results."

Graves would match Pollard's "longevity," but not his success. He compiled a 21-12-3 record, though with few victories against established rivals, before coaching Texas A&M for a season (1918). Despite this, there were still numerous items of note during those four years in Tuscaloosa.

In 1912, Alabama had the unusual distinction of having three brothers, the VandeGraafs, playing at the same time (something that wouldn't happen again until 2004): back Adrian, tackle Bully and end Hargrove. They also had another brother named Robert, who suffered a severe back injury and broken femur while playing quarterback in high school but went on to invent the generator used to split the atom. In a 52-0 victory against Marion Institute, Adrian and Hargrove both scored two touchdowns. Against Owentown College, Hargrove scored four touchdowns. Adrian's touchdown against Tennessee led to a 7-0 Thanksgiving victory.

Hargrove would be the team captain in 1913 when the game against Tennessee turned into the program's first unofficial night event. Due to a number of injuries, play lasted past sunset and spectators with automobiles were asked to encircle the Tuscaloosa field and turn on their headlights so it could continue. Alabama held on for a 6-0 victory, marking the seventh straight shutout against the Volunteers, who remembered Bully VandeGraaff more than the lighting problems.

"His ear had a real nasty cut and it was dangling from his head, bleeding badly," Tennessee lineman Bull Bayer said. "He grabbed his own ear and tried to yank it from his head. His teammates stopped him and the managers bandaged him. Man, was that guy a tough one. He wanted to tear off his own ear so he could keep playing."

The Crimson Tide won its first three games of 1914 by a combined score of 80-0 against Howard, Birmingham Southern and its first victory over Georgia Tech when talented quarterback Charlie Joplin was ruled ineligible because he had played professional baseball. Alabama still managed to crush Tulane 58-0 and

Chattanooga 63-0, but lost the other four games down the stretch including a 20-3 defeat against the Carlisle Indian Institute, to finish 5-4.

Joplin would later be killed in France during World War I.

It was during the Graves' era that one of the biggest developments in the football program occurred, and it had nothing to do with the coach. In 1912, Dr. George Hutcheson Denny was hired as president of the university. A massive football fan, he saw the sport as a way to gain notoriety and build enrollment. He improved the facilities, was instrumental in the creation of Denny Field on campus and was personally involved in the hiring of coaches.

When Denny arrived, the campus consisted of 652 students and nine principal buildings. When he retired in 1936, there were more than 5,000 students and 23 major buildings, which still form the central core of the modern campus.

The first era of Alabama football came to a close with Thomas Kelly's three-year coaching stint and the outbreak of World War I, which resulted in the cancellation of the 1918 season.

Kelly, a massive cigar-smoking alum of the University of Chicago, was the first of Denny's handpicked selections, but four games into the 1915 season came down with typhoid fever. With athletic director Lonnie Noojin and 1912 captain Farley Moody taking over the team, the yet-unscored-upon Crimson Tide faced a crucial test against Sewanee, which it hadn't defeated since 1894.

With the game tied 10-10 in the fourth quarter, and Alabama quarterback Griff Harsh ejected for cursing (when it actually had been a teammate), Bully VandeGraaff batted a pass in the air, caught it and ran 65 yards for a touchdown. Adding in field goals and extra points, Bully VandeGraaff scored 17 points to lead a 23-10 victory.

Alabama finished the first season at Denny Field, where modern Bryant-Stadium would be erected, 6-2 and outscored opponents 250-51. Known as the best kicker of his era, in addition to being a standout tackle on both offense and defense, Bully VandeGraaff became Alabama's first All-American selection and was also picked for the prestigious academic society Phi Beta Kappa. He eventually enrolled and graduated from West Point, but returned to be an Alabama assistant coach before becoming the head coach at Colorado College (1926-39).

Approximately 100 pounds lighter, Kelly returned in 1916 and again Alabama got off to an impressive start. It allowed just 13 points in its first six games, all victories, including an 80-0 win against Southern University, 7-6 vs. Sewanee and 16-0 over Florida in Jacksonville, the Crimson Tide's first game played in the Sunshine State. But Alabama didn't score in its final three games, losses to Georgia Tech, Tulane and Georgia, for a 6-3 record.

Despite World War I breaking out in Europe, Alabama managed to play the 1917 season, though the opponents were somewhat different and not because it went to Kentucky for the first time for a 27-0 victory. The Crimson Tide opened against the Second Ambulance Company of Ohio, which was training in Montgomery, and closed with a memorable 19-6 loss to Camp Gordon, Georgia, which boasted a number of former college standouts including Adrian VandeGraaff.

Alabama finished 5-2-1 and the season's biggest highlight was fullback Riggs

Stephenson scoring a record five touchdowns in a 64-0 victory against Ole Miss. Meanwhile, numerous Alabama players and former players took up military service. In addition to Joplin, center E.W. Maynor (1916) and Moody were killed in action. Moody, who died a month before armistice, was buried in a cemetery across the street from Bryant-Denny Stadium in Tuscaloosa.

Xen and Wade

1919–30

*W*hen football returned in 1919, Alabama was more than ready to take the next step in both regional and national prominence, though it would not be easy.

First off, the Crimson Tide needed yet another coach, No. 14 in 27 years, and when school president Dr. George Hutcheson Denny hired a horse-racing writer from Cleveland named Xen Scott, probably more than a few Tuscaloosa fans were shaking their heads.

They shouldn't have been. Though Scott had never played the game at a high level, he understood it well, evidenced by Alabama defeating its first five opponents by a combined score of 225-0, including an impressive 40-0 victory against Sewanee. Only a 16-12 loss to Vanderbilt in Nashville kept the Crimson Tide from both a perfect season and its first Southern Conference title, but it was considered the best season yet and a bit of a precursor of things to come. Backs Mulley Lenoir and Riggs Stephenson joined guard Ike Rogers as All-Southern Conference picks.

The 1920 season was even better. In recording the first 10-win season, Alabama avenged the loss to Vanderbilt, even though the Commodores were the only team to score in the Crimson Tide's first eight games. It outscored its opponents 377-35 with eight shutouts, and crossed the Mason-Dixon line for the first time in closing the season with a 40-0 pounding of Case College in Cleveland, Ohio.

Again, the Crimson Tide was led by Stephenson and Lenoir. Stephenson's 53-yard interception return keyed the 21-0 victory against Sewanee and he went on to have a successful career in Major League Baseball. Lenoir scored 25 touchdowns his senior year after recording 13 as a junior.

However, like in 1919, Alabama stumbled on the road, 21-14 at Georgia, with the Bulldogs returning two blocked kicks and a fumble for touchdowns. Consequently, the conference title went to regional powerhouse Georgia Tech.

Without his two star players, among others, and a sophomore captain in Al Clemons, Scott had to rebuild in 1921, but one of his key additions wouldn't be a player. Hank Crisp was hired as an assistant coach and despite never being the head football coach became an important fixture in Crimson Tide athletics and died at his State of Alabama Sports Hall of Fame induction in 1970.

Only a controversial 14-7 victory over Tulane in New Orleans secured a winning season at 5-4-2, with no big wins and no players honored with all-star selections. That wouldn't be the case in 1922, a turning point in Crimson Tide football despite numerous injuries. Alabama opened the season with a 110-0 victory against

11

Marion Institute and after losing 33-7 to Georgia Tech in Atlanta came back for a gritty 7-7 tie against Sewanee, only to subsequently fall 19-10 at Texas.

Until that point, Alabama's successes had almost entirely been limited to the South, a region that was still considered vastly inferior in football to the Northeast, where the game originated. On Nov. 4, the Crimson Tide was in Philadelphia to play highly-regarded Penn, which was considered a clear favorite to win (any team from the South would have been a huge underdog, that's how big the discrepancy between regions was regarded).

With approximately 25,000 on hand, Alabama refused to buckle. A field goal by Bull Wesley and the recovery of teammate's Pooley Hubert's fumble in the end zone by center Shorty Propst was all the Crimson Tide needed to pull off a remarkable 9-7 upset. According to numerous accounts, Scott and his players paraded through the streets of Philadelphia, and when they eventually got home were greeted at the Tuscaloosa Train Depot by thousands of fans.

It was not only the biggest victory in school history, but also one of the last for Scott, who had already turned in his letter of resignation. Unbeknownst to the players, the coach had throat cancer which would soon take his life. Alabama finished 6-3-1 after a 59-0 victory against Mississippi State, with Scott compiling a career mark of 29-9-3.

Again Denny had to find a replacement, but instead of hiring a popular coach like Scott, he went in the opposite direction with Vanderbilt assistant coach Wallace Wade in hopes of building a potential football dynasty. It turned out to be the right move at the right time.

Wade, who had lost his right hand in an agriculture accident, was known for his discipline, regimented practices and attention to detail. Although originally from Tennessee, he graduated from Brown and had been a cavalry captain in World War I. His first season produced a 7-2-1 record with Alabama getting pounded 23-0 at Syracuse, a game Wade claimed taught him more about football than any other. But the Crimson Tide also snapped the "Sewanee Jinx."

Asa Rountree wrote in a local newspaper: "It was a battle of battles—one that will go down with a red ring around it—not only because it marked the end of the prolonged regime of Sewanee, but as one that brought all of the ideal characteristics of red-blooded fighting young American."

The final score was 7-0.

Alabama won its first three games of 1924 by a combined 130-0, and didn't yield a point until its seventh game. A 17-0 loss to Centre College prevented perfection, but a dominating 33-0 Thanksgiving victory against Georgia in front of 20,000 fans in Birmingham gave Alabama (8-1) its first official championship season and Southern Conference title. Clemons, finally a senior, again served as captain and quarterback. Grant Gillis was named All-Southern Conference.

Alabama outscored its opponents 290-24 and recorded seven shutouts. Backs Johnny Mack Brown and Hubert along with guards Bill Buckler and Ben Compton—who one local writer called "a demon" after his strong performance against Georgia—were named All-Southern Conference, but it all paled in comparison to what the Crimson Tide accomplished in 1925—the season that would set the standard.

Through its first eight games, Alabama gave up just one touchdown while Brown and Hubert proved to be the best 1-2 combination in college football. A gut-wrenching 7-0 victory against Georgia Tech set up a rematch with Georgia with the Southern Conference title again at stake, and similar to the year before it was all Alabama, 27-0.

Only this time it didn't mean the end of the season. On hand for the victory were representatives of the Rose Bowl Committee from Pasadena, Calif., who essentially decided which teams would play in the national championship game. But the committee members left unimpressed and despite the Crimson Tide's undefeated record first invited Dartmouth, Yale and Colgate. Under pressure from the American Association of University Professors, who had issued a report that was unfavorable to the sport, all declined. Finally, the first offer was extended to a southern school, the Alabama.

The team left two weeks early for its appointment with the Washington Huskies, and with every train stop Wade worked his players. While the rest of the country expected a blowout and many sports writers predicted an easy two-touch-down victory for the West Coast representative, the South began to rally behind the Crimson Tide which suddenly carried the hopes of an entire region that had been struggling economically and even more so emotionally. Even Auburn president Dr. Spright Dowell, sent a telegram wishing the team luck.

For one half, it was all Washington. Led by fullback George "Wildcat" Wilson, the Huskies jumped out to a 12-0 lead, prompting Wade to walk into the locker room, growl "They told me boys from the South would fight," and walk out. But he also made adjustments to the defense and unleashed Hubert, who had not run with the ball for fear of injury. Alabama had nothing to lose, especially after Wilson unnecessarily twisted Brown's leg while finishing a tackle, which the Crimson Tide took as a cheap shot. Alabama, in turn, knocked Wilson, who finished with 134 rushing yards and completed five passes for 77 yards and two touchdowns, out of the game for the duration of the third quarter.

Hubert punched in one touchdown and Brown scored on both a 59-yard reception from Gillis (which sparked years of debate over how far the ball was actually thrown as statistics weren't precise) and a 30-yard catch from Hubert to give Alabama a 20-12 lead.

"When I reached the three I looked around and sure enough the ball was coming down over my shoulder," Brown said of Hubert's pass after being told to run as fast as he could toward the end zone. "I took it in stride, used my stiff arm on one man and went over carrying somebody. The place was really in an uproar."

Washington came back to score again and in the waning moments threatened another when Brown made an open-field tackle on Wilson to end the threat. Alabama won 20-19 to shock both the 50,000 on hand, and fans from coast-to-coast.

Although Alabama ended up sharing the national title with Dartmouth, the result shook the very foundation of college football. It was, and still is by some, considered the best Rose Bowl game ever played and the biggest victory in the South post-Civil War, which ended some 70 years pervious.

All the way home, the Crimson Tide was met by celebrating fans, especially once the train reached New Orleans. They came to not only applaud, but thank the young men who had given them a much-needed dose of both pride and glory.

The victory also had long-reaching affects for those involved as well. Brown was named the game's most valuable player and took advantage of the attention by returning to California two years later to become a successful movie star. In 1990, Wade was inducted into the Rose Bowl Hall of Fame, and he would be joined by Brown 10 years later. Both, along with Hubert, would be inducted into the College Football Hall of Fame.

It all begged only one question: Could the Crimson Tide do it again?

Even without Hubert and Brown, Alabama continued its winnings ways in 1926 and with a 33-6 Thanksgiving victory against Georgia won a third-straight Southern Conference championship. The only close game was a 2-0 victory against Sewanee decided by a blocked punt that went out of the end zone.

Led by All-Americans Fred Pickhard and Hoyt "Wu" Winslett, along with All-Southern Conference backs Herschel Caldwell and Emile Barnes and center Gordon "Sherlock" Holmes, the Crimson Tide outscored its opponents 242-20.

It was back to Pasadena, though this time Alabama didn't have to wait for an invitation to play Stanford, which was coached by the legendary Pop Warner. Because voting was often conducted at the conclusion of the regular season, both teams along with Lafayette and Navy had already been declared national champions by at least one significant poll prior to the game.

Jack James of the International News Service wrote in reference to Stanford's 13-12 victory against USC: "Football followers of this vicinity cannot forget the bewildering deception, the concentrated power, the grim determination of the afternoon. And because they remember, they figure that Alabama, or any other ball club, would have to be just short of super-human to deny a repetition of that attack."

Alabama was outplayed, but Stanford could never put the game away. In the closing minutes, the Crimson Tide scored a touchdown for a 7-7 standoff and 9-0-1 record. Pickhard was selected MVP of the Rose Bowl.

While school officials continued to promote the football team's success, its rise to national acclaim petered out over the next three years. Pickhard returned to earn All-Southern Conference honors, but the 1927 season ended with losses to Florida, Georgia and Vanderbilt for a 5-4-1 record. More memorable was that the Georgia game was Alabama's first at Legion Field in Birmingham.

Alabama finished 6-3 in both 1928 and 1929, disappointing fans who had been spoiled by Rose Bowl trips. In 1928, Alabama traveled to play a Big 10 school for the first time, a 15-0 loss at Wisconsin, though the season ended with a 19-0 victory against Georgia and 13-0 win over LSU. The 1929 season was highlighted by tackle Fred Sington and back Tony Holm named All-Americans, and Denny Stadium in Tuscaloosa was dedicated by Governor Bibb Graves on Sept. 28, 1929, a 55-0 victory against Mississippi College. Its initial seating capacity was 12,000.

Growing increasingly discontent, while at the same time being targeted by other schools, Wade turned in his resignation at the end of the 1929 season, but agreed to stay on for the final year of his contract before heading to Duke. Clyde Bolton of the Birmingham News called it the "greatest swan song in the history of football."

Alabama opened the season with a 43-0 victory against Howard and backed it up with two more shutouts, 62-0 against Mississippi and 25-0 vs. Sewanee. An 18-6 win against Tennessee and a 12-7 victory vs. Vanderbilt had the Crimson Tide 5-0, and it had already yielded the only points Alabama would give up all season.

The Mississippi victory was also when Alabama picked up the fierce elephant moniker that would eventually become the school mascot, "Big Al." Apparently inspired by comments yelled between fans, Everett Strupper of the Atlanta Journal wrote: "That Alabama team of 1930 is a typical Wade machine, powerful, big, tough, fast, aggressive, well-schooled in fundamentals, and the best blocking team for this early in the season that I have ever seen. When those big brutes hit you I mean you go down and stay down, often for an additional two minutes.

"Coach Wade started his second team that was plenty big and they went right to their knitting scoring a touchdown in the first quarter against one of the best fighting small lines that I have seen. For Ole Miss was truly battling the big boys for every inch of ground.

"At the end of the quarter, the earth started to tremble, there was a distant rumble that continued to grow. Some excited fan in the stands bellowed, 'Hold your horses, the elephants are coming,' and out stamped this Alabama varsity.

"It was the first time that I had seen it and the size of the entire eleven nearly knocked me cold, men that I had seen play last year looking like they had nearly doubled in size."

For years, the team would also be called the "red elephants," and before long seeing a real elephant on campus wasn't unusual despite the aquatic nickname, a practice that continued into the 1950s when school officials decided the massive mascots were too expensive.

A season-ending 13-0 victory against Georgia meant both a perfect season and Southern Conference championship, resulting in another invitation to the Rose Bowl to play Washington State. Even though the national championship was at stake, Wade again made the perplexing move of starting the second stringers, leaving his best players on the bench until the second quarter.

Washington State held its own against the backups, but not against the starters and Alabama easily won 24-0. Everyone on the Crimson Tide roster got into the game and Wade, who was carried off the field by his players, concluded his Alabama career with a 61-13-3 record and third national championship.

Sports writer Royal Brougham of the Seattle Post-Intelligencer wrote: "Out of the sunny southland came another great Alabama football team and it hit a bewildered Cougar from Washington State like a jug of Dixie gin. By a 24-to-0 score the banjo-plucking, mammy singing troubadours from the land of cotton won the annual Rose Bowl classic, and they were that much the better team. The vaunted defense of the western champions crumpled like the walls of Jericho before an amazing pass attack which caught the northmen flat on their heels.

"The Bammers unleashed a passing and cleverly masked running offense which the canny Coach Wade kept stored in the cooler all season long. And before it the touted cougars were just corn bone and possum pie. That freckled-necked southern gentleman who coaches the Tide won today's game with his noodle, and don't let anybody tell you different. Wade sat out there on the bench and out-figured the lads from the northwest all afternoon long."

John "Monk" Campbell was named MVP of the Rose Bowl. Halfback John Henry Suther was named All-American while guard John Miller and sophomore fullback John Cain were All-Southern Conference picks.

But by far the most unique honor went to Sington, who was a unanimous All-American selection in addition to earning Phi Beta Kappa honors. He had the song "Football Freddie" dedicated to him by Rudy Vallee.

Meanwhile, the football team's success was felt and seen all over Tuscaloosa. In 1929 Denny Chimes, an essential landmark located in the heart of campus, was dedicated and starting in 1948 team captains would have the honor of their names, handprints and footprints set in concrete around the bell tower on the "Walk of Fame."

Although the marching band was created in 1913 as a 14-person unit, it picked up the "Million Dollar Band" name in 1922 thanks to alumnus W.C. "Champ" Pickens, supposedly in reference to its early fund-raising prowess.

The one song the band plays most of all is simply titled "Yea Alabama," which mentions its early rivalries against Georgia and Georgia Tech (but not Auburn), and honors the team's heritage with the line "Remember the Rose Bowl, we'll win then."

Frank Thomas

1931–46

$\mathcal{T}$he early notice of Wallace Wade's departure gave Alabama president Dr. George Hutcheson Denny plenty of time to find a replacement, but he quickly focused on the person Wade recommended: Georgia assistant coach Frank Thomas, who had also been the roommate of George Gipp and called "Shrewd Tommy" at Notre Dame.

In addition to quarterbacking the Fighting Irish and his obvious link to the Four Horsemen, Naylor Stone in "Coach Tommy of the Crimson Tide" credited Knute Rockne with telling his coaches "It's amazing the amount of football sense that Thomas kid has. He can't miss becoming a great coach some day. I want him on our staff next fall."

Instead, Thomas went to law school before joining the Bulldogs. According to the Atlanta Journal, Denny said when hiring him: "Now that you have accepted our position, I will give you the benefit of my views, based on many years of observation. It is my conviction that material is 90 percent, coaching 10 percent. I desire to further say that you will be provided with the 90 percent and that you will be held to strict accounting for delivering the remaining 10 percent."

After leaving the meeting in Birmingham, Thomas said to writer Ed Camp: "Those were the hardest and coldest words I every heard."

Among his first moves was to adopt Rockne's "Box Formation" offense, in which the backfield players would shift left or right into a box, pause for a moment and then the ball would be snapped before the defense had time to adjust. Relying on speed and deception, not only did it give the running game greater versatility, but also helped open up the passing game.

Thomas couldn't be blamed for attempting to exploit every advantage possible, especially considering that 10 of the 11 starters from the 1930 national championship team were no longer at Alabama. However, the one player who returned was junior back Johnny "Hurry" Cain, who had a monstrous season leading the new offense and was named All-Southern Conference.

Alabama destroyed most of its opponents in 1931, including Clemson 74-7, Ole Miss 55-6 and Mississippi State 53-0. After a 14-6 victory at Vanderbilt, Blinkey Horn wrote in the Nashville Tennesseen: "Twas a savage struggle. Vanderbilt has encountered no rival which hit as hard as Alabama. Nor an enemy which tackled so surely. And so viciously."

The Crimson Tide pulled out a 9-7 victory against Kentucky, but the offense really struggled against Tennessee, resulting in a 25-0 defeat. Still, the 9-1 record remains the best debut season for a coach in school history, and the 36 points per game average was an Alabama record.

In 1932, Cain and guard Tom Hupke were the last Crimson Tide players to earn All-Southern Conference honors as the following year Alabama would join the offshoot Southeastern Conference, simply known as the SEC.

In part because of competition in track, the Southern Conference came together in 1920, with charter members Alabama, Auburn, Clemson, Georgia, Georgia Tech, Kentucky, Maryland, Mississippi State, North Carolina, North Carolina State, Tennessee, Virginia, Virginia Tech and Washington & Lee. Florida, Louisiana State, Mississippi, South Carolina, Tulane, Vanderbilt and Virginia Military quickly joined, while Sewanee and Duke became members in 1923 and 1928 respectively.

But the conference was obviously too big for most team sports, so the 13 members west and south of the Appalachian Mountains reorganized at a December 1932 meeting in Knoxville, Tenn., while the 10 coast members remained in the Southern Conference.

Comprising the new SEC were Alabama, Auburn, Florida, Georgia, Georgia Tech, Kentucky, Louisiana State, Mississippi, Mississippi State, Sewanee, Tennessee, Tulane and Vanderbilt. Sewanee withdrew in 1940, Georgia Tech in 1964 and Tulane in 1966. Arkansas and South Carolina joined in 1992, making it a 12-team conference.

Alabama didn't win the Southern Conference championship in its final year, but it came close. In his last game, Cain's spectacular 71-yard touchdown run gave the Crimson Tide a 6-0 victory against St. Mary's in San Francisco—Alabama's first regular-season game on the West Coast—and 8-2 record.

"John Cain is the best football player I have ever seen on a football field," Alabama line coach and 1924 All-American center Clyde "Shorty" Propst told Owen Merrick of the San Francisco News.

The two losses came against rivals Tennessee and Georgia Tech, and against the Volunteers Cain punted 19 times while his counterpart Beattie Feathers did so 21 times. (Note: The quick kick was much more in vogue then, especially during games played in poor weather.)

However, Alabama did win the first SEC championship in 1933, even after its first conference game was a 0-0 tie with Ole Miss. The Crimson Tide came back with an 18-6 victory against Mississippi State and then avenged the previous year's loss to Tennessee 12-6 in Knoxville, giving Thomas, who had been so nervous about the game he put the lit end of his cigar into his mouth, his first victory in three tries against the Volunteers.

Alabama finished undefeated against conference opponents, with the only loss a 2-0 controversial decision against Fordham in front of 60,000 fans at the Polo Grounds in New York. Hupke was named All-American, but the Crimson Tide also had an amazing collection of younger players, including fullback Joe Demyanovich, halfback Dixie Howell, end Don Hutson, tackle Bill Lee, quarterback Riley Smith and a rugged end named Paul W. "Bear" Bryant.

They came back in 1934 to form one of the greatest teams in college football history, and easily the best under Thomas. After beating Howard, which had hired Propst to be its head coach, 24-0, Alabama practically breezed through its SEC schedule, with the only close game against Tennessee, a hard-hitting 13-6 victory. Afterward, Volunteers coach General Neyland paid the Crimson Tide perhaps its greatest compliment ever: "You never know what a football player is made of until he plays against Alabama."

Although many sports writers thought Minnesota should have been chosen instead, Alabama was heading back to the Rose Bowl for the first time since 1926 to again face Stanford. The game was a sellout with 84,484, and like usual the Crimson Tide was considered the underdog. Thomas used it, and other things, to his advantage.

"I'll never forget going to the Rose Bowl," Bryant later said. "I remember everything about it. We were on the train and coach Thomas was talking to three coaches and Red Heard, the athletic trainer at LSU. Coach Thomas said, 'Red, this is my football player. This is the best player on my team.' Well shoot, I could have gone right out the top. He was getting me ready, and I was too. I would have gone out there and killed myself for Alabama that day."

Duly inspired, and aided by scouting reports from former standout Johnny Mack Brown, Alabama dominated 29-13.

Noted Will Rogers, who once referred to the Crimson Tide as the "Tusc-a-losers" before its first Rose Bowl appearance: "Stanford made a mistake in scoring first. It just made those Alabama boys mad."

Howell scored two touchdowns, one on a 67-yard run, and passed 59 yards to Hutson for another. He threw for 160 yards, ran for 111 and averaged 43.8 yards a punt to be named game MVP.

"That boy has ice water in his veins, if ever a competitive athlete had," said Thomas, who on the sideline was often more emotional than his players. "I've never seen him nervous before, but that morning he couldn't look at his breakfast, let alone eat it. And he couldn't eat lunch."

Thomas later called Howell's performance the "greatest I've ever seen."

In describing the performance, famous sports writer Grantland Rice wrote: "Dixie Howell, the human howitzer from Hartford, Ala., blasted the Rose Bowl dreams of Stanford today with one of the greatest all-around exhibitions football has ever known."

When he was presented with the Rissman Trophy at the Tuscaloosa Junior Chamber of Commerce's annual dinner for the football team, Denny joined in the praise.

"I've been making speeches to the Alabama football team for a great many years, and I've a barrel full of notes of former addresses," he said. "Looking back over the years, for example, I came upon the theme of the speech in 1927, and it was 'discipline.' And the next year, in 1928, it was 'loyalty.' Those, my friends, were the lean years. We had not much else to talk about.

"And now, we have an occasion which marks the close of a chapter that will be emblazoned for a hundred years, in the history of football and a chapter that stands today the most brilliant in the book of football in the southland."

Alabama had won its fourth national championship, averaging 31.4 points per game while yielding just 4.5. Howell was named SEC player of the year in addition to All-American with Lee and Hutson, who would go on to revolutionize the National Football League with the Green Bay Packers. Hutson was credited with inventing pass patterns, caught 99 touchdown passes and still holds the NFL record for points scored in a game, 29. He was named to the all-time college football team and has been enshrined into numerous different Halls of Fame, including Alabama, Arkansas, Rose Bowl, College, Pro, Green Bay Packers and Helms Foundation, Wisconsin.

Finding replacements for Howell and Hutson proved to be all but impossible, while the university would also soon be without Denny. After almost a quarter century of growth the president became somewhat a victim of his own success, resulting in disputes with both the state legislature and student faculty that would lead to his resignation.

The 6-2-1 season in 1935 would be equally disappointing, beginning with an unsatisfactory 7-7 tie with Howard and ending with a Thanksgiving 14-6 loss to Vanderbilt. Alabama would travel to Washington, D.C., to play George Washington, a 39-0 victory, and a 20-16 win against Georgia Tech in Atlanta kept the Crimson Tide near the top of the SEC standings, but short of a championship.

Smith, who earned All-American honors, was considered Alabama's best player and the first recipient of the Jacobs Trophy, given to the best blocker in the SEC (which today would be unheard of for a quarterback, though the year before Smith played fullback). Although he would score two touchdowns in a 25-0 victory against Tennessee, Bryant stole the show in arguably his best game as a player. In addition to catching a touchdown pass, he lateraled to Smith for another score, all while playing with a broken leg. Atlanta Constitution reporter Ralph McGill doubted the diagnosis and showed up early for the following week's game against Georgia and asked to see the X-ray. Indeed, it showed a broken fibula sustained against Mississippi State, from which Bryant was quoted as saying "It was just one little bone."

In 1936, Bryant joined Thomas' staff as an assistant coach and Alabama appeared poised for another title run. But after a 34-0 victory against Howard and a 32-0 win vs. Clemson, the offense sputtered. The Crimson Tide pulled out a 7-0 victory against Mississippi, only to see a 0-0 tie with Tennessee, in which the Red Elephants had first down at the Volunteers' 1 when time ran out in the first half, cost both the SEC championship and a bowl appearance.

In the final Associated Press poll, the first ever tabulated, Alabama (8-0-1) finished fourth. Guard Arthur "Tarzan" White, who went on to win the belt as the World Heavyweight Wrestling Champion, was a unanimous All-American selection, and future College Hall of Fame inductee Smith was named All-SEC. Smith was also the first Crimson Tide player selected in the National Football League, going in the first round to Boston, three rounds ahead of Bryant by Brooklyn.

Inspired by its bowl snubbing, Alabama came back in 1937 to record a perfect regular season, thanks to three narrow victories: 14-7 at Tennessee, 9-6 at Tulane and 9-7 at Vanderbilt. Otherwise, the Crimson Tide dominated, outscoring opponents 225-33 in clinching the SEC championship to secure another invitation to the Rose Bowl. But during a practice on the way to California, a lineman pulled the wrong way and collided with Leroy Monsky, with the All-American guard needing 25 stitches above his left eye. Monsky played, but the incident foreshadowed the game, won by California 13-0. It was the only loss Alabama suffered in the Rose Bowl.

"Alabama has a pass and a prayer," Mark Ehllinger wrote in the San Francisco Examiner. "California had the pass and the necessary power, they didn't need the prayer."

"It was a heartbreaker," Monsky said. "I still try and blank it from my mind."

Running back Joe Kilgrow and lineman Jim Ryba also earned All-American honors and for the second consecutive year Associated Press voters ranked Alabama fourth.

Unsettling finishes to the two previous seasons didn't sit well with Thomas, who decided Alabama needed to go back to the West Coast and get a victory. So for the 1938 season opener he scheduled a trip to Los Angeles to play Southern Cal.

With halfback Herschel Mosley running behind blockers Fred Davis, Walter Merritt and Bobby Wood, Alabama came home 19-7 winners, but it proved to be the season's biggest highlight. A 13-0 loss to Tennessee and a 14-14 tie with Georgia Tech resulted in a 7-1-1 record and No. 14 national ranking, while only fullback Charley Holm was named All-SEC. Meanwhile, USC went on to play in the Rose Bowl and upset Duke, which was coached by Wade and hadn't been scored on all season, 7-3.

The 1939 season had only one significant highlight as well, a 7-6 victory over national power Fordham, which was led by its incredibly tough "Seven Blocks of Granite" line including Vince Lombardi. Years later, after winning the 1966 Super Bowl as coach of the Green Bay Packers, Lombardi was asked what it felt like to be the greatest football team in the world. "I don't know," he said, "We haven't played Alabama yet."

Again, Tennessee proved to be the Crimson Tide's nemesis, with a 21-0 loss the team couldn't recover from. It was just one of three shutouts for Alabama, and a 7-7 tie to Kentucky particularly stung en route to a 5-3-1 record. Although the defense limited opponents to just 53 points, the offense could only muster 101, of which 39 came in the season finale against Vanderbilt. Only center Carey Cox could claim a major postseason award as an All-American, while end Harold Newman was second team.

Another good start in 1940 was derailed, again, by Tennessee, 27-12 in Birmingham, and a seconds-ending loss to Mississippi State, 13-0 in Tuscaloosa. Otherwise, Alabama was back on an upswing and its defense posted four shutouts and keyed a 14-13 victory against Georgia Tech in Atlanta. Tackle Fred Davis, who went on to have an impressive NFL career, was named All-SEC along with back Jimmy Nelson and end Holt Rast. Otherwise, the season was best remembered for the Crimson Tide's first official night game, a 26-0 victory against Spring Hill at Murphy High School Stadium in Mobile, and the departure of assistant coach Bryant, who left to join Red Sanders' staff at Vanderbilt.

With Nelson and Rast, who would be a unanimous All-American selection in 1941, Alabama appeared poised to make another run for at least the conference title only to suffer an early-season 14-0 loss to Mississippi State at Tuscaloosa. Still, the Crimson Tide had impressive victories against Tennessee (9-2), Georgia (27-14) and Georgia Tech (20-0) to stay high in the national rankings, even with a late-season 7-0 loss at Vanderbilt.

Alabama concluded the regular season by defeating the Miami Hurricanes 21-7 in the first meeting between the schools (and second night game for the Crimson Tide), and accepted an invitation to play Texas A&M in the Cotton Bowl.

In scouting the Aggies, assistant coach Harold "Red" Drew said they had "the greatest passing team I have ever seen, and Thomas, who almost never slept well the night before a big game, complained that studying the dynamic offense gave him headaches."

Playing in poor weather conditions, Alabama, in its first postseason appearance other than the Rose Bowl, created 12 turnovers, including seven interceptions, in a 29-21 victory that was nowhere near as close as the score indicated. Even though Texas A&M had a 13-to-1 advantage in first downs, the Crimson Tide still scored four touchdowns, attempted just seven passes and all 41 players who made the trip got into the game (in part leading to two late touchdowns by the Aggies).

"The boys really turned in some defensive work," Thomas told the Dallas Morning News. "It was the lifesaver for us. Our boys played a good, aggressive game—the best of the season."

Rast returned an interception for a touchdown, halfback Russ Craft twice reached the end zone and Nelson returned a punt 72 yards for one touchdown and added a second on a 21-yard run. Nelson, Rast and guard Don Whitmire shared game MVP honors, for what resulted in Alabama's fifth national title.

Although the majority of polls had Minnesota No. 1 at season's end, Alabama and Texas, neither of which won its conference title, were able to claim a share of the national championship thanks to the Houlgate System (1927-58), a mathematical rating system developed by Dale Houlgate of Los Angeles, which was syndicated in newspapers and published in Illustrated Football and Football Thesaurus (1946-58).

It wasn't pretty, but it counted. Considering how many times Alabama had not benefited from lady luck, like the undefeated 1936 team that didn't receive a bowl bid, fans were not complaining. Besides, the Cotton Bowl victory came less than a month after the attack on Pearl Harbor, plunging the country into World War II. Once again, football became secondary as many players enlisted and eventually headed overseas.

As was the case with World War I, Alabama's schedule included teams comprised of former college all-stars stationed at military bases. The Crimson Tide defeated the Pensacola Naval Air Station 27-0, but lost 35-19 to the Georgia Naval

Pre-Flight Skycrackers, who had Alabama assistant Hank Crisp as their head coach.

In SEC play, Alabama's only losses were to Georgia 21-10 and Georgia Tech 7-0, and after accepting the Heisman Trophy, the Bulldogs' Frank Sinkwich told United Press writer Jack Cuddy that the toughest team he played was: "Alabama, this season. They were awful tough. Yes, tougher than Auburn, which beat us."

Led by All-American linemen Joe Domnanovich and Don Whitmire, the Crimson Tide returned to Miami for its first appearance in the Orange Bowl. Boston College took an early 14-0 lead, but Domnanovich helped spark the comeback with a safety and Wheeler Leeth and Bobby Tom Jenkins both scored a pair of touchdowns in the 37-21 victory.

Covering the game, Boston Post columnist Bill Cunningham wrote: "When you're beaten as clearly and splendidly as was Boston College today, the only thing to do is stand and salute as the victors go by. It was a fine game, played in the truest tradition of sportsmanship, brilliantly won and gallantly lost in a magnificent setting, so in taste with the times that none who saw it ever forget it."

Alabama, which would not field a team in 1943 despite Thomas' efforts, finished 8-3 and ranked No. 10 in the final Associated Press poll. At season's end, Whitmire and Jenkins entered the Naval Academy and became All-Americans for the Midshipmen, with Whitmire eventually rising all the way to the rank of admiral.

Even though the war raged on, Thomas had enough players—20, down from the then-normal 50—to put together a team in 1944, which was appropriately nicknamed "The War Babies." Primarily, the Crimson Tide was made up of 17-year-olds who were too young to be drafted, students medically disqualified from military service and returning veterans. Thomas went from hoping the ragtag collection wouldn't "disgrace the University" to becoming his favorite of all the teams he coached.

Leading the Crimson Tide was a small all-around player from Woodlawn High School in Birmingham named Harry Gilmer, who might not have gone to college had Thomas not hired his high school coach Malcolm Laney to be a Crimson Tide assistant. With the SEC waiving it rule against freshmen playing with the varsity, Gilmer and his trademark leaping passes, in part because he otherwise couldn't see over his own linemen, would key the season. When he took a kick return 95 yards for a touchdown in the season opener against LSU, which resulted in a 27-27 tie, Alabama fans knew something special was at hand. The Crimson Tide followed with a 63-0 victory against Howard and 55-0 win over Millsaps. With a 5-1-2 record, the War Baby Tiders secured the school's first invitation to the Sugar Bowl in New Orleans, where Gilmer put on a dazzling performance in front of 72,000 fans. Though a much-older Duke pulled out a 29-26 victory in the final moments, Gilmer was named the game's MVP and Rice wrote he was "the greatest college passer I've ever seen."

Finally, with the successful conclusion of World War II in 1945, the Crimson Tide had a full roster again including Gilmer and returning center Vaughn Mancha, who would be named All-Americans. Even with two military opponents on the schedule, Alabama destroyed its competition with Georgia coming closest, 28-14. It outscored opponents 430-80 and among the lopsided games was a 41-0 victory against Kentucky in which Gilmer had 216 rushing yards—the first time in school history the 200-yard mark was eclipsed—on six carries in addition to more than 100 yards passing. The Crimson Tide also defeated LSU 26-7, Tennessee 25-7 and Vanderbilt 71-0 en route to the SEC championship.

The perfect season resulted in the sixth and final invitation to the Rose Bowl, and once again the Crimson Tide, with many of the grown up "War Babies," was considered an underdog to the West Coast representative, Southern Cal, which had won eight straight games in Pasadena going back to 1923.

At halftime, USC had minus-24 yards of offense on 21 plays while Alabama led 20-0. The Trojans didn't get a first down until the third quarter, when they trailed 27-0, but Thomas held back in the second half. Lowell Tew, who had had a broken jaw that had been taped and wired shut, was in from the start, but even Nick Terlizzi hobbled on to the field on a broken leg and could say he played in a Rose Bowl. It prompted USC coach Jeff Cravath to say: "There goes a great man. I'll never forget what he did today. If he wanted, he could have named the score."

Alabama won 34-14, but the game's outcome was never in doubt. The Crimson Tide had a 351-41 advantage in offensive yards, while USC's rushing attack compiled only 6 yards. Gilmer was named game MVP after running for 116 yards on 16 carries and two touchdowns. He was also SEC player of the year while Hugh Morrow won the national title for scoring by a kicker.

"Bama just took off and ran where she pleased—through tackle, through center or around the ends, it made little difference where the plays were directed," Braven Dyer of the Los Angeles Times wrote. "The Trojans? Well, let's be charitable and say they just didn't have it."

Amazingly, it didn't add up to a national title, even with the perfect 10-0 record. Although the National Championship Foundation, the Cliff Morgan Foundation and the Ray Byrne Foundation all had Alabama No. 1, it finished second in the rest of the polls to Army. Thus, it is not one of the 12 national championships the Crimson Tide claims.

However, Alabama does proudly boast of those who died serving in World War II, including tackle Tom "Hog" Borders (1939), tackle Cliff "Swede" Hansen (1940-41), end James "Babs" Roberts (1940-42), fullback Johnny Roberts (1937) and end Jimmy Walker (1935).

Thomas' reign at Alabama was also coming to a close due to his failing health. Because of high blood pressure he would lead practices during the 1946 season from an elevated position and had to use a loudspeaker so players and assistant coaches could hear him. Midway through the season, university president Raymond Paty suggested he give up his duties as head coach. Thomas declined but later admitted he probably should have, calling it his least enjoyable season.

Unable to continue the heroics of the previous season, road losses to Tennessee, Georgia, LSU and Boston College led to a 7-4 record. Among the victories was a 21-7 decision in Montgomery against Kentucky, which was coached by Thomas disciple "Bear" Bryant. Hal Self won the Jacobs Blocking Trophy and Gilmer led the nation in punt returns and bleachers were added to both end zones of the Tuscaloosa stadium, increasing capacity to 31,000. In Thomas' final game, Alabama defeated Mississippi State 24-7 in Tuscaloosa.

Thomas stayed on as athletics director and with a career record of 115-24-7 was elected to the College Football Hall of Fame in the same class with Hutson. In 1949, he was also unanimously voted to membership of the 82nd Airborne Division Association in Washington, D.C., the fifth civilian to receive the honor along with President Harry S. Truman, Gen. George Marshall, Winston Churchill and Gen. Dwight Eisenhower (who became president in 1953).

In 1952, Thomas resigned as athletic director. He died on May 10, 1954.

Red Ears

1947–57

$\mathscr{H}$alfback Harry Gilmer's last season with the Crimson Tide would be under the direction of Alabama's 17th head coach, who would have some monster-sized shoes to fill. From 1931 to 1946, Frank Thomas had gone 115-24-7 with two national championships, three trips to the Rose Bowl in addition to Alabama's first appearances in the Sugar, Cotton and Orange Bowls, with 17 All-Americans and 25 All-SEC selections. Before him, Wallace Wade won three national championships from 1923-30.

To say that the bar had been set a little high would be a tremendous understatement, but as athletic director Thomas had a large say on who would be his replacement and eventually the decision was made to hire someone already familiar with the program. Harold "Red" Drew, who had been an Alabama assistant for 14 years before heading Ole Miss for a season, took over a team full of veterans, both of World War II and the football field, including popular War Baby Tiders like center-linebacker Vaughn Mancha.

The 1947 season got off to a lackluster start with two close road losses, 20-7 to Tulane and 14-7 to Vanderbilt, when things began to click. Starting with a 26-0 victory against Duquesne, Alabama rediscovered its winning ways and rolled past Tennessee (10-0), Georgia (17-7), Kentucky (13-0), Georgia Tech (14-7) and LSU (41-12) before closing the regular season in Miami with a 21-6 triumph over the Hurricanes. At 8-2 and ranked No. 6 in the nation, the Crimson Tide returned to the Sugar Bowl to play Texas, where Gilmer's last game may have also been his worst. He completed just three passes in the 27-7 loss.

"I wouldn't swap the experiences, the thrills, the friendships and fellowships made in bowl games for anything," Gilmer later said. "Of course, a postseason game means a lot of additional work—practice, training and usually the sacrifice of Christmas vacations—but in the end it's worth even more."

Alabama wouldn't have a chance at bowl redemption for five years, an eternity in Tuscaloosa. Gilmer wasn't named an All-American, but for the second time he finished fifth in Heisman Trophy balloting (1945 the other), and with center John Wozniak was All-SEC. Gilmer ended his career as the Crimson Tide's all-time leader in rushing, passing, punt returns, kick returns and interceptions.

About the only thing he didn't do was play against state rival Auburn. In 1948, the debate on whether to renew the series finally came to an end after the state legislature got involved despite objections from Thomas and other school officials,

26

who believed nothing could be gained for the Crimson Tide by playing a team that had never finished better than third in the SEC. Citing problems, including brawls and other incidents, at rivalry games in Texas, Minnesota, Louisiana, Georgia, South Carolina, Maryland, Kansas and Tennessee, the Committee on Physical Education and Athletics report argued: "We hazard nothing in saying that the game would not make a single constructive contribution to education in the state." It concluded, "The fundamental question is: Do the people of Alabama need a tranquil, sane kind of athletics in their two major institutions, or an irrational rabid kind?"

When representatives threatened to hold back funding to both schools if they didn't meet on the football field each and every year, students met in Birmingham and buried a symbolic hatchet in Woodrow Wilson Park. On Dec. 4 at Legion Field, 46,000 attended the first Iron Bowl since 1907, with another 2,000 at the Birmingham Armory for a pay-per-view broadcast.

Gordon Pettus' touchdown pass to Butch Avinger set the tone. Ed Salem passed for three touchdowns, ran for another and kicked seven extra points as Alabama destroyed Auburn 55-0 to renew the rivalry and cap a 6-4-1 season.

Auburn would get some payback in the 1949 rematch. Similar to Drew's first season, Alabama opened the season with losses to Tulane and Vanderbilt before stringing together six straight victories, including solid back-to-back conference victories against Georgia (14-7) and Georgia Tech (20-7). But an interception return for a touchdown gave Auburn an early lead and Alabama missed a crucial extra point in the 14-13 decision. Avinger won the SEC's Jacobs Blocking Trophy though Ed Holdnak was the lone All-SEC selection.

The pattern would again be repeated in 1950, though with better results. Again, Alabama lost two early close games, to Vanderbilt 27-22 and Tennessee 14-9, before making a run through the rest of the SEC. Salem, a senior, had his best season and his favorite target, end Al Lary, caught a school record 10 touchdowns. Salem was named All-American and along with Lary, guard Mike Mizerany and center Pete O'Sullivan All-SEC. Avinger became the first player to win the Jacobs Trophy in back-to-back seasons.

Dominating victories against Mississippi Southern (53-0), Georgia Tech (54-19), Florida (41-13) and Auburn (34-0) moved the Crimson Tide to No. 16 in the final polls, but despite Alabama outscoring opponents 328-107, no bowls came calling. Instead, a 34-0 victory against Auburn and the emergence of sophomore halfback Bobby Marlow would have to suffice. Against Georgia Tech, Marlow had 180 rushing yards and set a modern school record with four touchdowns, three of which came in the first 4 minutes of the game. Yellow Jackets coach Bobby Dodd called him the best back he'd ever coached against, and Marlow's 882 rushing yards shattered the school's single-season record.

Marlow would be one of the few bright spots of the 1951 season, Alabama's first losing campaign since 1903. His 233 rushing yards against Auburn, a 25-7 victory, marked only the second time in school history the 200-mark had been reached, and set a school record that would stand for 35 years. But he would be the only Crimson Tide player named All-SEC as the rest of the season was considered a disappointment even though Alabama outscored opponents 263-188 (thanks in large part to a 89-0 thrashing of Delta State). During the 5-6 year, Alabama lost its first televised game, 27-13 to Tennessee in Birmingham.

In 1952, Marlow had a little more help with Bobby Luna joining him in the backfield and sophomore defensive back Hootie Ingram led the nation with 10 interceptions, still a school record. Bob Conway's 95-yard kickoff return for a touchdown helped the Crimson Tide squeak out a 21-20 victory at LSU, but defending national champion Tennessee thumped Alabama 20-0 in Knoxville and Georgia Tech pulled out a 7-3 win in Atlanta.

The Crimson Tide shrugged off the loss to the Yellow Jackets to beat Maryland, which finished No. 1 in numerous polls the year before and coached by the legendary Jim Tatum, 27-7, Auburn 21-0 and then destroyed Syracuse 61-6 in the Orange Bowl.

"I just couldn't stop them," Drew said of his own players, but someone else almost did. The first year bowl games were televised, an Orange Bowl official reportedly asked the timekeeper to speed things up because the network was about to cut off the game. Alabama rushed for 286 yards and passed for 300 in setting 15 bowl records. Ingram also returned a punt 80 yards for a touchdown and a young quarterback out of Montgomery named Bart Starr had a touchdown pass.

Wrote Charles Isreal of the Philadelphia Bulletin: "The game demonstrated the superiority of the Southern teams over any aggregation that the damn Yankees could send across the Mason-Dixon Line."

Drew was voted SEC coach of the year and joined Zen Scott, Thomas and Wade as the only Alabama coaches with double-digit wins. Marlow, who after being selected in the first round of the National Football League Draft would spurn a contract offer from the New York Giants to play in Canada, finished his career with 2,560 rushing yards and was named All-American and All-SEC with Ingram and guard Jerry Watford.

Starr would eventually, and unceremoniously, be selected in the 17th round of the 1956 NFL Draft and become the winningest quarterback in league history. He led the Green Bay Packers to five world titles including two Super Bowls, was the MVP of Super Bowls I and II, and went back to coach the team from 1975 to 1983.

Starr was selected to the first-ever All-SEC academic team in 1953, which would go down as one of the most unusual seasons in Crimson Tide history. Despite ties against LSU, Tennessee—which was the first home television game, with Alabama alum Mel Allen calling the game with Volunteers alum Lindsay Nelson—and Mississippi State, the Crimson Tide still managed to claim its first SEC championship in eight years when Luna's fourth-quarter field goal gave it a 10-8 victory against Auburn.

An invitation was extended to play Rice in the Cotton Bowl, which featured a play remembered much longer than the 28-6 final score. With Alabama already down 7-6, Owls halfback Dickie Moegle broke through the line at the Rice 5 and by the time he was racing past the Crimson Tide sideline it was apparent a touchdown was imminent. That is until fullback Tommy Lewis stepped on to the field and drilled the startled Moegle.

As if coming out of a daze, Lewis returned to the bench and covered his head with a towel as fans booed. Rice was awarded a touchdown and at halftime Lewis went to Rice's locker room and apologized. Lewis' fabled explanation of why he made his tackle was simply, "I'm just too full of Bama."

Despite the efforts of All-SEC halfback Corky Tharp, Alabama's fortunes dipped in the second half against Rice, much like they would in the approaching years. An injury-plagued 1954 season ended with a 28-0 loss to Auburn, though the 4-5-2 Crimson Tide had an impressive tackle tandem of All-American George Mason and Sid Youngleman. Other high points were a 27-0 win over Tennessee and a 12-0 victory at LSU, but it wasn't enough to save Drew, who resigned with a career record of 45-28-7.

Among those mentioned as a possible replacement was former Alabama player and assistant coach Paul W. "Bear" Bryant, who after serving as a naval officer in World War II had coached at Maryland, Kentucky and went 1-9 in his first year at Texas A&M. Instead, the Board of Trustees athletic committee selected former player J.B. "Ears" Whitworth, who was the head coach at Oklahoma State and had been the comedian of the Crimson Tide's 1931 Rose Bowl team.

With Starr struggling due to back problems and completing just 55 of 96 passes for 587 yards, 1955 was the worst season in Alabama history. Not only did the undisciplined Crimson Tide finish 0-10, but none of the games were close including a 26-0 loss to Auburn. Alabama was outscored 256-48 and only twice did the offense manage to reach double digits on the scoreboard.

Whitworth didn't get his first victory until his 15th game, 13-12 against Mississippi State, ending a non-winning streak of 20 that went back to Oct. 16, 1954 (27-0 vs. Tennessee). A win against Tulane and tie with Southern Miss helped the Tide to a 2-7-1 record, but the 1956 season ended with a 34-7 loss to Auburn, confirming the program was in disarray. The only comfort was that Alabama didn't finish last in the SEC, placing ahead of LSU and Georgia.

Only Kentucky would be worse than Alabama in 1957, the last of Whitworth's three-year contract. The Crimson Tide opened with a 28-7 loss at LSU, 6-6 tie at Vanderbilt, 28-0 defeat at Texas Christian and a 14-0 loss at Tennessee. Alabama finished 2-7-1, giving Whitworth a record of 4-24-2 at Alabama.

Auburn, which under the direction of coach Shug Jordan crushed Alabama 40-0, went on to win its only national championship. At the time, it was arguably the lowest point in Alabama football history.

In 1958, that would all change, along with the landscape of college football, and not because teams would be allowed to go for two-point conversions after scoring a touchdown. Rather, it was because of two simple words:

"Mama called."

The Bear

1958–82

*W*ith J.B. "Ears" Whitworth's fate already sealed, Alabama's coaching search started well before the end of the 1958 season, but for all practical purposes it came down to just one person, Paul W. "Bear" Bryant, who had Texas A&M on the verge of winning a national championship.

Bryant was born Sept. 11, 1913 in the community of Moro Bottom, outside Fordyce, Ark., the 11th of 12 children, three of whom died as infants. His father was a farmer, but after he became ill when Paul was a small child his mother Ida Mae took over and everyone helped out.

"His nickname was Bear. Now imagine a guy that can carry the nickname Bear," Joe Namath said on ESPN Classic's SportsCentury series. It went all the way back to the age of 13, when Bryant accepted a challenge to wrestle a bear at a carnival for $1. Despite his efforts, he didn't get the money and the bear bit his ear.

Bryant's football career began as an eighth-grader and he eventually helped lead the Fordyce High School Redbugs to a state championship. From there, it was on to Alabama, and while practicing with the Crimson Tide in the fall of 1931 he took high school classes to finish up his degree. In June 1935, while still a player, Bryant secretly married Mary Harmon. Their first of two children, Mae Martin, was born nine months later. Paul Jr., who would become a prominent businessman, was born in 1944.

After graduating in 1936, Bryant was an assistant coach with Alabama for four years and Vanderbilt for two. After serving in the Navy, he was named the head coach at Maryland, but resigned after one season. From there, he took over Kentucky and guided the Wildcats to their only SEC championship in 1950. In eight seasons, Kentucky went 60-23-5 and played in four bowl games.

After the 1953 season, Bryant signed a 12-year contract extension with the promise from school officials that football would be the athletic department's top priority. When it became clear that wouldn't be the case because of basketball, he quit. Texas A&M signed him to a six-year deal to be coach and athletic director for $25,000 a season and an unprecedented one percent of the gate receipts, one day before Southern Cal made a lucrative offer that almost certainly would have snared Bryant.

That first training camp with the Aggies, Bryant took his players 250 miles west to a barren army base in Junction and essentially ran a brutal boot camp in 100-degree heat with no water breaks that would begin to define his legacy as a hard-nosed disciplinarian. More than 100 made the initial trip, but after 10 days less than one-third remained, the "Junction Boys."

"I don't want ordinary people," Bryant was quoted as saying. "I want people who are willing to sacrifice and do without a lot of those things ordinary students get to do. That's what it takes to win."

The Aggies went 1-9 in 1954, the only losing season of Bryant's career. Two years later, they went 9-0-1 and won the Southwest Conference championship. In 1957, Texas A&M was ranked No. 1 in the country with a showdown against Rice looming when Crimson Tide officials met with Bryant in secret and offered the coaching and athletics director jobs at Alabama, with Bryant's friend Henry Crisp agreeing to step aside as athletic director. Bryant agreed to a 10-year contract with an annual salary of $17,000 and a house, declaring: "I ain't never been nothing but a winner."

"I left Texas A&M because my school called me," Bryant said. "Mama called, and when Mama calls, then you just have to come running."

Like he did at Texas A&M, Bryant put players through the wringer during his first training camp, causing many veterans to quit. But the change was immediate and noticeable in the first game of the 1958 season. LSU, which was led by Heisman Trophy winner Billy Cannon and would go on to win the national championship, was down 3-0 at halftime and struggled to a 13-3 victory.

Alabama would finish 5-4-1, with more victories than the previous three seasons combined. The other losses were all close, 14-7 to Tennessee, 13-7 to Tulane and 14-8 to unbeaten Auburn. The 14 points were the most given up in a game the entire season, and Alabama outscored the opposition 106-75, the fewest points allowed since 1935. Quarterback Bobby Jackson led the team offensively with 472 rushing yards, 408 passing yards and 44 points.

After a bit of a slow start with a 17-3 loss at Georgia things came together midway through the 1959 season and while riding a four-game winning streak handed Auburn a 10-0 loss to end a five-year drought against the inter-state rival. With the victory, Alabama received its first bowl bid in six years, to play Penn State in the inaugural Liberty Bowl. Beforehand, Bryant took the team to New York City where Alabama alum and announcer Mel Allen hosted a dinner that was also attended by New York Yankees legend Joe DiMaggio.

Played in frigid conditions in Philadelphia, a fake field goal was the difference as Penn State won 7-0. Notable was that leading the Nittany Lions' defense was Chuck Jenarette, the first black player the Crimson Tide ever faced. Alabama finished 7-2-2 and was ranked No. 10, but also started a string of 24 straight postseason appearances.

By 1960, the Crimson Tide was already knocking on the door of greatness despite not having an All-American or first-team All-SEC selection yet under Bryant. It opened the season with a 21-6 victory on national television against Georgia, which was led by quarterback Fran Tarkenton, with a 6-6 tie against Tulane and a 20-7 loss at Tennessee the only setbacks. Among the highlights was a dramatic 16-15 come-from-behind victory against Georgia Tech in which Bryant seemingly uncharacteristically walked into the locker room at halftime all smiles and told his players "Now we have them right where we want them," despite being down 15-0. Backup quarterback Bobby Skelton converted four fourth-downs on a touchdown drive and set up backup kicker Richard "Digger" O'Dell for the game-winning field goal that bounced off the crossbar and through the uprights with 3 seconds remaining.

A 3-0 victory against Auburn, with the only points scored by kicker Tommy Booker, led to an invitation to the Bluebonnet Bowl in Houston to play the Texas Longhorns. Alabama appeared to score what could have been a decisive touchdown when Skelton landed on the goal line, but an official ruled him down before reaching the end zone. Instead, the game ended a 3-3 tie.

"I was in there," Skelton said. "I had chalk all over my jersey when I got up."

When Bryant was first hired at Alabama, he told both the incoming recruiting class and the remaining players that if they weren't there to win a national championship, they were in the wrong place. With a number of key players returning, in addition to 12,000 seats along with a press box and elevator added to the Tuscaloosa stadium, including capacity to 43,000, 1961 had the potential to be that season.

Led by quarterback Pat Trammell, linebacker/center Lee Roy Jordan and lineman Billy Neighbors, Alabama simply destroyed the competition, beginning with a 32-7 victory at Georgia. Opponents scored 25 points all season, compared to 297 for the Crimson Tide, with North Carolina State, led by quarterback Roman Gabriel, managing the most points, seven.

"They play like it is a sin to give up a point," Bryant commented.

After Tennessee managed a field goal in a 34-3 loss, no more points were allowed during the regular season with shutouts against Houston, Mississippi State, Richmond, Georgia Tech and Auburn.

"I don't know if that's a great team, but they most certainly were great against us," Auburn coach Shug Jordan said after the 34-0 loss. "I don't guess anybody has ever hit us that hard."

After the Georgia Tech victory, Alabama was ranked No. 1 in the Associated Press poll for the first time, which it would maintain through a 10-3 victory against Arkansas in the Sugar Bowl for the national championship.

"Regardless of who was coaching them, they still would have been a great team," said Bryant, who was named national coach of the year. "I said early in the season that they were the nicest, even the sissyist bunch I'd ever had. I think they read it, because later on they got unfriendly."

Fullback Mike Fracchia was named MVP of Alabama's first victory at the Sugar Bowl in three attempts. Neighbors was a unanimous All-American, the Crimson Tide's first since 1954, while Jordan and Trammell were second-team picks, in addition to All-SEC selections with Fracchia.

"He can't run, he can't pass and he can't kick," Bryant said about Trammell. "All he can do is beat you."

Alabama continued to do a lot of beating in 1962 despite the SEC having one of its strongest years ever and sweeping three of the four major bowls. The Crimson Tide opened with a 35-0 victory against Georgia and fans were dreaming of back-to-back national titles, until Georgia Tech on Nov. 17. The previous year, linebacker Darwin Holt caught Yellow Jackets quarterback Emile Granning with an elbow on a late hit, fracturing his jaw. Georgia Tech didn't forget and pulled out a hard-hitting 7-6 victory when Alabama came inches short of completing a 2-point conversion.

Led by Jordan—a unanimous All-American who finished fourth in Heisman Trophy balloting—Alabama came back to destroy Auburn 38-0 and Oklahoma 17-0 in the Orange Bowl. Normally, most of Bryant's post-game praise went to Jordan, who had an amazing 31 tackles in the game, but this time it was directed at "potentially the finest quarterback I've ever coached," said Namath.

Alabama finished 10-1 and ranked No. 5. Fifteen seniors finished their careers after going 29-2-2 their last three seasons.

However, two off-field incidents got the dander up of Alabama fans. The first was at the Orange Bowl, when President John F. Kennedy visited Oklahoma coach Bud Wilkinson, who was on his physical fitness council, but not the Crimson Tide locker room. Just a year before, Kennedy attended the Hall of Fame dinner in New York to celebrate Alabama's national championship and was named an honorary Crimson Tide letterman, but many saw it as a snub due to the increasing hot issue of racial integration.

The other came in the spring of 1963 when the Saturday Evening Post, which Bryant was already suing regarding an article by an Atlanta-based sports writer for calling the Crimson Tide a dirty team (from the 1961 Georgia Tech game), accused Bryant and Georgia athletics director Wally Butts of fixing their game so they could bet on it. The article also alleged that Bryant had thrown the loss to Yellow Jackets. Both Bryant and Butts sued, and while investigating, attorneys found that the story had been based on false and fabricated evidence. A court awarded Butts $460,000 and Bryant later settled with Curtis Publishing for $300,000.

Back on the football field, 1963 was supposed to be a rebuilding year, but someone forgot to tell the Crimson Tide, which kept winning despite having no All-Americans and just one All-SEC player, running back Benny Nelson. Without most of the star players from the previous season, only a 10-6 loss to Florida and a 10-8 defeat by Auburn kept Alabama from running the table. However, when Namath violated the team's no-drinking policy, Bryant suspended him for the final two games of the season. The first was against Miami on Dec. 14, rescheduled after President Kennedy was assassinated on Nov. 22. With backup Jack Hulbert starting, Alabama pulled off a dramatic 17-12 victory before heading to the Sugar Bowl.

According to local legend, Bryant said his team's chances against SEC champion Ole Miss were the same as getting snow in New Orleans. The next day the Crimson Tide was welcomed by a city covered in the white stuff. Alabama didn't reach the end zone, but didn't have to. The defense made six fumble recoveries and three interceptions to offset the Rebels' statistical advantage of 248 yards to 194. Tim Davis' four field goals, of 31, 46, 22 and 48 yards led to a 12-7 victory and for the first time in Sugar Bowl history a kicker was named game MVP.

Namath returned in 1964, but during the fourth game of the season against North Carolina State sustained a knee injury that would limit him for the rest of the year. Steve Sloan would replace him and lead victories against Florida, Tennessee, Mississippi State and LSU. Against Georgia Tech in Atlanta, with Bryant wearing a helmet on the sideline for his own protection, Namath entered the game late in the second quarter with a 0-0 tie. By halftime, it was 14-0, en route to a 24-7 Alabama victory.

Namath performed similar heroics against Auburn on Thanksgiving Day. A touchdown pass to end Ray Perkins and Ray Ogden's 108-yard kickoff return added up to a 21-41 victory, a 10-0 record, and, combined with Notre Dame's loss to Southern Cal, a No. 1 ranking. Alabama was invited to play Texas in the first night Orange Bowl, a game remembered for its controversial officiating as much as anything else.

Once again, Namath came off the bench and completed 18 of 37 passes for 255 yards and two touchdowns. In the closing seconds, Alabama had the ball inches away from the goal line and was down 21-17. The call was a quarterback sneak behind center Gaylon McCollough, who with the snap plowed into the end zone. One official signaled touchdown, but another overruled. Namath said afterward: "I'll go to my grave knowing I scored."

Guard Wayne Freeman, tackle Dan Kearley and halfback/kicker David Ray were named to various All-American teams (back Mickey Andrews was second team) along with Namath, who went on to have a prolific career in the National Football League. Ironically, that year's Heisman Trophy winner, John Huarte of Notre Dame, would be one of Namath's backup quarterbacks with the New York Jets.

Also leaving the Crimson Tide was assistant coach Gene Stallings, who accepted the head coaching job at his alma mater, Texas A&M, where he had been one of Bryant's Junction Boys.

Even with the loss to Texas, Alabama was considered the national champion, but in 1965 the Associated Press poll decided for the first time it would hold its vote after the bowl games instead of at the conclusion of the regular season. Strangely enough, it again worked in Alabama's favor, but only after a controversial start to the season in which Georgia scored a game-winning touchdown on a play the receiver should have been called down for an 18-17 victory.

A 7-7 tie to Tennessee, in which young quarterback Kenny Stabler had Alabama in scoring range late in the game only to throw the ball away on fourth down when he mistakenly thought the scoreboard was correct and it was only third down, would be the only blemish the rest of the season. It was also able to steal a victory against Mississippi State with some hyjinks of its own.

Bryant was known for being innovative both on and off the field, even in something like recruiting. Before roster limits were enforced, he would give some recruits scholarships not so much to get them on the Crimson Tide, but to keep them off other teams. When recruiting rules became stricter, he was able to add players by making sure they acquired scholarships in other sports and then "walk on" the football team. On the flip side, many a story has been about told about how Bryant would walk into a recruit's house and simply say, "Welcome to Alabama," and the matter was settled.

On the field, he wasn't afraid to go for it on fourth down, would surprise the opposition with drop kicks and against the Bulldogs dusted off the tackle-eligible play. By having future radio announcer Jerry Duncan move off the line of scrimmage he could become a ball carrier or make a legal reception, a play the SEC would quickly deem illegal during the following offseason.

After beating LSU 31-7 and Auburn 30-3, Alabama was ranked No. 4 and turned down an opportunity to play in the Cotton Bowl to meet No. 3 Nebraska in the Orange Bowl and keep its dim national championship hopes alive. Thanks to No. 1 Michigan State losing to UCLA in the Rose Bowl and No. 2 Arkansas getting beat by LSU in the Sugar Bowl, the Crimson Tide had a chance to defend its title.

Despite being outsized, Alabama out-gained Nebraska 518 to 377 yards and Bryant utilized both the tackle-eligible play and more than one on-sides kick in completing a masterful 39-28 victory for his second consecutive national championship, and third overall. Sloan was named both game MVP and along with center/linebacker Paul Crane an All-American. All-SEC selections were fullback Steve Bowman, Crane, defensive end Creed Gilmer, defensive back Bobby Johns and split end Tommy Tolleson.

But could Alabama make it three-in-a-row?

With players like "Snake" Stabler—who at times gave Bryant fits, and like Namath was once suspended, prompting the quote: "You just can't tell about left-handed crapshooters and quarterbacks"—Perkins and lineman tackle Cecil Dowdy, the Crimson Tide destroyed every team it faced, allowing just 37 points all season with five shutouts, including 21-0 against LSU and 31-0 over Auburn. The one exception was at Tennessee, a game played in the rain. Down 10-0 at halftime, Bryant surprised everyone again by walking around the locker room patting them on the back and again the Crimson Tide responded. Stabler led Alabama back in the fourth quarter to take an 11-0 lead, and when Tennessee missed a game-winning field goal Bryant said: "If he'd kicked it straight, we would have blocked it."

Alabama went to the Sugar Bowl for a rematch with Nebraska, but the game was only more lopsided than the year before. On the first play from scrimmage, Stabler threw a 45-yard pass to Perkins to set up the Crimson Tide's first touchdown and the 34-7 route was on. Stabler completed 12 of 17 passes for 218 yards, to be named the game MVP ahead of Perkins. Johns also had three interceptions.

However, it didn't lead to the coveted three-peat. Going into the bowls, Alabama was ranked No. 3 behind Michigan State and Notre Dame, which had played to a 10-10 tie with the Fighting Irish running out the clock (prompting Bryant to gruffly declare, "At Alabama, we teach our men to win"). That year, both Associated Press and United Press International decided to have their final voting before the bowls, and some believed the state's racial issues including Governor George Wallace's "Stand in the Schoolhouse Door," the Rosa Parks bus incident in Montgomery and the Selma civil rights march were a factor in the snubbing.

Even though the National Championship Foundation, Clyde Berryman, Cliff Morgan, ARGH Power Ratings, Earl Jessen, and Soren Sorensen all had the 11-0

Crimson Tide No. 1, Alabama didn't count it, though Crimson Tide fans would later call it the "13th" national championship or the one that got away.

Defensive tackle Richard Cole, Dowdy, Johns and Perkins were all named All-Americans. Guard John Calvert, Dowdy, Johns, Perkins and back Dickey Thompson were named All-Conference, and more seats were added in Tuscaloosa, bumping stadium capacity to 60,000.

Maintaining that level of excellence was nearly impossible, though after tying Florida State 37-37 in the 1967 opener and equaling the number of points allowed during the entire previous regular season, the Tide won its next three games before suffering its first defeat in 25 games, a 24-13 upset to Tennessee.

Highlighting the season was a 7-3 victory against Auburn, won by Stabler's 47-yard run in the mud for a touchdown. At 8-1-1, Alabama was off to the Cotton Bowl to face Texas A&M and Stallings in a teacher vs. pupil matchup.

Five turnovers did the Crimson Tide in, including two interceptions by Northport native Curley Hallman for the Aggies. When the 20-16 game ended, Bryant gave Stallings a bear-hug at midfield and both had numerous stories to tell for years.

"It was a third-down situation, but coach Bryant thought it was a fourth down," Stallings was quoted in the book "Talk of the Tide." "At that time, the rules were that if you sent a player into the game he had to play one down. Coach Bryant sent his punter in, I knew that he was confused. Nevertheless, he sent his punter in so I sent in a safety who could only field punts—he wasn't a football player, but he could field punts pretty well. Then I saw the Alabama coaching staff talking to coach Bryant over on the sidelines and finally he sent another player in and the punter came out. So I send my safety in so my other guy can come out and the official over on the sideline says, 'Whoa! You can't do that, he's got to stay in one play.' So I said, 'Now wait a minute, fellow, I'm sitting right here watching coach Bryant send his punter in and then coach Bryant took him out.' He looked at me and said, 'You ain't coach Bryant.'"

Stabler, wide receiver Dennis Homan and Johns were named All-Americans. They along with defensive end Mike Ford, linebacker Mike Hall and guard Bruce Stephens were All-SEC.

Narrow conference losses to Ole Miss (10-8) and Tennessee (10-9) in 1968 were primarily the result of a lackluster running game. Sophomore quarterback Scott Hunter kept the Crimson Tide winning, but it was a far cry from the dominating fashion of the previous years. Otherwise, the defense carried the team, which posted a 14-6 victory at Miami in the first live prime time game on ABC.

Against Auburn, Hall had 16 tackles and two interceptions while also making a touchdown reception at tight end to lead a 24-16 victory. Afterward, Alabama presented the game ball to former quarterback Trammell a week before he succumbed to cancer. Bryant called it the saddest day of his life.

The season ended with a 35-10 loss to Missouri in the Gator Bowl, where Alabama had minus-45 yards rushing and a total offense of 23 yards compared to Missouri's 402 without having to complete a pass. Hall and nose guard Sammy

Gellerstedt were named All-Americans, and tackle Alvin Samples joined them as All-SEC.

Alabama made (late) history when Wilbur Jackson became the first black player to accept a scholarship to play football for the Crimson Tide, and was followed by Bo Matthews. For years, Bryant had taken criticism for not integrating the team, but he maintained that the local social and political climate wasn't ready. During a deposition for an anti-discrimination lawsuit filed against the school, Bryant testified that he had been actively trying to recruit black players for years, but had found no takers.

By 1973, one-third of the team's starters would be black.

Alabama's fortunes flip-flopped in 1969, with the offense setting records and the defense struggling. In one of the rare true shootouts in Crimson Tide history, Hunter completed 22 of 29 passes for 300 yards against Ole Miss quarterback Archie Manning, who was 33 of 52 for 436 yards and also ran for 104 more. Even though Bryant told his assistants they were fired numerous times while storming up and down the sideline, Alabama won 33-32 on George Ranager's game-winning touchdown reception.

It proved to be the lone highlight of the season. While Ole Miss went on to the Sugar Bowl, Alabama lost its next two games to Vanderbilt (14-10) and Tennessee (41-14). LSU and Auburn also posted solid victories against the Crimson Tide, which with a 6-4 record took a 47-33 pounding by Colorado in the Liberty Bowl. Samples was the team's lone All-American and also had the distinction of being voted outstanding lineman of the Liberty Bowl even though due to injuries he played the entire game at linebacker.

However, for the second straight year the season ended with tragedy when center Richard Grammer drowned in a hunting accident after his boat capsized. That was followed by former assistant coach Hank Crisp, who after 50 years with the university died of a heart attack approximately an hour before being inducted into the Alabama Hall of Fame. In 1991, the Hank Crisp Indoor Facility on the Tuscaloosa campus was dedicated in his honor.

Following the 1969 season, Bryant was offered a five-year, $1.7-million deal to coach the NFL's Miami Dolphins. He was tempted, but declined, saying he would never leave Alabama for financial reasons. Instead, the Dolphins lured Don Shula away from the Baltimore Colts.

Things didn't get much better in 1970, when Alabama posted a 6-5-1 record. Hunter was slowed by injuries, but junior running back Johnny Musso took up the slack and earned All-American honors. In the season opener, Southern Cal crushed the Crimson Tide 42-21 in Birmingham. Afterward, Bryant brought Trojans halfback Sam Cunningham, who had rushed for 135 yards and scored two touchdowns, into the Alabama locker room so his players could offer congratulations. Noted assistant coach Jerry Claiborne: "Sam Cunningham did more to integrate Alabama in 60 minutes than Martin Luther King did in 20 years."

Rough losses to Ole Miss (48-23) and Tennessee (24-0) had fans grumbling that maybe the game was passing Bryant by. A 30-21 upset of Houston in the Astrodome and a 35-6 victory over Mississippi State had Alabama above .500, but the Crimson Tide lost close games to LSU (14-9) and Auburn (33-28) and tied Oklahoma 24-24 in the Bluebonnet Bowl when a short field-goal attempt was deflected on the game's final play.

Uncharacteristically, Alabama had given up 264 points, after yielding 268 the previous season. Although he didn't say anything at the time, Bryant had seen enough and was ready to make sweeping changes.

THE BEAR CHARGES BACK

During the summer of 1971, Bryant quietly slipped out of Tuscaloosa to go visit his friend Darrell Royal at Texas. There, he studied the intricacies of the wishbone offense, which was designed to give the quarterback the option of handing off, throwing, running the ball himself or pitching out to a running back. Without a pure passer on the roster it would be the Crimson Tide's new offense, and players and coaches were sworn to absolute secrecy because Alabama's first game would be a rematch with Southern Cal.

Somehow, word didn't leak out and when Alabama arrived in Los Angeles, it was college football's equivalent of the Trojan Horse. Combined with a renewed emphasis on hard-hitting defense and bigger offensive linemen, the Crimson Tide surprised and shocked heavily-favored USC 17-10. It served notice to the rest of college football: 'Bama, and Bryant, was back.

From there, the Crimson Tide posted impressive victories over nationally-ranked Ole Miss (40-6), Houston (34-20), Tennessee (32-15) and LSU (14-7). For the first time, both Alabama and Auburn entered the Iron Bowl undefeated, and the Tigers were led by quarterback Pat Sullivan, who would go on to win the Heisman Trophy. But Alabama had Musso, a unanimous All-American whom Sullivan would have to share SEC player of the year honors with.

On national television, Alabama manhandled Auburn 31-7, prompting Bryant to say afterward: "I know one thing, I'd rather die now than to have died this morning and missed this game."

The only letdown of the season was a 38-6 loss to Nebraska in the Sugar Bowl, which was regarded as the national championship game. But joining Musso as an All-American was junior guard John Hannah, while linebacker Tom Surlas and defensive end Robin Parkhouse were second-team members. An even bigger accomplishment was defensive end John Mitchell became the first black player to start for the Crimson Tide.

Mitchell and quarterback Terry Davis both figured prominently in one of the greatest comebacks in Alabama history the following October at Tennessee. Down 10-3 with a little more than 2 minutes remaining, Davis led a rally with Jackson punching in a 2-yard touchdown. On the subsequent possession, defensive end Mike DuBose swatted the ball away from quarterback Condredge Holloway, with Mitchell recovering. A 22-yard run by Davis secured Alabama's 17-10 victory, and while Volunteers fans left Neyland Stadium in disbelief the Crimson Tide locker room was full of cigar smoke—a tradition started by Bryant against Tennessee.

Later that season, Alabama would be on the receiving end of a similar spectacular finish. After dominating Auburn all game long, the Crimson Tide had had two punts blocked and returned for touchdowns in the final minutes for a heartbreaking 17-16 final score.

With one loss, Alabama was again the SEC champion, but lost the "battle of the wishbones" against Texas in the Cotton Bowl, 17-13. Hannah, who would later be inducted into both the college and pro football halls of fame, would be named All-American along with center Jim Krapf and Mitchell, who was also named a team captain.

"I'll do it again in a minute," Mitchell said. "If you're a football player, you dream of playing for coach Bryant."

When Alabama opened the 1973 season with a 66-0 victory against a California team that featured quarterback Steve Bartkowski and running back Chuck Muncie, it was obvious that Bryant was ready to make another run for his fourth national championship.

Aided by halfback Randy Billingsley's blocks, Alabama had four players—Jackson, Richard Todd, Calvin Culliver and Jimmy Taylor—each reached 100 yards rushing during a 77-6 victory against Virginia Tech.

With a passing tandem of Gary Rutledge and Todd, the Crimson Tide laid waste to its SEC schedule, including a memorable 42-21 victory against unbeaten Tennessee in which Rutledge connected with wide receiver Wayne Wheeler for an 80-yard touchdown on the first snap of the game. Jackson, a team captain, capped the victory with an 80-yard score of his own.

On Thanksgiving, Alabama handled another unbeaten rival, LSU, 21-7 before pounding Auburn 35-0. Alabama would score a school-record 477 points and averaged 480.7 yards per game.

The season culminated at the Sugar Bowl with Alabama's first meeting against Notre Dame, in what might have been the most-hyped game in college football history. Bryant vs. Ara Parseghian lived up to the hoopla, but when Alabama couldn't put the game away in the third quarter, the Fighting Irish pulled out a 24-23 victory. Because UPI held its final rankings before the loss, the final time any poll was done so, Alabama was credited with the split, and unsettling, national championship. Guard Buddy Brown, linebacker Woodrow Lowe and Wheeler were named first-team All-Americans, while defensive end John Croyle, defensive tackle Mike Raines and cornerback Mike Washington were second-team.

Though Rutledge and Todd both suffered injuries, the 1974 season was almost an exact repeat of its predecessor. After winning a close 21-16 opener at Maryland, Alabama steamrolled through the SEC schedule with victories like 28-6 at Tennessee, 30-0 vs. LSU and 17-13 over Auburn, in which DuBose wrestled the ball away from quarterback Phil Gargis to secure the win. It set up a rematch with Notre Dame in the Orange Bowl, but this time only No. 1-ranked Alabama had a chance for the national championship with the Fighting Irish at No. 8. Still, in Parseghian's last game, the outcome was the same, with the final score 13-11. Defensive end Leroy Cook, center Sylvester Croom, Lowe and Washington were named All-Americans.

The 1975 season looked to be just as promising as the four before it, in which Alabama was an incredible 43-5, but after a surprising 20-7 opening loss to Missouri there was hardly any title talk in Tuscaloosa. From there, the Crimson Tide went on a tirade, allowing just 52 total points with no regular-season opponent finishing a game within 10 points. Along the way, Alabama beat Clemson 56-0, Washington 52-0, Tennessee 30-7 and Auburn 28-0. Against the Volunteers, the Tide defense, led by Cook, Lowe and tackle Bob Baumhower, sacked quarterback Randy Wallace 13 times.

During the Washington game, Alabama celebrated the 50-year anniversary of the original Rose Bowl victory, with each remaining player introduced by Bryant during an emotional halftime celebration.

With the SEC reaching an agreement for its champion to annually play in the Sugar Bowl, Alabama, which stunningly was winless in eight straight postseason games, was matched up against Penn State and coach Joe Paterno.

The game was 3-3 heading into the fourth quarter when Todd called a fortuitous time out.

"We had a sweep called to the left side, but I didn't like the defense they were in. I didn't want to take the chance of running a play," Todd said after the game. "So I called time. I went over to the sidelines and coach Bryant sort of winked at me. He called a pass."

Sophomore wide receiver Ozzie Newsome, who had been dazzling all season, ran a slant-and-go route and beat the single coverage for a 55-yard gain to set up the only touchdown of the game—an 11-yard sweep by halfback Mike Stock. Alabama won 13-6 and Todd, who completed 10 of 12 passes for 205 yards, was named MVP of the first Sugar Bowl played inside the Louisiana Superdome.

Afterward, reporters clamored to Bryant, but not about the time out. They wanted to know why he didn't wear his trademark houndstooth hat.

"My mother always taught me not to wear a hat indoors," he replied, much to the delight of Crimson Tide fans everywhere (especially the females).

With the 11-1 record, Alabama finished third in the polls while Oklahoma was credited with defending its national title. Cook and Lowe were named All-Americans, and nine players All-SEC, which had been the norm since 1971.

Prior to the 1976 season, Bryant warned fans and media alike that it would be a bit of rebuilding year, but most thought he was just expressing his usual summer pessimism. When the Crimson Tide lost its season opener 10-7 to Ole Miss, they realized he hadn't been exaggerating. Alabama came back to destroy SMU 55-3 and Vanderbilt 42-14, but then lost to Georgia in Athens 21-0.

Alabama won its next five games, including 20-13 at Tennessee, a come-from-behind 34-17 victory against Mississippi State and 28-17 over LSU, before it lost yet another close game to Notre Dame, 21-18. Still after soundly beating Auburn 38-7, the Crimson Tide received an invitation to play heavily-favored UCLA at the Liberty Bowl in Memphis. With high winds and below-freezing temperatures, the game was dubbed "The Refrigerator Bowl," which didn't suit the Californians at all. Led by its defense, Alabama took a huge lead and coasted to a 36-6 victory.

Sophomore linebacker Barry Krauss scored the first touchdown on a 44-yard interception return and was named game MVP.

"You gave us a good, old-fashioned butt-whipping and you know it," UCLA coach Terry Donahue told Bryant at midfield.

No one was sure what to expect in 1977, and an early-season 31-24 loss at Nebraska was cause for concern after quarterback Jeff Rutledge had five passes intercepted and the defense had given up its most points since playing the Cornhuskers in the 1972 Sugar Bowl.

But less than a month later, Alabama pulled off a 21-20 upset of No. 1 Southern Cal at the Los Angeles Coliseum when the Trojans decided to go for the last-minute victory and All-SEC defensive end Wayne Hamilton hit the quarterback, with Krauss intercepting the pass attempt on a two-point conversion. With the offense back in high-gear—led by Newsome, fullback Johnny Davis and halfback Tony Nathan—it served as a springboard with the Crimson Tide outscoring its next five opponents (including Tennessee, LSU and Miami) 176-26, and then handily defeated Auburn 48-21.

In another showcase matchup, Alabama drew Ohio State for the Sugar Bowl, which was hyped as featuring the game's two winningest active coaches between Bryant and Woody Hayes. Although they had combined for 503 wins, Bryant tried to deflect the attention, but when the Crimson Tide won a 35-6 rout, was quoted as saying: "Woody is a great coach . . . . and I ain't bad." Rutledge threw two touchdown passes to be named game MVP and Newsome ended up a unanimous All-American. He and guard Bob Cryder would be selected in the first round of the NFL Draft.

Alabama left New Orleans thinking it had made a good case for another national championship, but when Notre Dame upset No. 1 Texas in the Cotton Bowl the Irish leapfrogged the Crimson Tide from No. 5.

Similar to previous Alabama teams, the No. 2 finish motivated the 1978 squad even more, but this time it would really need it. Despite a preseason No. 1 ranking, the Crimson Tide had one of its toughest schedules ever with a murder's row of Nebraska, Missouri, Southern Cal, Washington, Florida, Tennessee, LSU and Auburn, followed by the presumably difficult bowl opponent.

The Crimson Tide cruised through the Cornhuskers 20-3, thanks in part to a 99-yard touchdown drive, and Missouri 38-20, but stumbled against Southern Cal 24-14—a loss that would in some ways come back to haunt Alabama. Still led by the defense, it didn't lose again during the regular season after defeating Auburn 34-16. No. 2-ranked Alabama was heading back to the Sugar Bowl to play No. 1 Penn State.

A 30-yard pass from Rutledge to split end Bruce Bolton with 8 seconds remaining in the first half gave Alabama a 7-0 lead, and the two teams traded touchdowns in the third quarter with running back Major Ogilvie following a block by tight end Rick Neal into the end zone.

However, in the final minutes Penn State recovered a misdirected pitchout at the Alabama 19 and soon found itself with third down at the 1.

"It was gut-check time," Krauss said. "We looked at each other. We knew this could be it. When they broke the huddle, everything got silent. Boy, talk about gut-checks."

Defensive back Don McNeal made the first stop roughly a foot away from the end zone and when Nittany Lions quarterback Chuck Fusina walked to the line of scrimmage to see how far the ball was from the goal line, defensive Marty Lyons warned him: "You'd better pass."

Instead, Paterno called Mike Guman's name for a run up the middle, where he was first met by Krauss and stopped cold short of the end zone—a dramatic image that would grace the cover of Sports Illustrated. Krauss was named game MVP and along with Lyons an All-American (both were also first-round NFL selections).

"That goal-line stand was something I'll never forget," Bryant said.

Alabama (11-1) thought the national championship was a slam dunk, but UPI voters had other ideas and promoted USC up from No. 3 in its poll, resulting in a split title.

There was only one thing to do, go undefeated in 1979 to cap the most dominating decade in college football. Led by three All-Americans—guard Jim Bunch, center Dwight Stephenson and McNeal—second-teamers E.J. Junior and Byron Braggs on the defensive line and five other All-SEC selections, that's exactly what the Crimson Tide did with Bryant winning his sixth national title.

With numerous starters returning, the Crimson Tide was the preseason No. 1 selection and it lived up to expectations by outscoring the first five opponents 219-9. The first scare of the season came against Tennessee, which had a 17-0 halftime lead. Bryant encouraged his players, but also put backup quarterback Don Jacobs in the game which Alabama dominated the second half for a 27-17 victory.

The second scare was at LSU, though the game wasn't as close as the 3-0 score indicated.

Turnovers led to the third and final scare, against Auburn. The Crimson Tide dominated statistically, but the Tigers still had a one-point lead in the fourth quarter when quarterback Steadman Shealy led an 82-yard drive on 13 plays for a 25-18 victory.

Before the Iron Bowl, Bryant commented that he would have to go back to Arkansas and plow if the Crimson Tide lost, prompting Auburn fans to yell "Plow, Bear, Plow!"

"Our winning drive was one of the finest I've ever seen," Bryant said. "We had to have it. I'm just thrilled to death with the win. We've got some mighty fine plow hands on his team."

(Note: Bryant understood the Iron Bowl rivalry better than anyone. Once when he was asked about the importance of getting a victory against Notre Dame, said: "Sure I'd like to beat Notre Dame, don't get me wrong. But nothing matters more than beating that cow college on the other side of the state.")

Once again the national championship would be settled at the Sugar Bowl, this time against Arkansas. After turning an early fumble into a field goal, the Razorbacks didn't know what hit them until it was 17-3 in the third quarter. Game

Men of good cheer? Hardly. The determined 1920 team finished 10-1 and outscored opponents 337-35. In 15 of the first 20 games under coach Xen Scott (top row, far left), Alabama didn't give up a single point. Leading the team was Riggs Stephenson (middle row, far left). Courtesy of the Paul W. Bryant Museum, the University of Alabama.

Harry Gilmer attempts one of his trademark leaping passes against Tennessee in 1945. Alabama won 25-7 at Legion Field in Birmingham. Courtesy of the Paul W. Bryant Museum, the University of Alabama.

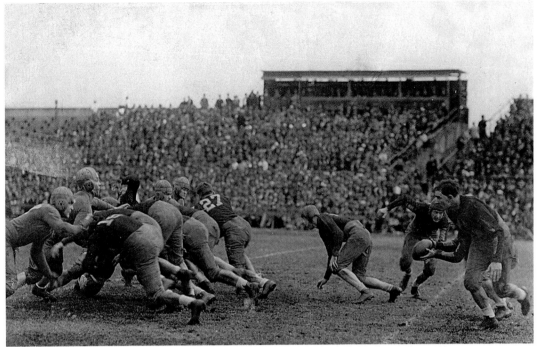

Johnny Mack Brown (in helmet) comes around for a reverse while Pooley Hubert steps forward to be his lead blocker. The 1925 team won 27-0 against Georgia at Rickwood Field in Birmingham and went on to win its first Rose Bowl game and national championship. Courtesy of the Paul W. Bryant Museum, the University of Alabama.

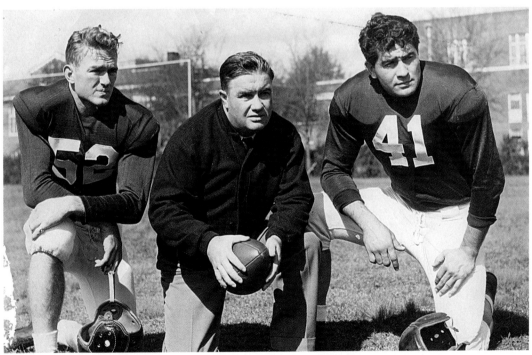

Harry Gilmer, coach Frank Thomas, and Vaughn Mancha pose in 1945. Alabama finished 10-0, but did not win the national championship. Courtesy of the Paul W. Bryant Museum, the University of Alabama.

What, no card? As university president, Dr. George Hutcheson "Mike" Denny was instrumental in making Alabama football a national power and used its success to improve the school's status. Courtesy of the Paul W. Bryant Museum, the University of Alabama.

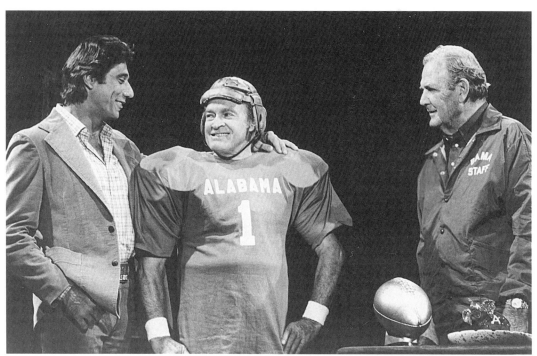

Joe Namath and coach Paul W. "Bear" Bryant joke around with Bob Hope in 1980. Courtesy of the Paul W. Bryant Museum, the University of Alabama.

William Gray Little is considered the father of Alabama football. Courtesy of the Paul W. Bryant Museum, the University of Alabama.

Joe Namath appears to be levitating as a North Carolina State player falls to his knees during a 21-0 victory in 1964. Later in the game, Namath suffered a knee injury that would limit his playing time the rest of the season. Courtesy of the Paul W. Bryant Museum, the University of Alabama.

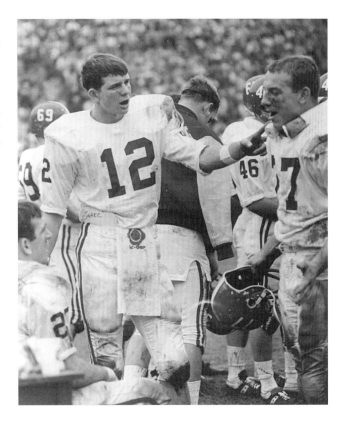

Kenny Stabler talks with Jerry Duncan and other teammates during the 1967 Sugar Bowl. Alabama defeated Nebraska 34-7 to finish 11-0, but did not win the national championship. Courtesy of the Paul W. Bryant Museum, the University of Alabama.

Coach "Bear" Bryant instructs quarterback Pat Trammell during the 34-0 Iron Bowl victory in 1961. The Crimson Tide went on to win the national championship. Courtesy of the Paul W. Bryant Museum, the University of Alabama.

Coach Paul W. "Bear" Bryant leans against the goalpost before career victory No. 314, which tied Amos Alonzo Stagg's record. Courtesy of the Paul W. Bryant Museum, the University of Alabama.

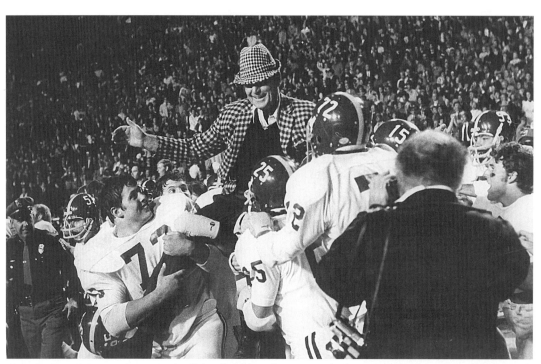

Coach "Bear" Bryant is carried off the field by players, including guard John Hannah (73) and linebacker Jeff Blitz (25), after Alabama defeated Auburn 31-7 in the 1971 Iron Bowl in Birmingham. Courtesy of the Tuscaloosa News.

Coach Paul W. Bryant wearing his trademark houndstooth hat. Courtesy of the Tuscaloosa News.

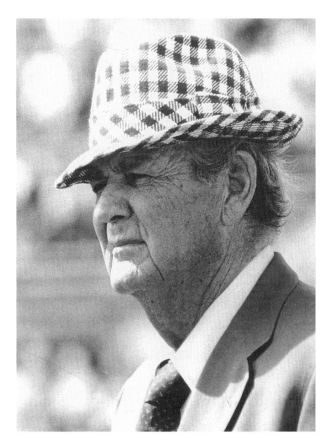

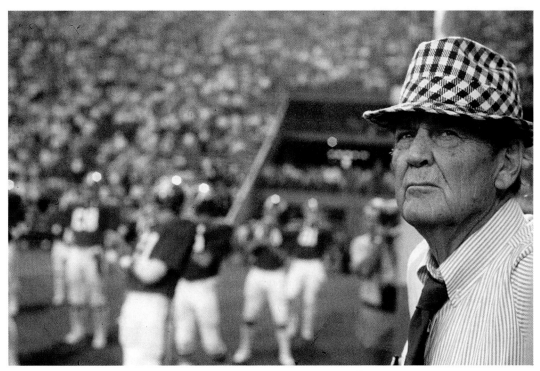

Coach Paul W. Bryant looks up into the stands near the end of his career as the Crimson Tide warms up for a game. Courtesy of the Tuscaloosa News.

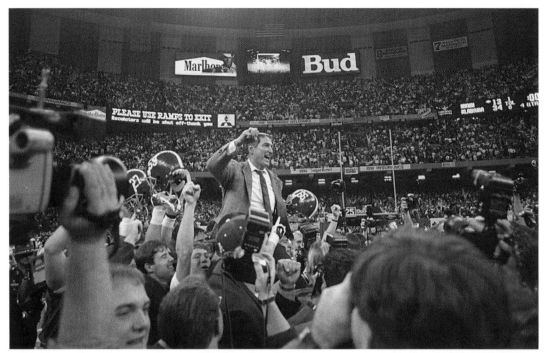

Coach Gene Stallings is carried off the field after Alabama beat Miami 34-13 in the 1983 Sugar Bowl. Photo by Kent Gidley. Courtesy of the Paul W. Bryant Museum, the University of Alabama.

Alabama players begin to celebrate winning the national championship after defeating Miami 34-13 in the 1983 Sugar Bowl. Photo by Kent Gidley. Courtesy of the Paul W. Bryant Museum, the University of Alabama.

MVP Ogilvie scored two touchdowns and had a 50-year punt return and Shealy led a 98-yard touchdown drive for a 24-9 victory.

This time, there would be no split national championship. At 12-0, Alabama was the only team in the country with a perfect record and a unanimous pick for No. 1, with USC second at 11-0-1. For the season, Alabama's defense yielded only 67 points, compared to 383 scored, with five shutouts.

For the 1970s, Alabama compiled an incredible 103-16-1 record with eight SEC titles and three national championships. It was considered the team of the decade, and when LSU fired Charles McLendon in 1979 for not being able to beat Alabama, Auburn's all-time winningest coach (176-83-6 from 1951-75) Jordan said: "You go by that and they'll have to fire us all."

Alabama thought it had a legitimate chance to make it three straight in 1980, but when Mississippi scored 35 points in the second game of the season (a 59-35 final), it appeared only a matter of time before the winning streak would end. It finally did at 28, a 6-3 loss at Mississippi State on Nov. 1. Two weeks later, Notre Dame won 7-0 in Birmingham, keeping the Tide winless against the Irish and opening the door for Georgia to win the SEC and national championships.

Led by Junior and linebacker Thomas Boyd, who were both named All-Americans, Alabama posted three shutouts, including 27-0 at Tennessee. Except for Auburn, which the Crimson Tide beat 34-18, none of the final seven opponents scored more than seven points.

Alabama capped the 10-2 season with a 30-2 victory against Baylor in the Cotton Bowl. While the defense limited the running combination of Walter Abercrombie and Dennis Gentry, who had nearly 2,000 yards during the regular season, to just 54 yards, Ogilvie became the first player to score a touchdown in four consecutive New Year's Day bowls and shared the MVP award with nose guard Warren Lyles.

In 1981, Bryant was chasing history of a different kind. At season's start, he was just eight victories away from Amos Alonzo Stagg's record of 314 wins over a 57-year career (he was a member of Walter Camp's original All-American team in 1889 at Yale and amazingly retired at the age of 90).

"All I know is, I don't want to stop coaching, and I don't want to stop winning, so we're gonna break the record unless I die," Bryant said.

But though only a few knew it at the time, Bryant's health was beginning to fail and he had coronary heart disease. Over the next year he would begin to develop heart problems and in 1978 had secretly checked himself in for alcohol rehabilitation, but left after a month and began drinking again.

"My life has been so tied up in football it has flown by," Bryant told the Tuscaloosa News. "Practice, recruiting and games. There hasn't been anything else but football."

This was also the man who once said, "There ought to be a special place in heaven for coaches' wives."

Still the record was a matter of when, not if. A 24-21 upset loss to Georgia Tech and a 13-13 tie to Southern Miss delayed the celebration, but during Alabama's first trip to Happy Valley to play Penn State, Bryant was finally in reach of tying the mark. Similar to the 1979 Sugar Bowl, the defense again made a goal-line stand and when the players walked off the field the coach tipped his hat to each of them.

Meanwhile, quarterback Walter Lewis and the offense had no such trouble in reaching the end zone as the Crimson Tide easily won 31-16.

Perhaps fittingly, Bryant would go for the record against Auburn, and it may have been the toughest ticket to get in state history. Not only did many former players attend, but the eyes of the nation were on Legion Field.

By the fourth quarter, Auburn was leading 17-14 when Lewis led a touchdown drive that had the sellout crowd chanting "315," and the emotions started to pour out of everyone, including legendary announcer Keith Jackson, who was also a close friend of Bryant's.

"I think it was the only time I saw him cry on the air," said Mike Swanson, who worked for years with Jackson on ABC broadcasts. "I think it was also the only time I heard him curse on the air as well."

When Alabama scored again in the closing moments, the celebration began early and after the clock reached zero Bryant was carried off the field. Two presidents, Ronald Reagan, who had been a sports reporter at the 1935 Rose Bowl that Alabama won, and Jimmy Carter, called to offer congratulations.

Perhaps experiencing a letdown, Alabama lost to Texas in the Cotton Bowl, 14-12, with the Longhorns scoring two touchdowns in the fourth quarter and then took a safety in the closing moments to secure the victory. Also overshadowed was that Alabama was co-champions of the SEC with Georgia, led by future Heisman Trophy running back Herschel Walker, giving Bryant his 13th conference title. Boyd and safety Tommy Wilcox were named All-Americans, with Lyles second team.

"I can honestly say that I didn't come to the University of Alabama because I thought it would be easy," Wilcox once said. "No, I came because I knew it would be hard."

It was about this time that Bryant came up with a new analogy, wanting players with a "Pete Rose mentality. He thinks baseball morning, noon and night. It's baseball, baseball, baseball."

At practice it was a different story. "I don't think we could beat anyone on our schedule today. So all I want you to do is the best you can."

Bryant's health continued to worsen in 1982, which would be his last season. After a solid 5-0 start, which included a 42-21 victory against Penn State, Tennessee pulled out a 35-28 victory in Knoxville. Three weeks later, the team suffered back-to-back losses to LSU (20-10) and Southern Miss (38-29), followed by a gut-wrenching 23-22 defeat against Auburn.

Two weeks later, on Dec. 15, Bryant announced his retirement, leaving a Liberty Bowl matchup against Illinois as the final game.

There was no way Alabama would lose. Led by cornerback Jeremiah Castille's three interceptions and a forced fumble, the Bryant era concluded with a 21-15 victory, and one last time players carried the Bear off on their shoulders.

Fullbacks Ricky Moore and Crain Turner, and flanker Jesse Bendross scored the touchdowns, all on runs, and a late interception by linebacker Robbie Jones sealed the victory. Castille was the game MVP, and along with Wilcox and defensive end Mike Pitts named an All-American, with center Steve Mott second team.

"I am proud they wanted to win this one for me," Bryant said.

Illinois quarterback Tony Eason gave Bryant one last great compliment when he said after the game: "Let's face it. Alabama just likes to hit you. They are the hardest hitting team I've ever played against."

Just 28 days later, Bryant's heart gave out on Jan. 26, 1983. He was 69.

The funeral was held in Tuscaloosa with the burial at Birmingham's Elmwood Cemetery. Eight players: Castille, Paul Ott Carruth, Paul Fields, Lewis, Mike McQueen, Jerrill Sprinkle, Darryl White and Wilcox, served as pallbearers. Hundreds of thousands watched the procession, not only as it went by Bryant-Denny Stadium and the university practice fields, but along the streets and interstate to Birmingham, more than 50 miles away. More than a man was gone, part of Alabama was laid to rest as well.

Statistically, Bryant's career legacy was a 323-85-17 record, 29 bowl appearances, 15 conference championships and six national championships. In the 1960s and 1970s, no school won more games than Alabama (193-32-5).

Off the field, plans were already under way for the Paul W. Bryant Museum, which would open in 1988, and Bryant had set up a scholarship fund for the children of his former players to attend Alabama (92 took advantage in the 2004-05 school year alone).

But he was more than the benchmark for coaching greatness. Bryant was an icon, a person who will forever be looked up to, beloved and admired in the South. It's said that his funeral could only be rivaled by those of Jefferson Davis, Elvis Presley and King.

"He literally coached himself to death," Hayes said at the funeral. "He was our greatest coach."

Perkins and Curry

1983–89

$\mathcal{R}$ay Perkins, who resigned his position as head coach of the National Football League's New York Giants (and replaced by Bill Parcells), had the nearly impossible task of trying to follow Paul W. "Bear" Bryant at Alabama. Selected by a search committee, which Bryant said he had no input with, Perkins had been an All-American receiver for him in the 1960s.

But that didn't stop Perkins from immediately attempting to distance himself from the Bear's legacy. One of Perkins' first moves was to take down Bryant's imposing coaching tower that stood over Thomas Field for practices. He was also the first Alabama coach to wear headphones on the sideline, like most other modern coaches, to communicate with assistants watching the game from the press box.

Everywhere Perkins went, he was reminded of Bryant, someone he too had emulated, but had to try and replace. Even players wore a little houndstooth hat on the back of their helmets in honor of their late coach.

At first the transition appeared to go as smoothly as possible, with the Crimson Tide winning its first four games of the 1983 season in impressive fashion and outscoring opponents a combined 148-44. But at Penn State, what should have been a touchdown catch by tight end Preston Gothard from quarterback Walter Lewis in the closing seconds was ruled otherwise, resulting in a controversial 34-28 loss. The following week, Tennessee pulled out a 41-34 victory in Birmingham, and Boston College followed suit with a 20-13 win.

Against Auburn, fans sat through a torrential rainstorm, only to see running back Bo Jackson lead a 23-20 victory. Alabama came back to upset No. 5-ranked Southern Methodist 28-7 in the Sun Bowl, with running back Ricky Moore recording his sixth-straight 100-yard performance.

His first season, which is normally difficult for any coach, Perkins' team went 8-4, with Lewis and Moore selected as second-team All-Americans. But there was also optimism for a quick return to greatness with the addition of a number of talented young players including outside linebacker Cornelius Bennett.

Unfortunately, it didn't carry over to the start of the 1984 team, which opened with a 38-31 loss to Boston College and future Heisman Trophy winner Doug Flutie, and running back Kerry Goode—who had 297 all-purpose yards after the second-half kickoff—was lost for the season with a knee injury. That was followed by losses to Georgia Tech, Vanderbilt and Georgia, plus heartbreaking defeats to Tennessee (28-27) and LSU (16-14).

With a losing season clinched and a bowl streak of 25 years ended, there were murmurs that Perkins' job might already be on the line, and against Auburn, which was targeting the SEC championship, the Crimson Tide was a clear underdog.

Perkins brought in every Alabama great he could, from Lee Roy Jordan and Joe Namath to Major Ogilvie and center Wes Neighbors' father, Billy. It worked. Alabama came out fired up and behind quarterback Mike Shula and running back Paul Ott Carruth had a 17-15 lead late in the fourth quarter. An interception gave Auburn a chance to win, but on fourth-and-goal at the 1-yard-line, coach Pat Dye went for a touchdown instead of a field goal and called for a toss sweep. When both Jackson and fullback Tommy Agee went the wrong way, safety Rory Turner dropped Brent Fullwood short of the end zone.

When asked about it after the game, Turner told reporters, "I just waxed the dude."

Bennett was named an All-American, but the victory was a potential turning point for the program. Further setting the tone was the 1985 season-opener at Georgia, a grinding, hard-fought game that was decided in the final moments. Down 16-13 with the ball at its own 29, the Crimson Tide went 54 yards on four plays and on the fifth Shula threw a 17-yard touchdown pass to junior college transfer wide receiver Al Bell for the 20-16 upset.

Alabama followed it up by beating Texas A&M, coached by Alabama alum Jackie Sherrill, 23-10 in its ESPN debut. Back-to-back last-second losses to Penn State (19-17) and Tennessee (16-14) cost a chance at the SEC championship, but the Crimson Tide was 7-2-1 going into the 50th anniversary of the Iron Bowl, and Auburn's Jackson was a week away from winning the Heisman Trophy.

It was one of the best games ever played between the rivals.

With Auburn leading 23-22 and less than a minute to play, Shula went to work. As if a replay of the Georgia game, he completed a pass to running back Gene Jelks, who had 192 rushing yards, handed off a reverse with Bell running 20 yards, and threw to wide receiver Greg Richardson to set up kicker Van Tiffin's dramatic 52-yard field goal with 6 seconds remaining.

At Alabama, it's simply known as "The Kick," and the antithesis to Auburn's "Punt, Bama, Punt," regarding the two blocked punts for touchdowns in 1972.

"A game like this, Alabama players will remember it for the rest of their lives," Dye said afterward. "Auburn players, it'll eat their guts out the rest of their lives."

For encores, defensive tackle Jon Hand and Bennett were named All-Americans and Alabama went to the Aloha Bowl and beat Southern Cal 24-3 after struggling with seven penalties for a 3-3 halftime score. Perkins called it: "The worst first half I have been associated with to play such a great second half."

Apparently back on track, Alabama was invited to participate in the 1986 "Kickoff Classic" in New Jersey against Ohio State, which would give the Crimson Tide an extremely difficult schedule. With the addition of young standouts like linebacker Derrick Thomas and running back Bobby Humphrey, who grew up across the street from Legion Field in Birmingham and had sold concessions at games, Alabama had an extremely talented team. It also suffered the tragic loss of two players when defensive tackle Willie Ryles collapsed during a practice and later died, and running back George Scruggs was killed in a car accident that also left cornerback Vernon Wilkinson in serious condition.

The Crimson Tide won its first meeting with the Buckeyes since the 1978 Sugar Bowl, 16-10, and after defeating Florida was 4-0 when it lined up for another shot at Notre Dame, which it still hadn't beaten in four attempts. Early on, Fighting Irish quarterback Steve Beuerlein faked a handoff and when he turned to his right immediately took the full brunt of a massive hit from Bennett.

"He knocked me woozy," Beuerlein said of "The Sack" after Alabama's 28-10 victory in Birmingham. "I have never been hit like that before and hopefully I'll never be hit like that again."

Bennett went on to be named an All-American for the third time, and SEC athlete of the year, but was also Alabama's first winner of the Lombardi Trophy, signifying him as the nation's best lineman. Tiffin, who finished his career making all 135 extra-point attempts, and Humphrey were also All-Americans.

Perhaps emotionally spent, the Crimson Tide came up short during the stretch run against Penn State (23-3), LSU (14-10) and Auburn (21-17), while rumors began to circulate that Perkins might leave to take over the head coaching job with the NFL's Tampa Bay Buccaneers. He initially denied them, but the scuttlebutt only gained momentum while Alabama headed to the Sun Bowl to handily defeat Washington 28-6. Led by Bennett, who was selected the game MVP, the defense yielded just 62 rushing yards. Humphrey scored three touchdowns to go with 159 rushing yards, and in his last game Shula completed 15 of 26 passes for 176 yards and two touchdowns.

After the dominating victory, Perkins resigned and left for Florida. While a 10-3 record his final season and 32-15-1 mark over four years despite the enormous pressures would have been considered impressive at most programs, Alabama wasn't like anywhere else. Fans and media had grown accustomed to championships, and try as he might Perkins wasn't Bear Bryant.

Nevertheless, another coaching search quickly began, with university president Joab Thomas instrumental in the selection of Bill Curry of Georgia Tech, who had a career record of 31-43-4. But in addition to also not being Bear Bryant, he had the double-whammy of being an outsider and the first head coach without an Alabama tie since Frank Thomas in 1937.

The beginning of the Curry regime appeared as unsettled as Bryant-Denny Stadium, which was being renovated to increase attendance to 70,123 fans, resulting in every home game played at Legion Field. A 38-6 opening victory against Southern Miss and a 24-13 win at Penn State eased immediate pressures, but the following week's 23-14 loss to Florida, in which Gators running back Emmitt Smith had a school-record 224 rushing yards and two touchdowns, set the tone for the season. Every accomplishment would seemingly be followed by a setback, and vice-versa.

A 13-10 loss to Memphis State was followed by a 41-22 victory against Tennessee. A 22-10 victory at LSU was nullified by a 37-6 pounding at Notre Dame. Somehow, the Crimson Tide still had a chance to be SEC champions, but only with a victory in the last Iron Bowl in which the schools evenly split the tickets at

Legion Field. But even with Thomas blocking a punt to give Alabama the ball at the Auburn 9, the offense still couldn't reach the end zone in a 10-0 defeat.

At 7-4, the Hall of Fame Bowl came calling with the Crimson Tide's first-ever matchup against Big 10 powerhouse Michigan, in which assistant head coach Gary Moeller replaced Bo Schembechler after he had a heart attack. All-American halfback Philip Doyle, who shared the honors with Humphrey (who had 149 yards on 27 attempts in the game), scored three touchdowns, and on fourth-and-3 at the Alabama 20, the Wolverines completed a touchdown pass with 50 seconds remaining to pull out a 28-24 victory.

Even before the 1988 season began, Curry had another setback when what was supposed to be Humphrey's run for the Heisman Trophy ended before it began. During spring practice, the prolific running back suffered a broken left foot, and while trying to play on it re-broke it during the home opener—a 44-10 blow-out of Vanderbilt—ending his Crimson Tide career. Also suffering a season-ending knee injury in that game was Jelks, whom Curry had moved to cornerback, during a kick return. He was joined on the sideline for three games by quarterback David Smith, who would come back and finish the season on a bad knee.

After an early season 22-12 home loss to Mississippi, Thomas put on a show against Penn State, with three sacks, eight individual tackles, one pass knocked down and eight additional quarterback pressures in an 8-3 victory. He would finish the season with 27 sacks, 12 tackles for a loss, 44 quarterback hurries and two blocked kicks, en route to setting school career records of 52 sacks and 74 tackles behind the line of scrimmage. Thomas was named both SEC male athlete of the year and the Butkus Award winner as the game's best linebacker, and finished 10th in voting for the Heisman Trophy.

"Whenever I see those crimson jerseys and crimson helmets, I feel humbled to have played football for Alabama," Thomas said. "Other players in the NFL talk to me about their schools and their traditions, I just smile knowing the immense love Alabama fans have for our school and its football program. I'm proud to be part of that Crimson Tide heritage."

After being selected by the Kansas City Chiefs in the first round (fourth pick overall after Troy Aikman, Tony Mandarich and Barry Sanders) of the 1989 NFL Draft, Thomas made nine consecutive Pro Bowl appearances before his career and life were both tragically cut short. While driving through a snowstorm and not wearing a seatbelt he lost control of his car, resulting in a broken back that left him paralyzed from the chest down. Thomas died from cardiorespiratory arrest 16 days later, on Feb. 8, 2000, at the age of 33.

Even with Thomas at his collegiate best in 1988, Alabama again failed to meet overwhelming and enormous expectations that were reflected in again-expanding Bryant-Denny Stadium, which opened the western upper deck for a 70,123 seating capacity.

A 19-18 loss to LSU and a 15-10 defeat against Auburn had fans grousing again and before the unique regular-season finale at Texas A&M, university president Roger Sayers called a press conference to deny rumors that Curry was about to be fired.

The "Hurricane Bowl" against the Aggies had originally been scheduled for Sept. 17, but postponed due to the threat of Hurricane Gilbert. Texas A&M even had a special queen and court of her "Seven Tropical Depressions" to mark the occasion, but it didn't help as Alabama won convincingly, 30-10.

At 8-3, the Crimson Tide headed to the Sun Bowl for its first meeting against Army. While Thomas blocked two kicks, Smith set two Alabama bowl records by completing 33 of 52 passes for 412 yards to be named MVP of the 29-28 come-from-behind victory. Joining Thomas on the All-American teams were guard Larry Rose and safety Kermit Kendrick.

Despite Sayers' vote of confidence, tension seemed to grow between Curry and almost everyone else in the state of Alabama, even as the Crimson Tide pulled out win after win during the 1989 season. A 47-30 victory against Tennessee followed by a 17-16 win at Penn State kept Alabama undefeated and with a 32-16 victory at LSU clinched the SEC championship, its first since Bryant. Tying an NCAA record that can never be broken, defensive back Lee Ozmint stepped in front of two-point conversion pass at his goal-line and returned it 100 yards.

"The first 50 yards I was praying no one would catch me," Ozmint said. "The last 50 yards I was praying that someone would."

With backup quarterback Gary Hollingsworth replacing injured starter Jeff Dunn, and setting a school record for passing yards, the Crimson Tide was ranked No. 2 heading into its first game at newly-expanded Jordan-Hare Stadium (85,000). In what was expected to be a low-scoring game, the two sides accumulated a combined 868 yards, but Auburn pulled out a 30-20 victory.

Outspoken fans and media didn't hold back, claiming that Curry couldn't even win a championship right, and, more importantly, couldn't beat Auburn. There were death threats and someone threw a brick through his office window. Unhappy and feeling unwanted despite winning the SEC title and flirting with a national championship, Curry decided he'd had enough. After Alabama lost 33-25 to Miami in the Sugar Bowl, clinching the national championship for the Hurricanes, he resigned and accepted the head coaching job at Kentucky.

"I knew Coach Curry was leaving when he came in the squad room with a blue jacket on and in its lapels were tickets to the Kentucky Derby," center Roger Shultz said after Curry told the team he was leaving.

His final season, the Crimson Tide finished 10-2, giving Curry a 26-10 record over three seasons. Senior cornerback John Mangum and junior linebacker Keith McCants were named All-Americans, and it would be both of their final years as McCants took advantage of a new rule that allowed him to declare himself eligible for the NFL Draft before his senior year. Running back Siran Stacy, tight end Lamonde Russell and Doyle were second-teamers while five other Crimson Tide players were All-SEC.

Once again, Alabama was adrift, but it wouldn't be for long as another member of the Crimson Tide family was called home.

Stallings

1990–96

*W*ith coach Bill Curry's departure, the University of Alabama didn't dare bring in another outsider to replace him, so it searched amongst its own, and even took a page from its own history in considering the reoccurring Texas A&M connection.

In retrospect, the decision by athletics director Cecil "Hootie" Ingram and university president Roger Sayers to hire Gene Stallings was essentially a no-brainer. He had been one of Paul W. "Bear" Bryant's original "Junction Boys" at Texas A&M ("All I know is that we went out there in two buses, and we came back in one," he said), and served as an Alabama assistant coach from 1958-64, including assistant head coach in charge of the defense his final season. From there, Stallings was the Aggies' head coach, compiling a 27-45-1 record before moving on to the National Football League for 14 years with the Dallas Cowboys and coach Tom Landry, and four seasons as the head coach of the St. Louis/Phoenix Cardinals (23-34-1).

"The expectation level is high at the University of Alabama and it should be," Stallings said. "What's wrong with people expecting excellence?"

Despite his losing record as a head coach, many believed that Bryant wanted Stallings to replace him at Alabama in 1982, but it took another eight years to become reality. By then, Bryant disciples were beginning to realize that their awaiting the second-coming of Bryant was probably in vain, but in many ways Stallings was close enough.

"I know that I picked up a great deal of things during my association with coach Bryant," Stallings said. "I know he influenced me as a coach by teaching me to never give up on your talent. And he told me there was no substitution for work. He convinced his people. And when players and coaches are convinced they can win, they're going to win."

It didn't seem that way when the 1990 team lost its first three games to Southern Miss (led by quarterback Brett Favre), Florida and Georgia, combined with season-ending injuries to running back Siran Stacy and wide receivers Craig Sanderson and Prince Wimbley. Though two of the losses had been close, Stallings agreed with fans and changed the direction of the team, focusing on power football.

Like the slow churning of a locomotive, the Crimson Tide started building momentum with a 59-28 victory against Vanderbilt and a 25-6 win at SW Louisiana. However, the proof that the program was back on track came at Tennessee, which was ranked No. 3 in the country. Tied 6-6 in the fourth quarter, defensive back Stacy Harrison blocked a field goal to set up a last-second 47-yard attempt by All-American kicker Phillip Doyle for a 9-6 victory.

"This has to rank right up there with the biggest wins I've ever had in my career," Stallings said.

Alabama lost the following week 9-0 to Penn State, the first shutout in Tuscaloosa since 1955, but rebounded to win its next four, including a 16-7 victory in the Iron Bowl, the first win against the Tigers since 1985. Despite a 34-7 loss to Louisville in the Fiesta Bowl, in which the Cardinals scored four touchdowns in the first quarter, hope had returned to Tuscaloosa. Besides, Louisville's head coach was Howard Schnellenberger, an assistant coach under Bryant at both Kentucky (1959-60) and Alabama (1961-65).

A 41-3 opening victory against Temple had fans expecting greatness in 1991, but the Crimson Tide responded with a flat 35-0 pounding at Florida. Although an SEC championship appeared out of reach, Alabama pursued it anyway and came close, with a 24-19 victory against Tennessee, the first of many narrow victories during the second half of the season. When quarterback Danny Woodson was suspended for violating team rules, freshman Jay Barker stepped in and led a 20-17 victory at LSU, followed by a nail-biting 13-6 win in the Iron Bowl.

At 10-1, Alabama drew defending national champion Colorado in the Blockbuster Bowl, where a young exciting player out of Birmingham named David Palmer helped inspire a 30-25 victory. After setting a school record with three punt returns for a touchdown during the regular season, "The Deuce" opened the scoring with a 52-yard return and was named the "Brian Piccolo Award" as game MVP. Touchdown passes from Barker to Stacy and wide receiver Kevin Lee highlighted the second-half comeback and had fans excited about 1992. Nose tackle Robert Stewart was named an All-American, but the Tide felt slighted in All-SEC voting, with just Stacy, Stewart and linebacker John Sullins named first-team, and defensive ends John Copeland and Eric Curry, and defensive back Antonio Langham and George Teague relegated to second-team status. Each would play huge roles during the season to follow.

The centennial season of Alabama football began with the Crimson Tide ranked anywhere from first to No. 9 in preseason polls, but was at the bottom end of that spectrum according to both USA Today/CNN and the Associated Press (Note: Only Corky Simpson of the Tucson Citizen, whom the author had the privilege of working with from 1998-2000, voted Alabama No. 1 in AP and refused to bump the Tide down until it lost).

The victories started piling up, though many were not pretty: 25-8 against Vanderbilt, 17-0 vs. Southern Miss, 38-11 at Arkansas, 13-0 vs. Louisiana Tech, 48-7 vs. South Carolina, 37-0 at Tulane. In the pivotal game of the season, which often determined which team would launch itself into contention for the SEC title, running back Derrick Lassic had 142 rushing yards and Alabama shut out Tennessee 17-0. The victory cigars were blazing in Knoxville.

"We finally got a little bit of respect," Lassic said.

It wasn't until three weeks later that Alabama would really start reaping rewards. While the defense limited LSU to just 22 rushing yards in a commanding

31-11 road victory, top-ranked Washington lost to Arizona (strangely enough the team Simpson covered) to put the Crimson Tide in contention for the national championship. It would come down to three games.

The first was the Iron Bowl on Thanksgiving, but Auburn came up with a turkey and not because coach Pat Dye announced one day before the game that it would be his last season with the Tigers. Early in the third quarter, Langham stepped in front of a pass and returned it 61 yards for a touchdown. With the defense yielding just 20 rushing yards and getting five sacks, Alabama won going away 17-0.

"Ten to nothing isn't a very big deal unless you've got a defense like Alabama's got, and then it's monumental," Dye said after his only shutout at Auburn. "Alabama may have the best defense I've seen in our conference."

For the season, Alabama outscored its opponents 366-122, prompting defensive coordinator Bill Oliver to say: "I wish Coach Bryant were here to see this defense play."

The second was the first-ever SEC championship game—after Arkansas and South Carolina entered the conference, splitting it into Eastern and Western divisions—played against Florida at Legion Field in Birmingham. Another Langham play would decide the outcome when in the final minutes he stepped in front of a Shane Matthews pass and retuned it 27 yards for a touchdown and 28-21 victory. Langham was named game MVP.

The third, and final test was the Sugar Bowl against No. 1 Miami, and riding a 28-game winning streak, the Hurricanes didn't believe the Crimson Tide deserved the same level of respect as the defending champions.

"We seek, we destroy," Miami linebacker Michael Barrow said. "We fear no one, but everyone fears us."

One pregame comment that especially attracted attention was Hurricanes wide receiver Lamar Thomas: "Alabama's cornerbacks don't impress me one bit. They're overrated. Real men don't play zone defense and we'll show them a thing or two come January 1st."

Just about everyone considered the Crimson Tide underdogs in the national championship game. That is, everyone outside the state of Alabama.

"Everyone says we can't beat Miami, but we are not just anybody. We are Alabama," Palmer said.

Led by its defense, the Crimson Tide began to take control in the second quarter. Unable to run, finishing with just 48 yards on the ground, the Hurricanes' hopes would ride the arm of Heisman Trophy winner Gino Torretta, but he had never faced a defense like Alabama's.

"In the second quarter, I saw Torretta look over at me and he froze for a second," Copeland said. "I saw fear."

After taking a 13-6 halftime lead, Alabama smelled blood. On Miami's first offensive play of the third quarter, cornerback Tommy Johnson intercepted a pass and returned it to the Hurricanes' 20. Six plays later, Lassic, who was named game MVP, scored from the 1.

Down 20-6, Miami didn't know how to react. On its next possession, Torretta found himself in shotgun formation with all 11 defenders on the line of scrimmage. The result was another interception, with Teague returning it for a 31-yard high-stepping touchdown.

That was followed by possibly the greatest play in college football history that didn't count. Torretta hit Thomas in a full sprint and the wide receiver appeared to be gone for a long touchdown, only Teague had other ideas. Not only did he chase down Thomas before reaching the end zone, but he ripped the ball away from him in mid-stride and started running the other way.

Even though nullified by a penalty, it's called the "Play of the Century" at Alabama.

"We had great respect for Alabama, especially its defense," Miami coach Dennis Erickson said after the 34-13 loss. "We knew they were a formidable opponent. But in retrospect, I think they were a lot stronger than a lot of our people thought."

The victory was so dominating that the Crimson Tide never even bothered to establish its passing game, with Barker throwing just four times for 18 yards. Meanwhile, the punishing ground game accumulated 267 rushing yards.

The celebration began with Stallings being carried off the field, and didn't end for months. More than 15,000 showed up at Coleman Coliseum for a congratulatory banquet and 60,000 were on hand for the victory parade and pep rally (including Simpson, who proclaimed "I was just that stubborn" for voting Alabama No. 1 in every poll). General Colin Powell, who was Chairman of the Joint Chiefs of Staff, visited Tuscaloosa and, in turn, the team traveled to Washington, D.C., to meet President Bill Clinton.

"There is a quote I've used before from Sir Isaac Newton," Stallings said in a speech during the on-campus "Salute to Champions" weekend. "It says, 'If I can see farther than most, it is because I have stood on the shoulders of giants.' Ladies and gentlemen, I have stood on the shoulders of giants."

Bookends Copeland and Curry, along with Langham, were named All-Americans, while linebackers Lemanski Hall, Antonio London and Derrick Oden, Lassic, center Tobie Sheils and Teague were first-team All-SEC. Stallings was a unanimous selection for coach of the year and was presented the Paul Bryant Award by the Football Writers Association of America.

"Even though we had a lot of guys from that team go to the NFL, talent-wise Miami had more talent," Hall said years later. "We had more heart and desire, and that's the major difference. What coach Stallings installed in us was that you can do anything if you set your mind to it. Be accountable. If you're accountable in life and work hard, good things will happen."

But even with its 12th national championship, not all was well with the Crimson Tide. After a night of celebrating, Langham, who had just finished his senior season, signed with a sports agent on a cocktail napkin making him eligible for the NFL Draft and a family member accepted a loan. Unsure what he had done, Langham contacted Stallings, who in turn tried to have the deal nullified.

Alabama was already on the radar of the National Collegiate Athletic Association after Gene Jelks, who many thought was still mad about being moved from running back to cornerback by coach Bill Curry and the affects it had on his curtailed career, said he had received loans from a booster based on his potential earnings as a professional. Nothing became of Jelks' case, though it did lead to numerous accusations that his attorney fess were paid by someone connected to Auburn (ratcheting up rivalry's intensity even higher), but Langham's would take years to unfold. When the agent produced the signature near the end of the 1993 season, it was a matter of what the NCAA penalties would be, not if.

Still, Alabama had an impressive 1993 season despite numerous injuries. After opening with a 31-17 victory against Tulane, it won the next four games by a combined score of 133-18. Thanks to a last-minute drive for a touchdown and a two-point conversion by Palmer, the Crimson Tide salvaged a 17-17 tie (the last in Alabama history as three years later the NCAA would adopt overtime) against Tennessee. But Alabama lost 17-13 to LSU without injured Barker and 22-14 to Auburn when he missed most of the fourth quarter. Ironically, the Iron Bowl couldn't be shown on network television due to NCAA sanctions against Auburn, but 55,000 showed up at Bryant-Denny Stadium to watch it on a giant screen.

The Crimson Tide still managed to reach the SEC Championship, only this time Florida was ready and won 28-13 at Legion Field. Alabama went on to the Gator Bowl, where backup quarterback Brian Burgdorf engineered a 24-10 victory over North Carolina and was named game MVP.

Although Alabama finished 9-3-1, two years later the NCAA ruled that every regular-season victory would have to be forfeited, making the Gator Bowl the only official "W" of the 1-12 season. Langham still won the Jim Thorpe Trophy, given to the best defensive back of the country, and Palmer finished third in Heisman Trophy voting before heading to the NFL a year early. Both were named All-Americans along with kicker Michael Proctor.

With NCAA sanctions hanging over the program in 1994, Alabama put together another title run by winning a number of close games. It pulled out a 17-13 win at Tennessee and despite a delay in the second quarter due to a thunderstorm beat Ole Miss 21-10 to remain undefeated. For the first time since 1971, the Iron Bowl featured unbeaten teams, though the Tigers had a tie. Despite playing with a bad shoulder, Barker led a 21-14 victory.

For the third straight year, the SEC Championship pitted Alabama against Florida, coached by Steve Spurrier, though the game location was new, Atlanta. The Crimson Tide rallied for a 23-17 lead when linebacker Dwayne Rudd returned an interception for a touchdown, but Gators quarterback Danny Wuerffel rallied back for a 24-23 victory and Sugar Bowl berth.

Alabama accepted an invitation for the Citrus Bowl, where it would play an extremely talented Ohio State squad that included quarterback Bobby Hoying, wide receivers Joey Galloway and Terry Glenn, tackles Korey Stringer and Orlando Pace, tight end Ricky Dudley, linebacker Craig Powell, cornerback Shawn Springs and 1995 Heisman Trophy winner Eddie George.

In a game featuring a stray dog running on to the field, Barker concluded his college career with a last-minute touchdown pass to senior running back Sherman Williams and 24-17 victory. With 166 rushing yards, 155 receiving yards and two touchdowns, Williams was named game MVP.

Not including the forfeited games in 1993 (which had yet to become official), the senior class finished 45-4-1, setting a school record for victories over a four-year period. Barker won the Johnny Unitas Award as the nation's best quarterback, and with Proctor was named All-American, with defensive end Dameian Jeffries and tailback Sherman Williams second team.

Prior to the start of the 1995 season, the NCAA finally announced a decision regarding Langham, but the Committee on Infractions also ruled that Alabama's faculty representative, professor Tom Jones, had lied to the governing body, resulting in further sanctions. In addition to the forfeits, the Crimson Tide was sentenced to a one-year bowl ban and ordered to give up 30 scholarships over a three-year period.

Even though no school had successfully appealed an NCAA penalty, Alabama did, and, thanks to further investigation, won, with the ethics charges dismissed. Seventeen of the scholarships were restored, but Jones went on to sue the NCAA for libel (and won, also in unprecedented fashion).

It wasn't until after the Iron Bowl that it became official Alabama wouldn't play in a postseason game, which only magnified problems on the field and a quarterback controversy between Burgdorf and Freddie Kitchens.

Against Arkansas, officials didn't notice that the Razorbacks had 12 players on the field in the final seconds of a 20-19 loss. At Auburn, Kitchens led a last-minute possession that stalled deep in Auburn territory, only photographs later showed that wide receiver Curtis Brown had caught a pass in the end zone that was incorrectly ruled incomplete in the 31-27 loss. Alabama's other defeat was 44-14 against Tennessee and quarterback Peyton Manning, the Volunteers' first victory against the Crimson Tide since 1985.

Thanks to three victories in particular: 10-3 against LSU, 31-0 at Georgia (with Stallings celebrating by commandeering a police motorcycle after crossing the state line) and 24-20 vs. Southern Miss when Burgdorf connected with wide receiver Toderick Malone for a 30-yard touchdown on the final play of the game, Alabama finished 8-3. But with no bowl game, the Auburn loss and upcoming scholarship reductions the season ended on a definite down note. Only defensive tackle Shannon Brown was second-team All-American.

Despite it all, Stallings still had some magic in him for 1996, though a shot at another national championship would likely be out of reach. Alabama opened with seven straight victories, including a 17-7 win against Arkansas on Sept. 21 that was the 1,000th game in school history, before another emotional roller-coaster began.

At Tennessee, a missed short field goal gave the Volunteers a chance to steal a 20-13 victory. A botched extra point gave Mississippi State a 14-13 win. Sandwiched between them was a dominating 26-0 victory at LSU in which running back Shaun Alexander had a school-record 291 rushing yards on 20 carries and four touchdowns.

Alabama still had a chance to play in the SEC Championship, but only with a victory against Auburn. Then the Monday before the game, Stallings informed a number of school officials that he would retire at season's end, primarily to spend more time with his son John Mark, who had Down's Syndrome. Though many have believed trouble with the NCAA had taken its toll on Stallings, and others have written that there were problems with the new athletic director Bob Bockrath, he's never confirmed either claim.

On terms of pure entertainment, it was one of the best Iron Bowls ever, going back-and-forth until the final minute when Auburn fans thought they finally had the game won. A 6-yard swing pass from Kitchens to tailback Dennis Riddle silenced them and the extra point by senior transfer Jon Brock provided the winning point, 24-23.

Stallings made his decision public after the victory, but immediately disliked the distraction it created. Less than two weeks later, on the Monday before the SEC Championship against Florida, defensive coordinator Mike DuBose was announced as his successor.

In the meantime, players hoped to get the coach win No. 70, a number he had mentioned when hired in 1990. It didn't happen against the Gators. Though coming in Florida was ranked No. 1 in the conference in offense and Alabama was No. 1 in defense, Wuerffel turned the game into a shootout. Despite wide receiver Michael Vaughn's school-record 94-yard touchdown reception, Florida won 45-30 and went on to win the national championship, with Wuerffel toping Heisman Trophy voting.

Stallings' last game would be the Outback Bowl against Michigan, which the following year would go on to win the 1997 national championship and cornerback/receiver Charles Woodson the Heisman Trophy. Like usual, Alabama was considered an underdog, which was seemingly confirmed by a 6-3 deficit heading into the fourth quarter. But with the Wolverines driving, blitzing strong safety Kelvin Silger's blindside hit of quarterback Brian Griese (who found out earlier that week he would start over Scott Dreisbach) forced an errant throw that Rudd grabbed at the 12 and returned all the way into both the end zone and Crimson Tide history.

Two possessions later, Alexander, who when being recruited had picked Alabama over Michigan and Notre Dame, broke a 46-yard touchdown run to effectively put the game away. Rudd was named game MVP and would later join safety Kevin Jackson and defensive tackle Michael Myers as the last of 21 All-Americans under Stallings, in addition to 58 All-SEC performers and 20 players who went on to the NFL.

"The locker room was very emotional," Jackson said. "Tears everywhere."

"It was real emotional," Stallings said after the coaching staff presented him with the game ball. "I can't think of a more fitting game."

Chaos

1997–2003

*A*fter being both a player and assistant coach for the Crimson Tide, becoming the head coach at Alabama had been a dream of Mike DuBose, who had been popular in his previous roles. But like those who attempted to follow Paul W. "Bear" Bryant, he had the supplemental distinction of not being Gene Stallings in addition to facing NCAA sanctions and scholarship reductions that sapped the team's depth.

In DuBose's case, the honeymoon with unforgiving fans ended almost immediately during the 1997 season, even though it began with another setback after preseason All-American defensive tackle Michael Myers, who was expected to be the cornerstone of the defense, was suspended for using an agent's credit card.

Alabama blew leads against Arkansas and Kentucky, lost decisively to Tennessee in Birmingham 38-21 and suffered an embarrassing homecoming loss to Louisiana Tech 26-20. Opposing quarterbacks like Tim Couch and Tim Rattay had big games, and after beating the Crimson Tide for the third time Peyton Manning celebrated by directing the Tennessee marching band during the playing of "Rocky Top."

With little continuity and even less focus, not even an Iron Bowl win could salvage the season. Though quarterback Freddie Kitchens came off the bench to rally the Crimson Tide to a 17-15 lead, a fumbled screen pass handed the game to Auburn, which won 18-17 on a last-second field goal.

Defensive end Chris Hood was second-team All-American, but the 4-7 record was the first losing season since 1984, the program's worst record since 1957 and marked the first time since 1955 that Alabama failed to win a game in Tuscaloosa.

DuBose likely had one chance to regain the team's focus and during the offseason promptly fired four assistant coaches who had been held over from Stallings. Among those he brought in were Ronnie Cottrell, who had been the recruiting coordinator at Florida State, and running backs coach Ivy Williams, who would both figure prominently in Alabama's future, only not the way either hoped.

The 1998 season began on an up note when running back Shaun Alexander scored five touchdowns against Brigham Young for a 38-31 victory in the first game played in renovated Bryant-Denny Stadium, which after the addition of the eastern upper deck and two levels of skyboxes had an 83,818 capacity.

But the good feelings didn't last when Alabama went to Arkansas and was humiliated 42-6. The following week against Florida, quarterback Andrew Zow came off the bench and though Alabama lost 16-10, stopped the hemorrhaging. The Crimson Tide won its first overtime game, 20-17 to Ole Miss, and squeaked by East Carolina 23-22, but only to lose again at Tennessee, 35-18.

With DuBose's job on the line, Alabama came from behind to win at LSU 22-16 and despite giving up four turnovers beat Auburn in the last real Iron Bowl, the series finale at Birmingham's Legion Field, 31-17. With both schools expanding their own stadiums, the game would permanently move to the campus sites.

At 7-4, Alabama was invited to play in the inaugural Music City Bowl in Nashville, against Virginia Tech. If the cold, wet conditions didn't foreshadow a gloomy performance, the school-record 287 points allowed by the Crimson Tide certainly did. Alexander, who had 1,178 rushing yards during the regular season, was held to just 55 and Zow could only reach the end zone once in a 38-7 loss.

If anything, it proved that Alabama needed to knuckle down and get tougher, and with 20 starters returning 1999 looked promising even with a brewing quarterback controversy between Zow and Tyler Watts. Additionally, Alexander came back for his senior season to make a run at Alabama's first Heisman Trophy, and was aided by massive left tackle Chris Samuels, who would join him earning All-American honors.

Just when it appeared that the Crimson Tide was poised for another great season, and could begin to put the stigma of NCAA sanctions behind it, rumors started spreading of DuBose having an affair with his secretary—and when it came to football, there was no such thing as a small rumor in Tuscaloosa. He denied the accusation, players didn't want to believe it and both Alexander and the school publicly backed the coach. That is until just before the start of fall practice, when DuBose admitted he had lied and the rumors were true. In addition to a lot of respect, it cost him $360,000 to settle the corresponding sexual harassment suit, but the coach still had his job.

In the opener against Vanderbilt, Alabama trailed through three quarters before Alexander proved to be too much for the Commodores, resulting in a 28-7 victory. For an encore, the Crimson Tide manhandled Houston 27-10.

And then it happened—again. Even after knocking Rattay out of the game, Alabama lost to Louisiana Tech for a second time in three years, 29-28, on an unbelievable last-second Hail Mary pass into the end zone.

It didn't appear as though DuBose would survive the season, much less the week when two days later, athletic director Bob Bockrath resigned and was replaced by former long-standing assistant coach Mal Moore, who played and graduated from Alabama before joining "Bear" Bryant's staff in 1964. DuBose received another brief reprieve while the team simply got mad.

That following Saturday, Alabama found itself in a similar situation against Arkansas, up 35-28 in the final seconds when Razorbacks quarterback Clint Stoerner threw one up for grabs in the end zone, only to see it hit the ground. The Crimson Tide then turned its attention to Florida, where the Gators had not lost at home in "The Swamp" in 30 games. In what can only be described as a wild and crazy afternoon, the lead changed eight times only to result in a 33-33 tie at the end of regulation. Florida led off overtime (each team got to start at the opponent's

25-yard line, with both sides guaranteed a possession) with a touchdown, but missed the extra point. Alexander responded by seemingly faking out the entire Florida defense to score on the first play, only to watch the extra point sail wide . . . until everyone saw the penalty flag on the field as a Florida player was called for being offside. Given a second chance, kicker Chris Kemp drilled the extra point for the 40-39 victory.

If that wasn't tumultuous enough, Alexander had 214 rushing yards and three touchdowns the next game against Ole Miss to put him among the leaders for a Heisman Trophy that was not meant to be. In the first Tuscaloosa meeting against Tennessee since 1930 (they had always played in Birmingham), both Zow and Alexander suffered ankle injuries in a 21-7 defeat. By missing Southern Miss and most of the LSU game, Alexander was no longer being considered for the coveted award.

But even without the two backfield standouts, Alabama managed to keep winning. Freddie Milons returned a punt 65 yards for a touchdown in a 35-14 victory against the Golden Eagles, and a controversial ending against the Tigers (in which a referee appeared to call an injury timeout in the final seconds, but after a lengthy debate was overruled) at Tuscaloosa had the Crimson Tide 7-2 and in position to win the Western Division of the Southeastern Conference.

Standing in the way was undefeated Mississippi State and archrival Auburn. The Bulldogs came to Tuscaloosa looking to even the score from years of poundings, but went home empty-handed 19-7 thanks to two Alexander touchdowns, three interceptions and a blocked punt.

Like usual, Auburn proved to be more than a worthy adversary and with a 14-6 lead in the third quarter appeared to make a decisive stand by stopping Alexander on four consecutive plays near the goal-line. But on the following play, Tigers quarterback Ben Leard was sacked in the end zone for a safety, and Milons' subsequent return had Alabama back within scoring range. This time, Alexander wouldn't be denied and he later added another touchdown for good measure and a 28-17 final score.

Alabama had another rematch with Florida in the SEC Championship with Gator fans calling for payback. Indeed, this time overtime would not be necessary. Alabama alternated between Zow and Watts in accumulating 426 offensive yards and Milons occasionally lined up at quarterback with a 77-yard touchdown on a keeper to be named game MVP. Defensive tackle Reggie Grimes also scored an unlikely touchdown when he grabbed a deflected pass and returned 38 yards into the end zone.

"I didn't come back to win the Heisman Trophy," Alexander said after the 34-7 victory. "I came back to play in games like this. The guys on this team wanted this championship so badly."

Without Samuels, middle linebacker Marvin Constant, linebacker Canary Knight and defensive tackle Kenny Smith, who were all injured, Alabama limped into the Orange Bowl to play Michigan and nearly pulled out a victory. Alexander had 161 rushing yards and three touchdowns, and Milons had for 107 yards on four punt returns, including a 62-yard return for a touchdown, to break Hootie Ingram's Alabama and Orange Bowl record for return yards in a game.

But after pulling even in the third quarter with three touchdowns only to see a potential game-winning field goal blocked by Crimson Tide linebacker Phillip Weeks, the Wolverines eventually won in overtime 35-34. After scoring 24 touchdowns Alexander was SEC Player of the Year and along with Samuels, who won the Outland Trophy for best lineman, named All-American. DuBose was named SEC coach of the year.

Despite all the distractions, Alabama finished 10-3 and won its 21st SEC Championship of the century. However, an even bigger controversy lay ahead, one neither DuBose nor the school would escape from. A number of rival coaches were complaining about Alabama's recruiting practices, among them Florida's Steve Spurrier and Tennessee's Phillip Fulmer. During the 2000 season, the NCAA would be back in Tuscaloosa to interview players and former coaches, and soon after a formal investigation was under way.

Alabama was ranked as high as No. 2 in the preseason polls, but with Alexander and Samuels both gone, it was pure folly. The Crimson Tide began the season at the Rose Bowl stadium playing UCLA, and promptly lost 35-24. Although Alabama handily beat two bowl teams, Ole Miss and South Carolina, by the time it lost 20-10 at Tennessee it was apparent that DuBose's inconsistent reign was coming to a close. The decision was finalized after another humiliating homecoming loss, this time 40-38 to Central Florida. From there the Crimson Tide had its first defeat at LSU's Tiger Stadium since 1969, 30-28, lost 29-7 at Mississippi State and 9-0 to Auburn in Tuscaloosa. Dubose posted a 3-8 record, 24-23 overall during his four years.

Thinking he was likely about to make his only coaching hire, Moore began an extensive search for someone to bring Alabama back to greatness, or at least an immediate bowl game, leading him to the person they called "The Great Rebuilder." Dennis Franchione had compiled an impressive 53-6 record at NAIA Pittsburg State in Kansas, and in three years transformed Texas Christian from a 1-10 team into a 10-1 conference champion. On Dec. 4, he left TCU without warning and accepted the job at Alabama.

"When Mal and I started talking about the possibility of me coming here, one of my first thoughts was, 'I can't wait until we're driving down the road one day and Mal starts telling Coach Bryant stories.' I'm in heaven," Franchione said.

"I didn't even visit the campus. I mean, this is Alabama. I didn't need to see the bricks on the buildings to know I wanted to coach here. I want to win a national championship one day and you have a chance to do that at Alabama."

Immediately, Franchione met with players and began a brutal offseason weightlifting program. He then went home to pack and also watched TCU lose 28-21 to Southern Miss in the Mobile Bowl.

But before Franchione could hold a practice, the NCAA investigation turned into a full-blown scandal in January when Milton Kirk, an assistant football coach at Trezevant High School in Memphis openly accused his head coach, Lynn Lang, of shopping defensive lineman Albert Means to numerous schools, with Alabama booster Logan Young the highest bidder.

Before long, former coaches Cottrell and Williams were implicated. Within six months both Lang and Kirk would be indicted by a federal grand jury of criminal charges and the NCAA would send the university a letter of inquiry listing 11 charges of major violations.

Some felt it was simply Alabama's turn.

Back on the field, DuBose hadn't left Franchione much to work with, but initially his biggest change came in attitude. For the second straight year Alabama opened against UCLA, and for the second straight year it lost, but only 20-17 in Tuscaloosa. Alabama would narrowly lose 37-36 to South Carolina and 27-24 to Ole Miss and quarterback Eli Manning, though it was competitive, even against Tennessee (35-24) and LSU (35-21).

The Crimson Tide capped the regular season with three straight victories, including a 31-7 victory to knock Auburn out of the SEC Championship. On the same day the NCAA Infractions Committee opened hearings on Alabama, Zow threw for 221 yards and two touchdowns including an off-balance 45-yard strike to wide receiver Jason McAddley, while the running game, led by Santonio Beard (199 yards) and Ahmaad Galloway (127), outgained the Tigers 328-41.

It followed with a 28-15 victory against Southern Miss, which had been rescheduled because of the Sept. 11 terrorist attacks, to narrowly qualify for the postseason and a first-ever trip to the Independence Bowl. Although Iowa State, which was led by quarterback Seneca Wallace, accumulated 456 yards of total offense and 23 first downs, the Cyclones only had a 13-10 lead late in the fourth quarter when Waine Bacon and Marc Miller combined to block a punt to set up a 27-yard touchdown pass from Zow to tight end Terry Jones Jr. for the 14-13 victory.

A 7-5 finish was more than respectable considering the circumstances, but in February 2002, the NCAA sentenced the loss of 21 scholarships over three years, a two-year bowl ban and five years of probation. The school would appeal, but this time there would be reprieve.

Still, even without a bowl game, expectations rose throughout 2003 despite a narrow 39-34 victory against Middle Tennessee State in the opener, followed by a tough 37-27 loss at Oklahoma. Dominating victories against North Texas, Southern Miss and Arkansas—in which running back Shaud Williams scored on an 80-yard run on the first play from scrimmage—were offset by a narrow 27-25 loss to Georgia, but Alabama was well on its way to a solid season. The following week against Ole Miss, a 42-7 victory, Beard scored five touchdowns to tie the school record set by Mulley Lenoir in 1920 and Alexander.

Linemen Jarrett Johnson, Kenny King and Kindal Moorehead led the defense while Watts and Brodie Croyle became the first quarterback combo to each pass for more than 1,000 yards in a season. Behind offensive linemen Wesley Britt, Alonzo Ephram and Marico Portis, Williams had four 100-yard performances.

A 34-14 victory against Tennessee and 31-0 win at LSU would normally have put Alabama into a prime position to play for the SEC Championship, but due to sanctions the Crimson Tide only had Auburn followed by a specially-scheduled game at Hawaii.

After lackluster performances in both games—a 17-7 loss to the Tigers in Tuscaloosa followed by a 21-16 victory in Honolulu—for a 10-2 record, Franchione literally disappeared from Tuscaloosa only to show up in College Station where without warning he was announced as the new coach of Texas A&M.

Crimson Tide fans were stunned, hurt and felt betrayed. It wasn't so much that Franchione left, rather how he left that was so upsetting even though he was hired at Alabama under somewhat similar circumstances. Granted, coaching the Crimson Tide was not his dream job and Franchione almost certainly didn't know how bad things would get with the NCAA, but he was immediately portrayed as a traitor and a sneak. Though Franchione was obviously a good coach, the prevailing feeling eventually came around to good riddance. If he didn't want to be in Tuscaloosa, then Alabama should have a coach who did.

Initially, rumors were rampant, spanning from Bill Parcells to Virginia Tech coach Frank Beamer, but Moore first turned to New Orleans Saints assistant coach Mike Riley, who had been the head coach at Oregon State and the National Football League's San Diego Chargers. He had played cornerback for Bryant from 1971-74 and helped lead the Crimson Tide to four Southeastern Conference titles and the 1973 national championship.

Alabama made a firm offer, but Riley, who obviously wasn't thrilled about the NCAA sanctions, didn't jump, waiting to see if there would be other suitors. A deadline was set and passed, resulting in the two sides going their separate ways.

Instead, Moore turned to Washington State coach Mike Price, who had a career record of 129-121 and badly wanted the job. Considering what the program had been through, it was music to everyone's ears.

But after Alabama had been through a decade of probation, controversy and unfulfilled expectations, Crimson Tide fans had yet one more surprise awaiting them. After spring practice was concluded, the 56-year-old Price attended a celebrity pro-am golf tournament in Pensacola, Fla., where he went on a drinking binge, visited a strip club and had dancers spend the night in his hotel room where they rang up a room-service bill exceeding $1,000. On May 5, less than five months after being hired, Price was fired by university president Robert Witt before ever coaching a game at Alabama.

Embarrassed and flabbergasted, Moore tried again, determined that the 26th head coach in Alabama history felt the same way about the program as he did. Three primary candidates emerged: Green Bay Packers running backs coach Sylvester Croom, Miami Dolphins quarterbacks coach Mike Shula and Carolina Panthers wide receivers coach Richard Williamson. All three had played for Alabama.

Shula had two advantages over the others: (1) He had already been on Alabama's radar as a potential head coach, and (2) of the three, school officials believed he would likely be the best option to give the program a jump-start in recruiting while at the same time providing much-needed stability.

When at age 37 Shula became the second-youngest head coach in Division I football, a year and two days older than Greg Schianno of Rutgers, he was also the youngest coach at Alabama since 1923. Of course, skeptics immediately accused school officials of trying to rent the Shula family name to restore the Crimson Tide image. They also ignored Shula's comment during his introductory press conference that he never would have accepted a head coaching job from any other school in a similar situation.

"I had some unfinished business," said Shula, who never won an SEC title as a player.

Of course, initially everything surrounding Shula was a complete mess. He had just 115 days until the season opener without the advantage of signing any recruits, spring practice or even the luxury of having time to access the coaching staff.

Not surprisingly, it was a disjointed season played by a divided team. Utilizing a pro-style offense that would feature Croyle, Alabama won the opener 40-17 against South Florida, and fought No. 1 Oklahoma and Heisman Trophy winner Jason White tooth-and-nail in a 20-13 home loss.

After beating Kentucky 27-17, in which Williams had 174 rushing yards and 192 of the team's 464 total yards, Alabama found itself ranked in the Top 25 only to suffer a humbling 19-16 home loss to Northern Illinois. A dramatic 34-31 double-overtime home loss to Arkansas, in which Croyle separated his shoulder, was followed by a 37-23 defeat at Georgia.

Essentially the season, like seemingly almost every other Crimson Tide season, would come down to two games: Tennessee and Auburn, and Alabama would be a heavy underdog against both.

Against the Volunteers, the Crimson Tide played the longest game in school history, but succumbed in the fifth overtime, 51-43.

Alabama outscored Auburn 21-10 in the second half, but couldn't stop running back Carnell "Cadillac" Williams, who totaled 204 rushing yards on 26 carries and two touchdowns to lead the 28-23 victory.

With a 37-29 loss at Hawaii, Shula's first "impossible" season ended with a 4-9 record. Due to injuries, he had been forced to use three quarterbacks, though Shaud Williams finished the year with 1,356 yards on 278 carries to lead the conference.

It could have been a lot worse. Considering that Alabama still had one more recruiting class limited by NCAA sanctions, the program had yet to bottom out, and wouldn't be at full strength for years, even without further setbacks.

"He's paying dues," said former Alabama defensive back Don McNeal, who also played for Don Shula in Miami. "Coming in like that is going to be tough. Give him some time . . . please give him some time and he'll be OK."

"We love winning, but we all have to be realistic too," legendary linebacker Lee Roy Jordan said. "How quick can you get the job done? It's going to take Mike two or three years to get things moving in the right direction with [players] his staff has recruited."

Yet fans were already clamoring for more. At Alabama, they don't measure success by steps, they measure it by championships.

"No one knows better than we do about lack of patience," Shula said. "We're not patient. We're never patient."

Neither are Alabama fans.

Part II

STORM

Logan's Legal Run

There's no such thing as a University of Alabama fan who hasn't heard of Logan Young, and all have a feeling about him one way or another.

It wasn't always that way, of course. It used to be that Young was one of Alabama's biggest supporters, seen at every home football game and at numerous road contests as well.

But in January 2005, Young was facing federal charges and looking at potentially 15 years jail time stemming from allegations that he bribed a high school coach $150,000 to influence a recruit to play for the Crimson Tide.

Throughout the trial, held in an 11th-floor courtroom of the Clifford Davis Federal Building in Memphis, Young's expressions almost never changed, as if to say "How on earth did we get to this point?" throughout the nine-day ordeal.

And all because of recruiting.

But first, a little backtracking and clarification.

Most people think that a booster of a college sports program is someone who contributes money. Technically, it is, but a booster can also be defined as anyone who ever purchased a ticket to watch a team play.

See? Just like that you're probably a booster of many teams and didn't even know it.

Beginning in 1993, the NCAA mandated that each Division I college football program could have up to 85 players on scholarship at any one time. An unlimited number of players were allowed to participate in spring practice, but the roster was limited to 105 players by the time fall practice began. Once the season started, the roster could be increased to 110.

Considering that there were 22 starting positions plus at least two-to-four special-teams positions, it basically worked out to three scholarships at each position in addition to a walk-on. Consequently, it's impossible to add a scholarship player at every position every year, so each recruit that didn't work out or lost due to injuries was magnified that much more.

Recruiting was intense between most Division I schools because it's the primary source of talent. At Alabama, it's considered the lifeblood of the program. In 2004, the most often-read articles on the Tuscaloosa News website were either Cecil Hurt's popular sports columns or had to do with recruiting, and three other successful websites—BamaOnline, TiderInsider and BamaMag—were dedicated to the subject year-round, sometimes exclusively.

In football, recruits were allowed to make as many visits as they wanted to attend games, but had to pay their way. Once there, the school could give them up to three tickets for free. At Alabama, recruits were encouraged to walk on the field during pre-game warm-ups and sat in a special section near midfield.

During a recruit's senior season, he's allowed to make official visits to five different schools, one each, in which the athletic department picked up the tab, but the student-athlete was limited to 48 hours on campus.

Once a recruit received a scholarship offer, he could make a "verbal commitment" at any time, which was supposed to signal that a decision had been made, but could still be changed. The entire process culminated on National Signing Day, the first Wednesday of February when recruits signed both their letter of intent and scholarship. After some quick rejoicing and chest-thumping, fans and recruiting junkies immediately turned their attention to the junior class and the "Who are we getting?" hype began anew.

Logan Young Jr., the son of a wealthy Arkansas family that made millions in margarine and invented the substance to turn it yellow, was one of those junkies. He got the football bug at an early age from this father, who had been friends with coach Paul W. "Bear" Bryant, and from there his love of the Crimson Tide developed. At one point, Young tried to spearhead an effort to purchase a team in the National Football League, but instead wound up co-owner of the Memphis Showboats of the United States Football League along with William Dunavant, head of Dunavant Enterprises cotton merchants.

Young reportedly even sold his Mid-South Pepsi-Cola Bottling Company to help with the financing. When asked what Bryant would think of his acquisition, Young reportedly answered: "He'd say I was crazier than hell. But he'd also say, 'Ah, what the hell. Do what you think you've got to do.'"

Much to the chagrin of University of Tennessee fans, the Crimson Tide had seemingly always recruited pretty well in the Volunteer state even though year-in, year-out the state of Alabama almost always had a better base of talent. The Tide especially had a foothold in Memphis, a sort of cultural crossroad for the region and approximately 170 miles closer to Tuscaloosa than Knoxville.

In 1998, Alabama won a major recruiting battle for Parade All-American defensive tackle Kindal Moorehead. (Note: Exceptional defensive linemen are very difficult to find, almost as much as gifted quarterbacks. That's primarily why so many are selected in the early rounds of the NFL Draft—scarcity.) The following year, the Crimson Tide again signed Memphis' best defensive tackle, David Paine. But the player every school coveted was Albert Means, whom some considered Memphis' best prospect ever. He was amazingly fast and strong for someone weighing 300 pounds, which in football is like finding a pitcher who can throw a 100-mph fastball.

When Means signed with Alabama, it immediately made Tennessee and other schools look bad, but also made people wonder. Already there had been more than whispers regarding illicit recruiting in the Memphis area, and with the Crimson Tide having so much success it didn't take a genius to figure out that something might be amiss. As the old saying goes, "Fool me once . . ."

In an effort of simplification, here's how things unfolded:

November 2000—Concerned about possible recruiting violations from 1997-2000, the NCAA began interviewing University of Alabama players on campus and former coaches.

January 2001—In Memphis, assistant coach Milton Kirk made allegations that fellow former Trezevant High School head coach Lynn Lang shopped Means to Southeastern Conference schools and others. Kirk later testified that Lang told him Alabama booster Logan Young paid him $200,000 for getting the former Parade All-American to accept a scholarship offer from the Crimson Tide. Young denied any wrongdoing. After one season, Means left Alabama and enrolled at the University of Memphis.

February 2001—Phone records obtained by the Tuscaloosa News showed numerous calls between assistant coach Ivy Williams and Young leading up to the 2000 signing day.

March 2001—Former Parade All-American David Paine claimed he was offered $25,000 by Kirk to make allegations of illegal recruiting tactics by the Crimson Tide. Later that month, University of Alabama compliance officials and NCAA investigators interviewed Young.

June 2001—Records at the office of the Clerk of Circuit Court in Leon County, Fla. indicated that former Alabama assistant coach Ronnie Cottrell received a $55,000 loan from Young to help secure the mortgage on a house in Tallahassee. Young admitted the loan, which was not an NCAA violation, which Cottrell paid back.

August 2001—Arkansas coach Houston Nutt confirmed that one of his assistant coaches told him that money was solicited for Means. Numerous SEC coaches would later do the same, though no other program other than Alabama was penalized (Kentucky was sentenced for a corresponding transgression).

September 2001—A federal grand jury indicted Lang and Kirk for violation of federal law including conspiracy, use of interstate facility to promote bribery and extortion under the color of official right. Later that month, Young was named in the NCAA's Letter of Inquiry, listing charges of 11 major violations against Alabama.

September 2001—Tennessee car salesman Wendell Smith denied that he delivered $20,000 to former recruit Kenny Smith, of which $10,000 allegedly came from Young. He later filed a lawsuit against the NCAA.

October 2001—Facing up to five years in prison and $250,000 in fines, Kirk changed his plea to guilty.

November 2001—The NCAA cleared Williams of any wrongdoing in the recruitment of Means. A violations charge regarding regulations on coaches' compensation against Cottrell was also dropped. Later that month, Alabama held hearings with the NCAA Infractions Committee in Indianapolis, beginning on the same day the Crimson Tide played at Auburn.

December 2001—Alabama agreed, either in whole or in part, with nine charges of major violations against the football program, of which Young was mentioned prominently in four. The school self-imposed a reduction of 15 football scholarships over three years, including eight for the February 2002 signing period.

February 2002—The NCAA nearly gave Crimson Tide football the death penalty, instead sentencing the loss of 21 scholarships over three years, a two-year ban on postseason play and five years probation. The penalties were announced just days before National Signing Day. Alabama appealed the ruling.

September 2002—The NCAA Division I Infractions Appeals Committee upheld all findings and penalties against the Crimson Tide.

November 2002—Facing a maximum prison term of 135 years, Lang changed his plea to guilty on one count and promised to cooperate with investigators, both from the government and the NCAA, in building a case against Young. He was not sentenced prior to Young's trial, which would start more than two years later, though he faced a maximum of five years in jail.

December 2002—Kirk was sentenced to six months in a halfway house, three years probation, 200 hours of community service and fined $1,000. Later that month, Cottrell filed a $60 million lawsuit against the NCAA and others. Williams would join the lawsuit.

October 2003—A federal grand jury indicted Young on charges of conspiracy, crossing a state line to commit racketeering and bribery of a state official, and structuring a financial transaction to evade reporting requirements.

January 2004—In an unprecedented move, a Tennessee judge ordered the NCAA to produce documents relating to its investigation of Alabama, making them public record. More lawsuits ensued.

February 2004—The Tuscaloosa News published the entire 424-page transcript of the NCAA Infractions Committee hearing on Alabama as a special report. More lawsuits ensued.

January 2005—Young's criminal trial began in Memphis.

By the time the NCAA Infractions Committee hearing transcript was published, most Crimson Tide fans just wanted to move on. The whole thing had reached the status of a bad car accident that everyone would slow down to check out as they drove by. For more than four years, headlines told of depositions, indictments and lawsuits, and many had exceeded the point of saturation and frustration.

Of course, that didn't stop them from reading about it. Anything about the case, including live updates from the trial, equaled or exceeded even the recruiting news in on-line popularity.

One of the more interesting items to come out of the Infractions Committee hearing was a statement by NCAA investigator Richard Johanningmeier, when he was asked about Young's friendship with Bryant and his influence in the athletic department.

"From the standpoint of their relationship, [former assistant] coach Jeff Rouzie, who I think has been around the Alabama program for some time, told us that at the time he was on Bear Bryant's staff, coach Bryant instructed those staff members to stay away from Logan Young. It was our understanding that he actually threatened their jobs if they got around Logan Young. Rouzie does believe, Rouzie and some other coaches certainly believed that there was a change when [Gene] Stallings left and [Mike] DuBose came in, that all of a sudden Logan became much more visible around the program with DuBose than he had been with Stallings."

Supposedly, the friction between Stallings and Young went back to when Young didn't show to pick him up at the Memphis airport for an alumni meeting and golf outing. Others believed Stallings just had a much better grasp of what was going with the program, like Bryant, even though the first round of NCAA sanctions happened under his watch.

Regardless, for nearly two weeks, Alabama's attention was fixated on Memphis.

Jury Selection Starts Monday in Young Trial

Jan. 23, 2005

When former University of Alabama booster Logan Young first was implicated in a bribery scandal to attract a football recruit to the Crimson Tide, Bill Clinton was still president, the World Trade Center was still standing and no one had heard of the television show "American Idol."

On Monday, jury selection in his criminal case will begin in Memphis, even though the player involved has completed his college eligibility, and Alabama already has served a two-year bowl ban and suffered scholarship reductions as part of sanctions imposed by the National Collegiate Athletic Association.

One way or another, it's the beginning of the end regarding Young's involvement, which has led to unparalleled speculation and sensationalism in Alabama and beyond.

"I think I'm going to be found innocent," Young said. "I'm extremely confident, but that's the same way I've felt for three years.

"Our strategy is simplicity. We didn't do it, and there's no proof that we did it."

The former booster is accused in a four-count indictment by a federal grand jury of conspiracy, crossing state lines to commit racketeering and arranging bank withdrawals to cover up a crime. The fourth count of forfeiture, only kicks in if Young is found guilty of the initial charges.

If convicted, Young, who turned 64 in November, could face a maximum penalty of 15 years in prison and a $900,000 fine, though federal guidelines call for a lighter sentence.

According to the government, the wealthy businessman paid coach Lynn Lang $150,000 to have high school recruit Albert Means of Trezevant High School attend Alabama. Means played one season for the Crimson Tide before transferring to Memphis.

Otherwise, the case—which will be tried in the U.S. District Court for Western

Tennessee in front of Judge Daniel Breen—is about as jumbled as an electronic football game, though with two imposing figures serving as head coaches.

Leading the prosecution is assistant U.S. Attorney Frederick Godwin, a former police officer with 20 years of experience and best known for a conviction in a case involving sports betting in Memphis.

Heading Young's legal team is Jim Neal, the former Watergate prosecutor who defended former Louisiana Gov. Edwin Edwards against corruption charges and was the first attorney to obtain a conviction of Jimmy Hoffa. Neal also was the chief counsel to a special U.S. Senate committee that investigated the Abscam bribery case among congressmen.

"I feel great," Young said. "They've been working all week and will work all weekend and show up bright and early Monday."

The government claims that Young made numerous cash withdrawals for a total of $291,000 during the time period named in the indictment, of which $150,000 allegedly found its way to Lang.

Young's attorneys, who only have to create reasonable doubt in a criminal case, will attempt to show that any withdrawals were for other purposes. There also doesn't appear to be a paper trail to Young (i.e. no cancelled checks).

The only person directly connecting Young to the alleged bribe is Lang, who initially denied the accusation and stated publicly that Alabama did nothing wrong, but changed his story after being indicted along with fellow coach Milton Kirk on charges of conspiracy, use of an interstate facility to promote bribery and extortion under the color of official right.

Kirk, who claims he never received any money for his part in Means' recruitment (though he says he was promised a share), also changed his plea and in December 2002 was sentenced to six months in a half-way house, three years probation, a $1,000 fine and 200 hours of community service.

Part of Lang's plea agreement was that he would aid prosecutors and testify against Young. However, he has yet to be sentenced and has been living in Michigan free on bond.

The case also has more subplots. Among them:

- Can the government use legislation devised to fight organized crime to prosecute someone for giving money to a football coach?

In May, Neal argued in a motion that even if Young did give money to Lang, it wasn't a federal crime. The motion to dismiss was rejected.

- If Lang shopped Means to six other schools as he claims, which ones offered money and why have none been investigated or penalized?
- Will race be an issue? While Young is white, both Means and Lang are black. If so, will both sides view jury selection as paramount?

In his 2000 book about Memphis-area recruiting entitled "Bragging Rights," Newsweek journalist Richard Ernsberger called Mean's recruitment "slave trading," which obviously did not reflect well on the city.

- What happened to the money? Did it exist or was it merely promised, and does Lang get to keep everything he received as part of his plea agreement?
- If the NCAA is a private organization without government authority, as the Supreme Court ruled regarding former UNLV basketball coach Jerry Tarkanian's lawsuit, how can governmental institutions be tied to its investigation?
- What kind of precedence does this set toward NCAA enforcement? Will college athletics continue to police themselves or could any coach or booster be prosecuted for illegal activity in the future?
- What other details and documents regarding the NCAA's investigation of Alabama, led by Richard Johanningmeier, might come out under oath?

Overall, it's estimated that the NCAA penalties cost Alabama more than $10 million and the football program still is recuperating from its black eye, both on the field and off.

Although Young's trial has little to do with Alabama football at this point, athletic director Mal Moore, who was hired Nov. 23, 1999, near the end of the time period in question, has been subpoenaed.

Neither former Alabama facility representative Gene Marsh, who is the chairman of the NCAA Infractions Committee, nor former compliance director Marie Robbins, have been subpoenaed.

Neither side has been required to divulge its strategy or whom it will have on the stand. Speculation has varied from Alabama State football coach Charles Coe, to former SEC commissioner Roy Kramer and University of Tennessee coach Phillip Fulmer.

The Tennessee connection is crucial, and not just because Kirk's brother was the prosecutor who ruled that Lang could be considered a federal employee or the role of rival Volunteers' booster Roy Adams, who helped point the finger at Young.

Fulmer was a secret witness for the NCAA in its investigation of Alabama, along with recruiting analyst Tom Culpepper and businessman Karl Schledwitz, who was recently named to Tennessee's Board of Trustees despite a somewhat-checkered past.

Schledwitz was convicted of three counts of mail fraud in 1992, which was overturned by a federal appeals court on his third appeal seven years later.

He also was tried on separate bank fraud charges along with former U.S. Rep. Harold Ford Sr. and two other men regarding the Butcher banking scandal—considered the largest bank failure since the Great Depression. All four were found innocent.

Aided by court-released documents in the Young case, former Alabama assistant coaches Ronnie Cottrell and Ivy Williams have sued the NCAA and others for $60 million. The case is scheduled for a June jury trial in Tuscaloosa.

"My case really has nothing to do with Logan Young's case," said Cottrell and Williams' attorney Tommy Gallion, who will have a representative in the courtroom. "They were accused of working with Logan to pay off Albert Means, but that's all fallen by the wayside."

Among the other related lawsuits, former Tennessee football player Kenny

Smith and his family also sued Fulmer and others for potentially hundreds of millions regarding testimony given to the NCAA and its disclosure.

In turn, Fulmer, in conjunction with the NCAA and the American Football Coaches Association, filed a counter complaint, asking a Knoxville judge to declare a coach's testimony to the NCAA off-limits to defamation lawsuits.

However, the prosecution of a booster who gave money to a high school athlete or coach isn't unique to Young.

For example, former Michigan basketball booster Ed Martin pleaded guilty to money laundering and running an illegal gambling operation in May 2002, in which he loaned four basketball players hundreds of thousands of dollars. However, Martin died before sentencing, and the Michigan basketball program won its appeal with the NCAA, returning its eligibility for the 2004 postseason.

In May 2000, Myron Piggie admitted that he schemed to defraud Duke University, UCLA, Missouri and Oklahoma State, their conferences and the NCAA by making payments to high school stars—including former Duke standout Corey Maggette—who played for him in summer league games.

Piggie was sentenced to three years and one month on one felony count of conspiracy to commit mail and wire fraud and one year on a misdemeanor count of failure to file income taxes. He also was ordered to pay more than $320,000 in restitution.

With Maggette, Duke won the national championship in 1999. Although coach Mike Krzyzewski said he was ready for any penalties the NCAA wanted to impose, the basketball program was never formally investigated.

"It's an unprecedented unique situation of facts, but some other NCAA investigations have spun out into some criminal proceedings," said Marsh, a professor of law. "I don't know which came first, it's like the chicken and the egg."

Court came to order at 9:35 a.m. on January 24 and less than 5 minutes later Judge Breen—who bore a striking resemblance to Syracuse men's basketball coach Jim Boeheim—applied a gag order that didn't allow attorneys on either side to talk to media during the course of the trial.

It was a good move and a solid attempt at keeping things on track as much as possible. That Breen didn't accept the request by both sides to end the first day at 3:30 p.m. after jury selection had been completed (and the dismissal of Elizabeth Donnelly as a potential alternate—her son Chris was a safety on the 1992 Alabama national championship team) sent a clear message that the case had festered long enough. Instead, opening statements got under way, with the prosecution going first.

"This case is about the buying and selling of a young man by men who had no right to do so," Godwin began his fiery presentation. "A high school football coach put a player on the block, and Logan Young Jr. bought him off that block."

Godwin also began to try to offset the coming character attack on Lang and other witnesses with, "There are no heroes in this case and even the victims are flawed."

Neal didn't even bother with an overview, using a significant part of his opening statement to attack Lang and installed the premise that Young couldn't be convicted unless jurors were convinced beyond a reasonable doubt. He also had an immediate answer regarding the bank figures.

"Those deposits don't show the source of the money and Mr. Lang had other sources of money as well," Neal said.

Meanwhile, Neal said Lang was frequently overdrawn and had to be ordered by a court to pay child support. How could that be if Lang had been given $150,000?

Moore was the trial's first witness. He clarified that Young had donated to the athletic department both a $500,000 life insurance policy and $50,000 toward the purchase of a $1 million audio/video system. Young had also leased a luxury box at Bryant-Denny Stadium that cost $35,000 a season plus the cost of tickets.

As a comparison, Moore said that Alabama's athletic department had received $43 million in donations over the last two years.

Lisa Mallory, Young's former girlfriend, testified that Young liked to put his hands on his chest when referring to Means and say, "He's mine," while drinking with friends. However, in cross-examination she said that he also said that about recruits who didn't end up at Alabama.

Mallory also testified that the gregarious Young had lavish spending habits, calling him a big tipper who gambled "a lot, and always with cash."

By the end of Day 2, it was apparent that the only witnesses who wouldn't come off the stand looking bad would likely be those who had nothing to do with college football. Even the used-car salesman who testified about a purchase Lang made was seen in a much better light.

The degeneration began with Means, who, with his college career concluded, admitted that he lied to a grand jury in 2001 and did not take his college entrance exam. Instead, Lang falsified documents and had someone else take it for him.

"I was afraid I might lose my education," said Means, who was set to graduate four months later. Immediately, University of Memphis officials were besieged with questions about playing an ineligible student.

Then Lang took the stand and began four hours of testimony. In addition to implicating Young, he also said he had been paid by Georgia and Kentucky, and was offered money by Arkansas, Michigan State and Tennessee. Later in cross-examination, he added Ole Miss.

Among the details:

- Lang specifically claimed to receive $3,000 from Kentucky, with recruiting coordinator Claude Bassett giving him another $4,000 after delivering Means for an official visit.
- Former Georgia coach Jim Donnan paid him $700, under the guise of working a summer camp, in addition to at least one $100 payment from a booster.
- Former University of Memphis coach Rip Scherer offered to get Lang's wife into law school at no expense.
- Arkansas assistant coaches Fitz Hill and Danny Nutt offered a job as a

defensive line assistant coach that would pay approximately $85,000, or $150,000 if Lang could deliver both Means and cornerback Leonard Burress, who wound up at Kentucky. Lang said he told Nutt that he would have to undo a previous agreement before he could entertain the Arkansas offer.

Lang also testified that during one of the visits to Young's house he received a phone call from Melrose High School coach Tim Thompson, who was trying to get money for one of his players. Thompson had also coached Moorehead.

"I asked Mr. Logan Young if he paid Tim Thompson for Kindal Moorehead," Lang said. "He told me he paid $10,000."

Since reaching a plea agreement in November 2002, Lang said he amended his tax returns from 1999 and 2000 to include the $150,000, and he was currently paying the Internal Revenue Service $1,200 a month to offset the additional amount owed, as well as penalties and interest.

"I got greedy," Lang said. "The more you have money like that, the faster it goes."

Neal's cross-examination concentrated on Lang's statements about when he was lying and when he was supposedly telling the truth. He also made it obvious to the jury that Lang was facing charges with a maximum sentence of 135 years when he plea-bargained down to one felony count for a maximum of five years.

By Wednesday, the trial had the makings of a bad movie script. Because defense attorney Robert Hutton had asked Mallory if Young had ever mentioned anything about paying any high school coaches to influence recruits (she said no), the prosecution was allowed to call Tennessee booster Duke Clement to impeach Mallory's testimony.

After Clement claimed Young had bragged about paying to get other Memphis-area recruits to Alabama, Hutton brought up previous testimony that both Clement and Young were extremely drunk at the time of those boasts.

"You said that when Mr. Young was talking to you at the Grove Grill about Alabama football, he had at least 10 scotch and sodas, did you not?"

"No, sir," Clement replied.

Dumbfounded, Hutton read testimony to the NCAA in which Clement said Young had downed 10 scotch and waters at dinner and was working on another 10.

"Oh, I thought you said scotch and sodas," Clement said.

The following morning, Adams—Young's rival booster for Tennessee, who was "covering" the trial for a website—was brought before Breen to answer questions about his report claiming he went out drinking with witnesses, jurors and media after the second day of the trial.

Adams told the court that his report had been "edited" and numerous people had his password to the fan site. He later changed his story while on the Paul Finebaum Show when it was pointed out that the website posted the times of all posts.

Then came the technical evidence; the phone records and bank statements.

An intelligence records specialist for the Federal Bureau of Investigation testified that there were 59 phone calls—most for a minute or less and Young had an answering service—between Young and Lang from June 5, 2000 to Feb. 13, 2001. However, there was no record of Young calling Lang until the scandal broke in the news. Phone representatives said that records before June 5, 2000 no longer existed. During the same time period, Young made 102 phone calls to Cottrell, with one returned, and 21 to Williams, of which two were returned.

Bank records showed that from July 1999 to October 2000, Lang had deposits totaling $76,799.84, of which $29,451.21 (after wages garnished) came from his employment as a teacher and coach. Otherwise, he made 74 cash deposits, often through an ATM, totaling $47,269.89. Of those, 16 were for $1,000 or more, with only one after July 31, 2000. After the $8,000 deposit, the largest were $4,000, $3,000, $2,800, $2,400 and $1,900. Almost half of the deposits were for $100 or less.

During roughly the same time period, Young made 64 withdrawals, all under $10,000, totaling $291,000. At least 12 times after Young made a withdrawal, Lang made a deposit. For example, on Sept. 2, 1999, Young took $6,500 out of the bank, with Lang depositing $1,400 soon after.

In comparing the transactions, the most eye-catching occurred on Feb. 14, 2000. Young withdrew $9,000 and then $4,000 more on the same business day. Lang deposited $8,000 that afternoon.

Young withdrawals		Lang deposits	
9/2/99	$ 6,500	9/2/99	$1,400
10/1/99	$ 3,500	10/4/99	$2,400
10/8/99	$ 9,000	10/11/99	$1,900
12/16/99	$ 9,000	12/17/99	$ 800
1/14/00	$ 9,000	1/18/00	$1,700
1/24/00	$ 9,000	1/25/00	$1,500
2/14/00-y	$13,000	2/15/00	$8,000
3/31/00	$ 9,600	4/3/00-x	$1,300
4/14/00-y	$13,000	4/17/00	$8,000
6/19/00-y	$13,000	6/20/00	$3,000
7/20/00	$ 9,500	7/20/00	$ 500
7/27/00	$ 3,000	7/27/00	$1,000

x—Includes deposits of $100 and $200 on 3/31/00, and $1,000 on 4/3/00.
y—Includes two different withdrawals, $9,000 and $4,000, but counted for the same business day.

With the jury out of the courtroom, Breen ruled that defense attorneys could admit Young's bank records from 1998 and the rest of 1999 to establish his financial habits (Note: It brought a burst of laughter from Godwin, who, in turn, wanted to admit evidence that Young bragged of paying another coach to influence recruits to Alabama. The prosecutor was immediately reprimanded). They showed Young made 10 cash withdrawals in 1998 and 12 the first six months of 1999, totaling more than $100,000 in both years, of which at least six were between $8,000 and $10,000.

Meanwhile, in the back of the courtroom, Tony Barnhart of the Atlanta-Journal Constitution, maybe the country's best college football writer, summarized the attorneys' roles in one word. For the prosecution, Godwin was the bulldog. For Young, Neal was the orator, Hutton the technician and Allan Wade the statistician (i.e. the money). The thought was repeated at the surreal lunch setting of Leonard's BBQ Downtown across the street where jurors, attorneys and media would all eat quickly (at separate tables and try to ignore each other except to say "excuse me" in the buffet line) to get back in time.

That was essentially the government's entire case, circumstantial bank and phone records and the word of one person who was trying to avoid potentially up to 135 years in jail. That the government didn't put many of Young's biggest accusers, like Kirk, Culpepper or anyone from the NCAA on the witness stand, spoke volumes.

Then came the first major twist in the trial. At 4:50 p.m. Thursday, the defense rested its case. Immediately thereafter, Hutton moved for a dismissal, arguing that the prosecution failed to put into the court record exactly what law Young had broken and whether Lang was acting in his official capacity as a public servant.

Already frustrated, Godwin appeared dumbfounded, but Hutton eloquently argued his point. Friday morning, the prosecution had little choice but to ask to re-open its case to call another witness.

"If the court allows them to re-open their case it would make a mockery of [the rule]," Hutton argued, later adding, "The rule of law is the law of rules."

Without initially ruling on the dismissal (a day later he denied it), Breen let the prosecution call former Memphis schools superintendent Dr. Johnnie B. Watson to demonstrate that Lang's solicitation of money was against school policy, though it was not specifically in the teacher's code of ethics. After Kirk had been suspended and Lang resigned, Watson recommended to the school board that the language be changed.

But before Watson, the defense had witnesses who had traveled from other states and were allowed to testify first, out of order.

Williams went first and flatly denied telling Lang to have someone take the ACT for Means. But Godwin showed during aggressive cross-examination that there were inconsistencies between statements Williams made to NCAA investigators and a federal grand jury. Williams admitted to actually talking with Young hundreds of times, though he claimed it was never about recruits. He also testified to hearing Kirk tell Lang he wanted an automobile when he walked in on a conversation.

Donnan testified that Lang received no money from Georgia other than $500 for working a summer camp in 1999 and a $194 expense check to Means for his official visit that was subsequently endorsed to Lang. He added that Georgia stopped recruiting Means after Lang asked for "SUVs," which was later discussed at an SEC compliance meeting for coaches.

"I told our coaches we were out of there," Donnan said. "He had his hand out."

To try and discredit Donnan, Godwin asked if he had made a lot of money as a head coach, and if anyone who admitted to paying a high school coach would be able to get a college coaching job ever again. Donnan was clearly upset with the insinuation that he had a reason to lie under oath. Meanwhile, outside the courtroom, Arkansas and Ole Miss officials publicly denied Lang's accusation and Michigan State issued a statement: "Our coaches were never alleged to be involved in any improper benefits or inducements for Means. In fact, the NCAA never contacted Michigan State regarding its brief recruitment of Means."

Also out of Michigan, news broke that Lang abruptly resigned from his job as assistant principal of Benton Harbor High School. Because he had yet to be sentenced, school officials were apparently unaware Lang had been indicted and pled guilty to federal charges, and immediately announced a change in the hiring policy.

The defenses' position boiled down to four words: "Lynn Lang is a liar," and Week 2 opened with six witnesses called to discredit Lang's testimony.

Scherer, who supposedly, and ironically, was one of the first people to accuse Alabama of illegal recruiting, denied offering to get Lang's wife into law school at no expense in exchange for Means: "Absolutely not."

Godwin used the same line of questioning he asked Donnan.

Melvin "Botto" Earnest denied Lang's claim that he drove him to Young's house for their alleged first meeting in 1999.

Godwin attacked inconsistencies in his statements and asked about a loan Young had given him, some of which was still owed.

Memphis attorney Bill Wade testified that he attended two meetings with Lang and Young in the fall of 2000 about a possible lawsuit against "Bragging Rights" author Ernsberger. Wade said Lang was "adamant" at the meeting that he and Young had never met, though phone records indicated that they had obviously talked.

Young's housekeeper Amy Hughey, 67, testified that she had never seen Lang before, disputing his claim that she had answered the door after Young had a heart procedure in November 1999. When asked if she could differentiate the difference between Lang and Williams, Hughey said yes. "You just brought Mr. Lang in here."

Godwin dramatically paused. "How did you know it was Mr. Lang?" he asked.

"I've seen him on TV," she replied.

George Wade, the owner of a Memphis personal-care service testified that a nurse was on-hand almost 24 hours a day after the heart procedure. Of the 12 corresponding bank transactions the prosecution highlighted, none were from that month.

And finally, similar to the movie "The Untouchables," only without all the shooting, the bookkeeper took the stand, David Pearson. He was familiar with

Young's yearly financial summaries, which were bigger than a metropolitan phone book, and also testified as an expert on accounting.

When asked about the bank transactions, Pearson said there was "no correlation between amounts. There is never a withdrawal that equals a deposit. The correlation of times would be difficult to answer because Mr. Lang made so many deposits that they are going to correspond in some fashion."

Interestingly, of the 74 cash deposits totaling more than $47,000 between July 1999 and October 2000, Lang also made 25 simultaneous withdrawals. No explanation to why was ever given. Pearson was also asked to examine Lang's amended tax returns in which $75,000 was added to both 1999 and 2000. Pearson noted that in 1999, Young only made 14 cash withdrawals for a total of $65,350.

"Not from those checks could he have given him $75,000," he said.

A final rebuttal witness for the prosecution was former Michigan State assistant coach Brand Lawing, who testified that in January 2000, Lang asked $200,000 for Means, of which he wanted $50,000 immediately to pay someone back. When asked who, Lang said: "I can't tell you, but if you don't get into the game, you will find out on National Signing Day."

That night, five of the newspaper journalists who were covering the trial had dinner at the famous Memphis restaurant Rendezvous, and after dinner made predictions on the trial outcome. Four voted acquittal. John Branston of the Memphis Flyer, the only local writer at the meal, voted guilty.

Three years to the day that the NCAA announced sanctions against Alabama, arguments concluded. Godwin called the complied evidence, "curiouser and curiouser" when put together. He asked that the jury look at the phone records and the bank records and see if the dates lined up.

"To them, this is a joke," assistant U.S. attorney Jerry Kitchen said during his rebuttal. "Use your common sense."

Between the co-counsels, they made references to the Declaration of Independence, Abraham Lincoln, Harry S Truman and Martin Luther King Jr. Godwin also played off Lawing's testimony in concluding, thanks to a coincidence of the calendar: "Ladies and gentlemen, tomorrow's signing day."

Neal, though it wasn't his finest moment, countered that in order to believe Lang the jury would have to disregard the word of six witnesses and a bank official, in addition to all the lies he had told beforehand.

Apparently they did, and in reading the young jury of seven women and five men the defense team knew beforehand what the verdict would be, reached after just 4 hours of deliberations (not including lunch and breaks).

As to count one, racketeering: "Guilty."

As to count two, bribery: "Guilty."

As to count three, structuring a financial transaction to avoid reporting requirements: "Guilty."

While suffering from the flu, Young had little reaction to the verdict, but within minutes appeared paler and more withdrawn.

The moment the jury left the room, Godwin and Kitchen shared a congratulatory handshake. Godwin then asked the court for a substantial bond to keep Young, who had been released on his own recognizance, from fleeing, and for an order banning him from drinking alcohol because he was a public risk. (Note: Young had been convicted of driving under the influence of alcohol and arrested twice, but not in more than 10 years.)

Breen declined the requests, but ordered Young, who was about to undergo kidney dialysis and had other health issues, to avoid excessive use of alcohol.

On the final day, Thursday, the jury deliberated the count of criminal forfeiture and ruled Young must pay $96,100 to the government.

"I'm upset, but there's a long way to go," Young said on his way out of the courtroom. None of the jurors talked to media, and the defenses' only other comment was Neal's "We'll appeal."

Adams, who threw a party after the initial guilty verdict, wore a bright orange blazer to "celebrate the Volunteers' recruiting class," on National Signing Day. He also added: "Humility is not my strongest point."

"Anyone who thinks about engaging in that practice ought to think twice about doing it," U.S. Attorney Terrell Harris said. "It's wrong to buy and sell 18-year-old student-athletes. It's wrong to bribe high school football coaches. It's wrong to structure banking transactions to avoid reporting requirements. What recruiting violations rise to the level that they constitute criminal acts, they should be investigated and prosecuted, and that's what was done here."

Almost a week later, on Feb. 8, Lang was finally sentenced to two years supervised probation, 500 hours community service and fined $2,500. He was able to keep whatever else Young may have given him.

Where Do We Go From Here?

February 13, 2005

It was supposed to be a landmark federal criminal case: A football booster standing trial for paying a high school coach $150,000 to influence where a recruit would attend college.

Prominent names were mentioned. Schools were implicated. A guilty verdict was obtained.

So naturally it will lead to sweeping changes, further charges and wide-ranging reforms. Won't it?

Actually, at this point probably not. In fact, the recent conviction of former University of Alabama booster Logan Young in the U.S. District Court for Western Tennessee likely will result in mountains of appeals and civil lawsuits and more questions rather than actual answers.

On Feb. 2, Young was found guilty on federal counts of conspiracy, crossing state lines to commit racketeering and arranging bank withdrawals to cover up a crime for paying former Trezevant High School coach Lynn Lang to steer defensive tackle Albert Means to Alabama.

The following day, the jury ruled he must also pay $96,100 in criminal forfeiture.

On face value, the verdict was in line with the National Collegiate Athletic Association's investigation of illicit recruiting practices at Alabama, which in 2002 resulted in five years probation with a two-year bowl ban and scholarship reductions.

"We applaud the federal government's efforts to protect the integrity of college sports," said Erik Christianson, director of public and media relations for the NCAA. "This was an important case because it puts rogue boosters on notice that they need to work within the same bylaws and principles as the institutions they support."

However, Lang implicated other universities as well with his testimony, specifically Arkansas, Georgia, Kentucky, Memphis, Michigan State, Ole Miss and Tennessee regarding Means' recruitment in 1999.

Though the NCAA does not comment about ongoing investigations, its statute of limitations regarding most cases is five years. In regards to Lang's allegations, none of the students involved are still playing college football (thus, no leverage for investigators), and many of the potentially implicated schools' officials have moved on.

Still, the government spent years investigating and prosecuting Young at significant taxpayer expense.

Memphis attorney Philip Shanks, who helps represent former Alabama assistant coaches Ronnie Cottrell and Ivy Williams in Tennessee, estimated that Young already has spent $3 million on his defense.

"It should deter this particular practice, of paying bribes to high school teachers," U.S. attorney Terrell Harris said. "Anyone who seeks or thinks about engaging in that practice ought to think twice about doing it."

As such, the trial only proceeded under the assumption that Lang was a public official per the Racketeering Influenced and Corrupt Organizations Act. To fall under RICO, an individual or group must commit two or more of a certain type of crime (some state, some federal), including embezzlement, extortion and bribery. Since the government wanted to prosecute Young for the harshest penalties possible, he was never charged with violating any state laws against bribing government officials.

Even Harris admitted that if Lang worked for a private school, charges likely could not have been brought against Young. The same would have been true had Young simply paid Means or his family directly instead of Lang.

On Wednesday, Young's attorneys filed a motion for a new trial and a motion for a judgment of acquittal.

The motion for a new trial claims that jury instructions concerning bribery incorrectly stated Tennessee law, violated the fair notice requirement of due process and repeatedly referred to an inapplicable provision of the state statute.

It argued that for Young to be found guilty of violating the travel act he first had to be found guilty of bribery, which did not happen.

Under Tennessee law, money paid by a private person to a public employee is only a bribe if the money is paid to influence the person's exercise of discretion in his official capacity. However, "official capacity" has never been defined in Tennessee.

Memphis attorney Robert Hutton argued during Young's trial that without that definition a coach could conceivably be prosecuted for accepting sponsorship money from a shoe company, working at a summer camp and bringing his players along or doing a radio show.

The motion for acquittal claimed that Young should not be subject to forfeiture when Lang wound up with the money in question, resulting in a greater punishment for Young.

The motion also contended that the forfeiture should not be enforced because the statute was not enacted until Oct. 26, 2001, as part of the Patriot Act—after the alleged crime occurred.

The motions are considered the first step toward the appeals process, which could conceivably take years.

For now, though, the basis for Young's appeal appears set, questioning whether there was actually a crime committed.

At some point there may also be a debate about using laws designed to fight organized crime and terrorism to prosecute and seize property from a football booster, issues that fall outside courtroom proceedings.

In the meantime, the NCAA has moved on to tackling other issues, like how to keep schools from trying to bypass new academic reforms that will be directly tied to scholarship penalties.

Specifically, the guidelines can result in scholarship reductions, recruiting limitations, ineligibility for NCAA team postseason or preseason competition including bowl games and NCAA championships, and, in the most extreme cases, restricted membership status.

"I don't think there's a whole lot of focus on the infractions process," said Alabama law professor Gene Marsh, who is also the chairman of the NCAA Infractions Committee and before being appointed to that post was Alabama's Faculty Athletics Representative during its NCAA troubles.

"There's always some tuning going on, but in terms of global specific proposals, I haven't seen any."

Since 1980, the NCAA committee has issued 160 penalties for impermissible recruiting inducements involving Division I men's basketball and football. Of them, Young is believed to be the first individual charged with breaking federal laws—even though the Supreme Court ruled the NCAA is not a public organization.

Schools comprising the Southeastern Conference have been among the organization's most frequent offenders. Since 1990, all 12 athletic departments in the league have served an NCAA probation for a major infraction, including nine football programs, of which Alabama leads with three.

As a proactive move, the SEC adopted the "Report of the Task Force on Compliance & Enforcement" last spring in an effort to better police itself. Consequently, as part of the so-called "Phillip Fulmer Rule" (the University of Tennessee head football coach is believed by some as one of the main people who implicated Alabama in 2001), coaches must first report allegations against other schools to their own athletic director, who in turn must notify the SEC office.

"I think that it reinforces the importance of what we've done with our task force and how we handle these things, and reinforces that we get beyond these matters in accordance with our goals to have none of our institutions on probation by 2008," SEC commissioner Mike Slive said. "I'm very pleased with the progress we've made."

Finger-pointing behind closed doors was a key component in how the NCAA built its case against Alabama. Once revealed, it also led to a number of civil lawsuits, which along with Young's appeal are now in the legal on-deck circle.

After numerous delays, NCAA officials, including chief investigator Richard Johanningmeier, will finally give their depositions in Indianapolis this week for the Team Cottrell defamation lawsuit for $60 million.

Alabama booster Ray Keller's defamation lawsuit against the NCAA recently survived numerous motions for dismissal and is about to begin the deposition process.

Alabama booster Wendell Smith and former Tennessee player Kenny Smith and his family have filed additional lawsuits. Even more lawsuits are expected in the months leading up to the Team Cottrell jury trial, scheduled for June in Tuscaloosa.

On Thursday, Slive took part in a state of Division I athletics symposium along with Marsh, former Tennessee official Linda Bensel-Meyers and television analyst Len Elmore at Vanderbilt University in Nashville.

Bensel-Meyers, who left Tennessee after making allegations of academic misconduct concerning football players (the NCAA ruled it was an academic and not an athletic issue), called for football and men's basketball to become true farm systems for the professional leagues. Marsh claimed that things were improving under the current enforcement and compliance system.

When asked specifically about the Young trial, Slive replied that it simply was in the league's "rear-view mirror."

Maybe it is for the SEC, but hardly anyone else.

Here a Lawsuit, There a Lawsuit,
Everywhere a Lawsuit . . .

*W*hen the National Collegiate Athletic Association began investigating the University of Alabama football program in earnest in 2000 and 2001, it focused on two people in particular: Ronnie Cottrell and Ivy Williams.

Cottrell was the assistant head coach/tight ends assistant under Mike Dubose, but his primary job was recruiting coordinator. Hired away from Florida State, where he had been for 10 years, Cottrell immediately came across as a likable person, someone who was good at remembering names and would always make a point to ask things like "How's your mother doing?" and mean it.

Williams was often considered soft-spoken, but stern and intimidating when he wanted to be.

Initially, both were singled out by investigators, but little came of it. In November 2001, Williams was cleared by the NCAA of any wrongdoing, while Cottrell was basically reprimanded for not coming forward about receiving a legal loan from booster Logan Young. When Young faced federal criminal charges for conspiracy, racketeering and bribery, neither former Alabama coach was indicted.

Still, they were seen as the fall guys, and the NCAA went so far as to have on its official web site that any school interested in hiring Cottrell first had to clear it with the NCAA. In December 2002, Cottrell, who couldn't find another job and probably felt he had nothing to lose, filed a $60 million lawsuit against the NCAA and others that immediately captured the attention of the football community, both locally and nationally. Williams soon signed on as well for one of the sensationalistic cases the state of Alabama had ever seen. It claimed everything from NCAA investigator Richard Johanningmeier threatening witnesses with criminal prosecution even though he didn't have the power to do so, to a vast conspiracy.

Of course, a major premise of the lawsuit was that the NCAA had it in for Alabama, and a number of reasons why were debated throughout the state.

One popular theory was that if the NCAA could take down a program like Alabama, it would enhance its power and send a clear message to the other schools (obviously this was denied by NCAA officials, with "Why would we want to weaken one of our member schools?").

Another was that the NCAA had been trying to get Coach "Bear" Bryant for years, but either couldn't or it didn't dare due to both his and the team's enormous success and popularity. Just before he took over the Crimson Tide in 1958, Bryant's

1956 Texas A&M squad didn't get invited to the Cotton Bowl because of a one-year bowl ban imposed by the NCAA for widespread rules violations, including players receiving money.

(Note: Incidentally, A&M got another one-year ban from postseason play when Gene Stallings' team was put on probation in 1966, and also received minor sanctions in 1969. Coach Jackie Sherrill, a former Alabama player, was cited in 1988 for violations that included improper employment and financial aid, extra benefits to student-athletes, improper recruiting and lack of institutional control. The Aggies were sentenced to two years of probation and a one-year ban on post-season play.)

When the NCAA investigated issues stemming from the 1992 championship team, it also made ethics charges against faculty representative Tom Jones, accusing the professor of lying to investigators in his report. While the school won the first successful appeal in NCAA history, Jones filed a lawsuit and took home a sizable settlement, while the NCAA had to publicly admit its errors.

Considering its history with other coaches and institutions, many fans believed the NCAA had a score to settle with Alabama, and already had means for doing so. Under its bylaws, prior record could be considered in determining penalties and this was Alabama's third major infraction in less than six years.

In 1995, the football program was penalized for impermissible bank loans made to defensive back Antonio Langham and for lack of institutional control during the NCAA investigation. For this, Alabama initially received a one-year bowl ban and penalized 30 scholarships over a 3-year period (though some were returned during the appeals process).

In 1999, Alabama self-reported recruiting violations by men's basketball coach Tyrone Beamon, who had attempted to obtain money from a booster in order to give money to a recruit's high school coach. The recruit had orally committed to Alabama and the school was not penalized.

Meanwhile, between 2002 and 2004, most of the other athletic programs in the Southeastern Conference went through their fair share of sanctions, investigations and inquiries, though nothing on the same level as Alabama. The closest were an academic fraud scandal with the Georgia men's basketball team, Arkansas lost football scholarships and was placed on three years probation after the NCAA determined a booster overpaid athletes for work at his trucking company and Kentucky was coming out of three years probation for recruiting violations that would overlap Alabama's investigation.

But two cases in particular fueled speculation that the NCAA had given Alabama "special" treatment.

Two Auburn assistant men's basketball coaches were accused of offering two recruits $50,000 and a car through their AAU coach. Unlike Alabama, Auburn was aggressive in its defense and the NCAA eventually penalized the program loss of a scholarship for two years, limits on off- and on-campus recruiting and two years probation.

Mississippi State also got a comparative slap on the wrist after the NCAA ruled that two former football assistants and several boosters broke recruiting rules between 1998 and 2002. The program was placed on four years probation, stripped eight scholarships over two seasons and banned from playing in a 2004 bowl game (which it wouldn't qualify for anyway).

Allegations of unethical conduct against former Bulldogs coach Sherrill were dismissed, but in December 2004 he filed a $15 million lawsuit, claiming NCAA investigators lied and fabricated charges that drove him out of college football and their subsequent publication defamed him.

When Alabama received its penalties, NCAA Infractions Committee chairman Tomas Yeager was quoted as saying the program was "staring down the barrel of a gun."

"God forbid, there's ever another appearance—ever," he said. "Should there be one—particularly within the five-year period—I don't know what's left."

Yeager then went out of his way to praise the efforts of two Alabama officials who bent-over-backwards to be accommodating and made sure even the most minute concern was covered, faculty representative Gene Marsh, a law professor, and Marie Robbins, who was in charge of compliance.

"Had this candor and cooperation been lacking, the death penalty (as well as substantial penalties in addition to those imposed in this case) would have been imposed," an NCAA press release said.

According to numerous school officials, their diligent work, in the face of incredible criticism and pressure from fans, did probably spare the football program from receiving the death penalty like Yeager claimed. Both Marsh and Robbins, were listed in the original Cottrell lawsuit, but removed when the Tuscaloosa News published the transcript from the infractions hearing when it became obvious they had essentially done exactly what they were supposed to.

Robbins took the sanctions hard and after five years of investigations and lawsuits had enough of compliance. The former Alabama gymnast was promoted to Associate Athletics Director and Senior Woman Administrator.

But many Alabama fans saw Marsh as someone who believed more in the system than the Crimson Tide, and thus felt he sold out the program in turn for self-betterment. Their proof: In 2004, Marsh replaced Yeager as chairman of the NCAA Infractions Committee.

In February 2005, Marsh attended a conference on "The State of Division I College Athletics" at Vanderbilt, and the following comments ran in the March 20th edition of the Tuscaloosa News as a commentary and the Vanderbilt Journal of Entertainment. (Note: His views; not intended to represent the NCAA or the Committee on Infractions.)

I have served as a member of the NCAA Division I Committee on Infractions since 1999. If you allowed it to happen (which I don't and won't), you could get a fairly twisted and sour view of college athletics, serving on the COI.

Given that our reason to exist as a committee is to deal with major infractions of NCAA rules, the experience is not unlike sitting in an emergency room in the hospital day after day and concluding that most of humanity has recently been touched by a car wreck, gunfight or has suffered a stroke.

If the only page you read in the newspaper is the obituaries, the world might appear to be a grim place. Similarly, if you form your opinion of college athletics by tracking major infractions and the attendant negative media coverage, without experiencing any more, you would have every right to become cynical and jaded. In college athletics, bad news travels fast, and good news travels almost not at all.

My personal antidote for serving on the COI—my "fix"—is to keep a sense of perspective and a sense of humor in what I see playing out before me as the cases are processed and the hearings occur. Although it is hard to imagine, there is some slight humor to be found in infractions cases as folks come in and explain how they managed to get themselves in such a tight spot. And there is a lot of "humanity" in the process and no little drama, especially in a case where the media has tracked the case as the hearing date approaches.

There's no question that you can find tragedy in some NCAA infractions cases. Individuals who cheated and lied, and held on to the lie may have had their careers in college athletics come to an end. Student-athletes who abused the system and who have been abused by overbearing coaches fall from grace and notoriety over-night. But the border between tragedy and comedy is porous in many places in life, and the thought holds true in college athletics.

At the University of Alabama, I served as faculty athletics representative from 1996 to 2003. I wrote a term limit in the job description in 1996, and unlike most politicians, I honored it. I was appointed in 1996 right on the heels of a major infractions case in football.

In 1998, I represented the university in a major infractions case in basketball, and as most of you know, the University of Alabama has just served out another sentence of scholarship losses and a multiyear bowl ban in a case involving boosters and football recruiting. Service at Alabama puts you right in the middle of what I think is the most rabid, football-crazy conference in the country—the Southeastern Conference. Alabama is a state where the Ten Commandments make big headlines and are mighty important, but to some folks, a clear second to SEC football.

So in addressing the question of whether there is further need for NCAA reform in college athletics, I come at it after having had too much experience at an NCAA institution that has been through the infractions process too often, and now as a member and chair of the Committee on Infractions.

Where Reform Begins

The NCAA is famous (and often subject to ridicule) for having committees, initiatives, commissions, cabinets and a sprinkling of a task force here and a task force there. I have always thought "faculty governance" was second to none in judging a good outcome by whether there has been sufficient mind-numbing process, without regard to product.

I was wrong. The NCAA takes the prize and makes faculty governance look like a well-oiled, lean and mean, result-driven machine.

All the national initiatives are important (and probably a necessary evil) in the multi-headed governance structure of the NCAA, but I have always believed that the fate of college athletics is being determined every day back on campus, where people who have the courage and instincts to do the right thing are far more important that any individual standing behind a podium or strutting like a rooster at a national press conference, announcing a new task force or initiative.

In the years that I served as faculty athletic representative, I was always puzzled and amused by university presidents, athletic directors, faculty athletic representatives and others who felt like they needed a national or conference push or initiative to find courage to do the right thing on their campus. Some of these folks were ignored on their campus, had been relegated to signing the occasional form and were ridiculed by people at their institution for being someone who would bend in a slight breeze.

But like the lion in "The Wizard of Oz," they'd come to a conference or NCAA meeting and say, "I need courage." I guess some faculty members and others have been so thoroughly run over on their campus, that they need the strength you draw in numbers at national and conference gatherings to go back to campus and have a bullet in the gun, like Barney on "The Andy Griffith Show." But I'm guessing that by about Wednesday following the big weekend meeting or announcement, the bluster is gone and the chamber is empty. The lion is once again in need of courage.

Although one might assume that watching people involved in the NCAA infractions process would lead you to believe that personal failings are the norm, my experience has been quite the opposite. Through the written response filed by institutions prior to a hearing before the COI, and at the hearing itself, I have met many people in different roles who have plenty of steel and who will never need to draw their strength from numbers or national initiatives.

These are some of the people I have come to know: Faculty members who would not change a grade for a student-athlete, in the face of great pressure. An assistant coach who would not "get with the program," because he did not believe in cheating and the follow-up lies to cover it up. A student-athlete who wouldn't take a handout or stand by while others did. An admissions officer who would not admit an academic disaster, no matter how much athletic talent existed. A university president who made a very unpopular personnel decision in the face of caustic public criticism and threats of litigation. A compliance director who refused to be run over by a power program and a power coach.

An especially important point to understand is that the people and the decisions noted above almost never receive any public attention. They'll never show up in The NCAA News, USA Today or talk-show radio. They will never be in front of a television camera to explain their grand initiative or agenda, because their personal agenda is not glitzy and does not require a PR handler or press release to set the stage for attention. At some point, all they were is honest and determined to maintain the academic integrity of the institution.

I go back to my point. The most important decisions that have the greatest impact on college athletics are not being made at the NCAA in Indianapolis but back on campus, in offices, classrooms and on the field. In my view, "reform" occurs every day on campus.

Failings of Faculty and Presidents

By far, most university presidents and faculty have the right instincts in balancing the academic mission of the institution and the interests of the athletic program. Most folks rightly assume that if "balance" and "reform" are needed, it will be the faculty and university presidents—especially the presidents—who will lead the way. I agree.

However, I have also been surprised and disappointed by the number of faculty and presidents who have caved in and lost their bearings. For example: University presidents who intervene to override admissions decisions, where the academic officers made it clear that granting admissions would be a disaster for the school. And when the decision blows up, the CEO is quick to say that he or she thought it important to provide an "opportunity" to the young man. The question that follows in my mind is how many 5-foot, 10-inch males who weigh 165 pounds would be granted a similar opportunity. University presidents who cry "academic freedom" when the NCAA comes calling to question a decision on an inexplicable grade change or decision to add a student way past a semester deadline. The stated rationale maybe "academic freedom," but it smells a lot like academic fraud. University presidents who personally intervene to keep a "problem child" in school, where it is clear that the student's status as an athlete is what is greasing the wheel. University presidents who "take the institution to the next level" to compete in Division I, even though the resources are not there and many faculty oppose the move. If such a school hires a marketing director to put more fannies in the stadium seats, but fails to put more resources in compliance and the academic offices responsible for certifying eligibility, a day with the Committee on Infractions is not far over the horizon. For such a school, when they set up their first big-time football schedule for a certain semester, they might as well call the NCAA and schedule a COI hearing. It will save time. Deans and faculty members who change grades, allow late adds and drops and permit a graded course to be changed to pass-fail, where non-athletes are not granted similar opportunities. These faculty members belong in the Hall of Shame, not any Hall of Fame. I am always surprised to see little or no reaction from the faculty senate at universities where academic fraud has occurred, linked to athletics. They should storm the Bastille. Faculty members whose classes are oversubscribed with athletes, and who give grades away. Some faculty members can be as silly and destructive as any renegade booster. Faculty members who travel with the team, accept gratuities and then respond to coaches who ask for a grade change or hint that a grade change would be appreciated. Faculty members who clamor to be appointed to "the athletic committee" and accept comp tickets while they are teaching student athletes, and then give away favors at grade time.

My own view is that among all the representatives who fill the table set aside for the institution at a COI hearing, the faculty athletic representative position is often the weakest. In some cases they are disengaged on a daily basis, disengaged from the investigation and clearly not identified as a player in the remedial and corrective measures outlined by the institution.

Some FARs do an outstanding job, but a surprising number could play the role of the lion in "The Wizard of Oz." Maybe we see a skewed sample—weak FARs at a COI hearing. Maybe that's partly the reason why the school ended up where it is. However, many FARs do an outstanding job in their position and in the face of all the internal and external pressures that are brought to bear.

I take it to heart and draw strength from the people who have courage, but I take note of people who don't. I applaud the many people I meet who make the right decision in the face of great pressure. They don't consider it newsworthy because it is just so obviously the right decision to make.

No matter what the setting, whether it is litigation, academics and even the NCAA, I am very leery of people who make a principled decision, then go off and look for ink and television coverage. Most of the folks who make the most important decisions receive no coverage.

I have been on the Committee on Infractions for roughly five years, and I have had the opportunity to take a pretty intimate look at more than 50 institutions across conferences and across the spectrum of large to smaller Division I schools.

I've seen a boatload of university presidents, athletic directors, compliance directors, faculty and other folks at their best and their worst, on paper and in person. And sometimes these people are under great stress in a hearing that can last more than 12 hours.

Despite all the gloom and doom stories about college athletics, despite all the committees, commissions and groups, most folks I meet have the right priorities and make good decisions. I've seen my share of meltdowns and have experienced several at my own institution, but I don't buy into the negative rants of people who watch this system from a distance or are the product of a difficult experience at one institution. Most of the folks in the system have backbone. They just don't get the ink and TV time that accompany major failings.

Radio show host Paul Finebaum was also in the lawsuit, but dropped after meeting with one of Cottrell's attorneys, the flamboyant Tommy Gallion, who is about as fascinating a person as one can ever expect to meet.

To quote the original lawsuit: "Cottrell has had his coaching career destroyed by this cannibalistic organization, that forces its subjects to submit to its above described dictatorial power, as it destroys and devours these individuals similar to the antics of the fictional character Hannibal Lector."

It continued: "Even during the era of Hitler's Gestapo and Mussolini's 'Storm Troopers' has a self-governed non-regulated committee of this nature ever been allowed to destroy the reputation and career of individuals based on hearsay, 'secret witnesses,' violations of their rules, and incredibly based on 'information developed or discussed during the hearing' without even informing the accused of what information developed and discussed that was a part of their finding.

"The citizens of this country, in particular athletes and coaches who participate in college athletic programs, should live in fear that this renegade and unbridled Gestapo type of agency could destroy their lives and athletic programs of their colleges with a stroke of its poisonous pen. The defendant NCAA and its agent defendants did in a malicious, unconstitutional and defamatory manner destroy the career of Cottrell."

When I finally had the opportunity to sit down with Gallion for the following story, I might have asked one question during the first 45 minutes of the interview. It was then interrupted by another remarkable man, Judge Charles Price, who stopped by to say hello.

Price, a former green beret who was the state's first black district attorney, made the controversial ruling that Judge Roy Moore must either place the Ten Commandments in a historical or educational setting, or remove them from his courtroom.

If I had a dollar for every time I've heard someone say Gallion is like something straight out of a John Grisham novel, I would be a rich man. That's why, in part, the initial headline on this story was "Is Tommy Gallion the Most Important Man in Alabama?" playing off the local phrase regarding the coach of the Crimson Tide.

Is Tommy Gallion the Most Important Lawyer in Alabama?

June 13, 2004

He's one of the biggest names in Alabama sports, but he was never an athlete. Thomas Gallion III is outlandish, bombastic, dynamic, arrogant, egotistical, theatrical, colorful, haughty, loud and boisterous. He's a bulldog. And that's according to people who like him.

The Montgomery-based lawyer leads what some consider the legal "Dream Team" of University of Alabama football—and what others believe could be UA's worst nightmare—even though neither the football program nor the university is a client.

Along with lawyers Delaine Mountain of Tuscaloosa, Tyrone Means of Montgomery and Philip Shanks of Memphis, Tenn., Gallion is representing former UA recruiting coordinator Ronnie Cottrell and former UA assistant coach Ivy Williams in a $60 million lawsuit against the NCAA and others. He doesn't care who may be losing sleep over it.

The group has been nicknamed "Team Cottrell," with Gallion its gang leader, and the team is picking a fight against the establishment.

"He's exactly like he was when he was an 18-year-old freshman at the University of Alabama," Mountain said. "He's not afraid to stir up controversy."

That's an understatement, especially after court records show that the secret witnesses used in the NCAA's investigation of Alabama's football program had ties to or were from the University of Tennessee.

"He's bad to the bone," Cottrell said. "I couldn't be more satisfied with the effort and the representation I've gotten. They've just been great."

Gallion has compared the Alabama-Tennessee rivalry to the Hatfields and the McCoys, likened the NCAA's lack of due process to Iraqi justice under Saddam Hussein and called the NCAA "one chromosome removed from the Gestapo."

In the lawsuit, he charged that Cottrell's "coaching career [has been] destroyed by this cannibalistic organization that forces its subjects to submit to its . . . dictatorial power."

Gallion called for a congressional investigation of the NCAA and denounced Tennessee football coach Phillip Fulmer while drawing mental images of riding into town on a white horse to save the day.

"For whatever reason, I've always been for the underdog," Gallion said. "I have a real, real big belief that everyone should be treated equally. Maybe it's because as a kid I watched too much of the Lone Ranger.

"That's what turns me on. I don't know psychologically why. I love a good fight, and I love to nail people who are doing harm, not only to other people and individuals, but also to society as a whole. I guess it comes from eating breakfast across from a prosecutor every morning. He taught me that when you're right, you fight."

His father, MacDonald Gallion, was an Alabama attorney general who ran unsuccessfully against George Wallace for governor. Consequently, his first experience with death threats came when his father battled organized crime in Phenix City, causing the family to hide in Sarasota, Fla.

"I was 10," Tommy Gallion said. "I've led a very interesting life."

A corporate litigator by trade, Gallion helped prove that Jett Williams was the adopted child of Hank Williams Sr. and win half the royalties from Williams' estate. He's gone after two Republican governors, Guy Hunt and Fob James, despite being a Republican.

He currently is representing the Retirement Systems of Alabama in a $70 million fraud case against the former officers of Enron. He has an even bigger case against WorldCom.

There are probably few things surrounding Gallion that aren't grandiose.

For example, Gallion's headquarters is imbedded in the heart of the state capital. Visitors don't have to be told that Haskell, Slaughter, Young & Gallion is one of the larger and more successful law firms in Alabama because its Montgomery office is the Governor Shorter House, where Alabama's governor lived during the Civil War.

But the NCAA case is different, in part, because Gallion, a fourth-generation UA graduate, has never faced an organization like the NCAA and vice-versa.

"They simply hate me," Gallion said, noting that NCAA President Myles Brand filed a grievance against him.

"I don't think anyone's going to take it seriously, with the bar association claiming that I'm trying it in the press. [Expletive], this thing has been in the press since 2000. Cottrell may be the biggest sports news story perhaps in the history of the state.

"They don't know how to handle it. That's why when they call, I hang up in their face. I don't like them, I don't like their lawyers."

Instead, Mountain deals with them.

Said NCAA spokesman Jeff Howard: "It's unfortunate that certain individuals feel the need to use the media as a pulpit for arguments, which many times are unfounded and flat-out false. The NCAA enforcement area is conducted with the utmost integrity, and membership would not stand for anything less.

"I think what people are missing the boat on, is that infractions occurred and the process that the association put in place was done correctly."

But Gallion isn't stopping there. He's claiming a conspiracy, with roots extending from the offices of Fulmer and recruiting analyst Tom Culpepper into the FBI and Justice Department.

Besides attempting to prove his clients were mistreated, Gallion also is trying to show that NCAA officials turned their backs on misdeeds at Tennessee in exchange for information to punish Alabama.

One advantage to being so outspoken about the case is that Team Cottrell has received numerous tips and information before it accepted confidential documents from the NCAA that can't be publicly disclosed.

"It's my opinion that investigation is nine-tenths of your case," Gallion said.

In short, Gallion's attempting to take the saying, "Where there's smoke, there's fire," to new heights, and by fanning the flames, hopes to have a full-blown inferno by the time the case goes to trial in Tuscaloosa.

Crimson Tide fans apparently can't get enough of the lawsuits surrounding the football program, although perhaps for the wrong reason.

"The real interesting aspect to a lawyer is that the public's perception appears to be that it's righting a wrong done to Alabama," said Montgomery lawyer Thomas Keene, who represented university officials Gene Marsh and Marie Robbins before they were dropped from the lawsuit. "The amount of media time this is getting is unbelievable. I think it shows the depth of interest in college football."

Meanwhile, Crimson Tide officials have been silent and have distanced themselves from the case. Alabama has completed its two-year bowl ban, but it is still in the middle of a five-year probation and reeling from the loss of 21 scholarships.

"I love Alabama, but they're not my client in this case," Mountain said. "They've thrown up roadblocks.

"We've subpoenaed them for telephone numbers which they refuse to give us. We have asked that they wave the attorney-client privilege for [attorney] Rich Hilliard so he can answer our questions fully. They have, to my knowledge, not even responded to that request, which came from Rich Hilliard's attorney. We're willing to drop Rich Hilliard from his lawsuit, if they are willing to do so. So far, we've had no response."

Initially, Gallion said that in addition to money for his clients, his goal was either to have the NCAA lift its sanctions against Alabama, reinstate all lost scholarships and offer a national apology or give Tennessee the death penalty. That has not changed, only now no one is laughing about it.

"They want to run me off," Gallion said. "They want to shut me down. I'll be 61 in July. I'm not afraid of them, and I'm afraid of very few things. I grew up in an atmosphere that I can almost relate to the streets of New York or something. I just won't live in fear. And when I get on something, whether it be the Montgomery city government, the governors, or something, and I think I'm right, I have one view, to represent my client. Screw everything else. When I stop doing that, I'll throw my license in the dump."

So the media circus will go on, with ringmaster Gallion grinning like he knows something no one else does.

"Stay tuned," Gallion said. "There's more to come."

Was there ever, but not in a way anyone expected.

Initially, Mountain, like so many other people, thought the lawsuit was probably a waste of time. But after a couple of phone calls from his former fraternity brother at Alabama, and Cottrell passed a lie-detector test, the Tuscaloosa-based attorney suddenly found himself listed as a co-counsel.

"I wanted people who wouldn't back out on me," Gallion said.

Shanks was the wild card. Though also an Alabama graduate, and a huge Crimson Tide fan, he was a criminal attorney and brought on board to represent Cottrell and Williams should charges be filed in Memphis as an extension of the Young case.

Five years to the day that Shanks' wife was killed in a car accident, he found himself back in a hospital.

Lawyer Mugged; Cottrell Files Stolen

May 07, 2004

The high-profile lawsuit brought forth by two former University of Alabama assistant football coaches against the NCAA and other defendants took an unexpected and dark turn Friday when a plaintiff lawyer was mugged, and documents relating to the case were stolen from his Memphis office.

Philip Shanks, who is part of the legal team nicknamed "Team Cottrell," was attacked from behind when he arrived early to work to prepare for a 10 a.m. hearing regarding another case.

Shanks was treated for a mild concussion and released from an area hospital to rest at home.

"I arrived at my office at about 7:10 this morning and really don't know what happened," said Shanks, who described the blow from behind as, "The lights just went out on me."

"At a little before 8, my assistant came in and found me unconscious, so she called 911. The first thing I recall is my assistant telling me, 'Hang on, the ambulance is on the way.'

"I have not yet seen my office because I was just discharged from the hospital, but according to my assistant the office was ransacked. She said the office was ransacked, and all the Cottrell files are gone. I'm just estimating, but that's probably 80-90 or 100 pounds of material."

A lawyer at the small firm of Philip T. Shanks & Associates, who asked not to be identified, confirmed that the office had been "trashed," and police had fingerprinted the entire area as part of its investigation.

Birmingham lawyer Thomas Gallion III, who also represents former Alabama assistant coaches Ronnie Cottrell and Ivy Williams, said Shanks told him that his wallet had also been taken.

"Also, some of my memorabilia was gone," said Shanks, who has an extensive collection of Alabama football items. "I definitely know that two SEC Championship rings were taken, but until I've seen my office, I won't know everything that is gone."

However, the lawyers said that all of the missing documents are believed to be replaceable because each lawyer on the case had shared information.

"It's gotten out of hand," Gallion said. "It's like the Hatfields and the McCoys.

"College football has sunk to a new low. I've been to his offices and it's in a very nice neighborhood, very prominent in Memphis. I don't think this was random."

Threats are not uncommon for lawyers. Co-counsel Delaine Mountain recalled one incident in which police removed a gun from a car parked in front of his Tuscaloosa office.

Both Gallion and Shanks have received numerous threats regarding this case, some more serious than others.

Last summer, Shanks said he came home to find dead cats on his front porch. The following day, someone broke through the back door, went through his files regarding the lawsuit and took some of his notes.

Gallion said that a "drunk" Tennessee fan wearing school memorabilia once showed up at Shanks' house and threatened to kill him. Shanks' dog chased him away.

"It certainly gets your attention," said Mountain, who hasn't received any specific threats regarding the case. "If that was the intent, I don't think it's going to work. I decided many years ago that I was going to do my job and not worry about those things. We're not going to back off."

Despite obvious concerns, Gallion echoed Mountain's sentiment.

"We're going forward full speed," Gallion said. "We have better evidence than we've ever had. When something like this happens to a colleague, it's tragic."

Gallion is hoping a positive might come out of the attack, that the NCAA will be more forthcoming to resolve the lawsuit, or "Assist rather than resist."

But he's not very optimistic.

"This is a typical day with this case," Gallion joked.

According to the police report, authorities had very little to go on, but Shanks, who retired from the courtroom because of the concussion, was absolutely convinced he knew who had attacked him—a person with local ties who then suspiciously and conveniently disappeared practically overnight—and what he had been looking for. Team Cottrell attorneys had just secured a copy of a taped conversation in which recruiting analyst Tom Culpepper allegedly claimed he would "get" Alabama.

Culpepper had been on Alabama's recruiting payroll until Cottrell fired him. Court records indicated that he went to Tennessee coach Phillip Fulmer with information on Alabama, who in turn went to the NCAA, and they were key secret witnesses in the investigation. Consequently, both were up to their ears in legal action.

Also filing lawsuits were former Tennessee player Kenny Smith and his family (Fulmer apparently told an NCAA investigator that he heard Smith's mother was having an affair with an Alabama assistant coach), along with former Alabama booster Ray Keller and Tennessee car salesman Wendall Smith, who had been implicated. The lawsuits were expected to take years to resolve.

Price-less

*W*ith coach Dennis Franchione's sudden departure in after the 2002 season finale, both University of Alabama officials and fans were simply stunned. Obviously, he didn't share their passion for the program, and athletic director Mal Moore had the unsavory task of trying to find not only a replacement who did, but someone to bring the kind of stability the Crimson Tide desperately needed despite sanctions imposed by the National Collegiate Athletic Association.

Moore eventually settled on an established veteran, 56-year-old Mike Price, who had spent nearly his entire coaching career in Washington, with 22 years between Washington State and Weber State (and seemingly always in the shadow of the Washington Huskies). Price's career record was 129-121 and he had never had more than two consecutive winning seasons. But when Price said during his introductory press conference that he wanted to become the second-best coach in Alabama history and end his career in Tuscaloosa, most skepticism dissipated.

Unfortunately, coaching Washington State was nothing like taking over the Crimson Tide both in terms of prestige and pressures. Perhaps Price fully understood that, but probably not. Either way, he was going to enjoy the fortuitous turn in his life.

After piecemealing together a recruiting class that paled in comparison to most Southeastern Conference teams, which frequently happened whenever there's a coaching change in the middle of recruiting, Price hired SEC stalwarts Joe Kines as defensive coordinator and Sparky Woods to handle the running backs. Kines had coached at Arkansas, Florida and Georgia in addition to a previous stint at Alabama in 1985-86, and Woods had been at Mississippi State, South Carolina and Tennessee. Both also had experience in the National Football League, which appealed to recruits who longed to play football as a profession. To complete his staff, Price hired his sons as offensive assistants, Aaron and Eric, though it was clear who would be calling the plays. Through spring practice, the pass-oriented offense was tweaked, and Tuscaloosa settled into its first quiet summer in years.

Or so everyone thought.

On April 16, 2003, while attending the Emerald Coast Classsic Pro-Am without his wife, Price got heavily intoxicated during a night out on the town in Pensacola, Fla. He also visited a topless club and eventually went back to his hotel room with at least two dancers. A room-service bill in excess of $1,000 was the proof that Price couldn't deny, though initially he tried.

Reports first started surfacing on the Internet and Sports Illustrated began to investigate, resulting in the article, "Bad Behavior: How He Met His Destiny at a Strip Club."

Destiny was the name of a dancer.

Instead of maintaining a low profile, Price had been seen out on the town in Tuscaloosa and rumors spread—some beforehand, many after. There were reports that Moore had confronted him about his behavior and habits, though the athletic director later downplayed their discussions and denied that he twice warned Price as the Sports Illustrated article indicated.

It also came out that Price claimed nothing happened in his room, nor could it because he hadn't taken his Viagra that day.

Price tried to spin the damage control as best he could while players, fans and even other coaches chimed in, asking that the school be lenient. But under the circumstances, another scandal was the last thing Alabama needed. Without ever coaching a game with the Crimson Tide, Price was fired on May 3, 2003, days before the Sports Illustrated article was published.

Naturally, he sued.

First it was the school, claiming everything from denial of due process to the violation of civil rights. But a U.S. district judge ruled that the university and the trustees were immune and the lawsuit was dismissed.

Then it was university president Dr. Robert E. Witt for fraud, breach of contract, misrepresentation and deceit. It too was dismissed because Price never signed his initial seven-year, $1.3 million contract. Witt also said during his deposition that although he had heard rumors Sports Illustrated was working on a story about Price, he had not read it or based his decision on the story.

Finally, it was Time, Inc. and Sports Illustrated author Don Yaeger for $20 million, and there were indications of possible mistakes in the story. It would lead to numerous odd twists and detours, beginning with the issue of confidential sources. On Dec. 8, 2003, U.S. District Court Judge Lynwood Smith ruled that Sports Illustrated was not eligible to protect its sources identities under Alabama's "Newspaper Privilege" law, which was amended in 1949 and 1975 to include radio and television broadcast stations. It wasn't specific to magazines.

Time, Inc., appealed to the Alabama Supreme Court, which on April 1, 2004 declined to answer the question. So it asked for another appeal, and Smith agreed that there were grounds for a difference of opinion.

On it went to 11th U.S. Circuit Court of Appeals and 15 national media organizations immediately filed a brief in support of Time, Inc., claiming "The district court's order tramples the media's First Amendment privilege to withhold confidential-source information under all but the most compelling circumstances." It also stated that if allowed to stand the ruling would result in 'immense arbitrariness and uncertainty in Alabama and beyond."

The court said no to the brief, but yes to the appeal, and was set to hear arguments in 2005.

Meanwhile, the longer the lawsuit stuck around, the more details were revealed about Price's night in Pensacola. In her affidavit filed with the court(s), Lori "Destiny" Boudreaux claimed that she did not leave "Arety's Angels," where she worked as a dancer, with Price on the night in question, but went home with her husband. Instead, she identified two other dancers, one of whom told her "that there was sex and they were screaming and jumping around and dancing for him."

Boudreaux was upset at the SI article title and that her real name was used. She also denied stating: "We started screaming 'Roll Tide' and he was yelling back, 'It's rolling baby, it's rolling.' I was not there. I did not spend the night in that room and I did not get up early and leave before Mike Price left to play golf."

Three employees of the Crowne Plaza Hotel in Pensacola described a young woman who ordered items for Price's room costing $1,123 including tip, and not Boudreaux.

One affidavit stated: "She kept using the name Tommy or Thomas when referring to the registered guest we knew was Mike Price. She said Tommy had said she could order what she wanted. It made us chuckle that she didn't even know his name. She looked to be in her 20s and looked disheveled."

After the young woman tried to leave the hotel with many of the ordered items, and denied by hotel employees, Price told the assistant general manager to give the food and alcohol to employees.

Even though it didn't come at Alabama, Price did get another chance at Texas-El Paso, accepting the head coaching job on Dec. 31, 2003. During the following season, he looked like a new man. No longer drawing comparisons to actor Wilford Brimley, he had lost weight, was tan and had ditched the glasses. The Miners went 8-4, narrowly losing 33-28 to Colorado in the Houston Bowl.

Both he and UTEP looked re-invigorated.

Can You Hear Me Now?

$\mathcal{O}$ne of the biggest complaints regarding the investigation of the University of Alabama's football program, and subsequent sanctions that would cripple the program for years, was that there was essentially no due process.

Specifically, Alabama was investigated by the National Collegiate Athletic Association's enforcement community, it was sentenced by the NCAA and its appeal was rejected by the NCAA. Because the U.S. Supreme Court ruled in 1998 that the NCAA is not a state actor and thus not bound by judicial due process standards, witnesses, without having their identities revealed, are not under oath to investigators, who can use that information to penalize schools and student-athletes.

Thus, Alabama was never able to confront its accusers and all avenues for appeal were exhausted.

But the NCAA was taking a number of public-relations hits both in and outside of Alabama, and not just because its rulings were seen as arbitrary and non-uniform.

For example, in December 2004 former Ohio State running back Maurice Clarett, in an interview with ESPN The Magazine, accused his former school of numerous $1,000 handshakes from boosters, giving high-paying jobs for doing nothing more than watching grass grow and free cars—not to mention free grades. His allegations were backed up by three players and came in the wake of a number of serious issues, including the firing of men's basketball coach Jim O'Brien after he admitted to giving $6,000 to a recruit. Additionally, quarterback Troy Smith was suspended from the Alamo Bowl due to allegations booster Robert Baker gave him unspecified illicit benefits, and numerous football players had been arrested for a variety of offenses. A search of court records by the Associated Press revealed at least 14 arrests involving 14 football players following coach Jim Tressel's hiring, from January 2001 to May 2004.

On Jan. 6, 2005, athletic director Andy Geiger, who was overseeing an annual operating budget of more than $85 million, announced his retirement.

"I find my work is no longer fun and I no longer look forward with enthusiasm each day," the 65-year-old Geiger said at his press conference. "I'm just tired. Just bone-weary. Not the tired that a good night of sleep fixes. Burnout, I guess, is what they call it in the industry."

When Clarett was initially suspended for lying to enforcement officials, Ohio State's athletic department and football program were cleared of any wrongdoing in a months-long investigation by the NCAA. One would assume, it was re-opened.

Maybe it was just Ohio State's turn.

At Colorado, the local district attorney accused the football program of using sex and alcohol as recruiting tools. That was followed by former female kicker Katie Hnida claiming she was raped by a teammate. Coach Gary Barnett was suspended, but kept his job even after criticizing Hnida for being a poor kicker. Instead, athletic director Dick Tharp resigned.

At least nine women said they were assaulted by Colorado football players or recruits between 1997 and 2004. The investigating grand jury said two female trainers alleged they were sexually assaulted by an assistant coach and that a "slush fund" was created with money from Barnett's football camp. However, the grand jury issued only one indictment, accusing former football recruiting aide Nathan Maxcey of soliciting a prostitute for himself and misusing a school-issued cell phone.

Although the NCAA wasn't directly involved in the Colorado investigation, it was in the decision to declare Buffaloes punt-returner Jerry Bloom ineligible because he accepted sponsorship money to compete and train as an Olympic skier. Bloom challenged the ruling and two weeks prior to his junior season had his final appeal rejected because NCAA rules stipulate that while athletes can accept salaries as professionals in other sports, like baseball, they are not allowed to accept money from sponsors.

USC wide receiver Mike Williams and Clarett were also declared ineligible when a court ruled that the NFL couldn't bar players who had been out of high school for less than three years, resulting in the sophomores signing with agents, only to have the appeal overturned.

Washington football coach Rick Neuheisel was fired for gambling when he entered betting pools on the 2002 and 2003 NCAA men's basketball tournaments (he spent $6,400), resulting in a another lawsuit that made just about everyone involved look bad. NCAA official David Price testified that blindsiding Neuheisel with gambling allegations in a June 2003 interview was necessary in order to obtain "the truth." As of April that same year, the bylaws had been amended so the NCAA was required to notify the subject of an investigation "prior to an interview being arranged or initiated by the enforcement staff" if an ethical conduct "allegation may be forthcoming."

Just before closing arguments were to be heard, Neuheisel reached a $4.5 million settlement with the NCAA and University of Washington. On the same day, Colorado president Elizabeth Hoffman resigned amid the football recruiting scandal and a national controversy over an activist professor who had compared victims of the Sept. 11 terrorist attacks to a Nazi. Incidentally, Neuheisel coached at Colorado before Washington.

There were also issues beyond the scope of enforcement and infractions, like two redshirt wide receivers at Michigan State arrested for planting homemade bombs outside of apartments, or the Alabama Legislative Black Caucus asking black athletes to refuse to attend Auburn until the school agreed to rehire two black administrators fired in a reorganization of the athletic department.

Meanwhile, the NCAA wouldn't admit that a playoff—which existed in every other sport, and on every other level of football—was the best way to determine its national champion at the Division I level. Instead, the Bowl Championship Series, which resulted in a split-title in 2003 after LSU and Oklahoma were matched up even though polls had Southern Cal No. 1, was utilized, with rankings determined by a formula so confusing that in comparison it made learning Japanese look easy. In 2004, the teams competing for the national championship at the Orange Bowl would be determined by a tweaked system featuring The Associated Press poll and the ESPN/USA Today coaches' poll, with six other polls also factoring.

In short, it was still a recipe for disaster that only added to the criticism, and not just by fans, but in Congress.

In part because there's no alternative, the NCAA was considered a voluntary organization comprised of approximately 1,200 schools from all 50 states. As an organization, it held 87 championships in 22 sports across three divisions, with more than 375,000 student-athletes competing.

Its impact on the country could not be measured. The television rights alone were worth billions of dollars. The NCAA estimated that the average Division I university spent almost $15 million on athletics. That increased to roughly $27 million for schools with football. The bigger the program, the more money spent.

Obviously, each person in Congress had at least one NCAA member that it represented, which made the organization incredibly influential.

NCAA Major Infractions through March 1, 2005 (All Sports)

8—Southern Methodist University.

7—Arizona State University, Auburn University, Texas A&M University (College Station), University of Minnesota (Twin Cities), University of Wisconsin (Madison), Wichita State University.

6—Florida State University, Kansas State University, University of California (Berkeley), University of California (Los Angeles), University of Georgia, University of Kentucky.

5—Michigan State University, Mississippi State University, North Carolina State University, University of Cincinnati, University of Illinois, Champaign, University of Kansas, University of Memphis, University of Miami (Florida), University of Oklahoma, University of Southern California, University of Texas at El Paso, University of Texas (Pan American), University of Washington.

4—Baylor University, Clemson University, Howard University, Jackson State University, New Mexico State University, Oklahoma State University, University of Alabama (Tuscaloosa), University of Arizona, University of Colorado (Boulder), University of Florida, University of Houston, University of Missouri (Columbia), University of Nebraska (Lincoln), University of Nevada (Las Vegas), University of Texas at Austin, University of Tulsa, West Texas A&M University, West Virginia University.

3—Alabama State University, Bradley University, California State University (Northridge), Centenary College (Louisiana), Grambling State University, Marshall Uni-

versity, Montana State University-Bozeman, Ohio State University, San Diego
State University, St. Bonaventure University, Tennessee State University, Univer-
sity at Buffalo (the State University of New York), University of Arkansas (Fayette-
ville), University of Dayton, University of Louisiana at Lafayette, University of
Louisville, University of Maryland (College Park), University of Mississippi, Uni-
versity of Nebraska at Omaha, University of Notre Dame, University of San Francisco, University of South Carolina (Columbia), University of Utah, Virginia
Polytechnic Institute & State University, Washington State University, Western
Kentucky University, Western State College of Colorado.

2—Alabama A&M University, Alcorn State University, Austin Peay State University,
Bethune-Cookman College, California Polytechnic State University, California
State University (Fresno), Cornell University, DePaul University, Drake University,
East Carolina University, East Tennessee State University, Florida A&M University,
Hampton University, Humboldt State University, Idaho State University, Indiana
University (Bloomington), Jacksonville University, Kentucky State University,
Louisiana State University, Louisiana Tech University, Loyola College (Maryland),
McNeese State University, Middle Tennessee State University, Mississippi Col-
lege, Morgan State University, North Carolina Central University, Northwestern
State University, Oral Roberts University, Oregon State University, Plattsburgh
State, University of New York, Prairie View A&M University, Purdue University,
Saint Louis University, San Francisco State University, San Jose State University,
Seton Hall University, Slippery Rock University of Pennsylvania, Southeast Mis-
souri State University, Southern University (Baton Rouge), Stetson University,
Tennessee Technological University, Texas Christian University, Texas Tech Uni-
versity, Tulane University, University of Alaska Anchorage, University of Hawaii
(Manoa), University of Idaho, University of Iowa, University of Louisiana at Mon-
roe, University of Michigan, University of New Mexico, University of North Carolina (Chapel Hill), University of Oregon, University of South Florida, University
of Southern Mississippi, University of Tennessee (Knoxville), University of West
Alabama, Villanova University, Wake Forest University, Westminster College
(Pennsylvania).

1—Adelphi University, Albany State University (Georgia), American International
College, American University, Arkansas State University, Ashland University,
Augustana College (South Dakota), Ball State University, Big Ten Conference,
Bloomsburg University of Pennsylvania, Brooklyn College, Bucknell University,
California Lutheran University, California State Polytechnic University (Pomona),
California State University (East Bay), California State University (Fullerton), Cali-
fornia State University (Sacramento), Canisius College, Central College (Iowa),
Cheyney University of Pennsylvania, Chicago State University, City College of
New York, Cleveland State University, Coastal Carolina University, Colorado Col-
lege, Dominican University (Illinois), Duke University, Eastern Kentucky Univer-
sity, Eastern Michigan University, Eastern Washington University, Elizabeth City
State University, Gallaudet University, Gardner-Webb University, Georgia Institute of Technology, Georgia Southern University, Gonzaga University, Gustavus
Adolphus College, Hamline University, Hardin-Simmons University, Illinois State

University, Iowa State University, Kenyon College, La Salle University, Lamar University, Lewis University, Lincoln University (Missouri), Lock Haven University of Pennsylvania, Long Beach State University, Marist College, McMurry University, Miami University (Ohio), Midwestern State University, Millersville University of Pennsylvania, Mississippi Valley State University, Montana State University-Billings, Morehouse College, Morningside College, Murray State University, New York Institute of Technology, Northern Arizona University, Ohio Valley Conference, Oklahoma Panhandle State University, Pfeiffer University, Portland State University, Robert Morris University, Rutgers (State University of New Jersey, New Brunswick), Saint Joseph's College (Indiana), Salem State College, Samford University, Savannah State University, Seattle University, Simpson College, South Carolina State University, Southeastern Louisiana University, Southern Illinois University at Carbondale, St. John's University (New York), St. Norbert College, Stephen F. Austin State University, Stony Brook University, Syracuse University, Texas A&M University-Kingsville, Texas Southern University, Texas State University-San Marcos, U.S. Military Academy, U.S. Naval Academy, University of Akron, University of Arkansas, Little Rock, University of Bridgeport, University of California (Irvine), University of California (Santa Barbara), University of Central Florida, University of Denver, University of Maine (Orono), University of Maryland (Eastern Shore), University of Massachusetts at Lowell, University of Massachusetts (Amherst), University of Minnesota Duluth, University of Montana, University of Nevada, University of New Haven, University of Pittsburgh, University of Portland, University of Redlands, University of Richmond, University of San Diego, University of South Alabama, University of Tampa, University of Tennessee at Chattanooga, University of Toledo, University of Virginia, University of Wisconsin (Milwaukee), University of Wyoming, University of the District of Columbia, University of the Pacific, University of the South, Utah State University, Vanderbilt University, Virginia State University, Virginia Union University, Waynesburg College, Weber State University, West Chester University of Pennsylvania, West Virginia Wesleyan College, Western Carolina University, Western Illinois University, Whitworth College, Winston-Salem State University, Yale University, Youngstown State University.

Among SEC teams, the breakdown was:
7—Auburn
6—Georgia, Kentucky
5—Mississippi State
4—Alabama, Florida
3—Arkansas, Mississippi, South Carolina
2—LSU, Tennessee
1—Vanderbilt

Quite often, when someone in Congress speaks up against the NCAA, it's a person with some sort of tie to one of the schools near the top of the penalties list. For example, when the Subcommittee of Commerce, Trade and Consumer

Protection held hearings on the problems facing amateur athletics on Feb. 13, 2002, the following testimony was given:

"Eraste Autin, a University of Florida recruit, collapsed during a so called 'voluntary' summer workout and later died. By NCAA rules, the University was not allowed to cover his hospital costs and his family could not even collect a death benefit. Surely the NCAA can allow a university to pay the hospital expenses for a student athlete who dies while practicing the sport that's making the NCAA incredible amounts of money. And why didn't this happen? Because the workout was categorized as 'voluntary.'"

Who made that statement? Congresswoman Shelley Berkley of Nevada, who as a formerly elected member of the Nevada University Board of Regents had first-hand knowledge of the NCAA targeting UNLV men's basketball coach Jerry Tarkanian and then spending millions defending itself in a lawsuit it would lose.

Maybe it was just a matter of time before Alabama's representatives added their voices to the numerous calls for Congress to get involved, especially since 2004 was an election year.

Congress to Hold Hearings on NCAA

May 14, 2004

A U.S. congressman's call for a formal investigation of the National Collegiate Athletic Association will apparently result in an oversight hearing by the House Judiciary Committee.

"Today I heard that we're going to have hearing on the matter," said Rep. Spencer Bachus, a republican from Vastavia Hills who is running for re-election in Alabama's 6th District. "It's going to happen."

Although a hearing has not been scheduled yet, Bachus, who sits on the Judiciary Committee, said he expects it to be held within 60 to 90 days.

Bachus formerly requested the hearing Tuesday in a letter written to House Judiciary Committee Chairman Jim Sensenbrenner, R-Wis.

"After reviewing several recent cases in which NCAA member institutions were investigated and sanctioned, I am alarmed by the lack of procedural due process the NCAA provides to some member institutions it investigates and sanctions.

"Unfortunately, the conduct of the NCAA raises serious questions as to whether it has strayed beyond this stated purpose. In recent investigations, the NCAA has allegedly concealed the identity of witnesses, manufactured evidence, threatened employees of schools being investigated, and condoned conflicts of interest between investigators and member schools. The effects of NCAA investigations and sanctions have profound consequences for member schools.

"Adverse decisions can have a devastating impact upon the academic programs, faculty, students, alumni, athletic programs, and revenue streams of targeted institutions."

The chairman was quick to respond:

"Your letter raises significant and timely questions regarding the adequacy of process accorded NCAA member institutions," Sensenbrenner wrote Thursday.

"Allegations that the NCAA has concealed the identity of witnesses, manufactured evidence, threatened member institutions' employees, and condoned investigator conflicts of interest are both serious and troubling.

"As a result, I agree that the Subcommittee on the Constitution should conduct a hearing to examine the important issues you have raised."

Although Bachus graduated from Auburn University and then the University of Alabama Law School, he said his concern regarding the NCAA did not stem from recent penalties imposed against both schools.

Alabama was penalized in 2002 following a lengthy investigation into football recruiting violations. The Crimson Tide was placed on a five-year probation, which included the loss of 21 scholarships and bans on both bowl appearances and television.

It also sparked a $60 million libel and defamation lawsuit by former assistant coaches Ronnie Cottrell and Ivy Williams against the NCAA and other defendants.

Last month, the Auburn men's basketball program was placed on two years' probation and revoked one scholarship for recruiting violations.

Bachus said his interest in the NCAA and its lack of due process was piqued last summer while considering Internet gambling legislation.

"I had discussions with people in Major League Baseball and the National Football League, and at that time it came to light that there were several instances of gambling on the collegiate level that the NCAA knew about," Bachus said. "But I was also aware that they weren't investigating those cases or prosecuting.

"What I found is that the NCAA has tremendous power and in many cases has overstepped its bounds and a lot of what they do goes against the public interest. They need to restore their credibility. That would be my goal in all of this."

Thursday, the NCAA announced the results of a gambling study that showed 35 percent of male athletes and 10 percent of female athletes have bet on college sports in the last year, and that gambling money has influenced the outcome of games.

The 2003 National Study on Collegiate Sports Wagering and the Associated Health Risks, surveyed more than 21,000 student-athletes. It found that gambling was most prevalent at the Division III level, and least prevalent in Division I, which includes the Southeastern Conference and Alabama.

Golfer, wrestlers, lacrosse and football players were the most likely male athletes to wager on college sports. Female athletes who gamble were more likely to compete in golf, lacrosse, basketball and field hockey.

"The scope of the sports wagering among intercollegiate student-athletes is startling and disturbing," NCAA president Myles Brand said in a statement. "Sports wagering is a double threat because it harms the well-being of student-athletes and the integrity of college sports."

The study showed that 1.1 percent of football players reported taking money for playing poorly in games.

While 2.3 percent of football players admitted they were asked to influence the outcome of games because of gambling debts, 1.4 percent acknowledged altering their performance to change the outcome.

Although most college gambling scandals have involved point shaving in basketball, the survey numbers for basketball were lower than those of football. Two Division I basketball players out of 388 surveyed (0.5 percent) said they took money to play poorly in a game.

The NCAA Sports Wagering Task Force has been charged with analyzing the study and will make recommendations. Notre Dame president Rev. Edward A. Malloy will head the task force, with American Football Coaches Association executive director Grant Teaff serving as vice chair.

The SEC will have three representatives on the 26-person task force: director of athletics designee Damn Evans of Georgia, Major Ricky Adams of the LSU Police Department, and Michael Munoz, a senior football player at the University of Tennessee.

"The NCAA is going to have to decide what it's going to investigate and what it's not going to investigate," Bachus said. "Are they going to accuse athletes of gambling? How will they do it? Will they hold hearings? Will they have secret witnesses? Will accused athletes have a chance to confront their accusers?

"There are only two instances in this country where someone doesn't have due process: The NCAA and espionage."

Bachus said he expects NCAA officials to arrive in Washington, D.C., today to begin lobbying for support.

"I haven't seen the letter that he wrote, but from what I've heard I support him," said attorney Phillip Jauregui, an Alabama graduate who's running against Bachus in the June 1 GOP primary. "The house judiciary committee also has the constitution restoration act, which has not been passed down to the House floor. That's why I'm running, to stop judges from making laws."

In July 2004, calls for congressional hearings gained momentum when Sen. Richard Shelby, also called for an investigation.

In his letter to Sen. Orrin Hatch, chairman of the Senate Judiciary Committee, the Alabama Senator wrote:

"The National Collegiate Athletic Association [NCAA] is an important entity in our society. It has the authority to severely sanction its member institutions, including the power to eliminate an institution's participation in intercollegiate athletics.

"With this enormous power to govern such a significant part of our economy, most observers would assume the NCAA is required to provide basic procedural safeguards while exercising its regulatory function; however, this may not be the case.

"During investigations resulting in the imposition of penalties, many institutions may have been denied basic due process to be able to receive timely notice of complaints, learn the identity of witnesses and be allowed to question and contest NCAA allegations.

"Given the economic and social impact of intercollegiate athletics in the United States, I would like to ask you as Chairman of the Judiciary Committee to schedule hearings into this matter. The committee should consider the proper role and methods of the NCAA in governing the athletic programs of its member institutions."

Like Bachus, Shelby avoided citing incidents at Alabama or Auburn as reasons for wanting investigations.

The NCAA maintained that it only enforced what's prescribed in the bylaws of a voluntary organization.

"Though the association has not reviewed or been privy to any letter from Senator Shelby, the association's enforcement staff is required to follow the procedures and policies instituted by the membership," said Jeff Howard, the NCAA's managing director for public relations. "It's important to recognize the bylaws that the membership follows are bylaws that are instituted by the individual colleges and universities that make up the NCAA."

In 1991, Congress held hearings on the NCAA's power to investigate, with Tarkanian testifying that the NCAA conducted a "reign of terror." No laws were changed, but in its own study, conducted by former Solicitor General Rex Lee, proposed 11 recommendations the NCAA should undertake, including the hiring of independent judges to hear infractions cases and the opening of those proceedings to anyone interested. Most of the recommendations were not implemented.

Thirteen years later, on Sept. 9, "Due Process and the NCAA" was called to order by the Subcommittee on the Constitution.

"This hearing is about fairness, particularly the fairness the NCAA displays in enforcing its rules," Chairman Steve Chabot of Ohio said. "Merited or not, the NCAA has at least the perception of a fairness problem."

Representing the NCAA's Committee on Infractions was vice-chairman Jo Potuto of the University of Nebraska. She argued that the NCAA offered college athletes due process because any athlete accused of a violation but sought reinstatement was allowed to testify before a committee and argue his or her case.

"An even playing field means more than an evenhanded and consistent application of the rules on the field," Potuto said. "It also means an evenhanded and consistent application of the rules off the field."

Strongly disagreeing with her were Bloom and David Ridpath, an associate professor of sport administration at Mississippi State who had previously been a compliance director at Marshall University. (Note: He had a pending lawsuit against Marshall, claiming he had been a scapegoat and reassigned after an improper employment scheme for athletes was uncovered and the school was placed on probation.)

"In the NCAA, the judgment of the dispute is formed exclusively within the organization by their own members," Bloom said. "They're the judge, the jury and the executioner."

"College athletics is a very seductive business that has forced good people to do bad things and bad people to do worse things," Ridpath testified, adding that infractions hearings should be open to keep committee members accountable. "Do not do something behind closed doors. It's a shroud of secrecy that makes it seem like something's wrong."

Ridpath also stated that member institutions were either afraid of the NCAA or too close to it. The result was people being able to use their influence to "settle scores or cash chips in."

The hearing lasted approximately 90 minutes. Like with its predecessor, no changes appeared imminent.

Part III

SURGE

The Turning Tide, the 2004 Season

*W*hen it comes to football, University of Alabama fans are simply nuts.

At least, that's the way it often appears from the outside.

OK, that's the way it can appear from the inside as well, but there's little doubt that there are no fans more devoted or dedicated than those that cheer for the Crimson Tide football team, anywhere.

Don't believe it?

Do you have a photo of yourself proudly sitting in the golf cart of your favorite coach more than 20 years after he passed away? (Obviously, Paul W. "Bear" Bryant)

Have you ever seen anything like a large headline "Tornadoes kill 69" just above an even bigger photo with the caption "One of few times when Tide did not function perfectly" five days after the team last played? (Birmingham News, 1930)

How about hearing the local executive sports editor saying, "The team could win the national championship and fans here would still be mad it wasn't by more than three touchdowns" and mean it? (David Wasson, Tuscaloosa News)

There's a reason why James Michener said in 1975 while writing his book "Sports in America," "I thought Nebraska was the most football-crazed state until I came to Alabama." It just so happened that he had been on hand for the 50th anniversary of the 1926 Rose Bowl celebration, in which all the remaining players were introduced by Bryant at halftime of a 52-0 drubbing of the Washington Huskies. "The people in the audience welcomed the team with an absolute admiration that is hard to describe."

Imagine for a second that the original signers of the Declaration of Independence dropped in on Washington, D.C., via a time warp for a weekend. That's how Alabama fans revered their Founding Fathers on that particular afternoon, and there were many tears shed in both joy and respect.

But in order to truly understand Crimson Tide football fans one first has to understand the place they consider the center of their universe, where they spend many Saturday afternoons in the fall.

Tuscaloosa is located in West Alabama on Black Warrior River, approximately 55 miles southwest of Birmingham. As of this writing, the university had a growing enrollment of approximately 20,000 students (with plans to quickly expand to more than 28,000), and the city population was roughly 78,000, representing nearly half of Tuscaloosa County's 165,000 residents. Many of the rest were living across the river in the community of Northport. Basically, the biggest difference between the communities is that one's on the north side of the river with a huge red dog statue made out of scrap metal while the other has a big school and a few more bars.

Originally, Tuscaloosa was built on top of a network of Indian trails as the river shoals were the southernmost site that could be forded year-round. When white settlers began to populate the area, they named it after the chief who had a fateful encounter with explorer Hernando DeSoto centuries before somewhere in Southwest Alabama, from the Choctaw words "tushka" meaning warrior and "lusa" meaning black.

In 1817, Alabama became a territory, and on December 13, 1819, the territorial legislature incorporated the town of Tuscaloosa, exactly one day before Congress admitted Alabama into the Union as a state.

From 1826 to 1846 Tuscaloosa was the state capital of Alabama, the ruins of which are located just up the street from the Tuscaloosa News at the appropriately named Capitol Park. But after the departure of the capital to Montgomery, the population fell from approximately 4,500 to less than 2,000 in 1850. Notable additions to the community were the Bryce State Hospital for the Insane in the 1850s and the construction of a system of locks and dams on the Black Warrior River by the U.S. Army Corps of Engineers in the 1890s, which boosted mining and metallurgical industries in the region.

Among the more modern economic impacts were manufacturing plants for Michelin Tires, JVC America and a Mercedes-Benz M-Class SUV assembly plant. It opened in 1997 and by 2004 employed approximately 4,000 people, bringing a steady stream of Germans to the area and forced the previously-mentioned bars to finally get some decent-tasting beer.

That's Tuscaloosa as seen though the eyes of the chamber of commerce. Its people are a completely different matter.

Author Pearl Buck once said, "Alabama, for some reason I cannot determine, seems to be the most Southern state of the South." It's a state that has been through decades of economic stagnation and racial politics, while keeping a continual link to antebellum society, which in some ways continues to give Alabama its charm and also make visitors wonder if they're still in the United States.

To over simplify, Tuscaloosa and its surrounding communities are the exact opposite of New York City. If you walk down the street in the Big Apple and look people in the eye as you pass, they'll probably think that you're weird, perverted or both. In Tuscaloosa, if you don't look people in the eye as you pass, they'll probably think that you're weird, perverted or both—or an Auburn fan.

Overall, the people of Tuscaloosa are incredibly friendly, and unlike most large communities every person makes a point of speaking to you, especially if they have no idea who you are. As a consequence, a local dictionary would be smaller than usual, primarily because some words and phrases have been consolidated.

For example, the phrase "How are you?" is actually one word, "Howru?" with a phonetic dip in the middle and emphasis on the "u." The only words spoken more often in Tuscaloosa are "Roll Tide!" which in addition to serving as a salute/ battle cry for any university program can also have numerous other meanings like "Good-bye," "No, we're not interested in buying any right now," and "I desperately want to marry/sleep with that woman/man."

That last one is extremely important because the women of Tuscaloosa are extremely gorgeous. The rest are even better looking.

It's very similar to Eskimos supposedly having more than 100 words for snow. However, in this case the only wrong answer is "War Eagle," which is what people from Auburn say.

By the way, as an important safety point, guns are very popular in Alabama.

The concept of dinner is also greatly simplified because instead of asking what kind of food you want, someone from Tuscaloosa might simply ask where you want to get barbeque that night. "Dreamland" is always a good answer, and many folks have been known to make the pilgrimage whenever they're within a 200-mile radius. Located on the outskirts of town, its walls are covered with Crimson Tide memorabilia (like just about every other establishment that serves food) and items of historical significance, like when President George W. Bush made sure to get Dreamland ribs the last time he campaigned in the area.

If you go there and ask to see a menu, be prepared to be laughed at. They offer a full slab of ribs, a half slab of ribs and a rib sandwich. That's it, other than white bread and sweet tea, commonly known to the rest of the world as iced tea with sugar. Newcomers to the area often suffer insomnia the first few weeks as their bodies grow accustomed to the daily sugar highs.

For breakfast, the Waysider was a favorite of the Bear's, and for lunch there's the ever-popular City Café in Northport, where you're as likely to eat too much as get sassed by a waitress. If it sounds like an unhealthy diet, there is that potential. In 2004, Alabama ranked No. 1 nationally in obesity and a number of other health-related issues and it wasn't too hard to figure out why. As writer Florence King once pointed out: "Southerners have a genius for psychological alchemy . . . If something intolerable simply cannot be changed, driven away or shot they will not only tolerate it but take pride in it as well."

The downtown and campus areas are actually off a ways form the main high-way that acts as a thoroughfare to Birmingham, hidden behind a mass of strip malls, burger joints and the type of various retail outlets that are popular in most college towns. But they also come with the Southern tradition of being a little more laid back than most other places, and even fast food can take a while.

Two things that Tuscaloosa seemingly has no shortage of are traffic lights and churches. Not only is there one at every intersection, in the community of Alberta there's actually a one-block area with three acting completely independently (now go back and read that sentence and try to figure out if its about traffic lights or churches).

Not surprisingly, the campus completely stands out and doubles as the heart of the community. The brick facades give the impression that it's all been there since well before the Civil War, when in reality the structures have been built at various times. The fraternities and sororities appear to be just as nice (well, at least on the outside) as some of the administration buildings, which is a clear tip-off to the Greek system's established presence and status. Every student knows that if you want to be someone on campus, you had best go Greek, unless you're an athlete.

The only thing people in Tuscaloosa may take more seriously than their religion and barbeque is football, though here they all go hand-in-hand. Not only do most folks have a picture of "Bear" Bryant hanging somewhere in their house and office, but he's usually displayed similar to a religious icon.

"Mama wanted me to be a preacher," Bryant once said. "I told her coachin' and preachin' were a lot alike."

Overall, the two biggest structures in town are a large bank building located downtown and Bryant-Denny Stadium. It's located on Bryant Drive, down the street from the amazing Bryant Museum and not too far from Bryant High School. You can't miss it. It's located next to the Bryant Conference Center, and within walking distance from the Bryant Drive Animal Hospital and Bryant Drive Apartments. There was talk of moving a statue of Bryant from Legion Field in Birmingham, where Alabama used to play its biggest home games, but some thought it might be a little overkill. Heaven knows the last thing a Southerner wants to be considered is gaudy.

Oh, and life is a lot easier in Tuscaloosa if you like the Southern rock band Lynyrd Skynyrd. The song "Sweet Home Alabama" is not only considered an anthem, but an absolute truth.

Tuscaloosa is similar to Green Bay, Wisconsin, in that the entire community seemingly revolves around football. A typical conversation will often include everything from the latest news in practice to tidbits like "I heard [athletics director] Mal Moore say the other day that he has so many rings from his 20-some years as an assistant coach he doesn't even know where they all are."

Of course, the correct response is to yell out, "Roll Tide!"

Ask someone about important dates in local history and they'll probably start listing national championships. Fans can tell you exactly where they where when "Bear" Bryant died and can often recite uniform numbers faster than their wedding anniversary (sometimes faster) and family birthdays. They love their football lore, even in some cases with players the Crimson Tide didn't get. For example, Dan Reeves, who would participate in an amazing nine Super Bowls as a player and coach, was approached by Alabama following an impressive appearance in a high school all-star game. But instead of heading to Tuscaloosa, Reeves decided to keep his commitment to South Carolina. Instead, the Crimson Tide recruited some guy named Joe Namath.

On game days, everything else shuts down and any radio station not broadcasting the Crimson Tide is simply wasting its time. By midweek, the town starts filling up with hundreds of mobile homes, driven by scores of fans who, until the Crimson Tide played in Hawaii, would drive to each and every game.

For a big game, like Auburn, it's practically an invasion. Parking lots cram in campers, which then open up like a piñata scattering everything from a portable living room fully equipped with large-screen televisions and barbeques, to anything imaginable with a Crimson Tide logo. Those that can't get into a designated parking lot are often forced to park roadside or might try and find some solitude amongst trees, which resembles an elephant trying to find a spot to do his business.

Come Sunday, the temporary neighborhoods pack up and move on to the next game, usually to the chagrin of the host community, especially if unequipped to handle the equivalent of a small army.

It's similar with some Southeastern Conference schools, but nowhere is the team connected to the community's soul quite like Alabama (suggested reading: "Rammer Jammer Yellow Hammer" by former New York Times writer Warren St. John).

True Alabama fans schedule their weddings during the bye week, decorate their homes with crimson and name their children after football heroes. It doesn't surprise anyone in Tuscaloosa that the annual Bryant Namesake Reunion has become a regular event at the Bryant Museum, advancing to the point where people named Bryant are naming their kids Bryant, even some of the girls.

Games themselves are the pinnacle events and the field at Denny-Bryant Stadium is considered sacred territory. When the grass was dug up to be replaced prior to the 2004 season, people stole it. Dirt security was actually a concern.

For your "average" games, the area known as "The Quad" turns into a giant tent city, promoting everything from alumni groups and souvenirs to Republican and religious supporters. The marching band puts on a show and with majorettes (called the Crimsonettes) out in front they lead the flocks of fans to the stadium in time for kickoff. For Homecoming, the festivities include anything from the annual bonfire to a block party.

Ideally, the atmosphere crescendos until the final moments of a victory, when the Million Dollar Band boldly plays the song/cheer everyone has been waiting to hear: Rammer Jammer.

> Hey Vols!
> Hey Vols!
> We just beat the hell out of you!
> Rammer Jammer Yellowhammer!
> Give'em hell Alabama!

The funny thing is that if you don't know the words, the only part you'll probably make out from the 80,000-plus people screaming is the "We just beat the hell out of you" line, which, of course, is the important part. Rammer Jammer was actually a campus magazine and inspired the name of a terrific burger joint across the street from the stadium, and Yellowhammer is the state bird. Anyone not from Alabama doesn't have a chance of figuring that out on his or her own, but is expected to contribute vocally anyway.

In many ways, 2004 had as much news off the playing fields as on. While the military was fighting campaigns in Iraq and Afghanistan, and President Bush won a tight re-election bid against Massachusetts Senator John Kerry, the Boston Red Sox pulled off the greatest comeback in baseball history to beat the New York Yankees in the American League Championship Series and then swept the St. Louis Cardinals in the World Series.

Lance Armstrong won his unprecedented sixth Tour de France, Maria Sharapova broke through at Wimbledon and the Tampa Bay Lightning brought the Stanley Cup to the beach. A massive steroids scandal overshadowed both the Olympic Games in Greece and the assault on baseball's home run records. Phil Mickelson finally won a major while Annika Sorenstam dominated women's golf by winning 10 of the 20 events she entered.

The New England Patriots won the Super Bowl in dramatic fashion, but all the water-cooler talk was about Janet Jackson's "wardrobe malfunction" resulting in her flashing the world. Kobe Bryant was charged with sexually assaulting a 19-year-old woman and even though the Los Angeles Lakers reached the NBA Finals they lost to the Detroit Pistons and then disintegrated with coach Phil Jackson retiring and Shaquille O'Neal traded to Miami. The Pistons went on to get into a skirmish with Ron Artest and the Indiana Pacers, who then brawled with fans.

Competing for the legal headlines were Scott Peterson, Michael Jackson and Martha Stewart, and none of them favorably. Pete Rose finally admitted he gambled on baseball, Jason Giambi admitted he used steroids and hockey players admitted that they were making too much money for the National Hockey League to survive, but still couldn't come to a labor agreement with owners, resulting in a lockout and the canceling of the 2004-2005 season.

In college sports, Connecticut swept the basketball tournaments (men's and women's); Cal-State Fullerton won the College World Series; UCLA defended its title in softball and also won the team championship in gymnastics; and Denver shocked the Frozen Four in hockey.

In football, 39-year-old Tim Frisby, a 20-year veteran of the U.S. Army and father of six, walked on to South Carolina as a wide receiver. A quarterback almost half his age named Alex Smith, who was academically so advanced that he entered college with enough credits to be a junior, led Utah to an undefeated season. Oklahoma running back Adrian Peterson was the game's most dominant freshman since Herschel Walker and almost put to rest the notion that a first-year player couldn't win the Heisman Trophy (he finished second).

In Alabama, everything except the war—per capita, Alabama contributed more members to the armed forces in the 20th century than any other state—and possibly the presidential election took a back seat to football, and this had the potential to be one of the worst seasons in Crimson Tide history.

. . . And Then There Was Football

A college football season doesn't begin when a team straps on the pads for the first game of the fall, or even the first practice of the spring when coaches get a month in the middle of the off-season to make sure everyone's doing what they're supposed to.

It begins long before that, with year-round recruiting, weight-lifting and game-planning that builds and climaxes during a three-month regular season that hopefully peaks with a postseason game of importance.

Having said that, for intensive purposes Alabama's 2004 season began the moment the previous season ended with a disappointing 37-29 loss at Hawaii. There was no bowl game. The Crimson Tide had been banned from the postseason by NCAA sanctions, but even so at 4-9 it was still short of the minimum six victories necessary to receive any invitation.

Alabama had also been in a constant state of flux with all the coaching changes, including going through 2003 spring practice learning Mike Price's high-flying passing attack and then having to switch gears in the fall to Mike Shula's more-deliberate pro-style offense. Not only where players trying to figure out the playbooks, as well as each other, but so were the coaches. Many had been hired by Price and held over by Shula, while others were getting their first taste of Tuscaloosa.

Overall, it was a veteran staff, laden with excellent recruiters like running backs coach Sparky Woods, secondary coach Chris Ball, offensive line coach Bob Connelly and defensive line coach Buddy Wyatt. Shula was also familiar with his coordinators. Offensive coordinator Dave Rader, the head coach at Tulsa from 1988-99, had been Shula's quarterbacks coach when he was a player at Alabama. Defensive coordinator Joe Kines, who took a lot of heat from fans in 2003 after the Crimson Tide gave up 333 points, was also on that staff.

"He is my people," Shula said. "He was my coach when I was here. We coached three years together at Tampa [Bay with the NFL's Buccaneers]. I knew a lot about Joe Kines. Made me feel good when I took this job that he was here. Now been around him another year, feel even better about Joe Kines and having him here as our assistant head coach and defensive coordinator, lucky to have him."

Charlie Harbison (receivers), Paul Randolph (defensive ends), Dave Ungerer (special teams and tight ends) along with director of football operations Randy Ross and his assistant Tim Bowens completed the staff, provided much-needed stability as Shula didn't have to make a coaching change through 2004. In addition to aiding recruiting efforts, which had seemingly fallen off since Gene Stallings left in 1996, they also helped with the mental turnaround, the highest priority of Shula's first full year heading the Crimson Tide.

Teams don't win championships unless they first believe they can.

Despite having the second-youngest coach in Division I, the re-unification of Alabama and Shula brought together names synonymous with football and coaching greatness. When Mike's father Don retired in 1995 he was the NFL's all-time winningest coach (347-173-6), held the record for having coached in six Super Bowls and engineered the only perfect season in league history. Older brother Dave had also been a head coach with the Cincinnati Bengals (1992-96).

"No one is going to expect more out of me than I do," Mike Shula said. "We put our jobs on the line every week, regardless of what our last names are."

When Alabama hired Mike Shula on May 8, 2003, Don came aboard as a sort of unofficial godfather to the program. That's just the way it was with the Shulas, who had a close family, though the father and sons had a relationship few could relate to.

For example, at age 33, Don Shula was the youngest head coach in NFL history with the Baltimore Colts.

Dave, who compiled a 19-52 record with Cincinnati, was the only coach in NFL history to oppose his father, on Oct. 2, 1994 and Oct. 1, 1995, with both games played at Riverfront Stadium.

"It was really a tough situation," Don Shula said. "My family made it known to me that week, 'Dad, we hope you understand, but we're going to be rooting for Dave.'"

Don won both games, the second of which was decided by a last-minute drive directed by Hall of Fame quarterback Dan Marino.

"I was happy for our team, but Dave was broken-hearted," Don Shula said.

The spotlight was nothing new for them, just the different stages. Dave and Mike had to deal with it at an early age, as did sisters Annie, Sharon and Donna.

"There was always tons of attention in whatever you did," said Dave Shula, who's six years older than Mike. "On the first day of school your name would be called out and everyone's head would turn. Some of the looks would be favorable, some would not."

"I benefited from being the youngest of five, so all the things that you were going to go through as a son or daughter of Don Shula I was going to be able to watch my brothers and sisters go through it," Mike Shula said. "I also had help along the way."

By help, Mike meant his mother Dorothy, who naturally was around more than her husband before she died in 1991. But there was also football, with the boys becoming gym rats.

"It was one way to spend time with him, a male-bonding type of thing," Dave Shula said.

Back then, not even pro teams had multi-million dollar facilities and training camps began right after July 4th. The Shula boys did everything from help plant grass seed and paint the locker room to cleaning the bathrooms and helping out with laundry. On game days, they worked their way up, from filling cups of water or Gatorade, to being a ball boy and eventually helping out some of the assistant coaches. Perhaps it was only a matter of time before they both took to the field themselves, with Mike becoming a quarterback at Alabama (even though growing up he was a big Notre Dame fan).

"The best thing was in high school, my senior year they had the [NFL] strike and every week they thought the strike would be resolved and they would game plan until Tuesday," Mike Shula said. "If it wasn't resolved they [would cancel] and go to the next week. So after Tuesday he would have a lot of time on his hands. He would bring the projector home and I would bring the film home and on Wednesday and Thursday we would watch film on my upcoming opponent.

"He taught me how to watch film and what to look for and this and that. Every now and then he'd have a suggestion."

Those sessions helped Mike's ability to see the big picture, encourage his calculating nature and attention to detail. He cherished those times, but they were also instrumental in his development as a coach.

"There are a lot of decisions that you have to make that aren't going to make everyone happy," Mike Shula said. "When I was an assistant or a coordinator, I wouldn't understand why the head coach made them. Now they're decisions that I have to make. Sometimes it's not the ideal decision, but it's the best one for everyone."

The same went for family life. Former Dolphins quarterback Bob Griese was once quoted saying that if a person wanted to disappear all they had to do is become a NFL assistant coach. Mike Shula was a NFL assistant coach or coordinator for 15 years, and the first time he saw his daughter Shari walk was on a field after practice.

"It's tough," he said. "Never enough time, and then the time you do spend with your family never seems like it's enough for the other people. You get past it. What I learned over the years, and just listening to people, is that you have to find a happy medium and what people are comfortable with."

In 2004, the Crimson Tide was far from being comfortable. Shula had 13 returning starters and 38 experienced lettermen, but scholarship reductions as part of the NCAA penalties would be severely felt. To put it into perspective, think of a hockey team with four lines that rotate, only no one could be added to the roster so for every player lost the others had to pick up the slack. Alabama's situation was like that only without a second line. The Crimson Tide had its fair share of starters, none of whom Shula had recruited, but little depth on the roster.

Consequently, whenever someone talked about how well the 2004 team might fare, he or she first had to preface it with "if everyone stays healthy."

But in addition to creating a new mindset, there had to be an equal commitment from the school as well.

Already a $100 million facilities improvement project was well under way that would include the renovation of Coleman Coliseum (where the basketball and gymnastic teams competed), the addition of a second deck beyond the north end zone of Bryant-Denny Stadium and the renovation of former football dormitory Paul W. Bryant Hall into an academic center for all student-athletes. The first part of the project to be completed was construction of a new football complex, transforming probably the worst weight room in the Southeastern Conference to among the very best in college football.

Under the direction of strength and conditioning coach Kent Johnston, a 17-year veteran of the National Football League who was arguably Shula's best hire in his first year at Alabama, players immediately began going through 6 a.m. workouts together as part of his "Pathway to Peek Performance." It not only made the Crimson Tide physically and mentally stronger, but brought the team closer together and impressed recruits. A commitment to excellence can't be fooled, and in this case led to a professional-type atmosphere, precision practices and pinpoint strategies. Well before the season started, the team had its tightest group of players Alabama fans had seen in years.

"Our view has definitely changed, it's more of a team atmosphere," junior center Taylor Britt said. "We have to get what needs to be done, there's no slacking around any more. We have to work toward perfection."

Though players had been working out and going through drills on their own, the Crimson Tide officially returned to the field in late February. Spring practice is not unique to Alabama, but few teams had their workouts so early.

According to National Collegiate Athletic Conference rules, every college football program was allowed 15 offseason practices, which usually culminated with a full scrimmage. At Alabama, it's called A-Day, and usually attracted more than 30,000 fans.

Though there are many reasons for having spring practices, three that stand out are:

- Practices are always a good thing.
- It's an ideal time to make major changes, like moving a player to a new position, ease someone into a starting role and get young players experience.
- It gives players a benchmark to measure their progress in preparation for the upcoming season.

Most programs don't have spring football until March, but Shula preferred not to have spring break interfere or break up the schedule, it also kept players from basically taking two months off after the end of the previous season and decreased the potential for getting in trouble (theoretically).

Here's how the 2004 Crimson Tide looked at each position:

Quarterback. Junior Brodie Croyle, who had become the first Alabama player to pass for 2,000 yards or more as a sophomore (and in the process broke a couple of school records set by Shula), was undoubtedly the starting quarterback, but after having offseason surgery on his non-throwing shoulder was held out of contact drills in the spring. Croyle, whose father John played for Paul W. "Bear" Bryant, was not only the first player to commit under Dennis Franchione, but arguably his lone standout recruit.

Most fans believed Croyle would be the key to the season, if he could stay healthy. He had missed his senior season in high school with torn anterior cruciate ligament in his knee, and his sister, Reagan, who had been a basketball player at Alabama and the 2000 homecoming queen, had also experienced knee trouble.

It's why some quietly called him Joe Jr., referring to another talented Alabama quarterback with knee trouble and a great arm, Joe Namath.

Also coming off surgery was backup Spencer Pennington, who went under the knife to fix his throwing shoulder. For him, the injury was a little more stressful because he was an even bigger baseball prospect.

As a high school duel-athlete, Pennington passed for 2,433 yards and 20 touchdowns as a senior to lead Fayette County High School—located 45 miles north of Tuscaloosa—to the Class 4A state championship. That same school year, he batted .476 (50-for-105) with 10 home runs and 55 RBIs, and after leading Fayette to the Championship Series turned down a six-figure offer from the Chicago Cubs on draft day to follow his brother Jeremy, who had been an offensive lineman.

Pennington dreamed of playing quarterback for the Crimson Tide and even though he would always be behind Croyle also turned down an opportunity to potentially be the No. 1 quarterback at Mississippi State. Besides, it had been years since Alabama's starting quarterback had made it through a season unscathed and in 2003 the Crimson Tide had three different players take snaps, including Pennington, due to injuries.

Also limited during spring practice, Pennington, a junior, had to compete with Marc Guillon for the No. 2 job after the sophomore took nearly every snap during spring practice. It gave him a slight advantage heading into the fall, when Guillon edged into the backup role. Otherwise, they appeared to have very little in common.

Pennington was a local favorite, an avid hunter who came from a religious family. Guillon was originally from California, had signed with Miami out of high school after playing two games as a true freshman and transferred to Alabama in August 2003 after injuries helped keep him from moving up the depth chart with the Hurricanes. He had family in the area, but his quiet nature also had fans wondering—possibly unfairly—if he possessed the fire necessary to lead the Crimson Tide, as the pressures of being Alabama's starting quarterback were immense.

They hoped not to find out in 2004, though it was more of a reflection of Croyle's potential than anything else.

Running Back. With limited options in 2003, Alabama gave the ball to Shaud Williams—a lot. As a senior, the small running back managed to accumulate 1,441 rushing yards to lead the SEC before moving on to the NFL's Buffalo Bills.

Senior Ray Hudson, the son of a minister from Bonifay, Fla., was the most experienced ball-carrier on the roster with 490 rushing yards in 2003, but no one knew if he could handle the workload of being the starter. Coming in, his best single-game performance was 82 yards on seven carries against North Texas as a sophomore. However, Hudson worked hard during the offseason and was impressive in scrimmages.

Hudson's backup was sophomore Kenneth Darby, who despite a nagging shoulder injury showed flashes of promise during his freshman season, including a 41-yard carry against Ole Miss. Originally out of Huntsville, he would get a chance to show what he could do as Hudson's relief.

One of the most popular players on the team and among fans was fullback Tim Castille, who had started 10 games as a true freshman and was arguably already Alabama's best clutch player. The sure-handed and gritty sophomore often had his number called on third-and-short and goal-line situations, and he rarely failed to come through.

He was also the son of an Alabama football legend, Jeremiah Castille, a first-team All-American cornerback in 1982 who also made three interceptions to win the MVP trophy in Bear Bryant's final game (21-15 over Illinois at the Liberty Bowl). The father was also on campus working with athletes through the Fellowship of Christian Athletes and served as the football team's minister.

Although Tim Castille almost went to Southern Cal, the Alabama heritage eventually won him over and prior to the start of the 2004 season changed his number from No. 29 to his dad's former No. 19.

"His influence is a major factor in everything I do here," the low-key Castille said.

Backing up Castille was sophomore Le'Ron McClain, who grew up across the river from Tuscaloosa in Northport and had excelled as a running back. His physical play had him challenging Castille for playing time and coaches devised a special "jumbo" formation with two tight ends and two fullbacks. With it, the Crimson Tide hoped to basically shove the ball down the opponents' throat, or catch the opposition off-guard with a pass that would be extremely difficult to defend, at crucial times.

Wide Receiver. Before fall practice began, Shula called this his scariest position, and rightfully so. Five of the top six receivers from 2003 were gone, with the lone exception being sophomore Tyrone Prothro, who would be heavily relied upon. Second on the "veteran" list was redshirt freshman Matt Caddell, though Antonio Carter was granted a rare sixth-year of eligibility since he hadn't played in a game since 2001 due to leg injuries. At minimum, Carter would serve as a sort of mentor, if not player/coach. The only other returning letterman receiver was Matt Miller, a special-teams standout who came from a long line of Alabama graduates and football players.

However, the Crimson Tide recruited a number of outstanding athletes, who would have an opportunity to play, if not start, as true freshmen. Leading the group was Keith Brown and DJ Hall (both from the Florida panhandle), Marcel Stamps, Ezekial Knight and Will Oakley. Knight was big enough to be a linebacker and Stamps would be moved to that position during the season, but it was obvious from the first day that the group had enormous potential.

Tight End. David Cavan, who grew up in Tuscaloosa and was the son of a former halfback under Bryant, played most of his junior season with a cast on his right hand, but it was a knee injury that finally sidelined him for the final three games of 2003. Still, at 6-foot-5, 252 pounds, he was an imposing run-blocker and tough to bring down after making a catch. Coaches viewed junior Clint Johnston (6-4, 245), whose father and uncle both played at Alabama, as more versatile, but it was one of the few positions where Alabama had some real experience.

Offensive Line. With three-year starting left guard Justin Smiley having left early for the NFL (and selected by the San Francisco 49ers in the second round), and senior left tackle Wesley Britt still recovering from a broken leg, the line was a primary concern heading into spring, with four players in new positions.

After Britt, who at 6-8 probably should have had his position listed as "small giant," Evan Mathis was Alabama's best offensive lineman, and coaches wanted a versatile player in Smiley's spot who could slide over to tackle in case Britt didn't make a full recovery. So Mathis moved from right tackle to left guard. The only other returning starter was junior center J.B. Closner, originally of San Antonio.

The real questions were on the right side. At guard, senior Danny Martz had a strong spring and won the starting job. Alabama didn't have anyone ready to step in to replace Mathis at right tackle and complete the unit, so during the offseason sophomore defensive tackle Kyle Tatum made the transition and started working at a position where coaches felt he had more long-term potential. Normally such a move would take at least a year to fully adjust, especially since the body types are vastly different (an offensive lineman wants more leverage down low and in the hind quarters). Tatum had months.

The depth chart had three freshmen listed as backups, and there was no third unit. If Alabama ran into injury problems on the line, the potential for disaster was enormous. By the time fall rolled around, Britt was still recovering, but still practiced through the pain. The unit began to click, on and off the field, and it wasn't long before they were as close as any group on the team, especially the seniors.

Defensive Line. Due to depth problems in 2003, the Crimson Tide had been forced to play a number of young and inexperienced players, including six in the defensive-line rotation. Both starting ends, Antwan Odom and Naughtyn McKay-Loescher, were gone, though Mark Anderson had started six games his sophomore season.

The key to the unit would likely be senior Todd Bates, who had missed his entire junior season after failing a random drug test. He had been taking a workout supplement that included the banned substance ephedra, though it wasn't listed as an ingredient. Bates found out about the suspension while in a hospital bed recovering from foot surgery, shortly after his grandfather, whom he was very close to, passed away.

"Initially, I didn't know what I was going to do," Bates said. "It hit me like a ton of bricks."

He leaned heavily on his family and friends, like Anderson, and Randolph, his defensive line coach who would visit the hospital after spring practices.

"I think that was a defining point in my life," Bates said. "I could have gone either direction. I was fortunate I had people to lead me in the right direction. I know I'm not a quitter, but during that time in my life I don't know what I would have done if I didn't have anyone in my life."

So Bates spent 2003 working with the scout team, trying to improve both his technique and his teammates. He then earned a pair of spring awards—the Billy Neighbors Most Improved Defensive Lineman" and the "Dwight Stephenson MVP Lineman" of the A-Day Game—in securing the starting job at left end.

At defensive tackle, Alabama appeared set, though again depth was a major concern. Instead of taking an early shot at the NFL, massive senior Anthony Bryant (6-3, 335) returned along with sophomore Jeremy Clark, and they would be backed up by sophomore Dominic Lee, sophomore Chris Harris and Rudy Griffin, a transfer from The Citadel who had been on the scout team with Bates.

Ideally, another player would earn a spot in the rotation because there's no such thing as having too many defensive linemen, and freshman Justin Britt did just that in the fall. In practice, he often lined up against one of his two older brothers, Taylor and/or Wesley, who, doing like brothers do, would try and beat the tar out of him.

Linebackers. If there was one position Alabama felt secure and could possibly even withstand an injury or two, it was this corps of fast hard-hitting players that was considered the strength of the defense.

Junior DeMeco Ryans led the team in tackles in 2003 with 126, which was second in school history to Woodrow Lowe's 134 in 1973, and included a record 25-tackle performance against Arkansas. But coaches moved him from weakside to strongside linebacker (in football-speak, the linebackers are called Will, Mike and Sam after the first letters of each position), which in theory meant he would likely be at the point of attack more and not chasing down as many ball-carriers.

The other two spots would be up for grabs between three players. Senior Cornelius Wortham missed the 2003 season after dislocating an elbow, and used his redshirt year to recuperate [Note: Student-athletes had five years to finish four years of eligibility. The first year he or she didn't participate in any game was called the redshirt year, meaning it was the year that didn't count against the four. A freshman who did not redshirt was called a true freshman]. Wortham was expected to compete with junior Freddie Roach, who had started 12 games and accumulated 85 tackles, at middle linebacker only it never happened. Roach had arthroscopic knee surgery in August, and Wortham essentially won the job by default.

On the weakside, Juwan Garth had been named to the All-SEC freshman team after playing in 12 games, with three starts. He still finished the season seventh in team tackles with 62, including two sacks. But for the most part, each of the four could play at any of the three positions, and coaches would flirt with a 3-4 alignment at times to get them all on the field together.

Among the backups, sophomore Terrance Jones was next on the depth chart. Junior Juke King had come back from a serious knee injury in 2002 to get playing time and earn a spot on special teams. There was also 5-11 freshman Demarcus Waldrop, who despite being on the small side showed a knack for being around the ball.

Secondary. With three of the four starters returning, the Crimson Tide could have been content to keep things as they were, but instead decided to move two players in order to get the most talent on the field.

Junior Roman Harper, who was second in tackles with 111 and blocked a field goal against Hawaii, returning it 73 yards for a touchdown, moved from strong safety to free safety (strong safety usually plays closer to the line while the free safety plays much deeper and helps the cornerbacks).

Junior Charlie Peprah, whose 183 career return yards off interceptions already ranked sixth on the school's all-time list, slid over from cornerback to strong safety, a transition that would be hindered by a nagging hamstring problem during fall practice.

That opened up a cornerback spot and sophomore Ramzee Robinson, who had a strong spring and was named the winner of the Jerry Duncan "I Like to Practice" Award, moved in on the left side. Opposite him was incumbent Anthony Madison, who had one interception, one fumble recovery and one blocked kick in 2003.

Madison had the look of being beyond his years. Growing up in the town of Thomasville, where he played five positions in football and was a two-time all-state selection, Madison was one of 12 children and four sets of twins. In less than a year, a close family friend died of natural causes, a brother died of a heart attack and his twin sister was diagnosed with cancer and died in January 1993 at the age of 11. Despite being a partial academic qualifier, Madison was on track to graduate with a marketing degree in spring 2005.

Among the backups, junior college transfer Jeffrey Dukes and freshman Marcus Carter were at safety, and freshmen Travis Robinson and Eric Gray worked their way on to the second unit. But electrifying freshman Simeon Castille made a big splash in the fall and immediately won the job as nickel back (fifth defensive back for passing situations). The younger brother of Tim, Simeon was the exact opposite in terms of demeanor. As kids growing up, Tim would run into the end zone and act like it was no big deal. Simeon made sure when he scored everyone knew it was.

Special Teams. Considering punter Bo Freelend (6-4, 260) was bigger than all of the linebackers and had a strong leg, there was little doubt that he would retain the job. The same was true for fellow senior Brian Bostick at kicker, though freshman Jamie Christensen proved to have a stronger leg and would handle kickoffs.

Coaches wanted 5-4 Brandon Brooks to concentrate on returns, and lined up Prothro with him deep on kickoffs. Otherwise, there were a lot of freshmen on all four return units who would have to grow up quickly if Alabama wasn't going to hurt itself.

After Nick Ridings had been the long-snapper for four years, a replacement needed to be found. Junior college transfer Drew Lane eventually won the job, while senior Alex Fox was the holder. Both would have solid seasons playing positions where getting noticed was usually a bad thing.

Not surprisingly, in the preseason media poll Alabama was picked to finish fourth in the Western Division behind LSU, Auburn and Ole Miss, while Georgia was favored to win the SEC title. Wesley Britt and Ryans were selected first-team All-SEC and Bryant, Roach and Peprah were named second-team.

Shula knew he might need 10 to 12 incoming freshmen to contribute immediately, and that's exactly what happened despite the obvious concerns. In the NFL, it's generally believed that every rookie in the starting lineup translates into a loss, and the same is often true in the college ranks as well (though more pure freshmen are winning jobs and making an immediate impact than ever before). Alabama would have only one true freshman win a starting job outright, but a number would be just a play away from being thrust into the lineup.

The one, it turned out, would be Hall at wide receiver, even though Prothro would take the most snaps and put up the unit's best numbers. When it became immediately apparent that the incoming freshmen receivers were too talented to keep on the bench, coaches essentially went with a six-man rotation.

Like with every team, there were injuries, setbacks, surprises and a whole lot of improvement once fall practice began. Of them, one of the most notable was at defensive tackle, with Griffin (6-0, 285) winning the starting job away from Bryant.

Even though he was a team captain for Hepzibah High School in Georgia, Griffin always wanted to play for Alabama, but wasn't recruited by the Crimson Tide. Instead, he signed on to The Citadel, a Division I-AA military school where former Alabama defensive coordinator Ellis Johnson coached. After starting two years, he decided to try again, transferred and walked on to the Crimson Tide.

Naturally, his favorite movie was "Rudy," the story of Daniel "Rudy" Ruettiger at Notre Dame, and when a newspaper reporter asked Ruettiger about Griffin, his interest was piqued. A couple of days later when Griffin was walking off the practice field, someone from the sports information office said he had a phone call.

"I thought they were kidding," Griffin said.

"Who knew Notre Dame and Alabama had something in common?" Ruettiger told him during their brief initial conversation, but they vowed to stay in touch.

Griffin went on to start 10 of 11 games for the Crimson Tide.

Going though two-a-day practices in the Alabama heat would take its toll on anyone, but at one point it seemed like half the team was wearing burnt-orange jerseys signifying no contact because of injuries. Normally, one would think that a few players were trying to duck practice, but Kent Johnston often worked those injured even harder on the sideline to keep up their conditioning.

As the opener approached, and excitement grew on campus and throughout the state, the number of burnt-orange jerseys decreased, in part because the standard rule on nearly every football team is if you can't practice, you can't play.

Finally, the curtain rose on the 2004 season, but unlike its predecessor optimism was creeping back into Tuscaloosa, primarily because this squad had something to focus on. Alabama was bowl eligible again, and with six victories could return to the postseason.

At least it was a start.

Good Guys

$\mathscr{T}$here are certain places where everything just seems to feel right the day a season opens. Cincinnati experiences that in baseball, Indianapolis in basketball and Montreal in hockey. Everything is suddenly different. The doldrums of a long offseason are over. Anticipation that has been building for months finally comes to a head. In short, the whole place comes alive.

Tuscaloosa is like that too, though 2004 was only the fifth season opener there since 1941 because most of the marquee games had been played at Legion Field in Birmingham. Still, the morning of Sept. 4 was simply a celebration waiting to happen. The town turned into a giant tailgate party, the air filled with the far-reaching aroma of barbeques and Bryant-Denny Stadium buzzed like an ultra-sweet beehive.

According to the tickets a swarm of scalpers were selling, the opponent was Utah State.

Now, for those who don't live and die college football, the Crimson Tide was opening its 110th season against a team it had never played before in an attempt to stack its win total and hopefully get the six victories necessary to qualify for a postseason bowl. Considering the program was coming off a two-year bowl ban, and still reeling from the reduced number of scholarships, it needed all the help it could get.

Besides, if Alabama didn't qualify for a bowl, fans would call for the firing of everyone from athletics director Mal Moore on down. It was six wins or bust.

In addition to it being the kickoff to the 75th anniversary of Bryant-Denny Stadium, the 1964 national championship team was honored at halftime with a ceremony fans seemingly got to see numerous times during a typical season. There were 82,033 in the stands that day, all with the same mentality regarding the visiting team, "Thanks for coming, now please be a nice opponent and take a good butt-kicking."

In short, probably Utah State didn't have a chance, and many of its players could be forgiven if they were more than a little intimidated. It was the third-largest crowd to watch a game in their school history.

About the only thing Utah State had going for it was that the previous five teams to make debuts at Bryant-Denny had somehow all won. The streak started with a 40-38 homecoming loss to Central Florida in 2000, and continued against Auburn, UCLA, Oklahoma, and the shocker to Northern Illinois the previous season.

Even though 26 players were making their debut with the Crimson Tide, including nine freshmen, the streak was doomed. Running backs Ray Hudson and Kenneth Darby both reached 100 yards rushing and the first time freshman corner-back Simeon Castille touched the football in a college game was on an interception he returned 31 yards for a touchdown. In comparison, older brother Tim needed two touches to score his first touchdown, prompting some good-natured teasing on the sideline.

Without a doubt, the play that jumped out at everyone was Alabama's first snap of the third quarter at its own 43-yard line. Junior quarterback Brodie Croyle faked a handoff and from his own 35-yard line unloaded with everything he had down the middle of the field where true freshman Keith Brown had beaten his man. The wide receiver caught the ball in stride at the 5 and easily scored. Time of the drive: 9 seconds.

It was pure bedlam in the stands. Never mind that Alabama used three quar-terbacks the season before, no one could remember the last time they had seen a pass like it at Bryant-Denny. Brown later said that he didn't know why he was on the field for the play, and when Croyle threw it figured there was no way he could catch up to it.

It was the first tangible sign on the field that the Crimson Tide was finally on its way back.

The 57-yard touchdown killed any hopes Utah State had of coming back and Alabama went on to win 48-17. Gone were the concerns about finding a replace-ment for running back Shaud Williams and whether Croyle was really the best quarterback at Alabama. For the first time in seven games, he didn't have a pass intercepted and running a highly-efficient offense completed 16 of 22 passes for 205 yards and two touchdowns. Perhaps the only negative was that the receiving corps' youth stuck out, with three drops and a missed block resulting in a sack.

Defensively, one of many players who stood out was Roman Harper. Making his first start at free safety, the junior had the first turnover of the season with an interception that led to the first touchdown. In some ways, it had been a long time coming for Harper, who had started at strong safety as a sophomore, but shinned at his new position during spring practice.

If the 2004 Crimson Tide had a version of the Three Amigos, it likely would have been Harper, junior strong safety Charlie Peprah and sophomore linebacker Juwan Garth, even though they came from vastly different backgrounds. The three were often seen together and extremely popular on campus, in part because they came across as being as nice as anyone you'll ever meet.

Although Peprah had represented the defense at the preseason press confer-ence known as "Media Days," Harper was the media darling of the team. On Tues-days, Shula had a weekly press conference and after the coordinators gave interviews players would filter in to answer the same questions over and over again. Usually, Harper would be one of the last to appear, sneaking into the back of the room while on his cell phone. It wouldn't take long before he would be the center of attention.

One exception was after a tough, hard-hitting loss just before an off week. Considering the game had been on the road, only two journalists had made it back in time to interview players on Sunday afternoon. Not surprisingly, only a couple of tired players made it too, prompting a school official to make reminder phone calls. Less than 5 minutes later, Harper came running in, out of breath, apologizing for being late. He was still in his pajama bottoms.

Not only was Harper polite, smart and articulate, but usually cheerful and expressing a great sense of humor—expect when someone put a snake in his sneaker in the locker room. But with every athlete, there's almost always another story, something you don't see on the field.

For Harper, the son of an assistant football coach and physical-education teacher at Prattville High School, it came on Sept. 21, 2002 as redshirt freshman. When the rest of the campus was celebrating a 20-7 victory against Southern Miss, Harper was visiting with his parents when they received the phone call. His aunt on his mother's side, Claudine Parker, had been shot along with Kellie Adams, while closing up an ABC Liquor Store in Montgomery. After numerous surgeries, Adams lived, but Parker died later that night after taking a single .223-caliber bullet in the head.

Harper took her death hard and like many other athletes coping with a loss, focused on the one thing he could control, football.

Two months later, thanks in part to a fingerprint on a magazine followed by ballistics tests, authorities linked the murder to the sniper attacks that terrorized Washington, D.C., for months. Former Gulf War veteran John Allen Muhammad and John Lee Malvo, who was 17 at the time, were eventually captured and prosecuted.

Harper wasn't the only player with someone in his daily thoughts.

Senior kicker Brian Bostick's phone call came after the end of the 2003 season, when he was taking final exams. It came from his father, who was a doctor, telling him that his mother had woken up with severe pain in her abdomen and was on her way to the hospital. She was diagnosed with a perforated bowel requiring emergency surgery, but the rupture of the intestinal wall was infected and beyond repair. A few days later, on Dec. 15, Betty Ruth Bostick died at Woodland Medical Center in the family's hometown of Cullman. She was 52.

The funeral held right before Christmas marked the end of a brutal year for the low-key Bostick. He had made 16 of 25 field goals (and 33 of 37 extra points), but missed game-winning attempts against Arkansas and Tennessee, both of which defeated Alabama in multiple overtimes. His grandfather had also passed away the week of the Tennessee game.

"If I lost my mother, it would kill me," senior punter Bo Freelend said.

Like Harper, the loss was devastating and took a toll on the family. With a degree in electrical engineering already in hand, Bostick thought seriously about not playing his senior season and heading home to Cullman, but he never got as far as telling the coaching staff. Instead, he opted to return for his final year of eligibility, enroll in graduate school and dedicated himself to improving as a football player.

The 2004 season would be one for mom, and it was off to a good start.

Against Utah State, Bostick made field goals of 32 and 28 yards and all six extra-point attempts.

"He's been one of those guys that, if I was a player on this team, I would look up to Brian Bostick for the way he carries himself," Shula said. "He's quiet. He's always going to be in the right place at the right time doing and saying the right things. He's worked hard. He's been through a lot on and off the field but has just kept his focus on how he can improve himself."

But no one's family associated with the Crimson Tide had been through anything like Peprah's.

Crimson Tide Strong Safety Has Rich Family Legacy

September 11, 2004

Along the humid, oceanfront road that stretches approximately 18 miles from the airport near the capital Accra to the city of Tema, Charlie Peprah couldn't help but look to his right when passing the landmark mound and wooden stakes lined up in a row.

About a dozen could be seen in the roped-off area, with the Gulf of Guinea in the background behind a scenic West African coastline.

This was where Peprah's grandfather, the former head of state of the Republic of Ghana, was executed.

"It was emotional," said Peprah, who is a University of Alabama junior strong safety. "To try to imagine what happened that day was kind of tough. It's just kind of weird, surreal.

"I think he was executed on [stake] No. 8. The numbers are still up."

*   *   *

About the size as Illinois and Indiana combined, Ghana is just a few degrees north of the equator with a population of approximately 20 million. It's the home of the world's largest man-made body of water, Lake Volta, and the official language is English, though most also speak an African language as well.

Peprah's parents speak Twi, though Peprah does not, but like a lot of American children of foreign parents, he can understand his mother even when she doesn't use English.

"I've talked with his mom and met his dad," junior free safety Roman Harper said. "Great people."

In Ghana, the life expectancy is 55.4 years for men, 57.2 for women.

Well endowed with natural resources, Ghana has roughly twice the per capita output of the poorer countries in West Africa. Its major sources of foreign exchange are gold, timber and cocoa. Before the slave trade was outlawed in the 19th century, it's believed that up to 10,000 slaves per year came from Ghana.

The country's more modern problems include poverty, unemployment, inflation and AIDS, but Ghana also boasts Kofi Annan, who studied economics at Macalester College in Minnesota and in 1997 was elected secretary general of the United Nations.

Very few of the Crimson Tide know much about Ghana, or Peprah's family history. In Peprah's personal bio in the media guide, sandwiched between the family names and his date of birth, Feb. 24, 1983, is a tidbit about the grandfather who once led a country where the political landscape was more turbulent than most hurricanes.

Yet those who have briefly talked with him about it, like coach Mike Shula and defensive coordinator Joe Kines, get wide-eyed at the mere mention.

"It's a tragic story," Harper said. "I always joke with him that he's going to move back to Ghana and get a couple of zebras, stuff like that. But he loves Ghana. He loves his country. He's very proud of it, his family and his tradition.

"It's cool to represent your heritage and know where you come from. I'm so proud that he's like that because a lot of people try and deny it."

Actually, Peprah—who is in his third year as a starter in the Tide secondary with eight career interceptions—doesn't often talk about his grandfather for one simple reason.

"There's so much, I can't remember it all," Peprah said.

*   *   *

Ignatius Kutu Acheampong, called "Ike" by some, could be Ghana's greatest rags-to-riches story.

Born Sept. 23 1931, as the son of a cocoa farmer, Acheampong taught himself to read and write, and at age 8 attended his first school. His first job was that of a teacher, but in 1953 he joined the military, unbeknownst to his father, who would have objected because the perception was that most soldiers died. Part of his training included studying abroad in Great Britain and at the U.S. Army's Command and General Staff College at Fort Leavenworth, Kan.

Formed from the merger of the British colony of the Gold Coast and the Togoland trust territory, in 1957 Ghana became the first country in colonial Africa to gain its independence.

However, self-rule came at a price as Kwame Nkrumah borrowed heavily to finance the country and projects. It marked the start of economic decline that would last nearly 25 years, during which Ghana had six different governments, five led by the military.

The first military coup occurred in 1966. Although most of the country was unable to reach a consensus on the type of government it wanted, elections in 1969 brought about the Second Republic of Ghana, which experienced many of the same economic problems.

In 1971, foreign debts equaled one-fourth of the gross national product, the currency had been drastically devalued and the economic reliance on cocoa was exposed when income from exports dropped. With the dramatic tightening of the defense budget and the reorganization of leadership, Prime Minister Dr. Kori Busia lost the support of the military.

On Jan. 13, 1972, Lt. Col. Acheampong, who was temporarily commanding the First Brigade near Accra, seized power in a bloodless coup and formed the National Redemption Council. The council promised to improve the quality of life through programs emphasizing nationalism, economic development and self-reliance.

*   *   *

According to Peprah's mother Elizabeth, family members used to joke that all one had to do was cry to Acheampong and he would try and help. She characterized him as warm, generous and forgiving, even to those who tried to assassinate or depose him. He abhorred violence and was against the death penalty.

Acheampong remained popular through 1974 as the government rescheduled Ghana's debts, but numerous factors worked against him. With rising oil prices the country had little to export and almost no credit. As food production decreased, by 1977 inflation reached 100 percent.

As opposition grew, and Acheampong now a general, he reorganized the NRC into the Supreme Military Council and wanted to create a union government composed of civilians, military personnel and police. Critics claimed it was a ploy to solidify power that had eroded due to mismanagement and corruption (of which the military leaders played a major role), resulting in strikes and demonstrations.

Acheampong's reign ended in July 1978 when he was forced to resign by the SMC and replaced by his chief of staff. Lt. Gen. Frederick Akuffo established a plan to return to democratic government, but was also unable to solve the economic problems or corruption.

In May 1979, less than five weeks before constitutional elections, a group of junior officers led by Flight Lt. Jerry John Rawlings attempted a coup that failed. They were jailed and court-martialed, only to be released by sympathetic military officers who overthrew Akuffo's regime in a violent coup and created the Armed Forces Revolutionary Council.

On July 16, 1979, 10 days after being moved to the Naval Officers Mess in Accra, Acheampong—who despite having numerous chances to flee the country—traveled down the same road his grandson would years later. According to family accounts, he gave his watch to the priest who read him his last rites, gave away his last remaining cigarette and waved his white handkerchief to the gathering crowd.

The 47-year-old was then tied to a stake and shot by a firing squad.

*   *   *

Later, people who saw his body in Nsawam said Acheampong had a smile on his face.

Seven others were executed, including Akuffo, at the Teshie military range. A special tribunal, held secretly and without due process, tried dozens of other military officers, government officials and private individuals, sentencing them to long prison terms and confiscated their property. Their offenses were not made public.

"A lot of it was blamed on my grandfather," Peprah said. "They were generals, they didn't know how to run a country like real politicians. But we think he did a pretty good job.

"It was all about power. Once you get that power, it can be hard to give it up."

Peprah's father Josh, who was in the military as well, left with Acheampong's daughter Elizabeth to Germany, Great Britain and then the United States. While Josh Peprah was getting a degree at Texas Christian in Fort Worth, Texas, Charlie Peprah was born. His middle name Yaw, literally means "Thursday born."

Peprah has two brothers. Older brother Richard played football at Wyoming while younger brother Josh Jr. is in the eighth grade. When it came time to be recruited by colleges, Peprah—who is on track to graduate from UA next summer with a degree in marketing—decided he wanted something different from Texas. The decision came down to Alabama and Kansas State, with the campus, tradition and the competitive Southeastern Conference winning him over.

Peprah's parents have since divorced and his father moved back to Ghana.

It wasn't until Dec. 27-30, 2001, after Rawlings had been voted out of office, that the family was able to perform a religious burial and proper memorial for Acheampong.

"We all still vividly remember how we received the news about Papa's murder," Elizabeth Peprah and her sister Rose wrote for the funeral. "We could not believe nor understand it. In fact, we still do not understand it today. We were unable to mourn or even bury him because of the conditions in the country at that time and have carried this pain with us ever since."

*   *   *

Today, Ghana has finally achieved some stability. Despite the coup deposing Acheampong, planned elections did take place in September 1979, but the government fell on Dec. 31, 1981 in another Rawlings-led coup. Rawlings won presidential elections in 1992 and 1996, but was constitutionally prevented from seeking a third term in the Fourth Republic. In 2000, he was succeeded by John Kufuor, who defeated Rawlings' hand-picked successor John Atta Mills.

According to the U.S. Department of State, Kufuor's government appears to enjoy broad support as it pursues a "domestic political agenda based upon public commitment to the rule of law, basic human rights and free market initiates."

On September 3, 2002, Ghana inaugurated its National Reconciliation Commission to investigate human rights abuses under former military regimes. It's alleged that more than 300 people "disappeared" during the Rawlings regime.

"It's such a sad deal because when I go visit [my father], I go past the shooting range," Peprah said. "The stakes are still there. I think the military practices on them, or something. But that's where they took him and shot him. I never met him, but it's part of my history.

"I'm glad of the background I come from. It gives me a lot of culture and I take pride in my parents and the background I have. I think it's helped me become a more well-rounded person, and getting to see Africa first-hand on many occasions . . . I recommend everyone go at least once.

"I will definitely go back."

The youth movement in full swing, Alabama's first significant test of the season came Week 2 against Southeastern Conference rival Ole Miss, which was also 1-0. Even though Alabama dominated the all-time series 40-9-2, the Rebels won the previous year's meeting 48-23 when quarterback Eli Manning threw three touchdowns in the first quarter in building an impressive 24-0 lead.

It was also the third anniversary of the terrorist attacks on New York City and Washington, D.C, and with Alabama being a state with strong military ties the evening began with a ceremony to honor the 22 school employees who had since served. Instead of running out of the tunnel to great fanfare as usual, the players walked out in single file with their helmets cradled in their left arms. They remained stoic in line for a moment of silence and the National Anthem, much like the Minnesota Vikings used to do every game under coach Bud Grant.

And then like against Utah State, the Crimson Tide knocked the stuffing out of Ole Miss.

Without Manning, the Rebels weren't the same team and Alabama took another step in putting the past in its rear-view mirror with a 28-7 victory. Led by the offensive line, which did not give up a sack, Alabama tallied 221 rushing yards, topped by Hudson's 116 yards on 14 carries and Darby's 90 yards on 17 carries. Croyle continued his efficient quarterbacking, completing 14 of 22 passes for 169 yards and two touchdowns, but most importantly had no interceptions. Brown again was his favorite target, and along with DJ Hall were the first true freshmen to start at wide receiver at Alabama since Ozzie Newsome in 1974.

Even better was the defense, which lost the shutout in the fourth quarter, but had the play of the game on one of Harper's 11 tackles. On third-and-6 at the Ole Miss 24, four players blitzed with one subsequently dropping into pass coverage along with a defensive end. Although quarterback Michael Spurlock had been in shotgun formation, he hesitated, with Harper beating two others for a 15-yard sack and fumble that was recovered by Garth.

Alabama needed only two plays to reach the end zone, with Croyle lofting the ball where only sophomore wide receiver Tyrone Prothro could get it. He made a terrific catch and planted a foot inbounds for the touchdown and 14-0 lead.

"The team was motivated and hungry," Peprah said. "We were embarrassed last season. Last year, we would have given up and fallen back. This year we are a different team and are ready to fight."

On what would have been coach Paul W. "Bear" Bryant's 91st birthday, Alabama was 2-0 for the first time in five years, and just four wins short of a bowl bid. Everything was still right in Tuscaloosa.

Disaster

$\mathcal{O}$n the morning of August 13, I received an e-mail from a journalist friend of mine who lived on Sanibel Island, Florida. Almost all of her life had been spent on the state's western coast in an area that was an ideal vacation spot, making her the envy of most of her friends.

She was scared out of her mind.

Immediately the television was on the Weather Channel. During the eight years I spent in the Fort Myers area, where my journalism career began, the closest we came to a major storm was Hurricane Andrew, which for practical purposes destroyed all of Homestead, just south of Miami, and then shot across the state toward Marco Island to terrify countless people including the author. Stupid me drove through some of it and quickly learned that it was as close as I ever wanted to be to a hurricane. Not only could I not see where I was going, but my car was not equipped to handle flooding, never mind the rather large items—for clarification we'll call them trees and even bigger items—that frequently flew by at high rates of speed.

For months, Homestead looked like Western Europe after the Allied advance in World War II. Homes had been completely blown apart, apartment buildings were missing entire walls, debris was scattered everywhere and none of basic services like water and electricity were available. Thousands of people lived in tent cities with nowhere else to go, and every night mosquitoes from the Everglades feasted.

On that morning, a hurricane was heading up the Florida coast, but suddenly had a change of heart and turned right for my former stomping grounds. A quick check among those I could reach found some hiding in their bathrooms while others had gathered their families in closets and were praying they would survive the day. Most had been on guard, but still received less than an hour of warning because of the course change.

With winds of 145 miles per hour, Charley, a category four hurricane, cut across Sanibel and went ashore at Punta Gorda, just north of Fort Myers. It destroyed 12,000 homes, damaged 19,000 more and 31 people died. Estimates had the insurance cost at approximately $7 billion, making it the fifth-most costly insurance disaster in the world since 1970 (No. 1 being the terrorist attacks on the World Trade Center and Pentagon at $21 billion).

My friends escaped unharmed, but extremely frazzled and much lighter in the pocket book, with some having to replace something like a roof or garage. Unfortunately for Florida, it was only the first of four hurricanes over a 44-day period, with

122 people dying, 79 in the Sunshine State alone. Four hurricanes hadn't hit the same state in one year since Texas in 1886.

Charley was followed by Hurricane Francis, a strong category two hurricane that struck near Stuart on September 5 and crept across the state for two days, and the copycat Hurricane Jeanne, a category three.

Between them was Ivan, and for a hurricane to affect the Tuscaloosa area, which is roughly 200 miles north of the coast, it would have to go ashore near the community of Gulf Shores and then basically head straight north.

On Thursday, September 16, that's exactly what Ivan was supposed to do.

This left the University of Alabama in a bit of a quandary. In addition to the safety of the fans, players and students, the football team had a home game scheduled Saturday against Western Carolina. The problem was it could not be rescheduled because the Catamounts played in Division I-AA, which went into its playoffs upon the completion of the regular season, and none of the remaining potential open weekends would work.

So school officials decided to wait and hope for the best. They also met with representatives of Alabama Power Company and law enforcement officials to find out, among other things, where the football stadium was on the list of priorities should the city lose power, and if enough police would be available to work the game. A lot would be decided by the course of the storm as damage, not to mention flooding, is usually worse on the eastern side of a hurricane than the western side.

All week, most of the questions at practice were directed at players from the Panhandle region, like freshmen wide receivers DJ Hall and Keith Brown, senior holder Alex Fox, freshman defensive end Wallace Gilberry and senior running back Ray Hudson. Hardly anyone asked about Western Carolina or Brown's knee injury which would sideline him for a game.

Although the vast majority of students fled, the football team gathered and like everyone else watched and waited. Along the nightlife area known as "The Strip," bars stayed open, but the mood of somber anticipation prevailed. Even downtown's Innisfree Pub made the rare move of turning off one of its recorded Crimson Tide classic victories that were almost always on in favor of storm reports.

Many went to bed Wednesday night knowing that the hurricane was already hitting Gulf Shores hard, and Pensacola, Florida, which was on the east side of the storm, had been taking a pounding. Forecasters still had the storm heading straight towards Tuscaloosa, but no one was giving odds.

Thursday morning, many awoke to no electricity, but also to no hurricane. While it was still packing sustained winds of 70 mph, 5 mph under the minimum to be considered a hurricane, the tropical storm had veered a little to the east and picked up speed in passing between Tuscaloosa and Birmingham. The glancing blow toppled trees and damaged buildings, but by evening much of the city's power had been restored and the college bars reopened. Many on the outskirts of town would go a week or two without power, but overall Tuscaloosa was extremely fortunate.

Ivan was credited with the deaths of at least 52 people after landfall: 19 in Florida, eight in North Carolina, six in Pennsylvania, four in Alabama, four in

Louisiana, four in Georgia, three in Mississippi, two in Maryland, one in Tennessee and one in Connecticut. It also killed 66 people in the Caribbean, including 39 in Grenada.

In Alabama, 32 countries were declared a hurricane disaster area, with Gulf Shores, Orange Beach and Fort Morgan taking the most damage. The peanut, cotton and oyster crops, among others, took severe losses, but not as bad as the citrus growers, most of whom lost entire crops.

Overall, the hurricanes had relatively little effect on the sports world. In Florida, the annual Florida State at Miami game was moved to a Friday night for safety reasons. In baseball, the Montreal Expos and Florida Marlins re-located games to Chicago and the Toronto Blue Jays at Tampa Bay Devil Rays season finale was canceled.

However, the Saturday after Ivan there were two public events in the entire state of Alabama, and both were football games: Western Carolina vs. Alabama and LSU at Auburn. To many fans of both schools, the decision to play was all but automatic.

It took Hall a couple of days to reach his family in Fort Walton Beach. Although a major section of the Interstate 10 Bridge near Pensacola had been completely destroyed, the family's house had suffered almost no damage and his parents would make the trip for the game. Other players had similar stories, but everyone was okay. So it was time to play football.

Meanwhile, many Western Carolina fans decided to stay home instead of attending the Catamounts' first appearance at Bryant-Denny Stadium. Just as the storm had struck a blow to Alabama, it kept going and pounded the western part of North Carolina. As of kickoff, reports indicated that approximately 219,000 customers were still without electricity, and in Canton, roughly 35 miles away from the Western Carolina campus in Cullowhee, water rose as high as 4 feet in places, with a National Guard helicopter used to aid swift water rescues. In part due to erosion, Interstate 40, the main east-west thoroughfare to Ashville, was closed for weeks.

Although coach Paul W. "Bear" Bryant's last national championship team in 1979 was honored at halftime, with 57 former players partaking in the festivities, the game quickly gave fans something else to worry about.

Bittersweet Victory

September 19, 2004

TUSCALOOSA | What was supposed to be the most meaningless game of the 2004 football season may have been the most pivotal one for the University of Alabama.

Playing overmatched Division I-AA Western Carolina with more than 10,000 empty seats at Bryant-Denny Stadium after Hurricane Ivan decimated parts of both Alabama and North Carolina this past week, Crimson Tide fans all but took it for granted that their team was going to start the year 3-0 for the first time since 1996.

It did, but the final score of 52-0 quickly became secondary when early in the third quarter junior quarterback Brodie Croyle went down with a knee injury and was lost for the season. Even before trainers reached him in front of the Alabama sideline, Croyle knew that he had suffered a torn anterior cruciate ligament in his right knee.

Croyle will undergo tests today to confirm the injury and likely have surgery on Tuesday. If the procedure goes well, he might be ready for 2005 spring practice.

"It just leaves a big hole in your stomach, for a lot of reasons," said coach Mike Shula, who was planning on pulling the quarterback after the drive.

Croyle sustained the injury on Alabama's first possession of the third quarter with his team up by 31 points. On third-and-7 at the Western Carolina 47, the quarterback couldn't find an open receiver and took off to his right.

"I was just going to the sideline," Croyle said. "I went to plant and my knee just went out. This isn't how I imagined it happening, but I've been through it before and I'll start over again."

Croyle, who missed two starts last season after sustaining a shoulder injury that required offseason surgery, completed 14 of 22 passes for 160 yards and two touchdowns before the injury.

For the season, he completed 34 of 66 passes for 534 yards, six touchdowns and no interceptions.

"I really feel for him," said junior center J.B. Closner, Croyle's roommate. "I know how much it means to him and how hard it works."

Sophomore Marc Guillon, a transfer from Miami who was the only healthy quarterback during spring practice, replaced Croyle and led two touchdown drives, completing 5 of 7 attempts for 71 yards.

"I was confident and I'm going to build on this and take it into next week," Guillon said. "As a backup, you prepare as a starter every week. No one wants to see that happen, but I'm going to keep going hard."

Junior Spencer Pennington, who was edged by Guillon for the backup job late in fall practice, also led a drive in mop-up duty.

All during the preseason, the prevailing belief was that if everything went right, Alabama would likely win six, maybe seven games. This fell into the "worst-case scenario" that everyone wanted to avoid. Immediately, some blamed Shula for having his quarterback on the field with such a lead. However, the offense had been sluggish in the first half and no one could have foreseen Croyle blowing out his knee without even taking a hit. In reality, there probably weren't too many coaches at the pro or college level that wouldn't have had him on the field.

Otherwise, Alabama dominated while using 74 players. Despite taking a number of hard hits in part to his decision-making, sophomore Brandon Brooks opened the game with an 87-yard kickoff return. The top three rushers all averaged 7 yards or more per carry. Having taken over the starting job a week earlier, junior tight end Clint Johnston caught his second touchdown pass. Redshirt freshman wide receiver Matt Caddell turned a corner route into a 41-yard touchdown.

Thanks to Western Carolina over-compensating for senior Chris James, freshman Marcel Stamps blocked a punt and returned it 14 yards for a touchdown.

Freshman cornerback Simeon Castille had another big interception by stepping in front of a screen pass to set up a field goal. Junior free safety Roman Harper had another outstanding game while backup freshman linebacker DeMarcus Waldrop had four tackles, 1½ for a loss, forced and recovered a fumble off a sack, broke up two passes and had two quarterback hurries.

But hardly any of that seemed to matter during the following days. In fact, hardly anyone noticed that Hudson, who ranked second in the SEC with 98.3 rushing yards per game, had taken a blow to the head and suffered a mild concussion.

After the impressive victory against Ole Miss, fans had been eye-balling the schedule and counting off potential victories. If the Crimson Tide could pull off a win at Arkansas after Western Carolina, there was potential to be 7-0 heading into the Tennessee showdown in Knoxville—which everyone in Alabama knew was almost always on the third weekend of October.

Without Croyle, they didn't know if their beloved Crimson Tide would win again all season, a situation fans knew all-too-well because it would be the third straight year Alabama would play its first Southeastern Conference road game with a first-time starter at quarterback.

With that, Guillon took over, ready or not. The 6-foot-3, 212-pound sophomore was a little bigger that Croyle, but didn't have the same zip on his passes, or, more importantly, near the experience. Suddenly, he went from being the quiet-spoken player on the sideline to being instantly recognized on campus.

Fortunately, coaches weren't about to put Guillon into a position where he would have to win the game (i.e., pass a lot) unless absolutely necessary. Though it was early in the season, Alabama led the SEC in rushing offense (averaging 241 yards per game) and in three crucial defensive categories—rushing defense, total defense and turnover margin (turnovers created minus turnovers lost). Coaches simply felt that if the Crimson Tide could run against Arkansas, it could run against anyone.

Although Arkansas had 24 players graduate off the previous team, with five leaving early for the National Football League, the Razorbacks were known for their big players, especially linemen, almost as much as the home crowd's non-stop hog calls and live mascot named "Big Red."

Arkansas was also led by 6-foot-6 senior quarterback Matt Jones, who inspired a mad comeback to steal a double-overtime 34-31 victory at Alabama the year before. Even more dangerous than his arm were Jones' legs, as his ability to run and make things happen gave defenses fits. Additionally, he was also a quality receiver. Simply put, Jones was a playmaker of the highest regard and with him Arkansas led the conference in both scoring offense (44 points per game) and total offense (525.7 yards).

For the second straight year, Jones was the difference.

For three quarters, Alabama pounded the ball. Hudson finished with a career-high 170 yards, and after making a defender miss in the backfield his 63-yard run through the left side resembled a jailbreak because there were so many bodies running down field looking over their shoulders. Of the 46 carries, only nine went away from seniors Wesley Britt and Evan Mathis, who dominated the left side in helping the Crimson Tide accumulate 271 rushing yards.

Guillon also showed poise in completing five of his first eight passes for 64 yards, but then had nine straight incompletions when coaches tried to open up the passing game in the second half. His one interception came when sophomore cornerback Michael Coe—son of Alabama State coach Charles Coe—took the ball away from sophomore Tyrone Prothro. Otherwise, the young receiving corps wasn't a factor as Hudson had the team's longest reception of 20 yards out of the backfield.

A pair of plays and a coaching decision proved critical. The first came on the opening possession, a bomb that Jones threw up for sophomore Cedric Washington that Harper, who had a staggering 14 tackles and one interception, had the ball knocked out of his hands and land on his hip, with the wide receiver then landing on the ball for a 41-yard completion. It set up a 6-yard touchdown run by Jones.

Alabama's defense kept it in the game until the fourth quarter, when down 14-10 it had to start forcing the issue. Because he was so concerned with Jones' playmaking ability, defensive coordinator Joe Kines hardly dared to blitz. However, the fifth and final time he did backfired with 7:50 remaining in the game. On third-and-4 at the Arkansas 26, Jones took off to his right and got around junior defensive end Chris Turner en route to a 50-yard gain that broke the Crimson Tide. Arkansas scored nine players later to put the game out of reach and later added another touchdown in the final moments after Alabama couldn't convert a fourth down at its own 23-yard line.

Jones' 50-yard run came shortly after Shula decided not to go for it on fourth-and-1 at the Arkansas 39, even though his running game was averaging 6 yards per carry. Instead, he opted to try and wedge the Razorbacks in deep, with Ezekial Knight making a freshman mistake in trying to perfectly down senior Bo Freelend's punt at the 1, only to see it take an odd bounce into the end zone for a touchback.

"Disappointing loss," Shula said after the 27-10 defeat. "Our guys fought hard. We didn't play well enough at times to win the game."

But the road to redemption had another big pothole named Lou Holtz.

The South Carolina coach was a legend, primarily of his success and 1988 national championship at Notre Dame—and perhaps ironically on the opposing side of one of Shula's biggest victories as a quarterback. His overall record was 246-128-1, which ranked third on the active list for coaching wins behind Penn State's Joe Paterno and Florida State's Bobby Bowden, and eighth all-time. Holtz was the only coach in the history of college football to lead six different programs to a bowl game: William & Mary, North Carolina State, Arkansas, Minnesota, Notre Dame and South Carolina.

Both teams were 3-1 overall, 1-1 in the conference, but the Gamecocks had 16 returning starters. If there was one home game Alabama fans felt uneasy about it was this one, and that was before Croyle got hurt.

The cause for concern was well founded as the Crimson Tide had a complete meltdown. It started early. Alabama tied to get Guillon into a rhythm with short passes on its first possession, but on third-and-4 near the end zone tried to force a pass to Johnston without first looking off defenders, who consequently knew exactly where the pass was going and freshman safety Bo Simpson made the interception.

The Crimson Tide came back to piece together a drive to tie the game 3-3, but just before the end of the half Guillon lofted a pass into the end zone toward Brown, who misjudged the ball and instead of catching it crashed headfirst into a fence, horrifying his mother who was seated nearby. Following a lengthy delay, during which Brown was taken off the field on a stretcher and straight to a hospital, Bostick hooked a 36-yard field goal for his first miss of the season.

Brown's blow proved to look much worse than it was, though it would still sideline him for a week. X-rays on his head, neck and shoulder all proved negative and after the game he was walking around the locker room. But the football team wasn't as fortunate, even after senior cornerback Anthony Madison ended South Carolina's first drive of the third quarter with an interception. That's because Alabama gave it right back, with Guillon again looking to Johnston, only this time sophomore cornerback Fred Barnett stepped in front of the pass and returned it 14 yards to the Crimson Tide 20.

"I thought their quarterbacks were telegraphing their passes," Barnett said. "We were ready for it."

South Carolina needed only three plays to reach the end zone for a 13-3 lead, and Shula pulled Guillon, who had completed 9 of 18 passes for 63 yards. However, instead of sparking the team, Pennington looked completely lost. His final numbers were 1 for 6 for 4 yards and two interceptions as South Carolina won 20-3. No one knew it at the time, but it was arguably Holtz's last big victory. At age 67, he walked away from the game at season's end, with his final game unfortunately marred by an ugly brawl against Clemson that caused South Carolina to reject any potential bowl bids.

Again, the defense kept the game close, giving up just 46 passing yards, but 223 rushing yards on 54 carries for a 3.8 average. It translated into a time of possession advantage of 34:00 to 26:00, and Alabama had the ball for just 3:01 of the fourth quarter.

Senior middle linebacker Cornelius Wortham led the team with 14 tackles, while both junior linebacker DeMeco Ryans and Harper played well again. But sophomore linebacker Juwan Garth hurt his shoulder when a 300-pound lineman landed on him, sidelining yet another player. Instead, Waldrop came off the bench to record an impressive 10 tackles.

In uncharacteristic fashion, fans started pouring out of Bryant-Denny Stadium early in the fourth quarter, numb from what they saw. The mood was similar in the Alabama locker room. The Crimson Tide's youth, passing game and lack of depth had all been exposed and exploited. In the span of nine days, the Bama faithful went from believing the team would easily accumulate the six victories necessary to receive a bowl bid to wondering if another disaster was at hand.

Legacies

$\mathcal{I}$n the state of Alabama, little boys don't necessarily dream of someday playing in the National Football League. Well, they do, but it's often not their first dream.

In many cases, they also don't necessarily dream of playing for the University of Alabama either unless their family has some connection to the school. Granted, it has a tremendous tradition that is incredibly appealing to most recruits, but unless they're surrounded by those who live, breath and die "Roll Tide," chances are they probably grew up hating the Crimson Tide.

That's part of everyday life in the state where the second question newcomers get after "Where are you from?" is "So are you Roll Tide or War Eagle?" It's in part from having so much success, but also because Alabama sees itself as a society school, attended by the upper-echelon of students—or more importantly, the children of the upper-echelon. The most powerful organization on campus is undoubtedly the Greek system, in which it's not so much what you know, but who you know.

Auburn, meanwhile, isn't just a rival, but seen as an unworthy challenger socially, academically and athletically. Nicknamed "Aw-barn," because the former Alabama Polytechnical Institute is more of an agricultural school, losing to the Tigers is almost seen as being beneath the Crimson Tide. The perception is that Auburn fans practically play into it by being insecure regarding their relationship with the school to the north (with the 12-to-1 ratio in national championships contributing).

However, once an Alabama tie is established in football, it's pretty much there for life.

Senior Wesley Britt was from Cullman, the same town as senior kicker Brian Bostick, about a 100-mile drive northeast of Tuscaloosa. Though he didn't grow up adoring, or even rooting for Alabama, he would become the unquestionable heart-and-soul of the Crimson Tide, especially after the Tennessee game his junior year.

Six plays in Alabama's starting left tackle shattered his left leg. The Bryant-Denny crowd was stunned with Britt strapped down to a stretcher and about to be taken to a hospital. In part because he didn't want anyone to know how badly he was hurt and also because it was Tennessee, Britt started yelling at his teammates not to give up and pumped his fist repeatedly at them and into the air.

The crowd went nuts and it literally brought tears to the eyes of thousands of the Crimson Tide faithful. Despite being heavily favored, the Volunteers needed five overtimes to pull off a 51-43 victory, but Britt became an Alabama legend.

140

His senior year, Britt was not only just the leader of a very close offensive line, who spent as much time together off the field as on, but one of three brothers on the Crimson Tide. Junior Taylor Britt was a backup offensive lineman while true freshman Justin was part of the rotation at defensive tackle. The only other time Alabama had a trio of brothers playing at the same time was Adrian, Hargrove and Bully VandeGraaff in 1912.

In Alabama, football isn't just a way of life, but also a family affair.

Family Matters

September 18, 2004

TUSCALOOSA | There was a time in the town of Cullman when kids could count on the Britt boys to come out and play. It didn't matter what the activity—football, basketball, capture the flag—as long as everyone understood that all the Britt boys would be participating even if no one else Justin's age was allowed.

Those were their rules, and despite the Britts being roughly four years apart in age, they often won, too.

Today, they're still at it, only with a few more people watching as senior left tackle Wesley, junior center Taylor and true freshman Justin are teammates at the University of Alabama.

"We all did the same things all the time," Wesley Britt said. "Taylor and Justin, they were always the same size. Growing up, people always thought they were twins.

"But that's why Justin is such a competitor. We didn't give him any slack, and he would mess with us too."

Extend that same mentality to 100-plus people and you have a pretty good idea what the Crimson Tide is about this season.

Not only does it have a strong survival sense following NCAA sanctions, numerous coaching changes and last season's sub-par 4-9 record, there's also a growing feeling of brotherhood, literally and figuratively.

Alabama's 2004 family tree reads like a depth chart, and vice-versa, with three sets of brothers, one set of cousins, one third-generation player and nine second-generation players.

On some teams, they would be splintered off like Scottish clans, fighting amongst themselves for influence. Instead, this band of brothers is out to re-establish the Crimson Tide's honor and winning ways.

"You kind of look at your teammates as kind of like your brother," junior quarterback Brodie Croyle said. "I'm sure there's something different with the Britt clan and the Castilles, but everyone on this team is tight. After everything that we've been through, we're going to be a close-knit team."

Croyle's legacy here includes his father John (defensive end, 1979-82), sister Reagan (basketball 1994-98) and brother-in-law John David Phillips (quarterback 1995-98).

That's a lot of people to answer to on top of teammates, coaches, students and fans, but doesn't top the next generation list. Junior wide receiver Matt Miller's grandfather Floyd lettered as a tackle (1948-49), his father Noah was a linebacker (1973) and older brother Marc was a linebacker and strong safety (2001-02).

"Growing up with the family, [we] loved Alabama football and its tradition," Matt Miller said. "Everyone hears about the tradition, but I lived it."

So did Tim and Simeon Castille. Their father Jeremiah was an All-American defensive back and the MVP of Coach Paul "Bear" Bryant's last game at the Liberty Bowl. He's still involved as UA's Fellowship of Christian Athletes director.

During this past offseason, Tim switched jerseys to wear his father's No. 19.

But while the brothers share the same hard-nosed playing style as their dad, they have contrasting personalities.

For example, when Simeon scored the first time he touched a ball against Utah State on Sept. 4, coaches couldn't immediately congratulate the true freshman cornerback because he was celebrating behind the Alabama bench.

"That's how we grew up playing the streets," said the more mild-mannered Tim Castille, a sophomore running back. "He would make a play, high-stepping down the sideline, practicing Deion [Sanders'] dancing. That's who he is."

Like the Britts and Castilles, junior linebacker Freddie Roach also has two family members on hand. Everyone knows about redshirt freshman wide receiver Will Roach, but assistant director of football operations Tim Bowens is their half brother.

"It's nice," Freddie Roach said. "It's less stressful for our parents to be able to come down here and see us all. It's a blessing. We've always been together and never far apart."

"There's a lot of legacy here and you'll see that in a lot of big-time programs where brothers will follow," Bowens said. "It definitely helps in recruiting, but it's always good to have family around."

For each player, the road to Alabama was a little different, yet the extra early exposure obviously didn't hurt the Crimson Tide's recruiting chances.

"There was never any doubt," said senior tight end David Cavan, formerly of American Christian Academy, whose father Pete was an UA running back (1975-77).

"You want to try and leave your options open, but I could never see myself going anywhere else."

In some cases, following in family footsteps was simply assumed. Other times, it was not, even when the father was a second-generation player like Noah Miller.

"He never said 'You're going to 'Bama,'" Marc Miller said.

Although the family heritage had a large impact on both Miller brothers, who almost certainly would have gotten more playing time at another school, Marc indirectly had an even greater influence on Matt.

"My brother's two years older and there's always that competitive older brother," Matt Miller said. "The biggest push for me was to try and be better than my older brother."

Simeon Castille's decision wasn't as clear-cut, but despite being heavily recruited by LSU, he believes Alabama would still have been his choice even if Tim had gone elsewhere.

"I couldn't imagine not having him on the same team to help me," Simeon Castille said. "Not only with football, but everything: school, where to go, little things about parking and where not to get a ticket, that kind of stuff. As football goes, it's just fun. We got to play in high school. Being back on the same team, I really enjoy it."

The younger Castille was also influenced by having an opportunity to earn immediate playing time, something that probably would not have happened elsewhere, with or without family connections.

"He's only going to get better as the year goes on," defensive coordinator Joe Kines said. "He's way ahead of probably where the average freshman would be. We knew that coming in. We bet on that. We had to have someone come through."

Then there are the Britts, who come from a self-created football family even though their father Tommy didn't play past high school, instead spending his days riding in back of a pickup truck to the farmer's market in Birmingham.

Their grandfather made sure Wesley knew what playing for the Tide meant throughout the state when he was deciding between Alabama and Florida. He also told Lou Holtz during a recruiting visit, "Never could beat the Bear, could you?"

Somehow it seemed only natural that the brothers followed, though Taylor wanted to play for Alabama regardless. Consequently, the Britts often line up opposite each other in practice.

"It's definitely a little weird," said Justin Britt, who was also way ahead of his peers at Cullman High School. "It's real personal because it's my brother. Anybody else I'm just thinking about playing football."

And that's where having so many family ties pays extra dividends, off the field. It helps lead to better practice habits and fewer distractions.

"When you're close to someone, you're willing to do a lot for them, and that goes along on the football field," Simeon Castille said. "You're willing to put it all out on the line for your teammate, and I look over and it's my brother so I'm willing to do whatever I can to make sure that we succeed and he does too."

"We're all like brothers," Cavan said. "We do things for each other. I guess it shows what this university means that so many family members come here to play, not because they're pressured to, but they want to."

"I know it makes me a better player knowing that my brothers are out there," Wesley Britt said. "I don't want to lose in front of my brothers. I want to show them how to work and how to improve with every drill every day. I don't want to be the one to bring them down.

"If we can get that mentality and our whole team playing like that, and no one on the team wants to lose because the guy next to him is his brother, it's an awesome thing."

"That attitude over the next couple of years is going to put Alabama back to where it wants to be," Kines said.

Perhaps it was fitting that Alabama's next game would be at Kentucky, where Shula's father Don had been the offensive backs coach in 1959 before going on to become the winningest coach in NFL history and a member of the Pro Football Hall of Fame. Kentucky also had a former head coach Alabama fans were familiar with, "Bear" Bryant, who led the Wildcats from 1946-53 and compiled a 60-23-4 record.

But first, the Crimson Tide had to get back on a winning track, and just a quick glance at the schedule was necessary to see how desperate the situation had become. To be bowl eligible, Alabama needed six victories but only had three with six games to go. Three of the opponents would almost certainly be nationally ranked, three would not. One more loss to an unranked foe and the season could be lost.

Led by the fast linebacking corps, the defense was solid, ranking first in the conference and looking better with each game. Even the line was proving to be better than expected while rotating players in and out to keep them fresh. In addition to starting ends Todd Bates and Mark Anderson, redshirt freshman Wallace Gilberry had been a surprise with two sacks and three tackles for a loss. The native of Baldwin County, who was Shula's first signee in August 2003, hadn't been seriously recruited until he had six tackles and two sacks in the Alabama-Mississippi All-Star Game.

However, large questions loomed over the offense, which was suddenly down to its third-string quarterback. Not only had starter Brodie Croyle suffered a season-ending knee injury, but backup Marc Guillon was experiencing back pain which turned out to be a painful muscle tear and herniated disc. Alabama had one scholarship quarterback remaining, Spencer Pennington, and on his arm the rest of the season would ride.

Through the first half of the season, Alabama was stronger in the backfield than anywhere else, and senior Ray Hudson was second in conference rushing, averaging 107.8 yards per game. Sophomore Kenneth Darby was right behind him at 67.6 yards per game. Sophomore fullback Tim Castille continued to be Mr. Clutch, making big plays in key circumstances, and his backup, sophomore Le'Ron McClain, was coming into his own. The offensive line was playing well. Senior Evan Mathis made the move from right tackle to left guard appear almost effortless. Senior Danny Martz had settled in at right guard and with Britt and Mathis the line was becoming a model for the rest of the team to emulate.

Naturally, coaches wanted to run the ball against Kentucky, and run the Crimson Tide did.

Alabama's opening possession went 56 yards on 11 plays, but failed to score when 6-foot-6 freshman Lonnell DeWalt freakishly leaped up and blocked a 46-yard field-goal attempt by Bostick. Undeterred, Alabama's next possession went 80 yards on 11 plays, all runs, capped by a 1-yard touchdown run by Tim Castille.

The following possession was even more impressive, 99 yards on 14 plays, with Hudson scoring on a twisting, tackle-breaking 20-yard run in which at one point he stiff-armed the ground to stay upright.

Kentucky went after undersized freshman linebacker Demarcus Waldrop, who started for injured sophomore Juwan Garth, but replaced by Roach, and came back just enough to make Alabama nervous, pulling to within 17-14 in the third quarter when the Crimson Tide finally got a break. On what should have been a blocked punt, senior Bo Freelend alertly tucked the ball and ran 24 yards for a first down. Special teams coach Dave Ungerer later jokingly called it "Bo run left," and at 6-4,

260 pounds Freelend was probably the biggest ball-carrier most of the Kentucky players had ever tried to tackle.

The momentum had shifted. Gilberry forced a fumble that senior middle line-backer Cornelius Wortham recovered at the 5 to set up a Darby touchdown. Senior cornerback Anthony Madison blocked a punt to set up another Darby score. Sophomore Tyrone Prothro broke a kick return for a 100-yard touchdown and Tim Castille punched in a final score for a 45-17 victory.

Blowing Kentucky off the line, Alabama accumulated 305 rushing yards, but once again the victory was costly.

Midway through the third quarter, Hudson went around the right end and into open field, when he had to make a split-second decision on whether to cut towards the more-safer sideline or back toward the middle of the field for extra yards. Hudson went for the yards only to find himself surrounded by three defenders including senior safety Mike Williams. The low helmet-to-knee hit blew out his right knee, ending Hudson's season and college career. The 11-yard carry gave him exactly 1,000 career rushing yards, while a couple of weeks later Williams was kicked off the Kentucky team.

Hudson wasn't the only player to sustain a painful injury. Junior tight end Clint Johnston took a shot to the head from a player he didn't see coming, resulting in a concussion. Madison fractured a bone in his left wrist and would wear a cast that made it difficult to catch the rest of the season. Alabama finished the game without its top two quarterbacks along with the leading running back, wide receiver, tight end, cornerback and a starting linebacker.

Obviously, there was cause for concern heading into Southern Miss, a regional matchup that Alabama had traditionally dominated (33-6-2). But the Golden Eagles were heading to Bryant-Denny Stadium ranked No. 24 in the country by the Associated Press and No. 25 in the USA Today coaches poll, and the Crimson Tide was vulnerable. Pressure was building and the one subject no one wanted to talk about at practice was if Alabama could get two more victories to secure a bowl bid with three of the five remaining games against tough rivals. Auburn was still undefeated and both Tennessee and LSU would be difficult road games. Yet the Crimson Tide didn't know if it even had a running back who could handle being a starter and the passing game had just 57, 67 and 83 yards in the three games since Croyle had been lost for the season.

With an umbrella of uncertainly overshadowing Tuscaloosa, homecoming festivities with the theme of "All Tide Together" kicked off, which seemed to re-assure fans that somehow the team would find a way to win, though almost no one knew how. Most of the annual events—including the bonfire, parade, block party and crowning of the king and queen—went off without a hitch. One of the fraternities managed to rent an elephant and taught it to hold a football. Of course, it only prompted thousands of Bama fans to wonder if the elephant was eligible for a football scholarship.

It turned out the Crimson Tide already had an intimidating ball-carrier on the roster. Despite a rash of penalties, Darby ran for 197 yards on 29 carries and two touchdowns, setting a school rushing record for a player making his first start.

With Southern Miss' quarterback sidelined the previous week with an injury, the defense was equally impressive allowing just 23 passing yards and kept the Eagles out of the end zone for a 27-3 victory. Despite lining up opposite All-American candidate Jeremy Parquet, senior end Todd Bates had his best game, with eight tackles, two sacks and nearly had an interception. Junior end Mark Anderson also had a strong game and Roach finished with a forced fumble and six tackles.

This time, there was nothing bittersweet about the victory, only a scare. Late in the game, junior safety Charlie Peprah made an interception and returned it 31 yards to Southern Miss 9 to set up Darby's final touchdown. While bodies were flying in an effort to get Peprah into the end zone, junior safety Roman Harper was leading the charge looking for a white jersey to take out—only he picked the biggest player on the field, 306-pound sophomore George Batiste.

Despite getting his shoulder into the massive guard, Harper bounced off and was a little slow to get up due to his head also bearing the brunt of the truck-sized hit. On the same return, Madison accidentally took a hard shot from Gilberry, and they both were a little shook up, but otherwise all right.

A couple of days later, Harper and Garth decided to catch Game 5 of the American League Championship Series between the Boston Red Sox and the New York Yankees at a local sports bar/restaurant called Will Hagen's. Garth was a Yankees fan and Harper was rooting for the Sox. When David Ortiz, who had won Game 4 with a walk-off home run, hit a dramatic single in the 14th inning to score the winning run, Harper jumped out of his seat and with a big toothy smile gestured at Garth in celebration.

He was still sore, but feeling a lot better. So were Alabama fans, who needed just one more victory to start making bowl plans.

The Most Hated Man in Alabama

$\mathcal{E}$veryone in Tuscaloosa knows what the third weekend in October means, and it has nothing to do with Halloween—though fans have been known to make unflattering references to the "Great Pumpkin," and they weren't talking about the cartoon "Peanuts."

Traditionally, that's when the Crimson Tide plays Tennessee, the dreaded rival to the north that invokes feelings of pure hatred, especially on the Alabama side.

As referred to earlier, Tennessee coach Phillip Fulmer was instrumental in promoting the NCAA's investigation of the Crimson Tide which resulted in probation and scholarship reductions that continued to affect the program in 2004. That was old news, but it was only half of the story.

For the most part, Fulmer did three things to raise the ire of most Alabama fans in 2004, and only one had to do with a football game. The other two occurred in July, engulfing the Southeastern Conference's annual Media Days in Birmingham, which was supposed to be a celebration of the upcoming season. The gathering of hundreds of reporters was structured so that a coach and two players rotated from room to room doing interviews that would be replayed numerous times in every way imaginable until the season started (TV, print, radio, Internet, etc.).

Only Fulmer decided he would rather pay $10,000 than set foot in Alabama.

In the days leading up to Media Days, Montgomery attorney Tommy Gallion notified SEC commissioner Mike Slive that he intended to issue Fulmer a subpoena to give a deposition in the Team Cottrell $60 million lawsuit against the National Collegiate Athletic Association and others. For more than a year, Gallion had been trying to get the deposition, and Fulmer had been able to avoid him because the case would go to trial in Alabama.

Previous to the letter, Tennessee officials publicly stated that they feared for Fulmer and the players' safety, and asked SEC officials for extra security (a request that was denied). Due to a strange quirk in the three-day schedule, Fulmer, offensive tackle Michael Munoz and linebacker Kevin Burnett were due to appear immediately after Alabama coach Mike Shula and players Charlie Peprah and Wesley Britt.

But attempting to maneuver public opinion to his client's side, Gallion made a strategic error. Citing the attack on attorney Phillip Shanks, who was knocked unconscious in his office, and the growing animosity between the schools, he requested that the commissioner "seriously consider" canceling the upcoming Alabama at Tennessee game. The mere suggestion was overwhelmingly scoffed at, as Gallion had overplayed his hand.

Or so it appeared. At approximately 2:45 p.m. on July 26, the Tuscaloosa News broke the story on its website that Gallion intended to serve the subpoena. Roughly 2 hours later, Fulmer announced he would not attend. Almost immediately, the SEC announced the $10,000 fine, which was automatic.

Tennessee went ahead and sent the players, but Fulmer stayed home and did his press conference via teleconference. Needless to say, the spacious interview room was jam-packed as it was by far the biggest story of the convention.

From his Knoxville office, and at least one lawyer at his side, Fulmer began his interview session with a prepared statement.

"I want to thank Commissioner Slive for allowing me this time. I regret that circumstances are such I can't be there with my players and kicking off the season as we have done for 12 seasons. I apologize for any distraction all this has caused.

"I will make a statement; answer some questions I'm sure you share, take your questions, then I want to talk about our football team.

"I am a football coach and not an attorney but will try to explain where I stand on some of the issues.

"It's very important to understand that a lot of people believe the entire NCAA enforcement process is at stake. If we have no enforcement process, all we have is chaos—much like a country with no army or a city with no police.

"It is well documented all that the University of Alabama has been through. It is not necessarily all their fault. We all fear uncontrolled boosters getting involved in our programs. There were good people trying to control it, but a few rogue boosters that took it on themselves to get involved in the recruiting process caused this problem.

"That brought on the investigation. Two coaches have pleaded guilty to federal criminal charges. Several boosters have been disassociated from the university. A federal grand jury indicted a man for racketeering. Coaches lost their jobs.

"Alabama accepted responsibility and [is] trying to move on. Some people do not want to move on.

"To blame me or any of the numerous coaches that told the NCAA about what they knew or heard about the cheating is wrong. All of us have an obligation and responsibility to our universities to run a clean program. If we hear a rumor, we report it. It's the NCAA's job to prove it or disprove it.

"We now have a small group of radical attorneys, who on their own, have undertaken their own agenda to smear the NCAA and anyone else they can along the way. These irresponsible people have alleged that there was a conspiracy between the Justice Department of the United States, the FBI, the NCAA, the University of Tennessee and me. These kinds of statements are absurd. These are the same people who sued two sitting Alabama governors.

"University presidents shaped the NCAA as our governing body some 100 years ago and we all participate voluntarily. In my 30 years of coaching, the people I have met from the NCAA seem to be bright and honorable people. I do not agree with everything they do, but they are our governing body and most of the rules we have has come from abuse and intended for the good of the whole body of members.

"Many coaches knew or suspected there was cheating going on and had challenged the suspect coaches to get it stopped. It was even addressed with all 12 SEC coaches in the same room at the SEC spring meeting a few years ago. It had been addressed long before the hammer finally fell.

"I strongly believe that this effort by an isolated group of irresponsible attorneys to somehow glorify or excuse illegal conduct at the expense of college football is hypocritical on their part.

"A lot of you have had the same questions, so I'd like to address the questions I've heard, take your questions and then talk football.

"Everyone wants to know why I'm not in Birmingham. Again, I'm not an attorney, but I will do my best to explain it. I am a defendant, along with the NCAA and the American Football Coaches Association—which in my opinion is pretty good company—in a frivolous lawsuit in Tuscaloosa.

"This could have been over weeks ago. Our motion to dismiss was continued several weeks ago to next Monday by the rogue lawyers and the timing of that is no coincidence.

"On the recommendation of my attorneys and those of the NCAA, AFCA and our university's general counsel. I am not going to fuel that lawsuit.

"I've heard it asked, 'Why not give a deposition and tell the truth?' That is actually two questions. First, through this entire affair, I have told the truth and will continue to tell the truth. Second, telling the truth is much different than agreeing to be a stage prop for a lawsuit that is for show.

"They have proven they are not interested in the truth. They only showboat and grandstand. They make wild charges—incredible exaggerations and tell half-truths to try and make their case.

"The truth is not on their side. I simply do not intend to play their game. I will not be drug into a deposition the week of the Florida, Georgia or Alabama game.

"I do not want this extended any longer. I do not want to go back and forth during the season at the whim of a lawyer. I have a duty and responsibility to my players and my university and all the fans and boosters that support it. I am going to fulfill my duties as the Tennessee coach and let the lawyers do their jobs.

"As for the attack, I plan to fight every step of the way and give nothing. I am in this, not by my own doing, unless you count doing what was right when asked by our governing body.

"A couple of you called me a coward. I was disappointed to see that. You can talk about my coaching if we lose. You can talk about my play-calling in games. You might talk about my physique if you chose to stoop that low, but coward is way over the line.

"The same people that used the space to call me a coward have used that same space to talk about cleaning up the SEC from cheating.

"I asked for this teleconference and have no problem meeting anyone, anywhere to talk about whatever—except when radical lawyers are trying to generate attention for themselves at the expense of a great city, a great conference and two great universities.

"I greatly appreciate our coaches' support. I understand some reluctance in some cases to get involved in this mess. I especially appreciate Houston Nutt and his comments. Most of the coaches have talked to me privately, and I appreciate their support.

"I'm trying to be as forthcoming as possible. I'll take time for a few questions, and then let's get on to talking about the team."

Though most journalists in the room accepted Fulmer's statement at face value and wanted to move on, those who had been closely following the case were stunned. Instead of just saying "no comment," or "my lawyers advise me not to talk about it," Fulmer instead fueled the fire, so to speak, and even Gallion later admitted it all but legitimized everything he had done.

Three things, in particular, stood out about Fulmer's statement:

1. Like it or not, because he was a defendant with the AFCA in a legal action against Gallion's clients, he had to give a deposition if asked. Either he got some bad legal advice or was too proud, but either way Fulmer wasted $10,000 after his appeal to the SEC regarding the fine was denied.
2. Whatever Fulmer told the NCAA, he wasn't under oath at the time and his testimony wasn't considered public record.
3. Summaries of NCAA investigator Richard Johanningmeier's interviews indicated that Fulmer went to the NCAA with allegation about Alabama, and not the other way around.

But in essence, that barely explains why Alabama fans felt so strongly in their dislike for the coach.

Why the Hostility?

October 23, 2004

TUSCALOOSA | To some people in the state of Alabama, University of Tennessee football coach Phillip Fulmer brings to mind an old "The Far Side" cartoon by Gary Larson that also made a popular T-shirt.

It's the one that's simply a view through a gun site of two bears. One is pretty much minding his own business, unaware of the impending danger.

The other bear is sheepishly pointing to the first bear.

These days, the shirt is no longer in widespread circulation. Instead, among those in vogue on the University of Alabama campus are, "Fat Phil likes to squeal," "Secret Witness," and "U CheaT: I still hate Rocky Top."

Without a doubt, Fulmer is perceived as the one person who has tried to damage, if not destroy, Crimson Tide football, and thus has arguably become the most hated man in Tuscaloosa.

Consequently, the rivalry between Alabama (5-2, 2-2 Southeastern Conference) and No. 11-ranked Tennessee (5-1, 3-1), which will play today for the 87th time, has degenerated to where threats and lawsuits have become almost commonplace.

In fact, the hatred has grown to the point that many Alabama fans were openly rooting for Auburn to beat Tennessee on Oct. 2.

"Honestly, before I got here, I didn't know the rivalry was that big," sophomore cornerback Ramzee Robinson said. "I always thought the biggest rivalry game was Auburn, but particularly this year you see a lot of fans, more people saying 'Beat Tennessee' than saying 'Beat Auburn.'"

Or maybe "Beat Phil" would be more appropriate, especially with Tennessee winning eight of the last nine matchups, including last year's gut-wrenching five-overtime game.

"It was disheartening," junior quarterback Spencer Pennington said. "As a kid growing up watching my brother play from '92-96, and grew up around Alabama football, this is what you play SEC ball for, games like this."

But mention Fulmer's name around Tuscaloosa and you might hear words like back-stabber, two-faced, hypocrite and coward—and those are some of the nicer comments.

And then there are the scores of jokes. For example, have you heard the one about if today's game was played at Bryant-Denny Stadium instead of Knoxville, the National Guard might have been needed in Tuscaloosa for the first time in 40 years?

Or if Fulmer and Osama Bin Laden were both hiding in Alabama, who would be first discovered by a manhunt? The answer, of course, is it depends on if the manhunt was issuing a subpoena from Montgomery attorney Tommy Gallion.

"Hitler, Mussolini and Tojo" said Tuscaloosa resident Bo Hines, 24. "How's that for a comparison?"

Others aren't quite so elaborate.

"[Expletive] him," added Brad Trousdale, 30.

Although the anti-Fulmer sentiment had been percolating for years, it came to a boil last year when court records from the Logan Young criminal case in Memphis indicated that Fulmer had been one of the secret witnesses in the National Collegiate Athletic Association's investigation of Alabama.

In 2002, the Crimson Tide was placed on five years probation, including a two-year bowl ban and the loss of 21 scholarships. The bowl ban and scholarship sanctions have already been completed.

Since then, the SEC has adopted the "Fulmer Rule," that requires coaches to report concerns about other league schools to their athletic director, who would then pass it on to the conference office.

Meanwhile, Fulmer's attorneys have been very busy.

Although not named as a defendant, Fulmer has been implicated in the impending $60 million "Team Cottrell" lawsuit against the NCAA and others brought forth by former Alabama assistant coaches Ronnie Cottrell and Ivy Williams.

Former Tennessee player Kenny Smith and his family named Fulmer along with the American Football Coaches Association and the NCAA in their $40 million defamation lawsuit.

Originally filed in Alabama and dismissed due to jurisdiction, the Smith lawsuit is expected to be resubmitted in Tennessee in the near future.

When told he would be subpoenaed by Cottrell attorneys Tommy Gallion of Montgomery and Delaine Mountain of Tuscaloosa, for a deposition at the preseason Media Days in Birmingham, Fulmer accepted a $10,000 fine from the SEC than risk crossing state lines.

Fulmer instead gave his interview via conference call and blasted both his legal opponents and critics in the media—in both states.

However, because Fulmer is named as a plaintiff in a complaint that would prevent coaches from being sued for their testimony, Gallion and Mountain recently filed their intention to make Fulmer give a deposition in Tennessee next month.

"I haven't spent any time worrying about that," Fulmer said. "My comments from the Southeastern Conference teleconference stand, and other than that we're just working and trying to do our job here."

But even though other coaches turned in Alabama to the NCAA, Fulmer has received the full brunt of disdain in part because Crimson Tide fans believe the NCAA has continually looked the other way for Tennessee's transgressions.

One example is the investigation regarding former Volunteers quarterback Tee Martin.

Former sportswriter Wayne Rowe told the Mobile Register that he wired $4,500 to Martin on behalf of insurance agent Dianne Sanford in February 1999. However, the NCAA enforcement staff found that neither Rowe nor Sanford was considered a booster at the time and no one considered a booster was involved.

Then there's Eric Locke, an Alabama wide receiver who transferred to Tennessee.

Violations ranged from Fulmer having illegal contact with Locke's father while Locke was still at Alabama, to Locke's father working for a UT booster. Locke was supplied with a vehicle while playing at Tennessee. For this, Tennessee penalized itself two football scholarships. UT also banned two boosters from contributing to the athletic department for three years.

Even more scathing was the allegation that Fulmer wanted Locke to go back to Alabama and act as a mole to help build a case against the Tide.

In 1996, trainer Jamie Ann Naughright filed a 33-point complaint against Fulmer and others in August 1996, alleging she was the victim of harassment, inappropriate behavior and discrimination.

Naughright recorded conversations with players and coaches, but the tapes were sealed as part of a $300,000 settlement. The NCAA has never heard the recordings.

Former Tennessee English professor Linda Bensel-Myers lodged complaints about academic misconduct concerning athletes for a decade. She eventually took her concerns to ESPN, casting a long shadow on Fulmer's 1998 national championship team.

Tennessee suspended four players during the investigation, but later cleared them, ruling that no NCAA rules were broken because it was an academic issue and not an athletic one.

[Note: This came as a terrific shock to Minnesota fans because in 2000 the Gophers' athletic department was sentenced to four years probation and the men's basketball team lost five scholarships due to academic fraud. The NCAA report said: "The violations were significant, widespread and intentional. More than that, their nature—academic fraud—undermined the bedrock foundation of a university and the operation of its intercollegiate athletics program."]

Alabama fans like to claim that Fulmer needs every advantage in recruiting in both Tennessee and other states, that he was accused of basically staging a coup to become head coach while Johnny Majors was recovering heart surgery in 1992, and so on.

Of course, little of this means anything to the players, who along with coaches have been trying to downplay the hype, though definitely feel the intensity.

"The Tennessee rivalry, that's all they talk about around here," junior free safety Roman Harper said.

"If anything it's going to get more intense," sophomore running back Kenneth Darby said. "I don't think it's ever going to change. Tennessee fans don't like us and Alabama fans don't like them."

Tennessee week has seemingly always been intense in Tuscaloosa. It's been about checkerboard end zones, the song "Rocky Top" and the color orange.

"The only time I want to wear it is hunting, and then not for very long," senior left tackle Wesley Britt said.

But now it's also about Fulmer, the man Tide fans love to not only hate, but passionately want to beat—especially before he gets too close to some of Paul W. "Bear" Bryant's SEC records, like 159 victories (Fulmer has 77).

"It's one of the biggest rivalries in the nation," Britt said. "If you can't give 110 percent for it, there's something wrong with you."

Needless to say, the article was a big hit in Alabama—which was the point of writing it, to explain where the hatred came from—especially because of the accompanying illustration. Instead of using a photo, our graphics guru Anthony Bratina did a cartoon illustration of Fulmer in front of a dartboard. We dropped off something like 50 copies in the Tennessee press box roughly 2 hours before kickoff. They were gone within minutes, and some even filtered down to the field.

But the article only scratched the surface. Yes, Alabama fans believed that Fulmer would have done anything to hurt the Crimson Tide, and were furious. Yes, Alabama had been penalized for its boosters cheating, yet there wasn't a single college football fan in the state, if not the country, who didn't believe that football players got extra benefits essentially everywhere. Yes, they thought the NCAA was turning a blind eye to Tennessee, which sold out Alabama to save itself.

But the real essence of their hatred came down to one thing: character. Everyone in sports knows that a coach often reflects upon his players and vice-versa, and when it came to the Volunteers critics routinely had plenty of ammunition.

For example, days before Alabama at Tennessee, Volunteers junior safety Brandon Johnson, a starter, was caught with a gun outside the off-campus apartment of tailback Cedric Houston. He had fired the weapon as well. Johnson was arrested and charged with reckless endangerment. Junior defensive back Chris Heath, who was in school on a medical scholarship, but not playing, was charged with misdemeanor unlawful carrying of a firearm. The charges were eventually dropped, but they were both kicked off the team.

Alabama had a similar instance just before the season opener against Utah State. Freshman middle linebacker Earnest Nance, who was third on the depth chart behind senior Cornelius Wortham and Freddie Roach, was arrested for disorderly conduct and resisting arrest when he ran away from police after dropping a gun in a Sheffield nightclub. Making matters only worse, an initial television report mistakenly identified him as Roach, who had been 120 miles away in Tuscaloosa that night. Nance was suspended from the team and didn't set foot on an Alabama football field the rest of the season.

Compared to some of the other things that have happened under Fulmer's watch, the gun incident wasn't even a blip on the radar. Here are a few of the more serious incidents regarding Tennessee football players, both during and after their college careers (in alphabetical order):

Daniel Brooks: Days before the 2004 SEC championship, a complaint was filed with the Knoxville City Police that the sophomore linebacker had punched another student in the face at a fraternity party in which, according to The Tennessean, up to 20 other players may have been present. None were suspended. In March 2005, Brooks was being investigated for his part in another brawl between a fraternity and football players, with a student treated for a broken jaw. Soon after, Brooks had surgery on an infected hand. The cause of the injury was not released.

Dale Carter: The four-time Pro Bowl defensive back was suspended indefinitely from the NFL in 2003 after numerous violations of the substance abuse policy. He also faced charges for drug possession, assault, gun possession and driving under the influence, and filed for bankruptcy.

Mondre Dickerson: The defensive tackle was suspended after being accused of rape in 2003. No charges were filed. In 2004 he was charged with raping a 30-year-old woman he met at a Knoxville nightclub.

Dwayne Goodrich: The defensive MVP of the 1999 national championship game was convicted in August 2002 of criminal negligent homicide after he hit and killed two people with his BMW who were trying to pull another person from a burning car and drove away. Goodrich was allegedly driving in excess of 100 mph and according to witnesses he made no effort to even slow down, dragging one victim approximately 150 feet. He was sentenced to more than seven years in prison.

Travis Henry: In 2001, Tennessee's career rushing leader pled guilty to attempted sexual misconduct with a 15-year-old girl.

Jamal Lewis: The former Tennessee running back was indicted on federal drug charges when he tried to help a friend buy cocaine in 2000. Lewis was released on $500,000 bond after being charged with conspiring to possess with the intent to distribute at least five kilograms of cocaine, and through a plea agreement would serve four months in prison and two months in a halfway house during the NFL's offseason. Incidentally, in 2001, Lewis violated the NFL's substance abuse policy for the third time, resulting in an automatic four-game suspension.

Leonard Little: In 1998, the former Tennessee linebacker ran a red light while drunk, resulting in an accident that killed a 47-year-old woman. Little was sentenced to 90 days in jail and community service. In 2004, he was arrested again for drunken driving. In 1999, he was arrested and charged for making harassing calls and threatening a former girlfriend.

Locke: In addition to being right in the middle of the growing Alabama-Tennessee rivalry, the wide receiver was caught withdrawing $2,400 from the ATM account of another student without permission. No charges were filed and Locke agreed to pay back the money. He was expelled.

Victor McClure: In 2004, the tight end was arrested on charges of disorderly conduct and resisting arrest after he shoved a religious studies professor and said "Hey Pop, you want to meet Jesus?" He stripped off his shorts (apparently he had trouble removing his underwear) while running around the lobby of the student recreation building, and grabbed a female student and tried to pull her down the stairs. After he was handcuffed, McClure pried himself loose from police only to run full speed face-first into a door. Two months later he was involved in a domestic dispute in which he reportedly pushed his girlfriend into a wall.

Tony McDaniel: The sophomore defensive tackle (6-7, 300) was suspended indefinitely after being charged with aggravated assault as a result of an altercation during a pick-up basketball game.

Leslie Ratliffe: In 1995, the offensive tackle was charged with assaulting his girlfriend, Antoinett Huntley, who also said that Ratliffe had accepted money from a booster. He was suspended one game.

Jason Respert: In 2000, he was charged with simple battery and trespassing while visiting the University of Florida as a recruit. According to the police report, Respert left a party with two women and at their apartment went into the room of a third woman who was ill. According to police reports, he pulled down the covers, pulled up her pajama top and put his hands down her pajama bottoms. The center pleaded no contest and was given a sentence of 40 hours of community service and two years probation.

Tony Robinson: Although a knee injury ended his Tennessee career before Fulmer took over as coach, the former quarterback was arrested for cocaine and paraphernalia possession shortly after his career ended in 2000. He also made a plea agreement for first-degree kidnapping.

Nilo Silvan: Once the nation's top kickoff returner, he was arrested in 1995 and charged with raping a 17-year-old. Silvan was kicked off the team, but later acquitted of the charges. After a brief stint in the NFL, he went back to school and completed his degree.

Onterrio Smith: In 2000 at the age of 19, Smith was arrested on a misdemeanor count of battery after a passing Sacramento police officer reportedly saw him strike the 18-year-old woman who was the mother of his 2-year-old child. After being kicked off the team for failing a drug test, Smith transferred to Oregon, where he was cited for driving under the influence, reckless driving, driving with a suspended license and underage drinking. In 2004, Smith was suspended four games for violating the NFL's substance abuse policy after testing positive for marijuana.

Antwan Stewart: In 2003, the defensive back was accused of raping a 16-year-old in a dormitory room. Fulmer and his attorney met with a friend of the victim, her mother and another relative, to "uncover the truth about the incident," and not influence a possible witness or impede the investigation. A police investigator called Fulmer's involvement "disruptive" and put "an odd light on the case." Stewart was disciplined for bad judgment in allowing the girl into his room and stayed on the team.

That doesn't include things like standout wide receiver James Banks being kicked off the team in December 2004 for attempting to taint a drug test (he had been suspended three times previously and later admitted to smoking marijuana), punter Britton Colquit arrested for the third time in less than seven months for underage possession of alcohol (twice cited for driving under the influence), and backup wide receiver Montrell Jones arrested twice for marijuana possession and kicked off the team in 2003. Kacy Rodgers, Dewayne Dotson and Keith Jeter were all investigated on a sexual assault charge in 1990 and reinstated when the complaint was dropped.

It also doesn't include former quarterback Peyton Manning being sued for defamation by Naughright after he wrote about mooning her in a locker room in the book "Manning: A Father, His Sons and a Football Legacy," with his father Archie, and called the incident "inappropriate—crude, maybe, but harmless." Naughright wasn't mentioned by name, but in 2003 asked for $15,000 in damages because Manning allegedly placed his "naked butt" on her face during the 1996 incident.

Unfortunately, some of those instances are generally not uncommon on any college campus (well, except getting sued for a mooning, that's a little unusual). But considering every year Tennessee seemed to have a top recruiting class and every year it had problems, it added up.

Team Cottrell attorneys were also doing what prosecutors suggested during Young's trial, and trying to follow the money. They claimed, among other things, to have a sworn affidavit from a former walk-on stating players received improper benefits while with the football team. They also alleged:

- While at Tennessee, Henry sent monthly checks of $2,000 to his mother for 14 months when he didn't have the financial resources to do so. Copies of the checks were subpoenaed.
- A $50,000 line of credit was established for defensive linemen John Henderson, with $30,000 for Henry and $2,200 to lineman Fred Weary. Gallion claimed he had documentation that Fulmer set up Henderson's account at Nashville SunTrust Bank. Henderson's agent, former NFL player Tim McGee, said he, not Fulmer, helped Henderson set up the line of credit in January 2002, a few days after Henderson played his final college game. McGee had been a wide receiver at Tennessee.

• Kenny Smith: In the fall of 2004, when his family was looking into re-filing his lawsuit against Fulmer in the state of Tennessee, Smith's attorneys were drawing up documents that an assistant coach offered him $130,000 to play for the Volunteers.

Meanwhile, Tennessee's graduation rate for football players had traditionally been on the bottom end, with only 38 percent of the football players from the freshmen classes of 1994-95 through 1997-98 graduating. It may have bottomed out with the incoming class of 1995, of which just 8 percent graduated (astonishingly, that was only second lowest in the SEC).

However, the numbers are somewhat misleading. Among Fulmer's quoted reasons for the low rate include:

1. Some Tennessee players became professionals and delayed their graduation (which is true).
2. The statistics don't accurately reflect the academic achievements of the players (which is ridiculous).
3. Players who transfer and graduate from another institution still count against Tennessee (and every other school as well).

Of the 15 incoming freshman in 1995, five went on to play professional football. Even if the other 10 all acquired degrees within five years, that still would have been a 67 percent graduation rate, which could have only gone up if players came back to acquire degrees.

FYI, the graduation rate of the 2004 team was again 38 percent, while Alabama, even with all its issues, was at 49 percent. Among bowl teams that season, Boston College (78), Syracuse (78), Notre Dame (77), and Virginia (75) led the way, but two-thirds of the 56 teams had graduation rates lower than the 54 percent average (Pittsburgh was last at 31 percent).

In January 2005, the NCAA passed the Academic Performance Program, which ensured that any team in any sport that did not graduate at least 50 percent of its athletes would be penalized scholarships with a 10 percent cap. So for a football team with 85 scholarships, the maximum it could lose was nine in any one year. Continued problems could lead to further recruiting and scholarship reductions, a postseason ban and possibly membership status.

In part because the pressures to win have been so great, problems in athletic programs are nothing new, and seemingly no school is immune. At Alabama, an NCAA investigation found that from 1997 to 1999, football recruits were entertained several times at on-campus parties that featured strippers (a practice that was not uncommon at the time). Former running back Sherman Williams was convicted of running a Texas-to-Alabama marijuana racket and plead guilty to passing counterfeit currency. In 2005, Michael Landrum, the first black man to play quarterback at Alabama, was convicted and sentenced to life in prison for having his 3-year-old daughter and her grandmother killed.

It just flabbergasted Alabama fans that it was Fulmer who pointed his finger at the Crimson Tide as if to cry out "heathen."

Of course, the best way to get back at the Volunteers was to beat them, and though few of the Alabama players fully understood the animosity, they knew that if they beat Tennessee, celebratory cigars would be smoked in the locker room (despite it being an NCAA violation). Besides, they had other things to worry about, like getting the passing game up to an acceptable level. Alabama was dead last in conference passing, and while the Crimson Tide had run over Kentucky and Southern Miss, this was Tennessee, ranked No. 11 in the nation despite losing its starting quarterback to an injury.

Hype was at a fevered pitch that week in Tuscaloosa, but a different attitude prevailed in Knoxville. Granted, it was Alabama, and you couldn't have an intense rivalry without two sides butting heads on a regular basis, yet the Tennessee campus was much more sedate. Fans either didn't understand the seriousness of the allegations against Fulmer, didn't care or had simply dismissed the issue as Alabama fans looking to blame others for their misdeeds. Those wearing crimson and white weren't overly harassed, there were no calls of "Go home" or signs venting against Alabama. In the press box, a few jokes were made by the local media, like "maybe Gallion should sue" when Alabama was flagged for a penalty, along with comments about "sour grapes."

An elderly lady who was waiting for an elevator before the game quickly put it all into perspective: "I like the media and think you all do a fine job. However, there's one of you and a lawyer I sure would like to get my hands on." She was referring to regional radio show host Paul Finebaum, a professional instigator who regularly gave Gallion a platform to state his case after he was removed from the initial lawsuit. Finebaum was nervous about appearing in the press box of his alma mater, but he made the trip.

On the field, Alabama may have had some nerves as well. On the second offensive play of the game, the Crimson Tide was in its "jumbo" package of two tight ends and a fullback. With the snap, senior right guard Danny Martz pulled to his right for a sweep and right tackle Kyle Tatum was supposed to push inside and take the defensive tackle out of the play. Only sophomore Turk McBride didn't follow the script, bursting into the backfield to interrupt junior quarterback Spencer Pennington's handoff to sophomore running back Kenneth Darby.

Junior defensive end Parys Haralson, who right before the series told teammates "Watch me go score a touchdown," picked up the fumbled ball and returned it 18 yards into the end zone. Just 45 seconds into the game Tennessee had a 7-0 lead.

Despite the setback, Alabama came right back. When Volunteers senior wide receiver Tony Brown bobbled a swing pass at midfield, junior linebacker DeMeco Ryans was able to react quickly enough to make a diving interception. With Tennessee focused on the run, Pennington bootlegged right for a 10-yard completion to junior tight end Clint Johnston, who returned from the concussion sustained against Kentucky, and swung a 22-yard pass to sophomore wide receiver Tyrone Prothro to set up a 2-yard touchdown run by sophomore fullback Tim Castille.

A 12-play, 43-yard drive resulted in a 34-yard field goal by senior kicker Brian Bostick, and Alabama had a 10-7 lead early in the second quarter.

However, when Alabama's next possession stalled, senior Derrick Tinsley took advantage of a missed tackle and returned a punt 45 yards to set up a 19-yard touchdown reception by sophomore wide receiver Jayson Swain, originally of Huntsville. It marked the only time in the first half that Tennessee had a possession in Alabama territory, and was the only touchdown the defense allowed.

The Volunteers didn't reach double digits in rushing until the third quarter, when they put together their best drive, going from its own 18 to the Alabama 4. But instead of going up by a commanding two touchdowns, Tennessee quarterback Erik Ainge made a freshman mistake. Looking over the middle with senior defensive end Todd Bates pressuring, he tried to force a pass, only Wortham read the play and made a sensational reaching catch for the interception.

Alabama's defense gave up only 63 yards rushing and 132 passing yards, which would leapfrog the unit into No. 1 status nationally in three categories: total defense (221.5 yards per game), passing defense (106.6) and pass-efficiency defense (86.3).

It all came down to one possession. With 4 minutes, 21 seconds remaining, Alabama was 72 yards away from the end zone and down 17-13.

And then it came down to one play, the wrong play, when sophomore cornerback Corey Campbell's interception off a poorly thrown ball stopped the drive 15 yards short. Fulmer had told his players to play the game like it was a championship because Alabama would give everything it had, and both players and Tennessee fans celebrated in the same manner.

"I really can't explain the feeling right now," Ryans said. "It feels someone just ripped your heart out. It's a bad feeling."

Even worse, once again, was the injury report. Senior left guard Evan Mathis hyperextended a knee and Martz sprained an ankle, but both returned to the game. He didn't say anything at the time, but Pennington had also suffered a mild concussion. Even more serious was sophomore fullback Tim Castille.

On the final drive, Castille caught a screen pass and while turning to run up field took a low hit from freshman cornerback Jonathan Hefney, whom he never saw coming from the blindside. Castille took the full force of the hit on his knee, tearing two ligaments that would require season-ending surgery. Yet somehow he had the presence of mind to get up and hop over to the sideline so Alabama wouldn't have to use a time out.

Heading into an off week during Halloween, the entire starting backfield was out for the season with major knee injuries. Tennessee week brought no treats, just another nasty trick.

"Coach, you just made Jeopardy!"

$\mathcal{T}$he first time I had the pleasure of crossing paths with Sylvester Croom was shortly after he had been hired by the Green Bay Packers in 2001 to be the team's running backs coach. After four seasons as the offensive coordinator of the Detroit Lions, where he had initially been hired by Bobby Ross, Croom found himself out of a job when Marty Mornhinweg took over as head coach and brought in a new staff.

Even though Kippy Brown had just left Green Bay to try his hand as a head coach with the Memphis Maniax of the XFL, Packers coach Mike Sherman could have gone in a number of directions with the vacancy, but jumped at the chance to hire Croom. His thinking at the time was that that not only was Croom too good of a coach to pass up on, but also too good of a person.

"Sylvester is a great football coach," Sherman said. "He is a salt-of-the-earth person who represents everything good."

Besides, among those on the long list of people he coached was running back Barry Sanders.

Just days before the season opener, I was walking with Croom after practice and enjoying the weather when I made the mistake of asking him if he was looking forward to getting a crack at Detroit in the season opener. He paused, sort of gave me a "What a stupid question, don't you know where I'm from?" look, and then gave me a quote I could use anyway.

I liked him immediately.

Green Bay went on to win the game 28-6 and Croom's newest pupil, Ahman Green, had a career-best 83-yard touchdown and finished with 157 rushing yards on 17 carries and two touchdowns. He went on to help the Packers finish 12-4 and was named both the team's MVP and to his first Pro Bowl.

Packers fans liked Croom immediately too.

Although Croom had coached 17 years in the National Football League, initially breaking into the league as a running backs coach with the Tampa Bay Buccaneers in 1987—on the same staff as Mike Shula, who was an offensive assistant for two years before being promoted to quarterbacks coach in 1990—his main purpose in going to Green Bay was to learn the West Coast offense as part of a long-term drive to become a head coach . . . at Alabama.

It came close to happening in 2003, when Alabama fired Mike Price and the two finalists for the job were Croom and Shula, and both were worthy candidates. Needless to say, Croom was extremely disappointed when athletics director Mal Moore chose Shula.

It set off a firestorm of controversy, both locally and nationally, including the administration being called out by activist Jesse Jackson. At the time, college football unbelievably had only four black head coaches out of 117 Division I programs and the Southeastern Conference had never had a black head football coach. Hardly anyone noticed that Shula had been on the school's coaching radar for years. Instead, headlines focused on the Shula family name, at age 37 he was the youngest coach in Division I football and the race factor.

Alabama's historical problems with civil rights—including Gov. George Wallace standing on the school's steps, proclaiming "segregation forever" to cheers while James Meredith had to be escorted by the National Guard—were gone, but not forgotten.

For example, in the spring of 2004, I wrote a story about there being a lack of black baseball players in the SEC, with only 14 out of 441 athletes listed on 12 rosters, including two who had not participated in any games that season. The story compared baseball to other sports and examined why it wasn't just a local, but national phenomenon that seemed to exist at every level, from Major League Baseball down to Little League.

It also pointed out that while Alabama did have successful black baseball players in the past, it didn't have any on the roster that year, while in comparison 63.6 percent of the football team was black.

The story ran as the Sunday front-page centerpiece of the newspaper, with supporting graphics, charts and sidebars. By Monday afternoon, I had received numerous phone calls and e-mails from readers who took issue with the story. Among them, one prevailing theme was "Well, why don't you do a story about basketball and about how the black players are taking the roster sports away from the white kids?" They completely missed the point of the story.

This is a letter that actually ran on the editorial page in the Tuscaloosa News:

Dear Editor: This letter is in response to the article written by Christopher Walsh published on May 2, 2004, titled "Striking out on diversity."

Mr. Walsh states there are only 14 black baseball players on SEC rosters and then goes on to show percentage figures of the entire NCAA Division I vs. the University of Alabama.

Why include the predominately white schools in the North, Chris?

It is the SEC and the University of Alabama that face the brunt of racial journalistic ridicule. You and your fellow writers continue to "slam dunk" UA with no front-page articles on the lack of diversity at black state-funded schools with zero percent of white athletes, coaches, etc.

Have you ever attended a sporting event at Alabama or other SEC schools? Look around the bleachers and coliseums, Chris. You talk about the lack of diversity. The stands are filled with white spectators supporting black athletes. Racial tensions in the South are kept at a fever pitch by you, the media, while opportunities are abundant to African-Americans through Affirmative Action, college funds, etc. One would think you would endeavor to publish more important subjects considering these troubled times we are facing. I suppose I should resort to reading the USA Today paper.

The Tuscaloosa News has become a real bore.

Unfortunately, racism and civil rights were something Croom had been dealing with his entire life. His parents were educators in Tuscaloosa, and his father was renowned as a civil-rights leader in addition to being a highly-respected Baptist minister who had almost been lynched as a youth. His grandparents were sharecroppers and Croom was the great-grandson of slaves.

Wilbur Jackson, the former Philadelphia Eagles running back, was the first black football player to play for Alabama, in 1970, a year before Croom arrived. During his two years starting at center, the Crimson Tide went 32-4 and won a national championship in 1973. The following year he was awarded the Jocobs Trophy, given annually to the SEC's best blocker, and named an All-American. Alabama won the SEC championship all three years he played, and played in the Cotton, Sugar and Orange bowls. As a senior, Croom was voted team captain by teammates.

Needless to say, Croom didn't have to wait much longer to get his head coaching job. A year after being Alabama's runner-up, he was interviewed by Mississippi State, another school facing NCAA sanctions, and hired to replace Jackie Sherrill. Geographically among SEC schools it was the closest to Tuscaloosa, where his mother and brother still lived, and his daughter was raising a grandchild within driving distance in Mobile. In terms of football tradition, it was among the most distant.

At his introductory press conference, in a room packed by media, the 49-year-old Croom diffused the issue with one simple statement: "I am the first African-American coach in the SEC, but there ain't but one color that matters here and that color is maroon."

Just like that, Mississippi State fans liked him.

Croom didn't waste any time setting forth not only changes in the football program, but installing a new attitude. Athletic director Larry Templeton liked to tell of the coach's first meeting with players when a cell phone rang. Croom calmly walked over and said, "Son, when I talk, I expect every eye in this room on my two eyes."

The coach sent another message during the summer semester when he decided to take in a health and nutrition class. After one of his players showed up late, Croom waited a few moments and then raised his hand to ask the professor a question.

"The player about fell out of his chair," Croom said during the preseason Media Days press conference, before mentioning that anyone who skipped class had detention runs at 5 a.m.

Needless to say, SEC officials and media immediately liked him too.

Of course, Alabama fans didn't need any winning over, and not just because of his playing days.

Croom also worked 11 seasons at his alma mater on the defensive side, during

Cornelius Bennett was one of Alabama's finest defenders and along with Derrick Thomas terrorized opponents in the 1980s. Courtesy of the Tuscaloosa News.

Left tackle Wesley Britt, who is being taken off the field on a stretcher after shattering his leg, raises his hand to cheers and tries to encourage teammates against Tennessee in 2003. The Crimson Tide eventually succumbed, 51-43, but not until the fifth overtime. Photo by Robert Sutton, Tuscaloosa News.

Joe Namath is all smiles on the way to the Alabama locker room after a 31-7 victory against Auburn at Jordan-Hare Stadium in 2001. Photo by Michael Palmer, Tuscaloosa News.

Crimson Tide fans have a message for Oklahoma during their game at Bryant-Denny Stadium in 2003. Alabama has won 12 national championships. Photo by Michael Palmer, Tuscaloosa News.

Running back Shaud Williams breaks through the defense for a touchdown against Arkansas in 2003. Photo by Robert Sutton, Tuscaloosa News.

Brodie Croyle throws a pass in the 2004 season opener against Utah State as defender Ronald Tupea closes in. Photo by Jason Getz, Tuscaloosa News.

Redshirt wide receiver Matt Caddell makes a diving catch for a 48-yard gain at LSU in 2004. Photo by Jason Getz, Tuscaloosa News.

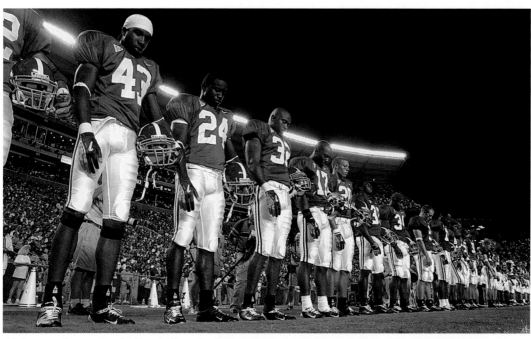

Alabama players, including Jeffrey Dukes (43), Travis Robinson (24), Chris James (32), and Ramzee Robinson (17), stand on the sideline during a moment of silence to mark the anniversary of Sept. 11 before defeating Ole Miss at Bryant-Denny Stadium in 2004. Photo by Jason Getz, Tuscaloosa News.

Senior left tackle Wesley Britt acknowledges a fan on the way to the Bryant-Denny Stadium locker room after the 28-7 victory against Ole Miss in 2004. Photo by Jason Getz, Tuscaloosa News.

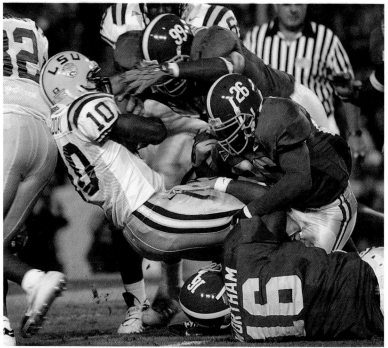

Jeremy Clark (99), Charlie Peprah (26), and Cornelius Wortham (16) converge on LSU running back Joseph Addai in 2004. Photo by Jason Getz, Tuscaloosa News.

Senior left tackle Wesley Britt comes off a snap ready to block LSU's Melvin Oliver in 2004. Next to him is senior guard Evan Mathis (51). Photo by Jason Getz, Tuscaloosa News.

The Crimson Tide takes the field at Bryant-Denny Stadium to play Western Carolina in 2004. Photo by Robert Sutton, Tuscaloosa News.

Junior quarterback Brodie Croyle leaves the field with the aid of crutches after sustaining a season-ending knee injury against Western Carolina in 2004. Photo by Jason Getz, Tuscaloosa News.

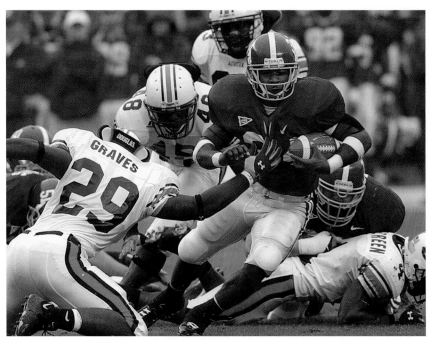

Sophomore running back Kenneth Darby is grabbed by Auburn linebacker Derrick Graves (29) in the 2004 Iron Bowl at Bryant-Denny Stadium. Photo by Jason Getz, Tuscaloosa News.

Junior quarterback Spencer Pennington gets away from Auburn's Stanley McClover long enough to attempt a pass during the 2004 Iron Bowl. Photo by Jason Getz, Tuscaloosa News.

Senior middle linebacker Cornelius Wortham makes a clutch interception near the goal-line as Roman Harper (41) and others look on at Tennessee in 2004. Photo by Jason Getz, Tuscaloosa News.

Junior Brandon Brooks is upended on a kickoff return at Tennessee's Neyland Stadium in 2004. Photo by Jason Getz, Tuscaloosa News.

A host of Alabama players, including defensive end Todd Bates (56) and linebacker Freddie Roach (8), tackle Tennessee running back Gerald Riggs Jr. during the 2004 meeting at Neyland Stadium. Photo by Jason Getz, Tuscaloosa News.

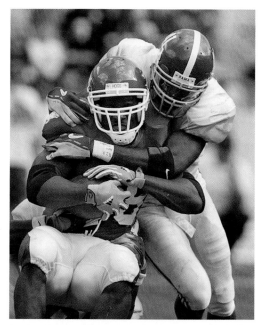

Junior free safety Roman Harper, with help from Cornelius Wortham, wraps up Arkansas tailback De'Arrius Howard after a short gain in 2004. Photo by Jason Getz, Tuscaloosa News.

Junior free safety Roman Harper celebrates after making a play in the 2005 Music City Bowl. Photo by Jason Getz, Tuscaloosa News.

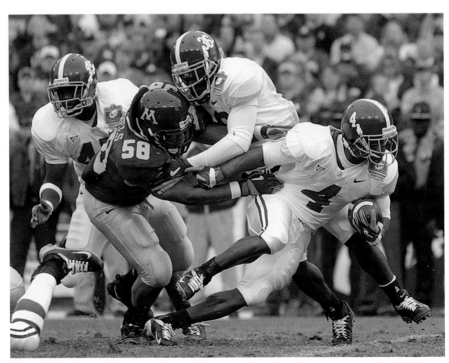

Tyrone Prothro spins away from Minnesota's Mike Sheets during the 2005 Music City Bowl. Photo by Jason Getz, Tuscaloosa News.

Alabama players come out of the tunnel to play Kentucky in 2003. Photo by Robert Sutton, Tuscaloosa News.

The Million Dollar Band plays during pregame festivities in 2003. Photo by Robert Sutton, Tuscaloosa News.

Alabama's Anthony Bryant (97) and Derrick Pope (6) tackle Auburn quarterback Tre Smith, while Charlie Peprah (26) contributes, during the 2002 Iron Bowl at Bryant-Denny Stadium. Photo by Robert Sutton, Tuscaloosa News.

Defensive back Charlie Peprah returns an interception for a touch-down against South Florida in 2003. Photo by Michael Palmer, Tuscaloosa News.

A bust of Paul W. Bryant greets visitors to the Tuscaloosa museum bearing his name. Photo by Robert Sutton, Tuscaloosa News.

Sophomore fullback Tim Castille eyes a touchdown on a 1-yard run at Kentucky in 2004. Alabama won 45-17. Photo by Michael Palmer, Tuscaloosa News.

Mississippi State's Sylvester Croom and Alabama's Mike Shula shake hands before their first meeting as head coaches in 2004. Photo by Jason Getz, Tuscaloosa News.

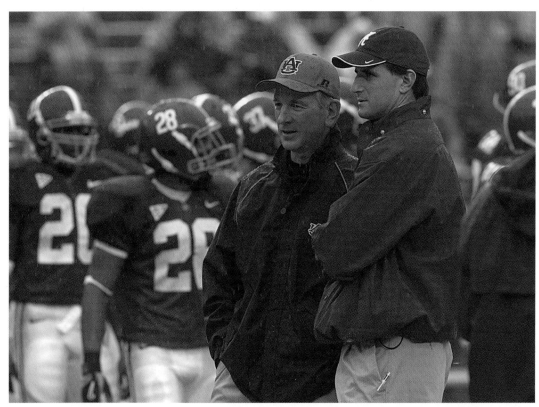

Head coaches Tommy Tuberville and Mike Shula talk at midfield before the 2004 Iron Bowl as a light rain falls on Bryant-Denny Stadium. Photo by Porfirio Solorzano, Tuscaloosa News.

Junior linebacker DeMeco Ryans hits Auburn's Cooper Wallace, forcing a fumble in the 2004 Iron Bowl. Photo by Robert Sutton, Tuscaloosa News.

Junior quarterback Spencer Pennington sits on the bench as the final seconds of the 2004 Iron Bowl tick off. Photo by Robert Sutton, Tuscaloosa News.

Minnesota's Justin Fraley gets the ball away from sophomore Tyrone Prothro in a controversial play during the 2005 Music City Bowl. Instead of a long gain, the play was ruled a fumble, with the Gophers recovering. Photo by Robert Sutton, Tuscaloosa News.

Junior quarterback Spencer Pennington looks for an open receiver against Minnesota in the second quarter of the Music City Bowl. Photo by Robert Sutton, Tuscaloosa News.

Spencer Pennington throws across the middle to wide receiver Triandos Luke during a 37-23 loss at Georgia in 2003. Photo by Robert Sutton, Tuscaloosa News.

which the Crimson Tide compiled a 102-28-2 record. As an assistant coach, he oversaw both the inside (1977-81, 1984-86) and outside (1982-83) linebackers and helped guide Alabama to back-to-back national championships in 1978-79. The 1979 defense was especially dominant, recording five shutouts and gave up just seven touchdowns all season while yielding just 180 yards of total offense per game. Of course, Croom's coaching career began under the direction of Paul W. "Bear" Bryant and he stayed in Tuscaloosa when Ray Perkins was hired. Croom only left when Perkins took him to Tampa Bay after being named the Buccaneers head coach. He was also honored upon the conclusion of each spring practice with handing out the Sylvester Croom Jr. Commitment to Excellence Award, one of 16 named after a former Crimson Tide standout.

That is except 2004.

Without making an announcement, Shula decided he didn't think it was right to honor someone who was now considered competition and when the list was handed out during the A-Day scrimmage no one noticed. Instead junior linebacker DeMeco Ryans received the first Bart Starr Commitment to Excellence Award. Most of the beat writers weren't even in the press box that day, instead covering the men's basketball team in the NCAA Tournament while it made an impressive run to the Elite Eight.

No one noticed for days, not even Croom until a local reporter asked about it after practice.

"I'm thoroughly disappointed that they chose to remove my name from an award that meant a lot to me because of the career I had at Alabama as a player," Croom was quoted. "To remove my name from that award because I achieved success in my coaching career is disappointing to me.

"I find it hard to believe that Coach Bryant would have ever done something like that."

Making matters worse for Shula, the story broke just as he was boarding an alumni cruise the school had been promoting for months, and was unavailable for comment. For days the outcry dominated everything from talk radio to newspaper columns throughout the state, and Alabama took a public-relations pounding both locally and nationally.

When he got back to land, Shula quickly realized the mistake, called Croom and issued a formal apology. The Sylvester Croom Jr. Commitment to Excellence Award was reinstated and the Bart Starr Most Improved Quarterback Award was created, with sophomore Marc Guillon the first recipient.

National attention remained focused on Croom when the season started, and ESPN2 broadcasted his first game, a 28-7 victory against Tulane. But then reality caught up to the Bulldogs with a 43-14 drubbing by Auburn and a humbling 9-7 loss to Division I-AA Maine, which prompted one newspaper to jokingly list in its weekly rankings of SEC teams Maine No. 12 instead of Mississippi State. That was followed by a 51-0 shellacking to LSU, a 31-13 defeat at Vanderbilt and a 27-13 loss against Alabama-Birmingham.

But those who looked closely saw changes, and three of the five losses had been to teams that would qualify for bowls. The rest of the college football world saw it the following week when sophomore Jerious Norwood's 37-yard touchdown run with 32 seconds remaining capped a stunning 38-31 victory over No. 20-ranked Florida, which had been favored by 24 points.

"This is embarrassing for us," said Florida coach Ron Zook, who was fired two days later.

"This is only the beginning for us," Croom said after charging off the field in jubilation. "We're building to a championship program."

After losing 27 of the previous 32 SEC games, fans stormed the field and tore down a goalpost. It was Mississippi State's biggest victory since 2000 when it snapped Florida's 72-game winning streak against unranked opponents with a 47-35 victory.

It also gave Croom the signature victory that Shula was still searching for, despite numerous near-misses.

"There have been a lot of good wins in my life, but for me this is No. 1," Croom said.

For an encore, the Bulldogs defeated Kentucky the following Saturday 22-7, setting up Croom's return to Tuscaloosa with both coaches desperately wanting the victory. Months before, Croom was asked about what it would be like to walk the sideline again at Bryant-Denny Stadium, and he called it a dream of his to be in Bryant's footsteps—which he literally would be because Alabama had swapped sidelines so the visiting team was now on the side Bryant had been.

"To say that I haven't thought about it would be a lie," Croom said. "I've thought about it. Any time you go back to play your alma mater, it's a big game. But we have a lot of games before then and I try and block it out."

The one thing Alabama didn't want to do was come out flat, and sure enough it did as Mississippi State needed only four plays to reach the end zone on a 50-yard run by Norwood. Later, defensive coordinator Joe Kines would characterize the slow start after an off week as "Too much sugar in the tea."

Moments after it was announced that Notre Dame had upset Tennessee, causing a loud roar from the stands, senior tight end David Cavan caught a bootleg pass and barreled his way through a player for a 13-yard gain and Alabama's first first down of the game. True freshman wide receiver Ezekial Knight's 9-yard reception converted a third down and a 22-yard carry by sophomore running back Kenneth Darby had Alabama threatening to score a touchdown, when all of the energy got sucked out of Bryant-Denny Stadium. During Darby's run, senior right guard Danny Martz was manhandling 310-pound defensive tackle Corey Clark, who happened to back step on senior left tackle Wesley Britt's left foot, causing him to not only leave the game, but head to the locker room.

Alabama settled for a 24-yard field goal by senior kicker Brian Bostick while the sellout crowd wondered about Britt. They remembered the shattered leg against Tennessee the year before, and only a serious injury would keep him out.

But just as the defense finished stonewalling Mississippi State's next possession, Britt came running back out of the locker room, pumping his fist into the air. Inspired, Alabama went 82 yards in four plays and scored on a rare trick play. Coming out of the huddle, junior quarterback Spencer Pennington lined up wide near the visiting sideline, with 5-foot-9 wide receiver Tyrone Prothro walking up behind center. Either the Bulldogs didn't see it quick enough or Prothro was almost invisible behind his linemen, but he took the snap and darted around the right side for a 21-yard touchdown.

For an encore, Alabama went 85 yards on six plays, with Pennington airing out a 40-yard pass to true freshman wide receiver Keith Brown, setting up a 15-yard touchdown run by Darby.

Mississippi State came back in the second half to close within 17-14, but a 47-yard field goal by Bostick—despite a poor snap salvaged by senior holder Alex Fox—kept the Bulldogs at bay [Note: When asked what the chances of the kick being good the year before, special teams coach Dave Ungerer said: "Zero, slim and none, and slim was walking out the door"]. Freshman defensive end Wallace Gilberry applied the finishing touches by recovering a fumble caused by junior end Mark Anderson to set up the final touchdown.

Gilberry totaled five tackles and three sacks, and true freshman Justin Britt come off a block to make a huge third-down sack when the game was still in doubt. Junior strong safety Charlie Peprah, who had aggravated his hamstring injury in practice, pulled himself after one play, but Mississippi State still managed only 114 passing yards.

"They had a great defense," Mississippi State sophomore quarterback Omarr Conner said.

Darby finished the game with a career-high 200 rushing yards, the 12th best single-game performance in school history, but there was equal buzz about sophomore fullback Le'Ron McClain, who on Prothro's touchdown flattened a linebacker, knocking him clean on to his back. McClain also completed the scoring with a 4-yard touchdown reception.

Finishing on an emotional high was sixth-year senior wide receiver Antonio Carter, who had been out since 2001 with leg problems. He was a team captain for the game and wearing his trademark No. 2 took the field for the final snaps to a loud ovation from the Bryant-Denny faithful.

"I really can't thank people enough," he later said. "To hear the crowd yell 'Deuce!' when I was out there, it made it all worthwhile."

After the 30-14 victory, the relief was obvious on Shula's face. Alabama had clinched a bowl game, and despite impending disaster on the injury front, including Britt suffering a painful sprained foot that made it extremely difficult to move, the season was a success.

"Everyone was jumping around, hollering and screaming everything, the fight song is always good," McClain said in describing the locker room and admitted to feeling some tears build up. "It was real emotional."

Croom could only say "good job" at midfield shortly after Shula received the Gatorade treatment. Later, Alabama players would quietly mention how impressed they were with Mississippi State, how hard the Bulldogs had played and that this was obviously the beginning of an impressive rivalry. Alabama wasn't the only team in the division on the way up.

Shula called it a "great night for Alabama football," as built-up frustration and frayed nerves regarding the direction of the program following sanctions and numerous off-field issue were swept away, even if only temporarily. Bama was going bowling.

The only question was which bowl game it would play. The Crimson Tide's most recent postseason appearance had been the 2001 Independence Bowl in Shreveport, La., and although things were lining up for a return visit, it wasn't Alabama's first choice. Traditionally, a team usually didn't attract the same number of fans to a bowl if it played there recently. However, because Alabama had not been bowling for two years and fans were clamoring for a trip, the Crimson Tide was like a star recruit searching for a place to play. Everyone wanted Alabama, especially the Peach Bowl and the Music City Bowl. The problem was, unless it won another game, the Peach Bowl, with a sizeable payout, couldn't justify inviting the Crimson Tide over other SEC teams that were more deserving because of their records.

In 2004, the SEC champion received an automatic invitation into the Bowl Championship Series and the Sugar Bowl, with a payout between $11-14 million, unless a conference team qualified to play in the national championship at the Orange Bowl.

From there, the SEC had an agreement for the Capital One Bowl ($5.187 million) to choose the next most-attractive team, followed by the Cotton Bowl ($3 million), the Outback Bowl ($2.75 million) and the Peach Bowl ($2.2 million), before the Music City Bowl ($780,000), the Independence Bowl ($1.2 million) and the Houston Bowl ($1.1 million) if eight teams qualified.

The team record was an important factor, but so was location and fan base. The Peach Bowl wanted Alabama because Tuscaloosa was just 200 miles away and amazingly it had never hosted the Crimson Tide. The Music City Bowl was foaming at the mouth because it was approximately 250 miles away and had never enjoyed a sellout. With Alabama, the stands would be full of crimson and white.

In order to qualify for the upper echelon of bowl games, Alabama had to win at either LSU (6-2), which won the 2003 national championship (a split title with Southern Cal, prompting further debate about how the BSC should be scrubbed for a playoff), and/or at home against undefeated Auburn.

Although Baton Rouge had a reputation for being a tough place to visit, with "Death Valley" full of raucous fans who had been known to occasionally throw things on to the field after hours of tailgating, Alabama was astonishingly 15-1-1 there since 1969. The lone loss came in 2000, 30-28, but since then the programs had gone in completely different directions. Even more strange was that LSU had won eight of its last 11 games at Alabama.

While Alabama's injury problems were beyond ridiculous—Cavan had suffered three cracked vertebrae in his back, Britt could barely play and junior center J.B. Closner missed the fourth quarter against the Bulldogs after suffering a painful neck stinger—LSU wasn't taking the game lightly. On Monday, Tigers coach Nick Saban told reporters he expected the game to be one for "tough guys," with a lot of hard hitting.

"This game is a war, you know what I'm saying?" McClain said in agreement.

Alabama treated it as such. Even though LSU, ranked No. 17, had a Bengal Tiger named "Mike" traditionally parked outside of the visiting locker room, it was Britt who walked out to the field and let out an animal-like war cry signaling the beginning of a brutal siege.

In some ways it was, with two plays crucial to the outcome.

Alabama's defense, still ranked No. 1 in the country, set the tone. LSU's first possession ended after three plays and the second saw ends Gilberry and Anderson combine on a sack and Bates get another.

Meanwhile, the offense went for broke when Pennington threw up a deep ball; redshirt freshman wide receiver Matt Caddell responded with a spectacular diving catch at the LSU 5 for a 48-yard completion. Three plays later, Darby fought his way into the end zone on second effort for a 1-yard touchdown and 7-0 lead.

The teams traded field goals, with Alabama holding a 10-6 halftime lead, and when LSU's first possession of the third quarter ended with a fumble recovery by Anderson at the Tigers' 9-yard-line, the Tide smelled a death blow.

Only it was Alabama's demise at hand.

With Brown isolated on the left side against senior cornerback Corey Webster, Shula called for a quick throw into the end zone, hoping that the freshman would be able to pull down the ball or at least draw a pass-interference penalty. But before the pass arrived, Brown was already down on the ground after being pushed by Webster, who easily made the interception and returned it 44 yards.

It was clearly pass interference, but no penalty was called. The following day, SEC officials apologized for the error, but it was like Alabama had the rug pulled out from underneath it. Aided by the swing in momentum and field possession, LSU was able to pin the Crimson Tide deep in its own territory and when Pennington tried to step out of the pocket, senior defensive end Marcus Spears, a preseason All-American, managed to get around a backup freshman tight end and catch the quarterback from behind, resulting in a fumble at the Alabama 13. Junior linebacker Cameron Vaughn picked it up at the 8 and scored for a 13-10 lead from which the Crimson Tide would not recover.

From that point, LSU's defense, which was ranked No. 4 in the nation, was merciless, sacking Pennington four times and yielding only 8 passing yards in the second half. The Tigers still couldn't throw effectively either, with only 44 passing yards in the second half, but with Alabama's defense forced to take more chances, turned a swing pass into a 35-yard touchdown and took advantage of a safety blitz to score a 47-yard run through the right side for a 26-10 final score.

It had been a gutsy performance by the offensive line, which had four of five starters limited by an injury, but in the end LSU was more opportunistic, experienced and out-manned Alabama, which had 20 fewer players under scholarship and was openly being referred to as the "Walking Wounded."

At quarterback, third-stringer Pennington had taken a brutal hit in the fourth quarter, resulting in shoulder and rib injuries. With junior Brodie Croyle out for the season and sophomore Marc Guillon ailing with a bulging disc and torn muscles in his back, fans wondered if Prothro might have to take over.

At running back, Darby had 109 yards on 35 carries to go over the 1,000-yard mark for the season, but also in the third quarter heard a "pop" in his midsection and also suffered an ankle sprain. It wasn't publicly known then, but he had suffered an extremely painful stress fracture on his pelvic bone and sports hernia, basically rendering him ineffective for the rest of the season.

At fullback, McClain had to be helped off the field with a sprained ankle in the fourth quarter after his foot got caught under Spears. His absence was immediately felt as Pennington was sacked and injured on the following play.

At tight end, junior Clint Johnston tried to play with his concussion problem, but struggled more as the game progressed. When Pennington tried to throw him a flare pass in the third quarter, Johnston couldn't tell which ball he was seeing was the real one, and was taken out of the game.

Sophomore linebacker Juwan Garth still hadn't fully recovered from a separated shoulder, Gilberry had a nagging strained calf muscle, junior free safety Roman Harper hurt his thumb, senior cornerback Anthony Madison was still playing with a cast on his wrist and Peprah was a surprise starter despite hamstring troubles.

Less than 24 hours later, none of it mattered. It was Auburn week.

The Rivalry of Rivalries

$\mathscr{T}$he morning of the Iron Bowl is like Christmas for the people of Tuscaloosa, not to mention just about everyone else in the state. Actually, in many ways it's better. Instead of dealing with in-laws, "some assembly required" and missing batteries, there's just a football game culminating a full year of anticipation.

Oh, there's also a week-long celebration with a parade, block party and other special events contributing to the fanfare and buildup for the biggest event of the year. Ask anyone in the state who Van Tiffin is and watch their reaction. If it's an Alabama fan, his or her face will probably light up and they'll say something like: "You don't know who Van Tiffin is? Oh you poor thing," as if you lost a puppy or just found out kidney stones run in your family. If it's an Auburn fan, expect the exact opposite reaction. That's because in the 1985 Iron Bowl, Tiffin kicked a 52-yard field goal as time expired to give Alabama a dramatic 25-23 victory after the lead changed hands four times in the final 15 minutes. The first person to reach the kicker from the bench in celebration was starting quarterback Mike Shula.

Fans take this game so seriously that heavy rains and the threat of a tornado didn't stop the 1983 game when running back Bo Jackson had 258 rushing yards and two touchdowns to lead Auburn to a 23-20 victory.

The series actually goes back to Feb. 22, 1893, when the two sides met at Birmingham's Lakeview Park and Auburn claimed a 32-22 victory. The following year, Alabama won 18-0, and a football rivalry was under way. However, following a 6-6 tie in 1907, the two sides refused to play again for 41 years in part because of animosity.

According to the Alabama sports information staff, in winning the 1906 game 10-0, the Crimson Tide used an offensive formation that Auburn coach Mike Donahue thought illegal. After Alabama implemented a similar formation again the following year, Auburn demanded that the next game should be officiated by an umpire from outside of the South, with no ties to either school. Alabama thought the idea ridiculous. Additionally, with 22 players allowed on each roster, Auburn wanted the per diem raised from $2 to $3.50. Alabama wanted 20 players with $3 each.

The two sides argued for months, but by the time a compromise had been reached both schedules had been set for 1908. Alabama suggested playing after Thanksgiving, which was rejected by Auburn's Board of Trustees. Attempts to revive the series in 1911, 1919, 1932 and 1944 all failed. In fact, the two schools stopped playing in all sports.

Finally, prior to the 1948 game, with the state legislature threatening to get involved, the student body presidents of both schools participated in a "burying the hatchet" ceremony, but it was obviously symbolic, or someone was crossing their fingers, because the two sides been going at each other non-stop since.

In addition to Tiffin's kick, four games in particular stand out:

- The 1971 game featured two 10-0 teams ranked in the top four in the country. The No. 3 Crimson Tide posted a lopsided 31-7 win over the No. 4 Tigers as Alabama halfback Johnny Musso outshined Auburn quarterback Pat Sullivan, who went on to win the Heisman Trophy, at Legion Field. However, Alabama lost the national championship game 35-31 to Oklahoma at the Orange Bowl.
- The following year, coach Paul W. "Bear" Bryant had his team 10-0 and heavily favored against Auburn. Alabama dominated most of the game, limiting the Tigers to just 57 yards of offense, and had a 16-3 lead in the fourth quarter. That's when Bill Newton became part of state lore when he blocked two consecutive Greg Gantt punts with David Langer grabbing both and scoring touchdowns for a 17-16 victory. The game is known as "Punt Bama, Punt."
- In 1981, Alabama defeated Auburn 28-17 to make Bryant the winningest coach in major college football history. The Tide's fourth-quarter rally provided win No. 315, moving him ahead of Amos Alonzo Stagg. It was also the first meeting between Bryant and former assistant coach Pat Dye.
- Finally, in 1989, SEC champion Alabama was 10-0 and ranked No. 2 nationally when it traveled to Auburn for the first time. The Tigers won 30-20 to knock the Crimson Tide out of the national championship.

The 2004 game would be a chance for Alabama to even a score because coming in Auburn was tied with Oklahoma at No. 2 nationally behind Southern Cal, and deservedly so. Auburn, which began the season ranked No. 18, was 10-0 for just the third time in school history, and had already clinched the Western Division title and berth for the SEC Championship game. Senior quarterback Jason Campbell was being mentioned as a serious contender for the Heisman Trophy, senior running backs Carnell Williams and Ronnie Brown were both up for running back of the year awards and the defense led the nation by limiting opponents to 9.3 points per game.

Auburn had outscored opponents 282-50 in the first three quarters, and 109-9 in the first quarter alone. In short, the Tigers got a lead and then throttled the opponent.

Their success was even more remarkable considering school officials attempted to replace coach Tommy Tuberville during the 2003 season while he was preparing for the Iron Bowl with a 6-5 record. With the Tigers falling short of expectations following preseason Top 10 rankings, a clandestine meeting was held in Kentucky to offer the job to Louisville coach Bob Petrino.

Neither Tuberville nor Louisville officials were informed of the meeting, which was leaked to the media much to the embarrassment of everyone involved. The university president who led the delegation to Louisville, William Walker, was forced out. The athletic director who accompanied Walker, David Housel, stepped down effective the end of the 2004 season. The trustees who accompanied Walker and Housel were cited in a report by the Southern Association of Colleges and Schools (SACS), which placed Auburn on probation with a threat to pull the school's accreditation as an academic institution in good standing.

Meanwhile, Tuberville received 15,000 e-mails of support and signed a contract extension. Alabama fans weren't about to root for Auburn, but many were sympathetic and quietly hoped he would do well and then tell the school to stick it.

Thus was the setting for the annual meeting, which would have a direct impact on the Bowl Championship Series and national championship scene for the first time in a decade. Although the two schools have never had losing records in the same season since the series revival in 1948, only once since 1989 had they met with both teams ranked (1995, No. 21 Auburn 31, No. 17 Alabama 27).

It begged a question regarding the status of the rivalry. Was it still considered the nation's best, or had it rusted a bit?

College Classics
Is Alabama-Auburn the biggest rivalry in college football?

November 20, 2004

TUSCALOOSA | Rivalries are the backbone of college football. They encompass every state, from the Magic City Classic between Alabama A&M and Alabama State, to the South's Oldest Rivalry of William & Mary vs. Richmond.

Since 1884, Lafayette and Lehigh have comprised the nation's oldest rivalry, in what is simply called "The Game."

Sometimes a trophy is involved. Minnesota vs. Iowa is for Floyd of Rosedale, which is a statue of a pig, while Hope vs. Kalamazoo in Michigan is for the Wooden Shoes.

However, anyone in the state of Alabama knows that the Iron Bowl is not just a college football game.

University of Alabama alumnus Scott Brown wrote in his book "The Uncivil War" that he had "never felt anything more intense than the hatred between Alabama and Auburn. Period."

Even though ESPN analyst Beano Cook once called Alabama vs. Auburn "Gettysburg South," we wondered if the rest of the country felt the same way.

Consequently, throughout this season 60 journalists from around the country were asked to list the three biggest rivalries in college football.

Of them, 10 were national reporters, the rest broken down equally into five regions that corresponded with at least one major conference—East (ACC), Southeast (SEC), South (Big 12), Midwest (Big Ten) and West (Pac-10). Almost all either voted in The Associated Press poll last year or are a current member of the Football Writers Association of America.

Oh, and here's the catch. No one currently working in the state of Alabama was included.

Our informal poll resulted in almost a dead-even tie between Alabama-Auburn and Michigan-Ohio State, primarily because the Iron Bowl has had little impact on the national championship in more than a decade.

Alabama-Auburn had more first-place votes (20-19), but Michigan-Ohio State appeared on four more ballots to finish with more points, 108-100.

Alabama-Auburn carried every region except the East and Midwest. In fact, no one in the Midwest voted the Iron Bowl first, and only three had it second.

"I was working the 1995 game at Jordan-Hare, which had zero championship implication, with a producer from another part of the country," ESPN's Rece Davis said. "He said, 'I can't believe how intense this is.' I said, 'You should see it when they're playing for something.'

"Actually, come to think of it, the intensity never changes with the circumstances."

Davis, an Alabama graduate, voted Michigan-Ohio State first because it has had more national significance of late, but said Alabama-Auburn was perennially the most intense.

"There is no rivalry like it because the Tiders and Tigers have to live within the same borders 365 days a year," Scott Rabalais of the Baton Rouge (La.) Advocate said. "That kind of pressure cooker is uncommon among college football rivalries. But the uneven nature of the programs of late—one year Alabama is up and Auburn is down, and vice-versa—makes the Iron Bowl suffer by comparison to Michigan-Ohio State."

Although voters referred to T-shirts like "Ann Arbor is a whore," and the Woody vs. Bo legacy, many who have actually attended an Alabama or Auburn game saw things differently.

"I knew it was intense, but have learned more about it since Arkansas joined the SEC and realize it really is life and death in the state of Alabama," Bob Holt of the Arkansas Democrat-Gazette said.

Kirk Bohls of the Austin (Texas) American-Statesman called the Iron Bowl: "Real football in the best conference in the land."

"The year-around obsession with this game is amazing," said Pat Forde, who recently left the Louisville Courier-Journal for ESPN.com. "I often tell people here that Kentucky-Louisville is the basketball equivalent of Alabama-Auburn football, for good and for ill."

"I don't know of any other place where one game can dominate sports talk 365 days a year," Jeff Shain of the Miami Herald said.

"Any game that causes married couples to divorce, or even worse in some psychotic cases, must be a pretty big deal," said Norm Wood of the Daily Press (Va.).

"Unquestionably for me, this is the most enduring of the nasty rivalries, elevated by recent coach firings, recent near-firing of coaches, cheating scandals, both schools, and the fact that no major-league pro teams reside in Alabama," said Alan Schmadtke of the Orlando Sentinel. "It's one side or the other. And—sorry [NCAA president] Myles Brand—fans don't care so much for things like satisfactory progress, graduation rates or faculty and salary arms races. Just, 'Who's controlling the rivalry.'"

A very distant third in the voting was Oklahoma-Texas, which finished in the same spot among voters in the South.

"The hatred between the teams is always evident, but when you throw in the fact that both teams are playing for BCS spots, that ratchets this rivalry into rare thin air," said Jenni Carlson of The Daily Oklahoman. "That could change, of course, if either program falls on hard times, but this game will always rank highly in my mind because they play a neutral spot, stadium split down the middle, crimson on one side, burnt orange on the other. Throw in the Texas State Fair going on at the same time and fans going at each other as they stroll down the midway, and it's always going to be grand fun."

Numerous voters went out of their way to give honorable mentions to games like Arizona-Arizona State, Notre Dame-Southern Cal and Oregon-Oregon State.

One person suggested that Tommy Gallion vs. Phillip Fulmer be counted.

"Alabama-Auburn is No. 1 on the field," John Adams of the Knoxville News-Sentinel said. "Alabama-Tennessee is No. 1 off the field."

Perhaps surprisingly, among those receiving no votes were Cal-Stanford, Kansas-Missouri or Clemson-South Carolina.

Naturally, Army-Navy got sentimental votes, in what one person called "The National Rivalry."

"Nothing else is even close," Michael Pointer of the Indianapolis Star said.

"I don't care if they're both 1-10," said Malcolm Moran of USA Today. "That never mattered, and it doesn't matter now more than ever."

Among in-state rivalries, only eight received votes, of which five, like Colorado-Colorado State, were listed on just one or two ballots.

"The [Pittsburgh] Steelers' Joey Porter, a Colorado State grad, got shot after last year's game," said Greg Archuleta of the Albuquerque Journal. "It may not have that elite program feel, but in terms of intensity and animosity, it has grown right up there with the rest."

Had the votes from the three Sunshine State powerhouses—Florida, Florida State and Miami—been combined it would have finished third overall. Instead, Florida State-Miami was fifth and Florida-Florida State sixth.

"This is the game that has defined college football's modern era," Barker Davis of the Washington Times said about Florida State-Miami. "The freakish combo of speed and strength in the state has dominated the game since 1983.

"Miami's move to the ACC combined with FSU's recent semi-slide has certainly hurt this rivalry. There was a 10-year stretch when this was unquestionably the No. 1 rivalry in sports, much less college football, from 1985-94."

Among the 10 dubbed national journalists, the Alabama-Auburn game received six first-place votes and one second. Michigan-Ohio State had two first-place votes and four seconds.

"I went to Auburn for a basketball game in 1986 shortly after Alabama won the football game, and some Auburn football players told me they hadn't shown themselves in public for three days," said John Henderson of the Denver Post. "Enough said."

Rivalries Chart

Three points were awarded for first, two for second and one for third.

Matchup (first-place votes)	Total votes
Michigan-Ohio State (19)	108
Alabama-Auburn (20)	100
Oklahoma-Texas (6)	40
Army-Navy (6)	37.5
Florida State-Miami (4)	35.5
Florida-Florida State (1)	15
Southern Cal-UCLA (1)	1
Texas-Texas A&M (1)	3.5
Harvard-Yale (1)	3
Florida-Georgia	3
Alabama-Tennessee	2
Grambling-Southern	1
Montana-Montana State	1
Nebraska-Oklahoma	1
Ole Miss-Mississippi State	1
Colorado State-Wyoming	1
Colorado-Colorado State	.5

Note: One voter did give a first-place vote. Another did not provide a third-place vote.

Voters: Kevin Acee, San Diego Union-Tribune; John Adams, Knoxville News-Sentinel; Parrish Alford, Northeast Mississippi Journal; Neil Amato, Durham (N.C.) Herald-Sun; Mark Anderson, Las Vegas Review & Journal; Greg Archuleta, Albuquerque Journal; Rus Baer, Columbia (Mo.) Daily Tribune; Tony Barnhart, Atlanta Journal-Constitution; Wendell Barnhouse, Fort Worth Star-Telegram; Rob Biertempfel, Pittsburgh Tribune-Review; Ty Blackledge, CBS; Mark Blaudschun, Boston Globe; Jack Bogaczyk, Charleston Daily Mail; Kirk Bohls, Austin American-Statesman; Jimmy Burch, Fort Worth Star-Telegram; Jenni Carlson, The Daily Oklahoman; Jim Carty, Ann Arbor News; Bill Cole, Winston-Salem (N.C.) Journal; Paul Coro, Arizona Republic; Tom D'Angelo, Palm Beach Post; Barker Davis, Washington Times; Ken Davis, Hartford Courant; Rece Davis, ESPN; Dennis Dodd, CBS Sportsline; Pat Dooley, Gainesville (Fla.) Sun; Charles Durrenberger, Arizona Daily Star; Pete Fiutak, College Football News; Pat Forde, Louisville Courier-Journal; Robert Gagliardi, Wyoming Tribune-Eagle; Vahe Gregorian, St. Louis Post-Dispatch; Tim Griffin, San Antonio Express-News; Todd Harmonson, Orange County Register; John Henderson, Denver Post; Bob Holt, Arkansas Democrat-Gazette; Todd Jones, Columbus Dispatch; Mike Kern, Philadelphia Daily News; Blair Kerkoff, Kansas City Star; Steve Kiggins, Casper Star-Tribune; Mark Long, The Associated Press (Miami); Ivan Maisel, ESPN.com; Ted Miller, Seattle Post-Intelligencer; Malcolm Moran, USA Today; John Niyo, Detroit News; Joseph Person, The State (S.C.); Michael Pointer, Indianapolis Star; Jeff Potrykus, Milwaukee Journal-Sentinel; Scott Rabalais, The (Baton Rouge) Advocate; Ray Ratto, San Francisco Chronicle; Brian Rosenthal, Lincoln Journal-Star; Alan Schmadtke, Orlando Sentinel; George Schroeder, Daily Oklahoman; Jeff Shain, Miami Herald; Sports Illustrated On Campus; Phil Stukenborg, Memphis Commercial Appeal; Bob Thomas, Florida Times-Union; Michael Wallace, Jackson (Miss.) Clarion-Ledger; Dan Wetzel, Yahoo Sports; Gene Wojciechowski, ESPN The Magazine; Norm Wood, Daily Press (Va.); Lee Zurik, WWL-TV New Orleans.

The hype kicked in that week on Tuesday, when media descended on Tuscaloosa—where strangely Alabama was 0-4 in Iron Bowls—for Mike Shula's press conference and the subsequent practice. Among players, the most-often heard answer was simply, "It's Auburn." But what they weren't talking about were some major problems that would put them at even more of a disadvantage than Auburn's abundant talent.

When offensive coordinator Dave Rader was asked if he could name a starter other than a wide receiver who was completely healthy, he had to think about it. After a long pause, he finally said, "I think Evan [Mathis] is. He actually ran sprints the other night."

The senior left guard was still coming off the hyper-extended knee suffered at Tennessee.

Although it was kept relatively quiet at the time, Alabama had 28 players with significant injuries. Among them, junior quarterback Spencer Pennington had a sore shoulder and ribs, but nothing broken. During Friday's practice, his arm hit a helmet on the follow-through, causing him to wear a support during the game.

Sophomore running back Kenneth Darby was another matter. After getting approximately 700 rushing yards in the previous five games to go over the 1,000-yard mark for the season, he suffered a sprained ankle and both a pelvic stress fracture and sports hernia against LSU that made it extremely difficult to twist or lift. Unable to cut, push off or accelerate like he wanted, Darby didn't practice the entire week prior to the Iron Bowl.

Sophomore fullback Le'Ron McClain's sprained ankle was bad. Any other week and he probably would have sat. The same was true for senior left tackle Wesley Britt, whose foot sprain was extremely painful and limited his movement.

Alabama would also be without tight ends David Cavan (back) and Clint Johnston (concussion). All together, the injuries made it extremely difficult for the Crimson Tide to try and run outside the tackles and the running backs probably wouldn't be able to take advantage of whatever holes they saw against a very fast defense. Alabama's hopes rested with Pennington, and his best performance had been 119 yards against Mississippi State.

Yet not once did anyone from Alabama make an excuse. No one was saying "What if?" or, at least publicly saying "Hey, we're beat up."

"There's not any point in thinking about that because it's not going to happen," Mathis said. "You might as well go what if we had 12 super heroes on the team, what would happen then?"

Mathis further pointed out that the source of that attitude largely stemmed from Shula, who never complained about scholarship reductions or taking over after spring practice the previous year.

"That's just Shula's mentality and he's our biggest leader," Britt said. "He's always 'no excuses,' 'keep your head high,' 'be proud of what you're doing,' and 'always look forward.'"

If Shula was worried, he wasn't letting on.

"There is definitely an excitement around campus," Shula said. "There is a buzz in the locker room. There is a buzz in the meeting rooms. There is a buzz on the practice field. I think the same thing for the coaches, too. It's probably worse for the coaches. I don't mean that in a bad way. I think it's really exciting.

"For whatever reason there is a lot more time spent, even when you are heading home after work, thinking about the game and all the situations that could come up. We kinda play the game to make sure that the staff has talked about as many things that could come up as possible and that you are ready to go with all the changes that may have taken place during the week. That is what makes it fun. Nothing is ever predictable as it seems. In this game, like a lot of other games, there are going to be certain plays that are going to be made that are going to change the momentum. Hopefully, we are on the top side of those and we take advantage of those when there are opportunities and, again, minimize our mistakes."

Oddsmakers opened with Auburn as a 7½-point favorite. By Saturday, the line was up to 10½ points.

November 20 was an overcast day in Tuscaloosa, but fans were out in force, even the ones that had been up most of the night as bars don't have a mandated last call on Fridays (it used to be that way every night).

The quad was packed, the marching band made its colorful procession with horns blaring and CBS was on hand to broadcast the game nationally. In a departure from the past, each of the 18 seniors were individually introduced, with Britt getting the loudest cheer until Joe Namath ran out the game ball. Even though there was a light rain at kickoff, the joint was jumping.

And then for two quarters, Alabama kicked the crud out of Auburn.

On the opening possession, senior All-American cornerback Carlos Rogers slipped and fell, with true freshman Keith Brown taking advantage by making a 40-yard diving catch to set up a 42-yard field goal by senior Brian Bostick.

Alabama went right back into the red zone thanks to a spectacular 40-yard punt return, the Tide's longest of the season, by sophomore Tyrone Prothro, who was aided by a brutal block by senior Matt Ragland on Rogers. After the teams traded interceptions, Alabama went up 6-0 on another Bostick field goal. Meanwhile, Alabama's defense was playing lights out. Auburn had minus-4 yards of offense in the first quarter and the Tide forced two turnovers.

Auburn finally pieced together a significant drive just before halftime, but after 78 yards on 12 plays, sophomore Joseph Vaughn sent a 21-yard field-goal attempt clanging off the left upright.

The sellout crowd went berserk. A television camera that was focused on the Alabama bench started bouncing around like an earthquake had hit and players charged off the field holding their helmets high in celebration.

But during the intermission Auburn seemed to remember that it was the No. 2 team in the country playing for a rendezvous with destiny while Alabama was relying on a third-string quarterback, running back, fullback and tight end.

Since the running game was going nowhere, Auburn offensive coordinator Al Borges turned to the play-action, which faked the run causing the linebackers to hesitate, and that was all Campbell needed. Four plays into the second half, he threw one up for 6-foot-2 junior wide receiver Devin Aromashodu, who was being defended by 5-9 Anthony Madison, and he easily out-jumped him for a 51-yard gain.

Auburn took the lead on the following play, a 5-yard run by Williams, deflating Bryant-Denny Stadium. Although the two senior running backs were held in check for 96 yards and Auburn averaged just 1.8 yards per carry, Campbell completed 10 of 11 passes in the second half and led two more touchdown drives en route to 224 passing yards, the most Alabama gave up all season.

The Crimson Tide's running game never got going. Darby had 19 yards on 14 carries and true freshman Aaron Johns had 24 yards on nine carries to go with an impressive 19-yard reception. Pennington, who almost doubled his career high in passing with 226 yards, managed to rally the offense in the fourth quarter, keying an 84-yard drive with true freshman DJ Hall out-jumping sophomore defensive back Montavis Pitts for an 18-yard touchdown, the first of his career, but it was too little, too late. Auburn won, 21-13.

Afterward, it wasn't too hard to figure out Shula's message in the locker room. This was supposed to be a team that could get six wins if everything went right. Well, nothing went right, and they still did it.

"There have been a lot of changes at this university over the last few years and these guys had to deal with a lot of things thrown at them, more so than any other kids in the country, maybe ever," Shula said during his press conference. "But they've been the one constant here, the way they stuck together. They had a chance to go somewhere else a couple of years ago. The way they fought through and the way they've come together as a football team, the way the upper classmen have led the freshmen and shown them how it's supposed to be done the right way; the way they've helped us recruit. And that's what makes me proud to be back here and to be associated with these guys."

"We are [close]," defensive coordinator Joe Kines said. "You could put all the plays in a shoe box that have been the difference in being undefeated and where we are."

"It's tough to take, but this team is something special," Pennington said. "We've come together more than any other team in the country."

While Pennington was taking questions from reporters, Brown stood with Bostick nearby, waiting for their turns. When someone asked how long it would take to get over such a heartbreaking loss, Pennington tried to put a positive spin on things, about how Alabama was going back to a bowl game and everyone was happy about that.

But Brown quietly said the correct answer under his breath: "Three hundred and sixty-five days."

For one player in particular, things only got worse the next day. The father of sophomore linebacker Juwan Garth, Walter Simpson, a sorting clerk for the U.S. Post Office, died of a heart attack. He was 49. Coaches and players alike attended the funeral, and the following spring Garth legally changed his last name to Simpson.

Perhaps fittingly, it rained almost non-stop for four days in Tuscaloosa, with heavy downpours and even some thunderstorms.

It finally stopped on Thanksgiving Day.

Epilogue: On the Roll Again

*R*oughly a month after the Iron Bowl, Alabama returned to the practice field to prepare for its bowl game, a session that ended with junior quarterback Spencer Pennington running extra sprints after being late.

"Stayed too long on a deer stand," he said, out of breath.

It didn't take long to get back into routines and the coaching staff worked the players hard in preparation for a team that seemingly always gave good effort in bowl games under its head coach, Minnesota and Glen Mason. They would meet in the Music City Bowl in Nashville on New Year's Eve, an inaugural matchup of college programs which had combined to win 18 national championships (though the Golden Gophers' most recent was 1960), but were about as different as can be.

Yanni vs. Forrest Gump? You Decide

December 31, 2004

NASHVILLE | Every week during the college football season, we've included in our Game Day section "The Call," where matchups are broken down so that it's easy to see where teams have an advantage on the field.

Well, the Music City Bowl is a unique circumstance because yours truly happens to hail from the opposition state, Minnesota. In fact, my first Division I college game as a spectator was watching the Gophers play my mother's alma mater, Northwestern (FYI, the second was coach Gene Stallings' last, the Outback Bowl vs. Michigan in 1997—how's that for a coincidence?).

It's been 18 years since I flew the Minnesota coop, so to speak, and started on the long road through New Hampshire, Florida, Arizona and Wisconsin that would finally take me to Alabama. However, I've always upheld my northern ties, and so for the first meeting between programs that have combined to win 18 national championships, here's how they compare off the field.

Alumni

Minnesota: Bronko Nagurski, Hubert H. Humphrey, Loni Anderson, Dave Winfield, Garrison Keilor, Walter Mondale, Christiaan Bernard (performed first heart transplant), Harry Reasoner, Deke Slayton (Mercury astronaut), Patty Berg, Herb Brooks, Tom Lehman, Kevin McHale, Verne Gagne (wrestling pioneer) and Yanni.

Alabama: Bart Starr, Ozzie Newsome, Joe Namath, Mike Shula, Shaun Alexander, Chris Samuels, Ken Stabler, Don Hutson, John Hannah, Dwight Stephenson, Cornelius Bennett, Sylvester Croom, Derrick Thomas, Lee Roy Jordan, Billy Neighbors, Paul "Bear" Bryant. You mean there are students who don't play football? Well, Winston Groom wrote Alabama football into Forrest Gump, and actress Sela Ward was a cheerleader.

Advantage: Alabama. Yanni was a deal-breaker, even if Minnesota does boast four Nobel Prize winners.

College football fans

Minnesota: The Gophers are No. 1 in hockey. Most don't realize the football team is still playing.
Alabama: Stressed about who the 25ᵗʰ recruit will be this year.
Advantage: Alabama.

Community celebrations

Minnesota: The Winter Carnival and St. Paul is filled with statues of Charles Schultz characters from the comic "Peanuts."
Alabama: Paul "Bear" Bryant Drive, Paul "Bear" Bryant High School, Paul "Bear" Bryant Museum . . .
Advantage: Minnesota.

Coping with winter

Minnesota: Either ice fish or jump into a freezing lake to join the Polar Bear Club.
Alabama: Put on a sweater and watch more football.
Advantage: Alabama (I don't get it either).

Driving

Minnesota: Too busy waving through other people at intersections.
Alabama: Going 80 mph on the highway is considered slow.
Advantage: Push.

Ethnicity and diversity

Minnesota: More blondes than Scandinavia.
Alabama: Still a touchy subject.
Advantage: Minnesota.

The fairer sex

Minnesota: Might smack you if called a snow bunny.
Alabama: Might hug you if called a Southern Belle.
Advantage: Alabama, even without factoring sundresses.

Friendliness/hospitality

Minnesota: Polite to a fault.
Alabama: Southern hospitality.
Advantage: Push.

Journalistic influence

Minnesota: Sports columnist Sid Hartman of the Minneapolis Star-Tribune.
Alabama: Radio talk-show host and professional instigator Paul Finebaum.
Advantage: Alabama. Hartman doesn't get sued or death threats.

Lawsuits

Minnesota: Parents of 11 girls sued because the girls' state hockey tournament is played at the only women's ice arena in the country, the university's Ridder Arena which seats 3,400 and has yet to sell out, instead of Xcel Center, which seats 18,000 and always sells out. (Seriously, I'm not making this up.)
Alabama: Tommy Gallion comparing the NCAA's lack of due process to Iraqi justice and the enforcement process to the Gestapo.
Advantage: Alabama.

Local cuisine

Minnesota: Walleyed pike and wild rice.
Alabama: Barbeque and sweet tea.
Advantage: Push (seriously, it blows catfish away).

Musical influence

Minnesota: Prince.
Alabama: Lynyrd Skynyrd.
Advantage: Minnesota.

Other sports

Minnesota: The state high school hockey tournament is the country's best.
Alabama: NASCAR.
Advantage: Push.

Politics

Minnesota: Jessie Ventura.
Alabama: George Wallace.
Advantage: Push.

Rivalries

Minnesota: Wisconsin and Iowa.
Alabama: Auburn and Tennessee coach Phillip Fulmer.
Advantage: Alabama.

School songs

Minnesota: "Hail! Minnesota" and the "Minnesota Rouser." They actually spell out Minnesota at the end.

Alabama: "Yea Alabama" and "Rammer Jammer" by the Million Dollar Band.
Advantage: Push. All sound better after a victory.

Shopping

Minnesota: Mall of America and gourmet grocery stores.
Alabama: Corners the market in Daniel Moore prints and elephant statues.
Advantage: Minnesota.

State motto

Minnesota: Land of 10,000 Lakes.
Alabama: Stars Fell on Alabama.
Advantage: Minnesota.

Tailgating

Minnesota: Before the team moved into the Metrodome, it was considered an art
    form.
Alabama: Fans could skip the Olympics and turn professional, especially those with
    RVs.
Advantage: Alabama.

Weather

Are you kidding me?

(As a personal footnote, I actually got complaints from people that I didn't include Alabama's real scholars and those really weren't the state mottos, just what's on the license plates. Considering the volume of guns in Alabama, I made sure to nod my head and agree to whatever they said, even if it was a humor column.)

One thing that didn't change during the off month was Alabama's injury problems. Although many of the 28 who were playing hurt at the end of the regular season were still limited, it seemed that for every player that returned another did not.

For example, senior tight end David Cavan fulfilled a promise to return despite three cracked vertebrae in his back, but junior tight end Clint Johnston had yet to be cleared due to lingering effects of concussions.

In addition, during conditioning drills at the end of the first practice, senior Bo Freelend sprained his right knee. Somehow, it was fitting. Even the punter was hurt.

Sophomore running back Kenneth Darby's initially reported abdominal strain, which was really a pelvic stress fracture, had yet to heal. Officially, his chances of playing were listed as "50-50," but the odds of Darby being able to make a significant contribution were next to none. With true freshman Aaron Johns next on the depth chart, the offense would again have to rely on Pennington to have a chance to win.

It almost did. When Minnesota fumbled on its second offensive play, with junior linebacker Freddie Roach recovering for first down at the 2, Alabama needed just one play to take a 7-0 lead—a flare pass to sophomore fullback Le'Ron McClain. But it would be one of the few things the 80, if not 90, percent of the stands filled with Alabama fans wearing crimson and white had to cheer that overcast day.

For the first time all season, an opponent controlled the line of scrimmage, which was magnified by the Crimson Tide's non-existent running game. Led by freshman wide receiver Keith Brown's 17-yard end-around, Alabama finished with 21 rushing yards on 21 carries.

Meanwhile, Minnesota's backfield combination of Marion Barber III and Laurence Maroney pounded away as the Gophers ran an astonishing 72 running plays for a time of possession advantage of 37:54 to 22:06. Although Alabama had not allowed a ball-carrier to reach 100 yards all season, Maroney finished with 105 yards on 29 carries and Barber overcame the early fumble for 187 yards on 37 carries and was named game MVP.

Even with the statistical mismatch, the Crimson Tide defense gave up only one offensive touchdown (Minnesota also scored a touchdown on a fumble recovery in the end zone). Four players finished with 10 or more tackles: junior safety Roman Harper (14), junior linebacker DeMeco Ryans (13), senior middle linebacker Cornelius Wortham (13) and Roach (11).

Pennington came out firing against the Big 10's lowest-ranked pass defense and completed 13 of his first 14 attempts, with Brown turning a quick out into a 40-yard gain when he completely faked out an opposing cornerback to set up a touchdown. But before McClain could complete the drive on a 1-yard dive, Pennington tried to run for the sideline on second-and-6, only to take a late hit with the back of his head slamming into the ground.

Pennington couldn't immediately see out of his left eye and was vomiting in the locker room during halftime from the concussion. He kept playing, but obviously wasn't the same in the second half, completing 6 of 16 passes. Despite it all, the quarterback still managed to lead Alabama on a last-minute drive to try and steal away a victory.

Down 20-16, sophomore wide receiver Tyrone Prothro's return off a self-imposed safety by the Gophers set up Alabama at midfield, and completed passes to Darby, freshman wide receiver Ezekial Knight, and redshirt freshman Matt Caddell put the Crimson Tide at the Minnesota 15.

On third down, Pennington spotted Prothro open over the middle in the end zone, and let fly what could have been a last-second game-winning touchdown. But the ball was just beyond the fingertips of Prothro, who wasn't able to leap for the pass.

Minnesota held on for the victory.

Statistically, it was Pennington's best game. He completed 22 of 36 passes for a career-high 243 yards and one touchdown. It upped his season statistics to 82 of 151 passes for 974 yards and four touchdowns.

It was also Pennington's last game. Two weeks later, he decided it was time to give up football and concentrate on baseball. Alabama would have Brodie Croyle back in 2005 and had recruited three quarterbacks who would challenge Marc Guillon. Besides, Pennington couldn't afford another injury sidetracking his promising baseball career. One to his throwing shoulder against Georgia in 2003 led to offseason surgery and limited Pennington to non-contact drills in the spring. During the 2004 season, he sustained shoulder and rib injuries on a brutal hit against LSU, and the concussion was his second of the season—the other against Tennessee.

"It was a very tough decision," Pennington said. "Playing football at the University of Alabama has been a dream come true. I was very fortunate to have the opportunity of play. To start seven games this season was unbelievable.

"It's a sad time, but an exciting time."

It was the same for Alabama's 18 seniors, many of whom had been recruited by Mike DeBose and been through three coaching changes, not to mention a number of other distractions. Many had become good friends, like Cavan and senior guard Danny Martz, who during their down time terrorized Tuscaloosa dartboards together.

But for every player like left tackle Wesley Britt and Todd Bates, who just before their final practice were elected as team captains for the season, there was someone like Matt Ragland—a walk-on from Huntsville who became a special teams standout, only to tear knee ligaments on the opening kickoff of the Music City Bowl—holder Alex Fox and fullback Josh Smith, who made his first and only start in his final game when Alabama lined him up in the backfield on McClain's touchdown. Those seniors may not have been the biggest or the strongest, but stuck with it just as much as the players who would go on to play in the National Football League.

They had the heart.

There was one consolation prize to the 2004 season for Alabama fans, and it was a big one: The Crimson Tide probably cost rival Auburn any chance of playing for the national championship.

The week of the Iron Bowl, Auburn had moved up to No. 2 in The Associated Press poll, and was closing in on Oklahoma in the Bowl Championship Series rankings that determined which two teams would play in the Orange Bowl for the national championship.

When Auburn struggled with Alabama and Oklahoma dominated Baylor 35-0, thanks in part to freshman running back Adrian Peterson racking up 240 rushing yards and three touchdowns before sitting for most of the fourth quarter, the Sooners locked down the No. 2 ranking heading into the conference championships.

Again, Auburn played well, but didn't do enough to sway voters. Although senior quarterback Jason Campbell threw for three touchdowns and accounted for more than 400 yards of offense (with the first 300-yard passing game of his career), and the Tigers dominated statistically, No. 15 Tennessee proved to be a handful.

With a 38-28 victory, Auburn had won its first SEC title in 15 years, but as the Tigers celebrated at the Georgia Dome, Oklahoma was capping an impressive 42-3 victory against Colorado in the Big 12 Championship. With Southern Cal and Oklahoma ranked 1 and 2 practically the entire season, Auburn was the odd team out.

At the Sugar Bowl, the Tigers pulled out a 16-13 victory to finish the season undefeated, but it seemed highly unlikely that it would be enough to leapfrog the winner of the Orange Bowl to finish No. 1 in any polls. While Auburn clearly outplayed No. 9 Virginia Tech, it also benefited from a dropped pass in the end zone and a short field goal that was missed. The Hokies also scored an 80-yard touchdown with 2 minutes remaining in the game.

The following night, Southern Cal—which had been left out of the national championship game the previous year—ended any debate about a split title when it destroyed No. 2 Oklahoma 55-19. In the first match up of Heisman Trophy winners, Matt Leinart threw five touchdown passes to outshine Jason White, and aided by four turnovers the Trojans scored 38 points in the final 20 minutes of the first half.

The final polls read like a landslide presidential election, No. 1 USC, No. 2. Auburn, though it was only one of two ongoing BCS disputes in the state of Alabama.

The Birmingham News, Mobile Register and Huntsville Times were all owned by Newhouse News Service, but had excellent beat writers covering the Crimson Tide in Steve Irvine, Thomas Murphy and Paul Gattis, respectively. Gattis was one of 65 sports writers selected to participate in the Associated Press poll, which was a major part of the BSC formula used to determine which teams played for the national championship. At the end of the regular season, Gattis had Auburn No. 3 and his newspaper asked him to write a column defending his rankings. He did so, and "Suffering from my cold, not my vote," had a tone of "Look, this is the way it is and that's pretty much it."

Raising the ire of sports journalists throughout the state and country was a rebuttal column by the paper's editor, Melinda Gorham, who on the front page of the whole paper, not just sports, apologized to fans. Besides the obvious issue of leaving a reporter twisting alone in the wind, it also sparked a huge debate nationwide about whether reporters should be helping influence news instead of just reporting it. In late December, the Associated Press told BCS officials to stop using the poll in its selection formula.

On January 15, 2005, Auburn held a "Parade of Champions," with more than 10,000 fans on hand for the celebration. Highlighting the event was the rolling of Toomer's Corner, where College Street and Magnolia Avenue met. The tradition is just like it sounds, fans throw rolls of toilet paper into trees to mark important events [Note: check out toomerscornerlive.com for live and archived pictures].

"I've been fortunate enough to be part of three national championship teams (at Miami)," coach Tommy Tuberville said. "This is the best team I've been around right here."

But Auburn fans didn't seem to be enjoying the 13-0 season like they should have. The fact that the Tigers didn't get a shot at the national championship overshadowed the perfect season, and when fans, players and coaches tried to portray themselves worthy of the title, most people outside of Auburn scoffed. It wasn't necessarily anything against Auburn, just Southern Cal had been that impressive. Besides, the Trojans played the Tigers in both of the previous seasons and won 23-0 in 2003 and 24-17 the year before.

The first jolt that Auburn was likely to come back to the pack happened just two days after the parade. Defensive coordinator Gene Chizik, whose unit gave up only one rushing touchdown during the regular season and led the nation in scoring defense for a good part of the year, left to accept the co-defensive coordinator position at Texas. Part of his reasoning was that it would be easier to get a head coaching job from Texas than Auburn, and Chizik had just won the Broyles Award for assistant coach of the year.

Meanwhile, Tuberville won the Paul "Bear" Bryant coach of the year award given by the National Sportscasters and Sportswriters Association. Considering what he had been though the previous 12 months, with his own school undermining him as much as anyone else, the selection was obvious.

Upon hindsight, 2004 was pretty much the year of the freshman. Peterson made a serious run at the Heisman Trophy, but finished second to Leinart. One of his favorite targets at USC, freshman Dwayne Jarrett, caught 12 touchdown passes. At North Texas, Jamario Nelson led the nation in rushing while Ohio State's Ted Ginn returned a Division I record four punts for touchdowns. Chad Henne and Mike Hart led Michigan to the Rose Bowl.

Otherwise, it was business as usual for the sport, which meant upheaval, turnover and controversy—and that's just the coaches.

Even before the season ended, the makeup of the SEC started to drastically change. At South Carolina, Lou Holtz retired and was replaced by none other than Steve Spurrier. Having jettisoned Ron Zook, Spurrier's former school, Florida, hired Urban Meyer, who many thought would end up at Notre Dame after Tyrone Willingham was (somewhat) surprisingly fired, after Utah finished undefeated.

Willingham ended up at Washington, Zook landed at Illinois and Notre Dame hired away New England Patriots offensive coordinator Charlie Weis.

That was just the beginning of the coaching carousel.

Ole Miss fired David Cutcliffe and hired Southern California defensive coordinator Ed Orgeron, causing a bit of an uproar when it was discovered that during a bar fight in 1992 he head-butted a bouncer, and had also been involved in a domestic violence judgment.

LSU coach Nick Saban, who flirted with the National Football League every year, finally made the jump and signed a five-year deal with the Miami Dolphins worth approximately $5 million per year. LSU, in turn, hired Les Miles from Oklahoma State.

Alabama, which didn't lose any assistant coaches, benefited when a prize recruit who had given a verbal commitment to LSU decided to instead join the Crimson Tide. It spoke volumes for the change in how Alabama was being perceived, that it was considered more stable than a top SEC rival a year off winning the national championship.

With Mick Dennehy out at Utah State, and Brent Guy in, Alabama had five opponents on its 2005 schedule with new coaches. Hopefully, if everyone stayed healthy it would lead to another bowl game, and fans were already clamoring for more and still sore that the Minnesota marching band, apparently to pay homage to their hosts in Tennessee, played a short version of "Rocky Top" after the Music City Bowl even though Vanderbilt, and not Tennessee, was located in Nashville.

More importantly, in the Gophers' locker room, Mason, as always after a game, walked in and asked his players, "What did you learn?" Sometimes, they just looked back, or struggled to come up with acceptable answers. After the Music City Bowl, about 10 players immediately yelled, "Alabama hits hard."

The spirit was willing . . .

Most fans remember 2004 as the "What if?" season. What if Brodie Croyle hadn't been hurt? What if the starting backfield of senior Ray Hudson and sophomore fullback Tim Castille made it through the season without injuries? What if Alabama had the same number of players as other teams? What if, what if, what if . . .

Could Alabama at full strength have affected the Bowl Championship Series? Perhaps, but we'll never know.

But comparatively, no Crimson Tide team—or maybe any in all of college football—had the deck stacked against it like the 2004 squad. Through the coaching changes, scandals, probation, scholarship reductions and injuries, while at the same time having the most demanding fans in college football, who not only yearn, but expect the glory years of coach Paul W. "Bear" Bryant to return, the players stuck together and never gave up.

Alabama's goals in 2004 were to reach a bowl game and re-establish a base for future teams to build on. It did that, and in many ways exceeded expectations. But if dealing with adversity is indeed a true measure of character, then this team will do down as being one of the Crimson Tide's finest.

Appendix A:
2004 University of Alabama Football Roster

No.	Name, Position	HT.	WT.	Class	Hometown/Previous school
2	Antonio Carter, SE	5-9	194	Sr.	Tallahassee, Fla./Rickards
3	Simeon Castille, CB	6-1	187	Fr.	Birmingham/Briarwood Christian
3	Alex Fox, K/Holder	5-9	179	Sr.	Pensacola, Fla./Pensacola Catholic
4	Tyrone Prothro, SE	5-8	176	So.	Heflin/Cleburne County
5	Brandon Brooks, SE	5-5	165	Jr.	Birmingham/Shades Valley
6	Marcel Stamps, SE	6-3	190	Fr.	Brantley/Brantley
7	Will Oakley, SE	6-1	192	Fr.	Ponte Vedra Beach, Fla./Nease
8	Freddie Roach, MLB	6-2	239	Jr.	Killen/Brooks
8	Adam Thrash, QB	6-4	215	Fr.	Little Rock, Ark./Pulaski Academy
9	Anthony Madison, CB	5-9	180	Sr.	Thomasville/Thomasville
9	A.J. Milwee, FL/QB	5-10	167	Fr.	Boaz/Boaz
10	Carlos Andrews, S	6-1	210	Sr.	Tallahassee, Fla./Godby
11	Matt Caddell, FL	6-0	181	Fr.	McCalla/McAdory
12	Brodie Croyle, QB	6-3	205	Jr.	Rainbow City/Westbrook Christian
13	Spencer Pennington, QB	6-4	224	Jr.	Fayette/Fayette County
14	Jeffrey Aul, P	6-2	208	So.	Daleville/Daleville
15	Brian Bostick, K	5-11	213	Sr.	Cullman/Cullman
16	Cornelius Wortham, MLB	6-1	233	Sr.	Calhoun City, Miss./Calhoun City
16	C.J. Rhody, K	6-0	175	Fr.	Jupiter, Fla./Martin County
17	Ramzee Robinson, CB	5-10	192	So.	Huntsville/Butler
17	Vic Horn, TB	6-1	233	Jr.	Huntsville/Huntsville
18	Marc Guillon, QB	6-3	212	So.	Chico, Calif./Miami (Fla.)
18	Danny Barger, S	5-11	182	So.	Tuscaloosa/Hillcrest
19	Tim Castille, FB	5-11	228	So.	Birmingham/Briarwood Christian
20	Marcus Carter, S	6-1	190	Fr.	Fort Payne/Fort Payne
20	Rashad Johnson, RB	6-1	183	Fr.	Sulligent/Sulligent
21	Bo Freelend, P	6-4	260	Sr.	Eutaw/Warrior Academy
21	Mookie Chaney, RB	6-0	208	Fr.	Birmingham/John Carroll
22	DJ Hall, FL	6-3	183	Fr.	Ft. Walton Beach, Fla./Choctawhatchee
23	Jake Wingo, LB	6-0	203	Fr.	Tuscaloosa/Hillcrest
23	Kyle Bennett, FB	6-2	231	So.	Boaz/Boaz
24	Travis Robinson, CB	5-10	180	Fr.	Tuscaloosa/Hillcrest
25	Aaron McDaniel, S	6-1	166	Fr.	Fort Payne/Fort Payne
25	Jeremy Schatz, P	5-7	151	Jr.	Homewood/Homewood
26	Charlie Peprah, S	5-11	193	Jr.	Plano, Tex./Plano East
26	Jake Collins, FL	6-0	190	So.	Homewood/Homewood
27	Ray Hudson, TB	5-11	203	Sr.	Bonifay, Fla./Holmes County
27	Zayne Smith, DB	6-2	197	Fr.	Cullman/Cullman
28	Aaron Johns, TB	5-10	185	Fr.	Thomasville/Thomasville
29	Theo Townsend, TB	5-9	172	Fr.	Antioch, Tenn./Brentwood Academy
29	Matt Grice, S	6-0	195	Sr.	Tuscaloosa/Hillcrest
30	Bryan Kilpatrick, S	6-4	193	Jr.	Monroeville/Monroe Academy

30	Patrick Eades, P	6-2	185	Fr.	Hoover/Hoover
31	Greg McLain, TE	6-2	243	Jr.	Lineville/Lineville
31	Forress Rayford, S	5-11	180	Fr.	Mobile/UMS-Wright
32	Chris James, CB	6-0	185	Sr.	Albany, Ga./Dougherty
32	JD Dailey, Jr., DB	6-2	190	So.	Daphne/Highland CC
33	Le'Ron McClain, FB	6-1	258	So.	Northport/Tuscaloosa County
33	Patrick Burch, TE	6-4	240	Fr.	Navarre, Fla./Navarre
34	Kenneth Darby, TB	5-11	205	So.	Huntsville/Butler
34	Courtney Moore, DB	5-10	185	Fr.	Florence/Bradshaw
35	DeMeco Ryans, LB	6-2	232	Jr.	Bessemer/Jess Lanier
35	Patrick Gordon, FL	6-6	194	Fr.	Houma, La./Vandebilt Catholic
36	Eric Gray, RCB	5-11	186	Fr.	Trinity/West Morgan
36	David Steakley, SE	5-10	182	Jr.	Huntsville/Huntsville
37	Matt Miller, FL	6-3	210	Jr.	Rainbow City/Gadsden
37	Trent Dean, DB	6-0	185	Fr.	Decatur/Decatur
38	Josh Smith, FB	5-11	201	Sr.	Birmingham/Mountain Brook
39	Brandon McAway, TB	5-10	184	So.	Anniston/Oxford
39	Justin Ballard, S	5-11	192	So.	Eutaw/Delta State
40	Kenneth Vandervoort, LB	6-3	210	Fr.	Anniston/Donoho School
40	Joseph McPhillips, P	5-10	175	Fr.	Cullman/Cullman
41	Roman Harper, F	6-1	197	Jr.	Prattville/Prattville
41	Nick Hudson, WR	6-0	198	So.	Muscle Shoals/Muscle Shoals
42	Juwan Garth, LB	6-2	220	So.	Decatur/Austin
42	Jason Reese, WR	6-2	215	Sr.	Birmingham/Briarwood Christian
43	Jeffrey Dukes, S	6-3	190	So.	Oxford, Miss./NW Mississippi CC
43	Ryan Saxby, K	6-1	180	Jr.	Jonesboro, Ga./Jonesboro
44	Demarcus Waldrop, LB	5-11	193	Fr.	Pinson/Pinson Valley
45	Juke King, LB	6-2	234	Jr.	Theodore/Theodore
45	Rob Germany, P	6-2	220	Fr.	Carrollton, Ga./Carrollton
46	Mike McLaughlin, K	6-2	201	Jr.	Gautier, Miss./Gautier
46	Allen Long, DT	6-2	280	So.	Addison/Addison
47	Mark Anderson, DE	6-5	253	Jr.	Tulsa, Okla./Washington
48	Curtis Dawson, MLB	6-1	276	Fr.	Hoover/Hoover
49	Damien Jones, WR	6-2	235	Fr.	Mobile/Vigor
50	Justin Britt, DT	6-4	285	Fr.	Cullman/Cullman
51	Evan Mathis, G	6-5	296	Sr.	Homewood/Homewood
52	Taylor Britt, G	6-4	278	Jr.	Cullman/UAB
53	Brent Nall, LB	6-0	213	Fr.	Andalusia/Straughn
54	Justin Johnson, DT	6-2	257	Fr.	Tuscaloosa/Central
54	Jon Freelend, OL	6-4	350	Fr.	Eutaw/Warrior Academy
55	Terrence Jones, LB	6-0	216	So.	Northport/Tuscaloosa County
56	Todd Bates, DE	6-4	263	Sr.	Heflin/Cleburne County
57	Earnest Nance, MLB	6-1	228	Fr.	Courtland/Courtland
57	Morgan Garner, SN/OL	6-2	245	Fr.	Deatsville/Stanhope Elmore
58	Kyle Tatum, T	6-7	298	So.	Prattville/Prattville
58	Bryan Hobbs, LB	5-11	175	Fr.	Selma/Selma
59	Antoine Caldwell, C	6-3	281	Fr.	Montgomery/Lee
60	Von Ewing, G	6-5	294	Jr.	Troy/Charles Henderson
61	B.J. Stabler, T	6-4	292	Fr.	Grove Hill/Clarke County
62	Dawson Brown, T	6-5	310	So.	Huntsville/UAB
63	Mark Sanders, T	6-7	328	Jr.	Ashville/Ashville
64	Layne Rinks, OL	6-2	275	Fr.	Florence/Bradshaw
65	Derrick Duke, G/SN	6-3	283	Fr.	Manassas, Va./Osbourne
66	Bennett Traylor, SN	6-2	230	Fr.	Pensacola, Fla./Tate
67	J.P. Adams, DT	6-3	267	So.	Northport/Tuscaloosa County
67	Joey Bragg, C	6-3	270	Fr.	Columbus, Miss./Columbus

68	Al Jefferson, G	6-2	275	Fr.	Mobile/Davidson
68	David Sears, SN	6-4	234	Jr.	Vestavia Hills/Vestavia Hills
69	Nick Emfinger, SN/P	6-3	248	Fr.	Kemp, Tex./Kemp
70	Wesley Britt, T	6-8	298	Sr.	Cullman/Cullman
72	Chris Capps, T	6-5	293	Fr.	Jonesboro, Ga./Landmark Christian
73	Justin Moon, G	6-5	296	Fr.	Guntersville/Guntersville
74	J.B. Closner, C	6-4	290	Jr.	San Antonio, Tex./Clark
75	Cody Davis, LT	6-7	282	Fr.	Tuscaloosa/Hillcrest
76	Travis West, C	6-3	280	Fr.	Laurel, Miss./Northeast Jones
77	David Brown, OL	6-7	320	Fr.	Birmingham/Sparkman
79	Danny Martz, G	6-4	288	Sr.	Gaithersburg, Md./DeMatha Catholic
80	Trent Davidson, TE	6-5	270	Fr.	Brewton/T.R. Miller
81	Keith Brown, FL	6-3	185	Fr.	Gulfport, Miss./Pensacola
82	Marcus McKnight, FL	6-2	186	So.	Callahan, Fla./West Nassau
83	Will Roach, SE	6-1	194	Fr.	Killen/Brooks
84	Ezekial Knight, SE	6-3	210	Fr.	Wedowee/Randolph County
85	Matt Ragland, SE	5-10	178	Sr.	Huntsville/West Alabama
86	Tramayne Wright, DE	6-3	240	Fr.	Saks/Arkansas Tech
86	Jamie Christensen, K	6-0	170	Fr.	Norcross, Ga./Naval Prep
87	David Cavan, TE	6-5	256	Sr.	Tuscaloosa/American Christian
88	Clint Johnston, TE	6-4	251	Jr.	Wetumpka/Wetumpka
88	Stephen Kulback, DE	6-3	255	Jr.	Birmingham/John Carroll
89	Nick Walker, TE	6-5	238	Fr.	Brundidge/Pike County
90	Rudy Griffin, DT	6-0	286	Jr.	Hepzibah, Ga./The Citadel
90	Barrett Earnest, TE	6-3	224	Fr.	Loretto/Loretto
91	Chris Harris, DE	6-5	251	So.	Tuscaloosa/Central
91	Will Denniston, TE	6-3	225	Fr.	Mobile/UMS-Wright
92	Wallace Gilberry, DE	6-2	251	Fr.	Bay Minette/Baldwin County
93	Matt Collins, MLB	6-1	236	Fr.	Pinson/Clay-Chalkville
93	Tanner Wickham, TE	6-5	225	Fr.	Clarksville, Tenn./Rossview
94	Keith Saunders, DE	6-3	242	Fr.	Willingboro, N.J./Holy Cross
95	Drew Lane, SN	6-1	230	Jr.	Braxton, Miss./Hinds JC
96	Dominic Lee, DT	6-2	283	So.	Birmingham/Huffman
97	Anthony Bryant, DT	6-3	336	Sr.	Newbern/Sunshine
98	Chris Turner, DE	6-3	288	Jr.	Jacksonville, Fla./NW Mississippi JC
99	Jeremy Clark, DT	6-3	296	So.	Daphne/Daphne

Depth Chart
Offense

Left Tackle: Wesley Britt, Chris Capps
Left Guard: Evan Mathis, Mark Sanders
Center: J.B. Closner, Travis West, Taylor Britt
Right Guard: Danny Martz, Justin Moon
Right Tackle: Kyle Tatum, Von Ewing
Tight End: Clint Johnston, David Cavan, Trent Davidson, Greg McLain
Quarterback: Brodie Croyle, Marc Guillon, Spencer Pennington, Adam Thrash
Tailback: Ray Hudson, Kenny Darby, Aaron Johns
Fullback: Tim Castille, Le'Ron McClain, Josh Smith
Flanker: DJ Hall, Tyrone Prothro
Split End: Matt Caddell, Keith Brown, Matt Miller
Kicker: Brian Bostick

Defense

Right Defensive End: Mark Anderson, Chris Harris, Keith Saunders
Right Defensive Tackle: Jeremy Clark, Chris Turner, Justin Britt
Left Defensive Tackle: Rudy Griffin, Anthony Bryant, Dominic Lee

Left Defensive End: Todd Bates, Wallace Gilberry
Weakside Linebacker: Freddie Roach, Juwan Garth, Demarcus Waldrop
Middle Linebacker: Cornelius Wortham, Matt Collins
Strongside Linebacker: DeMeco Ryans, Torrance Jones
Right Cornerback: Anthony Madison, Eric Gray
Free Safety: Roman Harper, Carlos Andrews, Jeffrey Dukes
Strong Safety: Charlie Peprah, Marcus Carter
Left Cornerback: Ramzee Robinson, Simeon Castille
Punter: Bo Freelend, Jeremy Schatz

Special Teams
Snapper: Drew Lane
Holder: Alex Fox
Kick Returner: Tyrone Prothro, DJ Hall, Ezekial Knight, Brandon Brooks
Punt Returner: Tyrone Prothro, DJ Hall, Brandon Brooks
Kickoffs: Jamie Christensen, Jeff Aul

2005 Signees

Name, Pos.	Ht.	Wt.	Hometown/Previous school
Jimmy Barnes, QB	6-5	225	Los Alamitos, Calif./Los Alamitos
Sam Burnthall, DB	6-2	190	Decatur/Decatur
Evan Cardwell, OL	6-3	290	Killen/Brooks
Glen Coffee, RB	6-0	207	Fort Walton Beach, Fla./Fort Walton Beach
Drew Davis, OL	6-6	300	Evergreen/Sparta Academy
Marlon Davis, OL	6-4	315	Columbus, Ga./Carver
Brandon Deaderick, DL	6-4	230	Elizabethtown, Ky./Elizabethtown
Scott Deaton, OL	6-5	270	Birmingham/Oak Mountain
Brandon Fanney, DL	6-5	270	Morristown, Tenn./Hargrave Military
Antonio Forbes, DL	6-4	265	Norcross, Ga./Meadowcreek
Mike Ford, RB	6-2	205	Sarasota, Fla./Sarasota
Bobby Greenwood, DL	6-6	245	Prattville/Prattville
Prince Hall, LB	6-0	240	Moreno Valley, Calif./Moreno Valley
Cole Harvey, OL	6-3	255	Tallahassee, Fla./Lincoln
Charles Hoke, TE	6-6	240	Birmingham/Briarwood Christian
Baron Huber, LB	6-4	238	Knoxville, Tenn./Powell
Desmond Jennings, WR	6-1	188	Pinson/Pinson Valley
Jimmy Johns, QB	6-2	225	Brookhaven, Miss./Brookhaven
Mike Johnson, OL	6-6	285	Pensacola, Fla./Pine Forest
Chris Keys, DB	6-2	205	Stevenson/North Jackson
Nick Kyles, WR	6-2	190	Milledgeville, Ga./Baldwin
Travis McCall, TE/DE	6-2	250	Prattville/Prattville
Lionel Mitchell, DB	6-2	180	Stone Mountain, Ga./Hargrave Military
Cory Reamer, DB	6-3	198	Hoover/Hoover
Michael Ricks, DB	6-2	185	Courtland/R.A. Hubbard
Chris Rogers, DB	6-1	178	Lakeland, Fla./Evangel Christian
Zach Schreiber, LB	6-2	220	Shreveport, La./Evangel Christian
Ali Sharrief, RB	5-10	190	Stevenson/North Jackson
Travis Sikes, WR/DB	6-3	190	Nashville, Tenn./Christ Presbyterian
Roy Upchurch, RB	6-0	207	Tallahassee, Fla./Godby
Byron Walton, DL	6-4	298	Trinity/West Morgan
Lorenzo Washington, DL	6-4	265	Loganville, Ga./Hargrave Military
John Parker Wilson, QB	6-2	215	Hoover/Hoover

Appendix B: Final 2004 Standings and Statistics

STANDINGS

Southeastern Conference					Overall			
	W-L	WP	PS	PA	W-L	WP	PS	PA
Eastern Division								
Tennessee	7-1	.875	215	199	9-2	.818	312	250
Georgia	6-2	.750	231	133	9-2	.818	311	177
Florida	4-4	.500	251	187	7-4	.636	372	226
South Carolina	4-4	.500	185	190	6-5	.545	243	229
Kentucky	1-7	.125	106	253	2-9	.182	173	341
Vanderbilt	1-7	.125	133	213	2-9	.182	212	286
Western Division								
Auburn	8-0	1.000	247	961	1-0	1.000	363	106
LSU	6-2	.750	220	131	9-2	.818	319	175
Alabama	3-5	.375	152	149	6-5	.545	279	169
Arkansas	3-5	.375	196	215	5-6	.455	328	270
Ole Miss	3-5	.375	142	200	4-7	.364	215	278
Mississippi State	2-6	.250	125	237	3-8	.273	173	280

Schedule/Results

Date	Opponent	Score	Attendance
Sept. 4	Utah State	48-17	82,033
*Sept. 11	Ole Miss	28-7	83,083
Sept. 18	Western Carolina	52-0	77,306
*Sept. 25	at Arkansas	10-27	72,543
*Oct. 02	South Carolina	3-20	82,141
*Oct. 09	at Kentucky	45-17	65,482
Oct. 16	No. 24 Southern Miss	27-3	82,094
*Oct. 23	at No. 11 Tennessee	13-17	107,017
*Nov. 06	Mississippi State	30-14	82,617
*Nov. 13	at No. 17 LSU	10-26	91,861
*Nov. 20	No. 2 Auburn	13-21	83,818
Dec. 31	vs. Minnesota	16-20	66,089

*—SEC game
Home game at Bryant-Denny Stadium

Record	Overall	Home	Away	Neutral
All Games	6-6-0	5-2-0	1-3-0	0-1-0
Conference	3-5-0	2-2-0	1-3-0	0-0-0
Non-conference	3-1-0	3-0-0	0-0-0	0-1-0

TEAM STATISTICS

	ALABAMA	OPP
SCORING	295	189
Points Per Game	24.6	15.8

FIRST DOWNS	194	166
Rushing	101	90
Passing	80	63
Penalty	13	13
RUSHING YARDAGE	2221	1589
Yards gained rushing	2484	2000
Yards lost rushing	263	411
Rushing Attempts	502	484
Average Per Rush	4.4	3.3
Average Per Game	185.1	132.4
TDs Rushing	21	11
PASSING YARDAGE	1699	1357
Att-Comp-Int	261-146-11	242-105-12
Average Per Pass	6.5	5.6
Average Per Catch	11.6	12.9
Average Per Game	141.6	113.1
TDs Passing	11	9
TOTAL OFFENSE	3920	2946
Total Plays	763	726
Average Per Play	5.1	4.1
Average Per Game	326.7	245.5
KICK RETURNS: #-YARDS	29-708	36-691
PUNT RETURNS: #-YARDS	33-270	22-150
INT RETURNS: #-YARDS	12-113	11-157
KICK RETURN AVERAGE	24.4	19.2
PUNT RETURN AVERAGE	8.2	6.8
INT RETURN AVERAGE	9.4	14.3
FUMBLES-LOST	16-9	21-14
PENALTIES-YARDS	70-614	65-501
Average Per Game	51.2	41.8
PUNTS-YARDS	65-2611	76-3133
Average Per Punt	40.2	41.2
Net punt average	37.9	37.7
TIME OF POSSESSION/GAME	31:59	28:01
3RD-DOWN CONVERSIONS	51/161	47/161
3rd-Down Pct	32%	29%
4TH-DOWN CONVERSIONS	4/12	6/14
4th-Down Pct	33%	43%
SACKS BY-YARDS	25-166	16-119
MISC YARDS	32	27
TOUCHDOWNS SCORED	35	23
FIELD GOALS-ATTEMPTS	16-19	10-14
PAT-ATTEMPTS	35-35	21-23
ATTENDANCE	573092	336903
Games/Avg Per Game	7/81870	4/84226
Neutral Site Games		1/66089

SCORE BY QUARTERS	1st	2nd	3rd	4th		Total
Alabama	65	97	48	85	—	295
Opponents	38	46	62	43	—	189

Individual Statistics

RUSHING	GP	Att	Gain	Loss	Net	Avg	TD	Long	Avg/G
Kenneth Darby	12	219	1101	39	1062	4.8	8	45	88.5
Ray Hudson	6	92	650	12	638	6.9	4	63	106.3
Tim Castille	8	62	247	0	247	4.0	6	40	30.9

Aaron Johns	8	53	223	23	200	3.8	0	44	25.0
L. McClain	12	17	67	1	66	3.9	2	14	5.5
Tyrone Prothro	12	13	76	10	66	5.1	1	21	5.5
Keith Brown	10	3	52	0	52	17.3	0	18	5.2
Bo Freelend	12	1	24	0	24	24.0	0	24	2.0
Josh Smith	12	4	12	0	12	3.0	0	5	1.0
DJ Hall	12	1	4	0	4	4.0	0	4	0.3
Marc Guillon	4	1	0	1	−1	−1.0	0	0	−0.2
Brodie Croyle	3	9	11	38	−27	−3.0	0	7	−9.0
Team	8	7	0	41	−41	−5.9	0	0	−5.1
S. Pennington	9	20	17	98	−81	−4.1	0	7	−9.0
Total	**12**	**502**	**2484**	**263**	**2221**	**4.4**	**21**	**63**	**185.1**
Opponents	**12**	**484**	**2000**	**411**	**1589**	**3.3**	**11**	**50**	**132.4**

PASSING	GP	Effic	Att-Cmp-Int	Pct	Yds	TD	Lng	Avg/G
S. Pennington	9	105.93	152-82-8	53.9	974	4	48	108.2
Brodie Croyle	3	164.63	66-44-0	66.7	534	6	57	178.0
Marc Guillon	4	77.54	43-20-3	46.5	191	1	39	47.8
Total	**12**	**116.10**	**261-146-11**	**55.9**	**1699**	**11**	**57**	**141.6**
Opponents	**12**	**92.85**	**242-105-12**	**43.4**	**1357**	**9**	**51**	**113.1**

RECEIVING	GP	No.	Yds	Avg	TD	Long	Avg/G
Tyrone Prothro	12	25	347	13.9	1	35	28.9
Matt Caddell	12	17	331	19.5	1	48	27.6
Keith Brown	10	17	295	17.4	1	57	29.5
DJ Hall	12	17	186	10.9	1	23	15.5
Kenneth Darby	12	15	74	4.9	1	14	6.2
Tim Castille	8	14	104	7.4	0	20	13.0
Ray Hudson	6	11	78	7.1	1	20	13.0
Ezekial Knight	12	10	98	9.8	0	39	8.2
L. McClain	12	8	55	6.9	3	24	4.6
Clint Johnston	9	6	80	13.3	2	22	8.9
Aaron Johns	8	3	24	8.0	0	19	3.0
Marcus McKnight	3	1	14	14.0	0	14	4.7
David Cavan	10	1	13	13.0	0	13	1.3
Matt Miller	12	1	0	0.0	0	0	0.0
Total	**12**	**146**	**1699**	**11.6**	**11**	**57**	**141.6**
Opponents	**12**	**105**	**1357**	**12.9**	**9**	**51**	**113.1**

PUNT RETURNS	No.	Yds	Avg	TD	Long
Brandon Brooks	25	128	5.1	0	39
Tyrone Prothro	6	98	16.3	0	40
Anthony Madison	1	15	15.0	0	0
Marcel Stamps	1	29	29.0	1	14
Total	**33**	**270**	**8.2**	**1**	**40**
Opponents	**22**	**150**	**6.8**	**0**	**45**

INTERCEPTIONS	No.	Yds	Avg	TD	Long
Anthony Madison	4	22	5.5	0	19
Roman Harper	3	26	8.7	0	26
Simeon Castille	2	34	17.0	1	31
DeMeco Ryans	1	0	0.0	0	0
Charlie Peprah	1	31	31.0	0	31
C. Wortham	1	0	0.0	0	0
Total	**12**	**113**	**9.4**	**1**	**31**
Opponents	**11**	**157**	**14.3**	**0**	**44**

KICK RETURNS	No.	Yds	Avg	TD	Long
Tyrone Prothro	17	452	26.6	1	100
Brandon Brooks	10	244	24.4	0	87
Trent Davidson	1	2	2.0	0	2
Matt Caddell	1	10	10.0	0	7
Total	**29**	**708**	**24.4**	**1**	**100**
Opponents	**36**	**691**	**19.2**	**0**	**44**

FUMBLE RETURNS	No.	Yds	Avg	TD	Long
Freddie Roach	1	8	8.0	0	8
Rudy Griffin	1	24	24.0	0	24
Total	**2**	**32**	**16.0**	**0**	**24**
Opponents	**3**	**27**	**9.0**	**3**	**18**

SCORING	TD	FGs	Kick	Rush	Rcv	Pass	DXP	Saf	Points
Brian Bostick	0	16-19	35-35	0-0	0	0-0	0	0	83
Kenneth Darby	9	0-0	0-0	0-0	0	0-0	0	0	54
Tim Castille	6	0-0	0-0	0-0	0	0-0	0	0	36
L. McClain	5	0-0	0-0	0-0	0	0-0	0	0	30
Ray Hudson	5	0-0	0-0	0-0	0	0-0	0	0	30
Tyrone Prothro	3	0-0	0-0	0-0	0	0-0	0	0	18
Clint Johnston	2	0-0	0-0	0-0	0	0-0	0	0	12
Marcel Stamps	1	0-0	0-0	0-0	0	0-0	0	0	6
Matt Caddell	1	0-0	0-0	0-0	0	0-0	0	0	6
Simeon Castille	1	0-0	0-0	0-0	0	0-0	0	0	6
Keith Brown	1	0-0	0-0	0-0	0	0-0	0	0	6
DJ Hall	1	0-0	0-0	0-0	0	0-0	0	0	6
Team	0	0-0	0-0	0-0	0	0-0	0	1	2
Total	**35**	**16-19**	**35-35**	**0-0**	**0**	**0-0**	**0**	**1**	**295**
Opponents	**23**	**10-14**	**21-23**	**0-0**	**0**	**0-0**	**0**	**0**	**189**

TOTAL OFFENSE	G	Plays	Rush	Pass	Total	Avg/G
Kenneth Darby	12	219	1062	0	1062	88.5
S. Pennington	9	172	−81	974	893	99.2
Ray Hudson	6	92	638	0	638	106.3
Brodie Croyle	3	75	−27	534	507	169.0
Tim Castille	8	62	247	0	247	30.9
Aaron Johns	8	53	200	0	200	25.0
Marc Guillon	4	44	−1	191	190	47.5
L. McClain	12	17	66	0	66	5.5
Tyrone Prothro	12	13	66	0	66	5.5
Keith Brown	10	3	52	0	52	5.2
Bo Freelend	12	1	24	0	24	2.0
Josh Smith	12	4	12	0	12	1.0
DJ Hall	12	1	4	0	4	0.3
Team	8	7	−41	0	−41	−5.1
Total	**12**	**763**	**2221**	**1699**	**3920**	**326.7**
Opponents	**12**	**726**	**1589**	**1357**	**2946**	**245.5**

FIELD GOALS	FGM-FGA	Pct	01-19	20-29	30-39	40-49	50-99	Lg	Blk
Brian Bostick	16-19	84.2	0-0	5-5	7-8	4-6	0-0	47	1

PUNTING	No.	Yds	Avg	Long	TB	FC	I20	Blkd
Bo Freelend	62	2516	40.6	54	7	17	17	0
Jeremy Schatz	3	95	31.7	40	0	0	1	0
Total	**65**	**2611**	**40.2**	**54**	**7**	**17**	**18**	**0**
Opponents	**76**	**3133**	**41.2**	**57**	**4**	**9**	**22**	**2**

KICKOFFS	No.	Yds	Avg	TB	OB
J. Christensen	62	3844	62.0	24	2
Total	**62**	**3844**	**62.0**	**24**	**2**
Opponents	**45**	**2688**	**59.7**	**13**	**4**

ALL PURPOSE	G	Rush	Rec	PR	KOR	IR	Tot	Avg/G
Kenneth Darby	12	1062	74	0	0	0	1136	94.7
Tyrone Prothro	12	66	347	98	452	0	963	80.2
Ray Hudson	6	638	78	0	0	0	716	119.3
Brandon Brooks	10	0	0	128	244	0	372	37.2
Tim Castille	8	247	104	0	0	0	351	43.9
Keith Brown	10	52	295	0	0	0	347	34.7
Matt Caddell	12	0	331	0	10	0	341	28.4
Aaron Johns	8	200	24	0	0	0	224	28.0
DJ Hall	12	4	186	0	0	0	190	15.8
L. McClain	12	66	55	0	0	0	121	10.1
Ezekial Knight	12	0	98	0	0	0	98	8.2
Clint Johnston	9	0	80	0	0	0	80	8.9
Anthony Madison	12	0	0	15	0	22	37	3.1
Simeon Castille	11	0	0	0	0	34	34	3.1
Charlie Peprah	12	0	0	0	0	31	31	2.6
Marcel Stamps	12	0	0	29	0	0	29	2.4
Roman Harper	12	0	0	0	0	26	26	2.2
Bo Freelend	12	24	0	0	0	0	24	2.0
Marcus McKnight	3	0	14	0	0	0	14	4.7
David Cavan	10	0	13	0	0	0	13	1.3
Josh Smith	12	12	0	0	0	0	12	1.0
Trent Davidson	12	0	0	0	2	0	2	0.2
Marc Guillon	4	−1	0	0	0	0	−1	−0.2
Brodie Croyle	3	−27	0	0	0	0	−27	−9.0
Team	8	−41	0	0	0	0	−41	−5.1
S. Pennington	9	−81	0	0	0	0	−81	−9.0
Total	**12**	**2221**	**1699**	**270**	**708**	**113**	**5011**	**417.6**
Opponents	**12**	**1589**	**1357**	**150**	**691**	**157**	**3944**	**328.7**

DEFENSIVE LEADERS	GP	Tackles				Sacks	Pass Def			Fumbles		Blkd	
		Solo	Ast	Total	TFL/Yds	No-Yds	Int-Yds	BrUp	QBH	Rcv-Yds	FF	Kick	Saf
16 C. Wortham	12	39	60	99	3-8	1.0-3	1-0	—	3	1-0	—	—	—
35 DeMeco Ryans	12	46	32	78	7-12	—	1-0	1	2	1-0	2	—	—
41 Roman Harper	12	45	32	77	7-33	1.0-15	3-26	4	1	2-0	1	—	—
8 Freddie Roach	12	28	29	57	9-26	2.0-10	—	1	5	1-8	2	—	—
26 Charlie Peprah	12	34	17	51	2-5	—	1-31	1	—	—	—	—	—
56 Todd Bates	12	23	25	48	8-30	5.5-26	—	—	4	1-0	—	—	—
17 Ramzee Robinson	12	27	18	45	1-3	—	—	4	—	—	—	—	—
47 Mark Anderson	12	23	18	41	11-40	1.5-9	—	2	8	2-0	2	—	—
42 Juwan Garth	10	18	14	32	4-5	0.5-1	—	1	3	1-0	—	—	—
92 W. Gilberry	12	14	14	28	13-50	6.5-44	—	—	7	2-0	2	—	—
9 Anthony Madison	12	15	11	26	2-5	—	4-22	10	—	—	—	1	—
97 Anthony Bryant	12	10	12	22	3-8	1.5-7	—	—	2	—	—	—	—
44 D. Waldrop	12	9	13	22	4-20	1.0-13	—	1	2	1-0	1	—	—
99 Jeremy Clark	12	6	14	20	2-8	0.5-6	—	1	—	—	—	—	—
55 Terrence Jones	12	9	9	18	1-1	—	—	—	—	—	—	—	—
90 Rudy Griffin	12	4	13	17	3-2	—	—	—	—	1-24	—	—	—
91 Chris Harris	12	6	10	16	3-13	1.5-11	—	1	1	—	—	—	—
3 Simeon Castille	11	7	7	14	2-6	1.0-5	2-34	4	—	—	—	—	—
96 Dominic Lee	8	2	11	13	1-0	—	—	—	—	—	—	—	—
50 Justin Britt	11	3	9	12	2-10	1.0-9	—	—	—	—	—	—	—
98 Chris Turner	8	5	5	10	4-12	1.0-7	—	—	—	—	—	—	—

No.	Player	GP												
10	Carlos Andrews	11	5	5	10	—	—	—	—	—	—	—	—	—
84	Ezekial Knight	12	5	5	10	—	—	—	—	—	—	—	—	—
6	Marcel Stamps	12	3	6	9	—	—	—	—	—	—	—	1	—
85	Matt Ragland	12	5	3	8	—	—	—	—	—	—	—	—	—
43	Jeffrey Dukes	12	6	1	7	—	—	—	—	—	—	2	—	—
36	Eric Gray	9	3	1	4	1-0	—	—	—	—	1-0	—	—	—
20	Marcus Carter	11	2	1	3	—	—	—	—	—	—	—	—	—
37	Matt Miller	12	—	3	3	—	—	—	—	—	—	—	—	—
45	Juke King	12	2	—	2	1-3	—	—	—	—	—	—	—	—
93	Matt Collins	12	—	2	2	—	—	—	—	—	—	—	—	—
34	Kenneth Darby	12	2	—	2	—	—	—	—	—	—	—	—	—
24	Travis Robinson	5	1	—	1	—	—	—	—	—	—	—	—	—
TM	Team	8	1	—	1	—	—	—	—	—	—	—	—	—
38	Josh Smith	12	—	1	1	—	—	—	—	—	—	—	—	—
39	Justin Ballard	7	—	1	1	—	—	—	—	—	—	—	—	—
86	J. Christensen	12	1	—	1	—	—	—	—	—	—	—	—	—
19	Tim Castille	8	1	—	1	—	—	—	—	—	—	—	—	—
81	Keith Brown	10	1	—	1	—	—	—	—	—	—	—	—	—
11	Matt Caddell	12	1	—	1	—	—	—	—	—	—	—	—	—
58	Kyle Tatum	12	1	—	1	—	—	—	—	—	—	—	—	—
51	Evan Mathis	12	1	—	1	—	—	—	—	—	—	—	—	—
33	L. McClain	12	—	1	1	—	—	—	—	—	—	—	—	—
46	Allen Long	1	—	1	1	—	—	—	—	—	—	—	—	—
21	Bo Freelend	12	1	—	1	—	—	—	—	—	—	—	—	—
	Total	**12**	**415**	**404**	**819**	**94-300**	**25-166**	**12-113**	**31**	**38**	**14-32**	**12**	**2**	**1**
	Opponents	**12**	**452**	**450**	**902**	**78-242**	**16-119**	**11-157**	**22**	**11**	**9-27**	**9**	**1**	**—**

2004 AWARDS
Crimson Tide
Collegesportsreport.com SEC Team of the Week (vs. Ole Miss, Sept. 11)
Collegesportsreport.com SEC Team of the Week (vs. Mississippi State, Nov. 6)
Todd Bates, senior, defensive end
SEC Defensive Lineman of the Week (vs. Southern Miss, Oct. 16)
Brian Bostick, senior, kicker
First-Team All-SEC (AP, Coaches, Rivals.com)
Semifinalist for the Lou Groza Award
SEC Special Teams Player of the Week (vs. Mississippi State, Nov. 6)
Wesley Britt, senior, left tackle
2004 Jacobs Award Winner (SECs Most Outstanding Blocker)
First-Team All-SEC (AP, Coaches, Rivals.com)
CNN/SI Honorable Mention All-American
College Football News Midseason All-American
SI.com Midseason Honorable Mention All-American
SEC Football Good Works Team (vs. Kentucky, Oct. 9)
Kenneth Darby, sophomore, tailback
Second-Team All-SEC (AP)
SEC Offensive Player of the Week (vs. Mississippi State, Nov. 6)
Collegesportsreport.com SEC Player of the Week (vs. Mississippi State, Nov. 6)
Bo Freelend, senior, punter
Semifinalist for the Ray Guy Award (Nation's Best Punter)
Wallace Gilberry, freshman, defensive end
Freshman All-American Team (Rivals.com)
First-Team Freshman All-SEC (Coaches)
Roman Harper, junior, free safety
Second-Team All-SEC (AP, Coaches)
SEC Defensive Player of the Week (vs. Ole Miss, Sept. 11)
Ray Hudson, senior, tailback
Collegesportsreport.com SEC Player of the Week (vs. Ole Miss, Sept. 11)

Clint Johnston, junior, tight end
Honorable Mention All-SEC (AP)
Danny Martz, senior, right guard
SI.com Midseason Honorable Mention All-American
Evan Mathis, senior, left guard
First-Team All-SEC (AP, Rivals.com)
Second-Team All-SEC (Coaches)
SI.com Midseason All-American
Tyrone Prothro, sophomore, wide receiver/kick returner
First-Team All-SEC (Rivals.com)
Second-Team All-SEC (Coaches)
SEC Special Teams Player of the Week (vs. Kentucky, Oct. 9)
Freddie Roach, junior, linebacker
Second-Team All-SEC (Coaches)
CNN/SI Honorable Mention All-American
DeMeco Ryans, junior, linebacker
Second-Team All-SEC (Coaches)
Honorable Mention All-SEC (AP)
CBS Sports Scholar/Athlete of the Game (vs. Auburn, Nov. 20)
Cornelius Wortham, senior, linebacker
First-Team All-SEC (AP, Coaches)

Appendix C: The 2004 University of Alabama Football Program

The University of Alabama (2004)

President Dr. Robert E. Witt

Football

Mike Shula, Head Coach
Joe Kines, Assistant Head Coach/Defensive Coordinator/Linebackers
Dave Rader, Offensive Coordinator/Quarterbacks
Chris Ball, Secondary
Bob Connelly, Offensive Line
Charlie Harbison, Receivers
Kent Johnston, Strength and Conditioning
Paul Randolph, Defensive Ends
Dave Ungerer, Special Teams/Tight Ends
Sparky Woods, Running Backs
Buddy Wyatt, Defensive Line
Randy Ross, Director of Football Operations
Tim Bowens, Assistant Director of Football Operations
Paul Hogan, Offensive Graduate Assistant
Jason Jones, Defensive Graduate Assistant
Steadman Campbell, Video Graduate Assistant
Danny Kimble, Video Graduate Assistant
Josh Lawson, Recruiting Graduate Assistant
Jeremy Gsell, Athletic Trainer Graduate Assistant
Allen Ishmael, Head Student Trainer
Mary Spybey, Head Coach's Secretary
Alecia Price, Operations Coordinator
Brenda Swindle, Football Administrative Secretary
Glenda Foreman, Football Administrative Secretary
Terri Nolan, Football Administrative Secretary

Athletics Department

Mal Moore, Director of Athletics
Joe Hornsby, Faculty Athletics Representative
Wes Allen, Assistant Director of Athletic Marketing and Trademark Licensing
Finus Gaston, Senior Associate Athletics Director
Johnny Williams, Senior Associate AD/External Operations
Kevin Almond, Associate AD for Support Services
Jon Dever, Director of Academic Services for Intercollegiate Athletics
Frank Dykes, Manager of Football Facilities
Jon Gilbert, Associate AD for Events
Daniel Hopper, Director of Marketing and Promotions
Wendell Hudson, Associate AD for Alumni Relations

Carol Keys, Assistant AD/Business Office
Chris King, Associate AD for Compliance
Karin Lee, Director of Student Development/Lifeskills
Kirk Miller, Manager Computer Services
Sarah Patterson, Associate AD/Community/University Relations/Gymnastics Coach
Andy Rainey, Athletic Web Communications Director
Bobby Rice, Director of Athletic Facilities
Marie Robbins, Associate AD and Senior Woman Administrator
Thad Turnispeed, Director of Athletic Capital Projects
Scott Urbantke, Director of Athletic Grounds and Outdoor Facilities
Rhonda Vaughn, Director of Athletic Ticket Office
Steve Wilson, Manager of Athletic Facilities
Tank Conerly, Athletic Equipment Director
Terry Jones, Assistant Head Strength and Conditioning Coach
Steve Martin, Strength and Conditioning Coach
Don Rawson, Video Coordinator
Patrick McDonald, Assistant Manager of Video Services
Carey Sutton, Gameday Security, Alabama State Trooper
Jessie Peoples, Gameday Security, Alabama State Trooper
Libby Austin, Eligibility and Financial Aid Coordinator
Cedric Burns, Player Relations Coordinator
Bryant Carter, Assistant Director Event Manager
Jana Morrison, Assistant Director Event Manager
Rusty Holley, Assistant Athletic Equipment Manager
Telisa Blanton, Athletic Development
Lee Leonard, Assistant Athletic Equipment Manager
Joe Whitehead, Assistant Coleman Coliseum Manager
Jill Bender, Skybox Coordinator
Melanie Gray, Administrative Secretary
Judy Tanner, Administrative Secretary

Athletic Trainers and Team Physicians

Bill McDonald, Director of Sports Medicine
Rodney Brown, Head Athletic Trainer
Clint Haggard, Assistant Athletic Trainer
James Andrews, Orthopedic Consultant
Craig Buettner, Team Physician
Lee Cain, Team Physician
Jeff Laubenthal, Team Physician
Rick McKenzie, Team Neurosurgeon
Les Fowler, Team Orthopedist
Bryan Givhan, Team Neurosurgeon
Jimmy Robinson, Team Physician
Rush Smith, Team Dentist

Tide Pride

Tommy Ford, Director
Melissa Mitchell, Brenda Vaughn, Misty Smith, Mary Turner, Rhonda Moore, Jo Davis and Dude
    Hennessy
Lance Covan, Director of Crimson Tradition Fund

Broadcasting

Eli Gold, Play-By-Play Announcer
Ken Stabler, Color Analyst
Tom Roberts, Director of Broadcasting

David Crane, Assistant Director of Broadcasting
Tom Stipe, Butch Owens, Brian Roberts and Bert Bank, Producers
Chris Stewart, Postgame Host
Michael Alford, General Manager Crimson Tide Sports Marketing

Media Relations

Larry White, Associate AD/Media Relations
Becky Hopf, Associate Media Relations Director
Barry Allen, Assistant Media Relations Director
Kent Gidley, Photography Coordinator Athletics
John Hayden, Assistant Media Relations Director
Brent Hollingsworth, Assistant Director of Marketing/Public Relations
Brian Morgan, Assistant Media Relations Director
Roots Woodruff, Assistant Media Relations Director
Brenda Burnette, Media Relations Administrative Assistant
Karen Deaver, Media Relations Office Associate

University Jet Flight Crew

Danny Dubose, Chief Pilot/Manager
William Carter, Pilot
Butch Lary, Pilot
Tommy Brown, Mechanic

Various Staffers

Henry Walls, Kent Harris, Jackie Craig, Stephen Spraddling, Tommy James, Rhoda Vaughn, Barbara House, Virginia Crump, James Lott, Garrett Klassy, Kristy Trimm, Kristi Dyer, Patsy Stewart, Melissa Barnett, Lourie Clements, Pam Thompson, Marie Johnson, Carol Lucas, Donna Graham, Ronnie Browning, Skip Newell, Carlton Posey, Troy Trimm, Terry Cook, Willie Thompson, Joe Page, James Smith, Elaine Whitson, James Simms, Benn Hammonds and Sandi Keller.

Appendix D: Crimson Tide Tradition

The National Championships (12): 1925, 1926, 1930, 1934, 1941, 1961, 1964, 1965, 1973, 1978, 1979, 1992.

The "Other" Five: In addition to the 12 recognized national championships, the Official NCAA Football Records Book recognizes Alabama as producing national champions in 1945, 1962, 1966, 1975 and 1977. In 1945, the 10-0 Tide was recognized as champions with Army by the National Championship Foundation. The 1962 Crimson Tide, 10-1, was chosen by Billingsley and Sagarin, while the 1966 team, 11-0, was selected by Berryman. The 11-1 Tide team in 1975, along with Ohio State, was selected by Matthews. In 1977, Football Research picked Alabama, 11-1, and Notre Dame as co-national champions.

SEC Championships (21): 1933, 1934, 1937, 1945, 1953, 1961, 1964, 1965, 1966, 1971, 1972, 1973, 1974, 1975, 1977, 1978, 1979, 1981, 1989, 1992, 1999.

Bowl Games (Overall record 29-20-3)

1926	Rose	Alabama 20, Washington 19
1927	Rose	Alabama 7, Stanford 7
1931	Rose	Alabama 24, Washington State 0
1935	Rose	Alabama 29, Stanford 13
1938	Rose	California 13, Alabama 0
1942	Cotton	Alabama 29, Texas A&M 21
1943	Orange	Alabama 37, Boston College 21
1945	Sugar	Duke 29, Alabama 26
1946	Rose	Alabama 34, Southern Cal 14
1948	Sugar	Texas 27, Alabama 7
1953	Orange	Alabama 61, Syracuse 6
1954	Cotton	Rice 28, Alabama 6
1959	Liberty	Penn State 7, Alabama 0
1960	Bluebonnet	Alabama 3, Texas 3
1962	Sugar	Alabama 10, Arkansas 3
1963	Orange	Alabama 17, Oklahoma 0
1964	Sugar	Alabama 12, Mississippi 7
1965	Orange	Texas 21, Alabama 17
1966	Orange	Alabama 39, Nebraska 28
1967	Sugar	Alabama 34, Nebraska 7
1968	Cotton	Texas A&M 20, Alabama 16
1968	Gator	Missouri 35, Alabama 10
1969	Liberty	Colorado 47, Alabama 33
1970	Bluebonnet	Alabama 24, Oklahoma 24
1972	Orange	Nebraska 38, Alabama 6
1973	Cotton	Texas 17, Alabama 13
1973	Sugar	Notre Dame 24, Alabama 23
1975	Orange	Notre Dame 13, Alabama 11
1975	Sugar	Alabama 13, Penn State 6
1976	Liberty	Alabama 33, UCLA 6

1978	Sugar	Alabama 35, Ohio State 6
1979	Sugar	Alabama 14, Penn State 7
1980	Sugar	Alabama 24, Arkansas 9
1981	Cotton	Alabama 30, Baylor 2
1982	Cotton	Texas 14, Alabama 12
1982	Liberty	Alabama 21, Illinois 15
1983	Sun	Alabama 28, SMU 7
1985	Aloha	Alabama 24, Southern Cal 3
1986	Sun	Alabama 28, Washington 6
1988	Hall of Fame	Michigan 29, Alabama 24
1988	Sun	Alabama 29, Army 28
1990	Sugar	Miami 33, Alabama 25
1991	Fiesta	Louisville 34, Alabama 7
1991	Blockbuster	Alabama 30, Colorado 25
1993	Sugar	Alabama 34, Miami 13
1993	Gator	Alabama 24, North Carolina 10
1995	Citrus	Alabama 24, Ohio State 17
1997	Outback	Alabama 17, Michigan 14
1998	Music City	Virginia Tech 38, Alabama 7
2000	Orange	Michigan 35, Alabama 34 (OT)
2001	Independence	Alabama 14, Iowa State 13
2004	Music City	Minnesota 20, Alabama 16

College Football Hall of Fame
Name, Years Played, Position, Year Inducted
Cornelius Bennett, 1983-86, linebacker, 2005
Johnny Mack Brown, 1923-25, halfback, 1957
Paul Bryant, 1933-35, right end, 1986
Johnny Cain, 1930-32, fullback, 1973
Harry Gilmer, 1944-47, quarterback/defensive back, 1993
John Hannah, 1970-72, guard, 1999
Frank Howard, 1928-30, guard, 1989
Dixie Howell, 1932-34, halfback, 1970
Pooley Hubert, 1922-25, quarterback, 1964
Don Hutson, 1932-34, end, 1951
Lee Roy Jordan, 1960-62, linebacker, 1983
Vaughn Mancha, 1944-47, center, 1990
Johnny Musso, 1969-71, halfback, 2000
Billy Neighbors, 1959-61, tackle, 2003
Ozzie Newsome, 1974-77, split end, 1994
Fred Sington, 1928-30, tackle, 1955
Riley Smith, 1934-35, quarterback, 1985
Frank Thomas, 1931-46, coach, 1951
Wallace Wade, 1923-30, coach, 1955
Don Whitmire, 1941-42, tackle, 1956
[Note: Alabama has six players inducted into the Pro Football Hall of Fame: Don Hutson (1963), John Hannah (1991), Joe Namath (1985), Ozzie Newsome (1999), Bart Starr (1977) and Dwight Stephenson (1998).

National Honors
Cornelius Bennett, 1986 Lombardi Award (Most Outstanding Lineman)
Derrick Thomas, 1988 Dick Butkus Award (Most Outstanding Linebacker)
Antonio Langham, 1993 Thorpe Award (Most Outstanding Defensive Back)
Jay Barker, 1994 Johnny Unitas Golden Arm Award (Best Quarterback)
Chris Samuels, 1999 Outland Trophy (Best Interior Lineman)
[Note: Alabama has never won a Heisman Trophy, with 17 players finishing in the top 10 of voting and nine in the top five. David Palmer came closest at third in 1993, while Lee Roy Jordan and

Johnny Musso were fourth in 1962 and 1971, respectively. However, Bryant did coach a Heisman winner with halfback John David Crow at Texas A&M in 1957.]

First-Team All-Americans
Shaun Alexander, 1999, tailback
Jay Barker, 1994, quarterback
Cornelius Bennett, 1984-86, linebacker
Thomas Boyd, 1980-81, linebacker
Buddy Brown, 1973, offensive tackle
Jim Bunch, 1979, offensive tackle
Johnny Cain, 1931-32, fullback/punter
Jeremiah Castille, 1982, cornerback
Richard Cole, 1996, defensive tackle
Leroy Cook, 1974-75, defensive end
John Copeland, 1992, defensive end
Carey Cox, 1939, center
Paul Crane, 1965, center
Sylvester Croom, 1974, center
Eric Curry, 1992, defensive end
Joe Domnanovich, 1942, center
Cecil Dowdy, 1966, offensive tackle
Phillip Doyle, 1990, kicker
Wayne Freeman, 1964, offensive guard
Sam Gallerstedt, 1968, nose guard
Harry Gilmer, 1945, halfback
Mike Hall, 1968, linebacker
Jon Hand, 1985, defensive tackle
John Hannah, 1972, offensive guard
Tony Holm, 1929, fullback
Dennis Homan, 1967, split end
Millard "Dixie" Howell, 1934, quarterback
A.T.S. "Pooley" Hubert, 1925, quarterback
Bobby Humphrey, 1986-87, tailback
Tom Hupke, 1933, offensive guard
Don Hutson, 1934, split end
Kevin Jackson, 1996, safety
Bobby Johns, 1966-67, defensive back
Lee Roy Jordan, 1962, linebacker
E.J. Junior, 1980, defensive end
Dan Kearley, 1964, defensive tackle
Kermit Kendrick, 1988, defensive back
Joe Kilgrow, 1937, halfback
Jim Krapf, 1972, center
Barry Krauss, 1978, linebacker
Antonio Langham, 1992-93, cornerback
Bill Lee, 1934, defensive tackle
Woodrow Lowe, 1973-75, linebacker
Marty Lyons, 1978, defensive tackle
Keith McCants, 1989, linebacker
Don McNeal, 1979, cornerback
Vaughn Mancha, 1945, center
John Mangum, 1989, cornerback
Bobby Marlow, 1952, halfback
George Mason, 1954, offensive tackle
John Mitchell, 1972, defensive end
Leroy Monsky, 1937, offensive guard

Johnny Musso, 1970-71, halfback
Michael Myers, 1996, defensive end
Joe Namath, 1964, quarterback
Billy Neighbors, 1961, offensive tackle
James "Bubber" Nesbit, 1936, fullback
Ozzie Newsome, 1977, split end
David Palmer, 1993, flanker
Ray Perkins, 1966, split end
Fred Pickhard, 1926, offensive tackle
Mike Pitts, 1982, defensive end
Michael Proctor, 1993-94, kicker
Holt Rast, 1941, defensive end
David Ray, 1964, kicker
Larry Rose, 1988, offensive guard
Dwayne Rudd, 1996, linebacker
James Ryba, 1937, defensive tackle
Ed Salem, 1950, halfback
Alvin Samples, 1969, offensive guard
Chris Samuels, 1999, offensive tackle
Fred Sington, 1929-30, offensive tackle
Steve Sloan, 1965, quarterback
Riley Smith, 1935, quarterback
Kenny Stabler, 1967, quarterback
Dwight Stephenson, 1979, center
Robert Stewart, 1991, nose tackle
John Henry Suther, 1930, halfback
Derrick Thomas, 1988, linebacker
Van Tiffin, 1986, kicker
W.T. "Bully" VandeGraaff, 1915, offensive tackle
Mike Washington, 1974, cornerback
Wayne Wheeler, 1973, split end
Arthur "Tarzan" White, 1936, offensive guard
Don Whitmire, 1942, offensive tackle
Tommy Wilcox, 1981-82, safety
Hoyt "Wu" Winslett, 1926, defensive end

Academic All-Americans
1961   Tommy Brooker, end
          Pat Trammell, quarterback
1964   Gaylon McCollough, center
1965   Dennis Homan, end
          Steve Sloan, quarterback
1967   Bob Childs, linebacker
          Steve Davis, kicker
1970   Johnny Musso, tailback
1971   Johnny Musso, tailback
1973   Randy Hall, defensive tackle
1974   Randy Hall, defensive tackle
1975   Danny Ridgeway, kicker
1979   Major Ogilvie, halfback
2002   Kenny King, defensive tackle

Alabama's All-Century Team (selected by fans)
Offense
E: Don Hutson, 1932-1934
E: Ozzie Newsome, 1974-77

L: Fred Sington, 1928-30
L: Vaughn Mancha, 1944-47
C: Dwight Stephenson, 1977-79
L: Billy Neighbors, 1959-61
L: John Hannah, 1970-72
QB: Joe Namath, 1962-64
QB: Ken Stabler, 1965-67
RB: Bobby Marlow, 1950-52
RB: Johnny Musso, 1969-71
RB: Bobby Humphrey, 1985-88
K: Van Tiffin, 1983-86

Defense
L: Bob Baumhower, 1973, 1976
L: Marty Lyons, 1975-78
L: Jon Hand, 1982-85
LB: Lee Roy Jordan, 1960-62
LB: Barry Kraus, 1976-78
OLB: Cornelius Bennett, 1983-86
OLB: Derrick Thomas, 1985-88
DB: Harry Gilmer, 1944-47
DB: Don McNeal, 1977-79
DB: Jeremiah Castille, 1979-82
DB: Tommy Wilcox, 1979-82
P: Johnny Cain, 1930-32
Coach: Paul W. "Bear" Bryant

NCAA All-Century Team (by Sports Illustrated)
First team (starters)
G: John Hannah, 1970-72
WR: Don Hutson, 1932-34
LB: Lee Roy Jordan, 1960-62
Coach: Paul W. "Bear" Bryant
Second team (backup)
Dwight Stephenson, 1977-79

Unofficial All-Name Team (Selected by the Author)
E: Hoyt "Wu" Winslett, 1924-26
E: G.H. "Hub" Kyser, 1893
L: C.B. "Foots" Clement, 1928-30
L: Calhoun "Sunbeam" Saul, 1916
L: Ken "Tank" Mitchell, 1964
L: James "Goofy" Bowdoin, 1927-28
L: Arthur P. "Tarzan" White, 1934-36
QB: Ken "Snake" Stabler, 1965-67
QB: Laurien "Goobie" Strapp, 1958-60
RB: John "Hurry" Cain, 1930-32
RB: Margan Oslin "Major" Ogilvie, 1977-80
FB: A.T.S. "Pooley" Hubert, 1922-25
K: Fred Benjamin "Bucky" Berrey, 1974-6
U: Alvin "Pig" Davis, 1937-38

Defense
L: Nautyn McKay-Loescher, 2001-03
L: John "Brownie" Sides, 1966-67
L: Allen "Bunk" Harpole, 1965-67

L: W.T. "Bully" Vandegraaff, 1912-15
L/LB: Haywood Eugene "Butch" Norman, 1973
LB: Canary Knight, 1998-99
LB: Woodward A. "Woodie" Husband, 1969-70
DB: Cecil "Hootie" Ingram, 1952-54
DB: Frank "Chesty" Moseley, 1931-33
DB: William "Brother" Oliver, 1960-61
DB: Edward McGruder Tutwiler, 1898
P: Woody Umphrey, 1978-80
Coach: Paul W. "Bear" Bryant, 1958-82
Assistant coach: Tillden "Happy" Campbell, 1935-42, 1947-55
Honorary: President John F. Kennedy, 1961

All-Time Assistant Coaches (through 2004)

Jody Allen (Catawba) 1986; Bruce Arians (Virginia Tech), 1981-82, 1997; Butch Avinger (Alabama), 1954-55;

Sam Bailey (Ouachita) 1958-59; Chris Ball (Missouri Western State), 2003-04; Jim Blevins (Alabama) 1962-63; Lew Bostick (Alabama) 1942, 1944, 1946-57; Tommy Bowden (West Virginia) 1987-89; Charley Bradshaw (Kentucky) 1959-61; Paul W. "Bear" Bryant (Alabama) 1936-39; Paul Burnum (Alabama) 1930-42;

Neil Callaway (Alabama) 1997-2000; Louis Campbell (Arkansas) 1975-76, 1980-84; Tilden "Happy" Campbell, 1935-42, 1947-55; LeBaron Caruthers (North Carolina State) 1990-96; Ron Case (Carson-Newman) 2001; Pete Cawthon (Southwestern University) 1942; Andy Christoff (Idaho) 1987-89; Jerry Claiborne (Kentucky) 1958-60; Russell Cohen 1923-27; Bob Connelly (Texas A&M-Commerce) 2003-04; Ronnie Cottrell (Troy State) 1998-2000; Paul Crane (Alabama) 1974-77; Hank Crisp (VPI) 1941-42, 1950-57; Sylvester Croom (Alabama) 1976-86; John David Crow (Texas A&M) 1969-71; Don Cochran (Alabama) 1960; Phil Cutchin (Kentucky) 1958-62);

Paul Davis (Ole Miss) 1981-82; Ken Donahue (Tennessee) 1964-82; Red Drew (Bates) 1931-41, 1945; Mike DuBose (Alabama) 1983-86, 1990-96; Pat Dye (Georgia) 1965-63;

Stan Eggen (Moorehead State) 2001-02; Ben Enis (Alabama) 1965-73;

Rocky Felker (Mississippi State) 1983-85; Jeff Fitzgerald (Cal State) 1987-89; Jack Fligg (Oglethorpe) 1987-89; Lee Fobbs (Grambling) 2001-02; Bob Ford (Memphis State) 1959-60; Danny Ford (Alabama) 1972-73; Jess Foshee (Alabama) 1942; Jimmy Fuller (Alabama) 1984-96;

Ralph Genito (Kentucky) 1965; Dorsey Gibson (Oklahoma State) 1956-57; Tom Goode (Mississippi State) 1983; Jim Goostree (Tennessee) 1957-83; Clem Gryska (Alabama) 1960-76; John Guy (North Carolina A&T) 1987-89;

Steve Hale (East Carolina) 1982-86; Curley Hallman (Texas A&M) 1973-76, 1996-97; Charlie Harbison (Gardner Webb) 1998-2000, 2003-04; Jim Bob Helduser (Texas Lutheran) 2001-02; Dude Hennessey (Kentucky) 1960-76; George Henshaw (West Virginia) 1983-86; Dixie Howell (Alabama) 1946;

Rob Ianello (Catholic) 1987-89;

Pat James (Kentucky) 1958-64; Ellis Johnson (Citadel) 1990-93, 1997-2000; Howard Johnson (Georgia) 1955-57; Kent Johnston (Stephen F. Austin) 1985-86; 2004; Amos Jones (Alabama) 1990-91; Terry Jones (Alabama) 1988-2004;

Bobby Keith (Texas A&M) 1958-59; Elwood Kettler (Texas A&M) 1960; Joe Kilgrow (Alabama) 1938-39, 1946-57; Al Kincaid (Virginia Tech) 1974-75, 1989; Joe Kines (Jacksonville State) 1985-86, 2003-04; Larry Kirksey (Eastern Kentucky) 1990-93; Les Koenning Jr. (Texas) 2001-02;

Malcolm Laney (Alabama) 1944-57; Carney Leslie (Alabama) 1932, 1958-69; K.J. Lazenby (Alabama) 1979-80; Murray Legg (Alabama) 1981-82; Walter Lewis (Alabama) 1989; Tom Lieb (Notre Dame) 1946-50; Don Lindsey (Arkansas A&M) 1987-89; Bobby Luna (Alabama) 1958;

Bobby Marks (Texas A&M) 1972-82; Mike Marks (Oklahoma State) 1977-82; Ken Martin (Alabama) 1971-74; Woody McCorvey (Alabama State) 1990-96; Mac McWhorter (Georgia) 1987-88; Ken Meyer (Dennison) 1963-67; Al Miller (NE Louisiana) 1982-84; John Mitchell (Alabama) 1973-77; Bud Moore (Alabama) 1972-74; Mal Moore (Alabama) 1964-82, 1990-93;

Jess Nelly (Vanderbilt) 1928-30; Larry New (Illinois) 1987-89; James Nisbet (Alabama) 1949-55; Charley North (Panhandle State) 2001-02;

Bill Oliver (Alabama) 1971-79, 1990-95;

Julius Papais (Alabama) 1942; Charley Pell (Alabama) 1963; Danny Pearman (Clemson) 1992-97; Ben Pollard (Texas Tech) 2001-03; Bryant Pool (East Texas State) 1997-82; Barney Poole (Ole Miss) 1956-57; Kenith Pope (Oklahoma) 2001-02; Dee Powell (Texas A&M) 1958, 1964-82; Jerry Pullen (Livingston) 1986;

Dave Rader (Tulsa) 1983-86, 2003-04; Paul Randolph (Tennessee-Martin) 2003-04; Rick Rhoades (Central Missouri) 1989; Charley Richards (Livingston) 1966-67; Hayden Riley (Alabama) 1958-69; Tom Rogers (Delta State) 1966-70; Randy Ross (St. Bernard) 1990-98, 2002-04; Jeff Rouzie (Alabama) 1976-81; 1991-2000; Jack Rutledge (Alabama) 1968-82;

Rip Scherer (Penn State) 1987; Howard Schnellenberger (Kentucky) 1961-65; Jimmy Sharpe (Alabama) 1963-73; Jackie Shipp (Langstone) 1998; Steve Sloan (Alabama) 1968-70; Homer Smith (Princeton) 1988-89, 1994; Melvin Smith (Millsaps) 2001-02; Rick Smith (Florida State) 1986; Mike Solari (San Diego State) 1990-91; Gene Stallings (Texas A&M) 1958-64; Rodney Stokes (Delta State) 1984-86; Charlie Stubbs (BYU) 1998-2000; Dabo Swinney (Alabama) 1996-2000;

Joe Thomas (Oklahoma State) 1955-57; Lance Thompson (The Citadel) 1999-2000; John Thompson (Central Arkansas) 1987; Chris Thurmond (Tulsa) 2001-02; Mark Tommerdahl (Concordia) 2001-02; Carl Torbush (Carson-Newman) 2001-02; Bob Tyler (Ole Miss) 1971;

Dave Ungerer (Southern Connecticut State) 2003-04;

Lance Van Zandt (Lamar) 1990;

Steve Walters (Arkansas) 1985; Shorty White (Jacksonville State) 1975-80; Ivy Williams (Xavier) 1994-2000; Richard Williamson (Alabama) 1964-71; Perry Willis (Alabama) 1978-80; Rich Wingo (Alabama) 1987-88; Chip Wisdom (Georgia) 1987-88; Sparky Woods (Carson-Newman) 2003-04; Buddy Wyatt (TCU) 2003-04.

Appendix E: All-Time Results

Coach E.B. Beaumont (Penn, 2-2)
1892 (2-2)

Nov. 11	Birmingham H.S.	Birmingham	56-0
Nov. 12	Birmingham A.C.	Birmingham	4-5
Dec. 10	Birmingham A.C.	Birmingham	14-0
Feb. 22, 1893	Auburn	Birmingham	22-32
Captain: William G. Little			96-37

Coach Eli Abbott (Penn, 7-13)
1893 (0-4)

Oct. 14	Birmingham A.C.	Tuscaloosa	0-4
Nov. 4	Birmingham A.C.	Birmingham	8-10
Nov. 11	Sewanee	Birmingham	0-20
Nov. 30	Auburn	Montgomery	16-40
Captains: G.H. Kyser, William Walker			24-74

1894 (3-1)

Oct. 27	Mississippi	Jackson	0-6
Nov. 3	Tulane	New Orleans	18-6
Nov. 15	Sewanee	Birmingham	24-4
Nov. 29	Auburn	Montgomery	18-0
Captain: Samuel Byron Slone			60-16

1895 (0-4)

Nov. 2	Georgia	Columbus, Ga.	6-30
Nov. 16	Tulane	New Orleans	0-22
Nov. 18	LSU	Baton Rouge	6-12
Nov. 23	Auburn	Tuscaloosa	0-48
Captain: M.H. Bankhead			12-112

Coach Otto Wagonhurst (Penn, 2-1)
1896 (2-1)

Oct. 24	Birmingham A.C.	Tuscaloosa	30-0
Oct. 31	Sewanee	Tuscaloosa	6-10
Nov. 14	Mississippi State	Tuscaloosa	20-0
Captain: Samuel Byron Slone			56-10

Coach Allen McCants (Alabama, 1-0)
1897 (1-0)

Nov. 13	Tuscaloosa A.C.	Tuscaloosa	6-0
Captain: Frank S. White Jr.			6-0

1898 (no team)

Captain: T.G. Burk

W. A. Martin (Virginia, 3-1)
1899 (3-1)

Oct. 21	Tuscaloosa A.C.	Tuscaloosa	16-5
Nov. 11	Montgomery A.C.	Tuscaloosa	16-0
Nov. 24	Mississippi	Jackson	7-5
Nov. 25	New Orleans A.C.	New Orleans	0-21
Captain: Thomas William Wert			39-31

M. Griffin (2-3)
1900 (2-3)

Oct. 21	Taylor School	Tuscaloosa	35-0
Oct. 26	Mississippi	Tuscaloosa	12-5
Nov. 3	Tulane	Tuscaloosa	0-6
Nov. 17	Auburn	Montgomery	5-53
Nov. 29	Clemson	Birmingham	0-35
Captain: Earl Drennen			52-99

M.S. Harvey (Auburn, 2-1-2)
1901 (2-1-2)

Oct. 19	Mississippi	Tuscaloosa	41-0
Nov. 9	Georgia	Montgomery	0-0
Nov. 15	Auburn	Tuscaloosa	0-17
Nov. 16	Mississippi State	Tuscaloosa	45-0
Nov. 28	Tennessee	Birmingham	6-6
Captain: Earl Drennen			92-23

Eli Abbott and James Hayworth (Yale)
1902 (4-4)

Oct. 10	Birmingham H.S.	Tuscaloosa	57-0
Oct. 13	Marion Institute	Tuscaloosa	81-0
Oct. 18	Auburn	Birmingham	0-23
Nov. 1	Georgia	Birmingham	0-5
Nov. 8	Mississippi State	Tuscaloosa	27-0
Nov. 11	Texas	Tuscaloosa	0-10
Nov. 27	Georgia Tech	Birmingham	26-0
Nov. 29	LSU	Tuscaloosa	0-11
Captain: James R. Forman			191-49

W.B. Blount (Yale, 10-7)
1903 (3-4)

Oct. 10	Vanderbilt	Nashville	0-30
Oct. 16	Mississippi State	Columbus, Miss.	0-11
Oct. 23	Auburn	Montgomery	18-6
Nov. 2	Sewanee	Birmingham	0-23
Nov. 9	LSU	Tuscaloosa	18-0
Nov. 14	Cumberland U.	Tuscaloosa	0-44
Nov. 26	Tennessee	Birmingham	24-0
Captain: W.S. Wyatt			60-114

1904 (7-3)

Oct. 3	Florida	Tuscaloosa	29-0
Oct. 8	Clemson	Birmingham	0-18
Oct. 15	Mississippi State	Columbus, Miss.	6-0
Oct. 24	Nashville U.	Tuscaloosa	17-0
Nov. 5	Georgia	Tuscaloosa	16-5
Nov. 12	Auburn	Birmingham	5-29
Nov. 24	Tennessee	Birmingham	0-5
Dec. 2	LSU	Baton Rouge	11-0
Dec. 3	Tulane	New Orleans	6-0
Dec. 4	Pensacola A.C.	Pensacola, Fla.	10-5
Captain: W.S. Wyatt			100-62

Jack Leavenworth (Yale, 6-4)
1905 (6-4)

Oct. 3	Maryville	Tuscaloosa	17-0
Oct. 7	Vanderbilt	Nashville	0-34
Oct. 14	Mississippi State	Tuscaloosa	34-0
Oct. 21	Georgia Tech	Atlanta	5-12
Oct. 25	Clemson	Columbia, S.C.	0-25
Nov. 4	Georgia	Birmingham	36-0
Nov. 9	Centre	Tuscaloosa	21-0
Nov. 18	Auburn	Birmingham	30-0
Nov. 23	Sewanee	Birmingham	6-42
Nov. 30	Tennessee	Birmingham	29-0
Captain: Auxford Burks			178-113

J.W.H. "Doc" Pollard (Dartmouth, 21-4-5)
1906 (5-1)

Oct. 6	Maryville	Tuscaloosa	6-0
Oct. 13	Howard	Tuscaloosa	14-0
Oct. 20	Vanderbilt	Nashville	0-78
Nov. 3	Mississippi State	Starkville	16-4
Nov. 17	Auburn	Birmingham	10-0
Nov. 29	Tennessee	Birmingham	51-0
Captain: Washington Moody			97-82

1907 (5-1-2)

Oct. 5	Maryville	Tuscaloosa	17-0
Oct. 12	Mississippi	Columbus, Miss.	20-0
Oct. 21	Sewanee	Tuscaloosa	4-54
Oct. 25	Georgia	Montgomery	0-0
Nov. 2	Centre	Birmingham	12-0
Nov. 16	Auburn	Birmingham	6-6
Nov. 23	LSU	Mobile	6-4
Nov. 28	Tennessee	Birmingham	5-0
Captain: Emile Hannon			70-64

1908 (6-1-1)

Oct. 3	Wetumpka	Tuscaloosa	27-0
Oct. 10	Howard	Birmingham	17-0
Oct. 17	Cincinnati	Birmingham	16-0
Oct. 24	Georgia Tech	Atlanta	6-11
Oct. 31	Chattanooga	Tuscaloosa	23-6
Nov. 14	Georgia	Birmingham	6-6
Nov. 20	Haskell Institute	Tuscaloosa	9-8
Nov. 26	Tennessee	Birmingham	4-0
Captain: Henry Burks			108-31

1909 (5-1-2)

Oct. 2	Union	Tuscaloosa	16-0
Oct. 9	Howard	Tuscaloosa	14-0
Oct. 16	Clemson	Birmingham	3-0
Oct. 23	Mississippi	Jackson	0-0
Oct. 30	Georgia	Atlanta	14-0
Nov. 13	Tennessee	Knoxville	10-0
Nov. 20	Tulane	New Orleans	5-5
Nov. 25	LSU	Birmingham	6-12
Captain: Derrill Pratt			68-17

Guy Lowman (Springfield, 4-4)
1910 (4-4)

Oct. 1	Birmingham Southern	Tuscaloosa	25-0
Oct. 8	Marion Institute	Tuscaloosa	26-0
Oct. 15	Georgia	Birmingham	0-22
Oct. 22	Georgia Tech	Tuscaloosa	0-36
Nov. 5	Mississippi	Greenville, Miss.	0-16
Nov. 12	Sewanee	Birmingham	0-30
Nov. 19	Tulane	New Orleans	5-3
Nov. 24	Washington & Lee	Birmingham	9-0
Captain: Owen Garside Gresham			65-107

D.V. Graves (Missouri, 21-12-3)
1911 (5-2-2)

Sept. 30	Howard	Tuscaloosa	24-0
Oct. 7	Georgia	Birmingham	3-11
Oct. 14	Birmingham Southern	Birmingham	47-5
Oct. 21	Mississippi State	Columbus, Miss.	6-6
Oct. 29	Georgia Tech	Atlanta	0-0
Nov. 4	Marion Institute	Marion	35-0
Nov. 11	Sewanee	Tuscaloosa	0-3
Nov. 18	Tulane	Tuscaloosa	22-0
Nov. 30	Davidson	Birmingham	16-6
Captain: R.H. Burmgardner			153-31

1912 (5-3-1)

Sept. 28	Marion Institute	Tuscaloosa	25-0
Oct. 5	Birmingham Southern	Tuscaloosa	62-0
Oct. 12	Georgia Tech	Atlanta	3-20
Oct. 18	Mississippi State	Aberdeen, Miss.	0-7
Oct. 26	Georgia	Columbus, Ga.	9-13
Nov. 2	Tulane	New Orleans	7-0
Nov. 9	Mississippi	Tuscaloosa	10-9
Nov. 16	Sewanee	Birmingham	6-6
Nov. 28	Tennessee	Birmingham	7-0
Captain: Farley W. Moody			156-55

1913 (6-3)

Sept. 27	Howard	Tuscaloosa	27-0
Oct. 4	Birmingham Southern	Tuscaloosa	81-0
Oct. 11	Clemson	Tuscaloosa	20-0
Oct. 18	Georgia	Birmingham	0-20
Oct. 25	Tulane	New Orleans	26-0
Nov. 1	Mississippi College	Jackson	21-3
Nov. 9	Sewanee	Birmingham	7-10
Nov. 14	Tennessee	Tuscaloosa	6-0
Nov. 27	Mississippi State	Birmingham	0-7
Captain: C.H. VandeGraaff			188-40

1914 (5-4)

Oct. 3	Howard	Tuscaloosa	13-0
Oct. 10	Birmingham Southern	Tuscaloosa	54-0
Oct. 17	Georgia Tech	Birmingham	13-0
Oct. 24	Tennessee	Knoxville	7-17
Oct. 31	Tulane	Tuscaloosa	58-0
Nov. 7	Sewanee	Birmingham	0-18
Nov. 13	Chattanooga	Tuscaloosa	63-0
Nov. 26	Mississippi State	Birmingham	0-9
Dec. 2	Carlisle	Birmingham	3-20
Captain: Charles Allen "Tubby" Long			211-64

Thomas Kelley (Chicago, 17-7-1)
1915 (6-2)

Oct. 2	Howard	Tuscaloosa	44-0
Oct. 9	Birmingham Southern	Tuscaloosa	67-0
Oct. 16	Mississippi College	Tuscaloosa	40-0
Oct. 23	Tulane	Tuscaloosa	16-0
Oct. 30	Sewanee	Birmingham	23-10
Nov. 6	Georgia Tech	Atlanta	7-21
Nov. 13	Texas	Austin	0-20
Nov. 25	Mississippi	Birmingham	53-0
Captain: William L. Harsh			250-51

1916 (6-3)

Sept. 30	Birmingham Southern	Tuscaloosa	13-0
Oct. 7	Southern University	Tuscaloosa	80-0
Oct. 14	Mississippi College	Tuscaloosa	13-7
Oct. 21	Florida	Jacksonville	16-0
Oct. 28	Mississippi	Tuscaloosa	27-0
Nov. 4	Sewanee	Birmingham	7-6
Nov. 11	Georgia Tech	Atlanta	0-13
Nov. 18	Tulane	New Orleans	0-33
Nov. 30	Georgia	Birmingham	0-3
Captain: Lowndes Morton			156-62

1917 (5-2-1)

Oct. 3	Ohio Amer. Corp.	Montgomery	7-0
Oct. 12	Marion Institute	Tuscaloosa	13-0
Oct. 20	Mississippi College	Tuscaloosa	46-0
Oct. 26	Mississippi	Tuscaloosa	64-0
Nov. 3	Sewanee	Birmingham	3-3
Nov. 10	Vanderbilt	Birmingham	2-7
Nov. 17	Kentucky	Lexington	27-0
Nov. 29	Camp Gordon	Birmingham	6-19
Captain: Jack Hovater			168-29

1918 (no team)

Captain: Dan Boone

Xen Scott (Western Reserve, 29-9-3)
1919 (8-1)

Oct. 4	Birmingham Southern	Tuscaloosa	27-0
Oct. 11	Mississippi	Tuscaloosa	49-0
Oct. 18	Howard	Tuscaloosa	48-0
Oct. 24	Marion Institute	Tuscaloosa	61-0
Nov. 1	Sewanee	Birmingham	40-0
Nov. 8	Vanderbilt	Nashville	12-16
Nov. 15	LSU	Baton Rouge	23-0
Nov. 22	Georgia	Atlanta	6-0
Nov. 27	Mississippi State	Birmingham	14-6
Captain: Isaac J. Rogers			280-22

1920 (10-1)

Sept. 25	Southern Military Acad.	Tuscaloosa	59-0
Oct. 2	Marion Institute	Tuscaloosa	49-0
Oct. 9	Birmingham Southern	Tuscaloosa	45-0
Oct. 16	Mississippi College	Tuscaloosa	57-0

Oct. 23	Howard	Tuscaloosa	33-0
Oct. 30	Sewanee	Birmingham	21-0
Nov. 6	Vanderbilt	Birmingham	14-7
Nov. 11	LSU	Tuscaloosa	21-0
Nov. 20	Georgia	Atlanta	14-21
Nov. 25	Mississippi State	Birmingham	24-7
Nov. 27	Case College	Cleveland	40-0
Captain: Sid Johnston			377-35

1921 (5-4-2)

Sept. 24	Howard	Tuscaloosa	34-14
Oct. 1	Spring Hill	Tuscaloosa	27-7
Oct. 8	Marion Institute	Tuscaloosa	55-0
Oct. 15	Bryson (Tenn.)	Tuscaloosa	95-0
Oct. 22	Sewanee	Birmingham	0-17
Oct. 29	LSU	New Orleans	7-7
Nov. 5	Vanderbilt	Birmingham	0-14
Nov. 11	Florida	Tuscaloosa	2-9
Nov. 19	Georgia	Atlanta	0-22
Nov. 24	Mississippi State	Birmingham	7-7
Dec. 3	Tulane	New Orleans	14-7
Captain: Al Clemens			241-104

1922 (6-3-1)

Sept. 30	Marion Institute	Tuscaloosa	110-0
Oct. 7	Oglethorpe	Tuscaloosa	41-0
Oct. 14	Georgia Tech	Atlanta	7-33
Oct. 21	Sewanee	Birmingham	7-7
Oct. 28	Texas	Austin	10-19
Nov. 4	Pennsylvania	Philadelphia	9-7
Nov. 10	LSU	Tuscaloosa	47-3
Nov. 18	Kentucky	Lexington	0-6
Nov. 25	Georgia	Montgomery	10-6
Nov. 30	Mississippi State	Birmingham	59-0
Captain: Ernest E. Cooper			300-81

Wallace Wade (Brown, 61-13-3)
1923 (6-2-1)

Sept. 29	Union	Tuscaloosa	12-0
Oct. 6	Mississippi	Tuscaloosa	56-0
Oct. 13	Syracuse	Syracuse	0-23
Oct. 20	Sewanee	Birmingham	7-0
Oct. 27	Spring Hill	Mobile	56-0
Nov. 3	Georgia Tech	Atlanta	0-0
Nov. 10	Kentucky	Tuscaloosa	16-8
Nov. 16	LSU	Montgomery	30-3
Nov. 24	Georgia	Montgomery	36-0
Nov. 29	Florida	Birmingham	6-16
Captain: Al Clemons			222-50

1924 (8-1, Southern Conference champion)

Sept. 27	Union	Tuscaloosa	55-0
Oct. 4	Furman	Greenville, S.C.	20-0
Oct. 11	Mississippi College	Tuscaloosa	55-0
Oct. 18	Sewanee	Birmingham	14-0
Oct. 25	Georgia Tech	Atlanta	14-0
Nov. 1	Mississippi	Montgomery	61-0
Nov. 8	Kentucky	Tuscaloosa	42-7
Nov. 15	Centre College	Birmingham	0-17
Nov. 27	Georgia	Birmingham	33-0
Captain: A.T.S. Hubert			294-24

1925 (10-0, national champions, Southern Conference champions)

Sept. 26	Union College	Tuscaloosa	53-0
Oct. 2	Birmingham Southern	Tuscaloosa	50-7
Oct. 10	LSU	Baton Rouge	42-0
Oct. 17	Sewanee	Birmingham	27-0
Oct. 24	Georgia Tech	Atlanta	7-0
Oct. 31	Mississippi State	Tuscaloosa	6-0
Nov. 7	Kentucky	Birmingham	31-0
Nov. 14	Florida	Montgomery	34-0
Nov. 26	Georgia	Birmingham	27-0
Jan. 1, 1926	Washington	Rose Bowl	20-19
Captain: Bruce Jones			297-26

1926 (9-0-1, national champions, Southern Conference champions)

Sept. 24	Millsaps	Tuscaloosa	54-0
Oct. 2	Vanderbilt	Nashville	19-7
Oct. 9	Mississippi State	Meridian	26-7
Oct. 16	Georgia Tech	Atlanta	21-0
Oct. 23	Sewanee	Birmingham	2-0
Oct. 30	LSU	Tuscaloosa	24-0
Nov. 6	Kentucky	Birmingham	14-0
Nov. 13	Florida	Montgomery	49-0
Nov. 25	Georgia	Birmingham	33-6
Jan. 1, 1927	Stanford	Rose Bowl	7-7
Captain: Emile "Red" Barnes			249-27

1927 (5-4-1)

Sept. 24	Millsaps	Tuscaloosa	46-0
Sept. 30	So. Presbyterian U.	Tuscaloosa	31-0
Oct. 8	LSU	Birmingham	0-0
Oct. 15	Georgia Tech	Atlanta	0-13
Oct. 22	Sewanee	Birmingham	24-0
Oct. 29	Mississippi State	Tuscaloosa	13-7
Nov. 5	Kentucky	Birmingham	21-6
Nov. 12	Florida	Montgomery	6-13
Nov. 27	Georgia	Birmingham	6-20
Dec. 3	Vanderbilt	Birmingham	7-14
Captain: Freddie Pickhard			154-73

1928 (6-3)

Oct. 6	Mississippi	Tuscaloosa	27-0
Oct. 13	Mississippi State	Starkville	46-0
Oct. 20	Tennessee	Tuscaloosa	13-15
Oct. 27	Sewanee	Birmingham	42-12
Nov. 3	Wisconsin	Madison	0-15
Nov. 10	Kentucky	Montgomery	14-0
Nov. 17	Georgia Tech	Atlanta	13-33
Nov. 29	Georgia	Birmingham	19-0
Dec. 8	LSU	Birmingham	13-0
Captain: Earle Smith			187-75

1929 (6-3)

Sept. 28	Mississippi College	Tuscaloosa	55-0
Oct. 5	Mississippi	Tuscaloosa	22-7
Oct. 12	Chattanooga	Tuscaloosa	46-0
Oct. 19	Tennessee	Knoxville	0-6

Oct. 26	Sewanee	Birmingham	35-7
Nov. 2	Vanderbilt	Nashville	0-13
Nov. 9	Kentucky	Montgomery	24-13
Nov. 16	Georgia Tech	Atlanta	13-0
Nov. 28	Georgia	Birmingham	0-12
Captain: Billy Hicks			196-58

1930 (10-0, national champions, Southern Conference champions)

Sept. 27	Howard	Tuscaloosa	43-0
Oct. 4	Mississippi	Tuscaloosa	64-0
Oct. 11	Sewanee	Birmingham	25-0
Oct. 18	Tennessee	Tuscaloosa	18-6
Oct. 25	Vanderbilt	Birmingham	12-7
Nov. 1	Kentucky	Lexington	19-0
Nov. 8	Florida	Gainesville	20-0
Nov. 15	LSU	Montgomery	33-0
Nov. 27	Georgia	Birmingham	13-0
Jan. 1, 1931	Washington State	Rose Bowl	24-0
Captain: Charles B. Clement			271-13

Coach Frank Thomas (Notre Dame, 115-24-7)
1931 (9-1)

Sept. 26	Howard	Tuscaloosa	42-0
Oct. 3	Mississippi	Tuscaloosa	55-6
Oct. 10	Mississippi State	Meridian	53-0
Oct. 17	Tennessee	Knoxville	0-25
Oct. 24	Sewanee	Birmingham	33-0
Oct. 31	Kentucky	Tuscaloosa	9-7
Nov. 7	Florida	Birmingham	41-0
Nov. 14	Clemson	Montgomery	74-7
Nov. 26	Vanderbilt	Nashville	14-6
Dec. 2	Chattanooga	Chattanooga	39-0
Captain: Joe Sharpe			360-51

1932 (8-2)

Sept. 24	Southwestern	Tuscaloosa	45-6
Oct. 1	Mississippi State	Montgomery	53-0
Oct. 8	George Washington	Washington, D.C.	28-6
Oct. 15	Tennessee	Birmingham	3-7
Oct. 22	Mississippi	Tuscaloosa	24-13
Oct. 29	Kentucky	Lexington	12-7
Nov. 5	Virginia Tech	Tuscaloosa	9-6
Nov. 12	Georgia Tech	Atlanta	0-6
Nov. 24	Vanderbilt	Birmingham	20-0
Dec. 3	St. Mary's	San Francisco	6-0
Captain: John Cain			200-51

1933 (7-1-1)

Sept. 30	Oglethorpe	Tuscaloosa	34-0
Oct. 7	Mississippi	Birmingham	0-0
Oct. 14	Mississippi State	Tuscaloosa	18-0
Oct. 21	Tennessee	Knoxville	12-6
Oct. 28	Fordham	New York	0-2
Nov. 4	Kentucky	Birmingham	20-0
Nov. 11	Virginia Tech	Tuscaloosa	27-0
Nov. 18	Georgia Tech	Atlanta	12-9
Nov. 30	Vanderbilt	Nashville	7-0
Captain: Foy Leach			130-17

1934 (10-0, national champions, SEC champions)

Sept. 29	Howard	Tuscaloosa	24-0
Oct. 5	Sewanee	Montgomery	35-6
Oct. 13	Mississippi State	Tuscaloosa	41-0
Oct. 20	Tennessee	Birmingham	13-6
Oct. 27	Georgia	Birmingham	26-6
Nov. 3	Kentucky	Lexington	34-14
Nov. 10	Clemson	Tuscaloosa	40-0
Nov. 17	Georgia Tech	Atlanta	40-0
Nov. 29	Vanderbilt	Birmingham	34-0
Jan. 1, 1935	Stanford	Rose Bowl	29-13
Captain: Bill Lee			316-45

1935 (6-2-1)

Sept. 28	Howard	Tuscaloosa	7-7
Oct. 5	George Washington	Washington, D.C.	39-0
Oct. 12	Mississippi State	Tuscaloosa	7-20
Oct. 19	Tennessee	Knoxville	25-0
Oct. 26	Georgia	Athens	17-7
Nov. 2	Kentucky	Birmingham	13-0
Nov. 9	Clemson	Tuscaloosa	33-0
Nov. 16	Georgia Tech	Birmingham	38-7
Nov. 28	Vanderbilt	Nashville	6-14
Captain: James Walker			185-55

1936 (8-0-1)

Sept. 26	Howard	Tuscaloosa	34-0
Oct. 3	Clemson	Tuscaloosa	32-0
Oct. 10	Mississippi State	Tuscaloosa	7-0
Oct. 17	Tennessee	Birmingham	0-0
Oct. 24	Loyola (N.O.)	New Orleans	13-6
Oct. 31	Kentucky	Lexington	14-0
Nov. 7	Tulane	Birmingham	34-7
Nov. 14	Georgia Tech	Atlanta	20-16
Nov. 25	Vanderbilt	Birmingham	14-6
Captain: James "Bubber" Nisbet			168-35

1937 (9-1, SEC champions)

Sept. 25	Howard	Tuscaloosa	41-0
Oct. 2	Sewanee	Birmingham	65-0
Oct. 9	South Carolina	Tuscaloosa	20-0
Oct. 16	Tennessee	Knoxville	14-7
Oct. 23	George Washington	Washington, D.C.	19-0
Oct. 30	Kentucky	Tuscaloosa	41-0
Nov. 6	Tulane	New Orleans	9-6
Nov. 13	Georgia Tech	Birmingham	7-0
Nov. 25	Vanderbilt	Nashville	9-7
Jan. 1, 1938	California	Rose Bowl	0-13
Captain: Leroy Monsky			225-33

1938 (7-1-1)

Sept. 24	Southern Cal	Los Angeles	19-7
Oct. 1	Howard	Tuscaloosa	34-0
Oct. 8	North Carolina State	Tuscaloosa	14-0
Oct. 15	Tennessee	Birmingham	0-13
Oct. 22	Sewanee	Tuscaloosa	32-0
Oct. 29	Kentucky	Lexington	26-6
Nov. 5	Tulane	Birmingham	3-0
Nov. 12	Georgia Tech	Atlanta	14-14
Nov. 24	Vanderbilt	Birmingham	7-0
Captain: Lew Bostick			149-40

1939 (5-3-1)

Sept. 30	Howard	Tuscaloosa	21-0
Oct. 7	Fordham	New York	7-6
Oct. 14	Mercer	Tuscaloosa	20-0
Oct. 21	Tennessee	Knoxville	0-21
Oct. 28	Mississippi State	Tuscaloosa	7-0
Nov. 4	Kentucky	Birmingham	7-7
Nov. 11	Tulane	New Orleans	0-13
Nov. 18	Georgia Tech	Birmingham	0-6
Nov. 30	Vanderbilt	Nashville	39-0
Captain: Carey Cox			101-53

1940 (7-2)

Sept. 27	Spring Hill	Mobile	26-0
Oct. 5	Mercer	Tuscaloosa	20-0
Oct. 12	Howard	Tuscaloosa	31-0
Oct. 19	Tennessee	Birmingham	12-27
Nov. 2	Kentucky	Lexington	25-0
Nov. 9	Tulane	Birmingham	13-6
Nov. 16	Georgia Tech	Atlanta	14-13
Nov. 23	Vanderbilt	Birmingham	25-21
Nov. 30	Mississippi State	Tuscaloosa	0-13
Captain: Harold Newman			166-80

1941 (9-2, national champions)

Sept. 27	SW Louisiana	Tuscaloosa	47-6
Oct. 4	Mississippi State	Tuscaloosa	0-14
Oct. 11	Howard	Birmingham	61-0
Oct. 18	Tennessee	Knoxville	9-2
Oct. 25	Georgia	Birmingham	27-14
Nov. 1	Kentucky	Tuscaloosa	30-0
Nov. 8	Tulane	New Orleans	19-14
Nov. 15	Georgia Tech	Birmingham	20-0
Nov. 22	Vanderbilt	Nashville	0-7
Nov. 28	Miami (Fla.)	Miami	21-7
Jan. 1, 1942	Texas A&M	Cotton Bowl	29-21
Captain: John Wyhonic			263-85

1942 (8-3)

Sept. 25	SW Louisiana	Montgomery	54-0
Oct. 3	Mississippi State	Tuscaloosa	21-6
Oct. 10	Pensacola N.A.S.	Mobile	27-0
Oct. 17	Tennessee	Birmingham	8-0
Oct. 24	Kentucky	Lexington	14-0
Oct. 31	Georgia	Atlanta	10-21
Nov. 7	South Carolina	Tuscaloosa	29-0
Nov. 14	Georgia Tech	Atlanta	0-7
Nov. 21	Vanderbilt	Birmingham	27-7
Nov. 28	Georgia Pre-Flight	Birmingham	19-35
Jan. 1, 1943	Boston College	Orange Bowl	37-21
Captain: Joe Domnanovich			246-97

1943 (no team)

1944 (5-2-2)

| Sept. 30 | LSU | Baton Rouge | 27-27 |
| Oct. 7 | Howard | Birmingham | 63-7 |

Oct. 14	Millsaps	Tuscaloosa	55-0
Oct. 21	Tennessee	Knoxville	0-0
Oct. 27	Kentucky	Montgomery	41-0
Nov. 4	Georgia	Birmingham	7-14
Nov. 11	Mississippi	Mobile	34-6
Nov. 18	Mississippi State	Tuscaloosa	19-0
Jan. 1, 1945	Duke	Sugar Bowl	26-29
Captain: None (game-by-game)			272-83

1945 (10-0, SEC champions)

Sept. 29	Keesler AAF	Biloxi, Miss.	21-0
Oct. 6	LSU	Baton Rouge	26-7
Oct. 13	South Carolina	Montgomery	55-0
Oct. 20	Tennessee	Birmingham	25-7
Oct. 27	Georgia	Birmingham	28-14
Nov. 3	Kentucky	Louisville	60-19
Nov. 17	Vanderbilt	Nashville	71-0
Nov. 24	Pensacola NAS	Tuscaloosa	55-6
Dec. 1	Mississippi State	Tuscaloosa	55-13
Jan. 1, 1946	Southern Cal	Rose Bowl	34-14
Captain: None (game-by-game)			430-80

1946 (7-4)

Sept. 20	Furman	Birmingham	26-7
Sept. 28	Tulane	New Orleans	7-6
Oct. 5	South Carolina	Columbia	14-6
Oct. 12	SW Louisiana	Tuscaloosa	54-0
Oct. 19	Tennessee	Knoxville	0-12
Oct. 26	Kentucky	Montgomery	21-7
Nov. 2	Georgia	Athens	0-14
Nov. 9	LSU	Baton Rouge	21-31
Nov. 16	Vanderbilt	Birmingham	12-7
Nov. 23	Boston College	Boston	7-13
Nov. 30	Mississippi State	Tuscaloosa	24-7
Captain: None (game-by-game)			186-110

Harold "Red" Drew (Bates, 54-28-7)
1947 (8-3)

Sept. 20	Mississippi Southern	Birmingham	34-7
Sept. 27	Tulane	New Orleans	20-21
Oct. 4	Vanderbilt	Nashville	7-14
Oct. 11	Duquesne	Tuscaloosa	26-0
Oct. 18	Tennessee	Birmingham	10-0
Oct. 25	Georgia	Athens	17-7
Nov. 1	Kentucky	Lexington	13-0
Nov. 15	Georgia Tech	Birmingham	14-7
Nov. 22	LSU	Tuscaloosa	41-12
Nov. 29	Miami (Fla.)	Miami	21-6
Jan. 1, 1948	Texas	Sugar Bowl	7-27
Captain: John Wozniak			210-101

1948 (6-4-1)

Sept. 25	Tulane	New Orleans	14-21
Oct. 2	Vanderbilt	Mobile	14-14
Oct. 8	Duquesne	Tuscaloosa	48-6
Oct. 16	Tennessee	Knoxville	6-21

Oct. 23	Mississippi State	Starkville	10-7
Oct. 30	Georgia	Birmingham	0-35
Nov. 6	Mississippi Southern	Tuscaloosa	27-0
Nov. 13	Georgia Tech	Atlanta	14-12
Nov. 20	LSU	Baton Rouge	6-26
Nov. 27	Florida	Tuscaloosa	34-28
Dec. 4	Auburn	Birmingham	55-0
Captain: Ray Richeson			228-170

1949 (6-3-1)

Sept. 24	Tulane	Mobile	14-28
Oct. 1	Vanderbilt	Nashville	7-14
Oct. 7	Duquesne	Tuscaloosa	48-8
Oct. 15	Tennessee	Birmingham	7-7
Oct. 22	Mississippi State	Tuscaloosa	35-6
Oct. 29	Georgia	Athens	14-7
Nov. 12	Georgia Tech	Birmingham	20-7
Nov. 19	Mississippi Southern	Tuscaloosa	34-26
Nov. 26	Florida	Gainesville	35-13
Dec. 3	Auburn	Birmingham	13-14
Captain: Doug Lockridge			227-130

1950 (9-2)

Sept. 23	Chattanooga	Birmingham	27-0
Sept. 30	Tulane	New Orleans	26-14
Oct. 7	Vanderbilt	Mobile	22-27
Oct. 13	Furman	Tuscaloosa	34-6
Oct. 21	Tennessee	Knoxville	9-14
Oct. 28	Mississippi State	Tuscaloosa	14-7
Nov. 4	Georgia	Birmingham	14-7
Nov. 11	Mississippi Southern	Tuscaloosa	53-0
Nov. 18	Georgia Tech	Atlanta	54-19
Nov. 25	Florida	Jacksonville	41-13
Dec. 2	Auburn	Birmingham	34-0
Captain: Mike Mizerany			328-107

1951 (5-6)

Sept. 21	Delta State	Montgomery	89-0
Sept. 29	LSU	Mobile	7-13
Oct. 6	Vanderbilt	Nashville	20-22
Oct. 12	Villanova	Tuscaloosa	18-41
Oct. 20	Tennessee	Birmingham	13-27
Oct. 27	Mississippi State	Starkville	7-0
Nov. 3	Georgia	Athens	16-14
Nov. 10	Mississippi Southern	Tuscaloosa	40-7
Nov. 17	Georgia Tech	Birmingham	7-27
Nov. 24	Florida	Tuscaloosa	21-30
Dec. 2	Auburn	Tuscaloosa	25-7
Captain: Jack Brown			263-188

1952 (10-2)

Sept. 19	Mississippi Southern	Montgomery	20-6
Sept. 27	LSU	Baton Rouge	21-20
Oct. 3	Miami (Fla.)	Miami	21-7
Oct. 11	Virginia Tech	Tuscaloosa	33-0
Oct. 18	Tennessee	Knoxville	0-20

Oct. 25	Mississippi State	Tuscaloosa	42-19
Nov. 1	Georgia	Birmingham	34-19
Nov. 8	Chattanooga	Tuscaloosa	42-28
Nov. 15	Georgia Tech	Atlanta	3-7
Nov. 22	Maryland	Mobile	27-7
Nov. 29	Auburn	Birmingham	21-0
Jan. 1, 1953	Syracuse	Orange Bowl	61-6
Captain: Bobby Wilson			325-139

1953 (6-3-3, SEC champions)

Sept. 18	Mississippi Southern	Montgomery	19-25
Sept. 26	LSU	Mobile	7-7
Oct. 3	Vanderbilt	Nashville	21-12
Oct. 10	Tulsa	Tuscaloosa	41-13
Oct. 17	Tennessee	Birmingham	0-0
Oct. 24	Mississippi State	Tuscaloosa	7-7
Oct. 31	Georgia	Athens	33-12
Nov. 7	Chattanooga	Tuscaloosa	21-14
Nov. 14	Georgia Tech	Birmingham	13-6
Nov. 21	Maryland	College Park	0-21
Nov. 28	Auburn	Birmingham	10-7
Jan. 1, 1954	Rice	Cotton Bowl	6-28
Captain: Bud Willis			178-152

1954 (4-5-2)

Sept. 17	Mississippi Southern	Montgomery	2-7
Sept. 25	LSU	Baton Rouge	12-0
Oct. 2	Vanderbilt	Mobile	28-14
Oct. 9	Tulsa	Tuscaloosa	40-0
Oct. 16	Tennessee	Knoxville	27-0
Oct. 23	Mississippi State	Tuscaloosa	7-12
Oct. 30	Georgia	Birmingham	0-0
Nov. 6	Tulane	New Orleans	0-0
Nov. 13	Georgia Tech	Atlanta	0-20
Nov. 19	Miami (Fla.)	Miami	7-23
Nov. 27	Auburn	Birmingham	0-28
Captain: Sid Youngleman			123-104

J.B. "Ears" Whitworth (Alabama, 4-24-2)
1955 (0-10)

Sept. 24	Rice	Houston	0-20
Oct. 1	Vanderbilt	Nashville	6-21
Oct. 8	Texas Christian	Tuscaloosa	0-21
Oct. 15	Tennessee	Birmingham	0-20
Oct. 22	Mississippi State	Tuscaloosa	7-26
Oct. 29	Georgia	Athens	14-35
Nov. 5	Tulane	Mobile	7-27
Nov. 12	Georgia Tech	Birmingham	2-26
Nov. 18	Miami (Fla.)	Miami	12-34
Nov. 26	Auburn	Birmingham	0-26
Captain: Nick Germanos			48-256

1956 (2-7-1)

Sept. 22	Rice	Houston	13-20
Oct. 6	Vanderbilt	Mobile	7-32
Oct. 13	Texas Christian	Tuscaloosa	6-23

Oct. 20	Tennessee	Knoxville	0-24
Oct. 27	Mississippi State	Tuscaloosa	13-12
Nov. 3	Georgia	Birmingham	13-16
Nov. 10	Tulane	New Orleans	13-7
Nov. 17	Georgia Tech	Atlanta	0-27
Nov. 24	Mississippi Southern	Tuscaloosa	13-13
Dec. 1	Auburn	Birmingham	7-34
Captains: Jim Cunningham, Wes Thompson			85-208

1957 (2-7-1)

Sept. 28	LSU	Baton Rouge	0-28
Oct. 5	Vanderbilt	Nashville	6-6
Oct. 12	Texas Christian	Fort Worth	0-28
Oct. 19	Tennessee	Birmingham	0-14
Oct. 26	Mississippi State	Tuscaloosa	13-25
Nov. 2	Georgia	Athens	14-13
Nov. 9	Tulane	Mobile	0-7
Nov. 16	Georgia Tech	Birmingham	7-10
Nov. 23	Mississippi Southern	Tuscaloosa	29-2
Nov. 30	Auburn	Birmingham	0-40
Captains: Jim Loftin, Clay Walls			69-173

Paul W. "Bear" Bryant (Alabama, 232-46-9)
1958 (5-4-1)

Sept. 27	LSU	Mobile	3-13
Oct. 4	Vanderbilt	Birmingham	0-0
Oct. 11	Furman	Tuscaloosa	29-6
Oct. 18	Tennessee	Knoxville	7-14
Oct. 25	Mississippi State	Starkville	9-7
Nov. 1	Georgia	Tuscaloosa	12-0
Nov. 8	Tulane	New Orleans	7-13
Nov. 15	Georgia Tech	Atlanta	17-8
Nov. 22	Memphis State	Tuscaloosa	14-0
Nov. 29	Auburn	Birmingham	8-14
Captains: Dave Singleton, Bobby Smith			106-75

1959 (7-2-2)

Sept. 19	Georgia	Athens	3-17
Sept. 26	Houston	Houston	3-0
Oct. 3	Vanderbilt	Nashville	7-7
Oct. 10	Chattanooga	Tuscaloosa	13-0
Oct. 17	Tennessee	Birmingham	7-7
Oct. 31	Mississippi State	Tuscaloosa	10-0
Nov. 7	Tulane	Mobile	19-7
Nov. 14	Georgia Tech	Birmingham	9-7
Nov. 21	Memphis State	Tuscaloosa	14-7
Nov. 28	Auburn	Birmingham	10-0
Dec. 19	Penn State	Liberty Bowl	0-7
Captains: Marlin Dyess, Jim Blevins			95-59

1960 (8-1-2)

Sept. 17	Georgia	Birmingham	21-6
Sept. 24	Tulane	New Orleans	6-6
Oct. 1	Vanderbilt	Birmingham	21-0
Oct. 15	Tennessee	Knoxville	7-20
Oct. 22	Houston	Tuscaloosa	14-0

Oct. 29	Mississippi State	Starkville	7-0
Nov. 5	Furman	Tuscaloosa	51-0
Nov. 12	Georgia Tech	Atlanta	16-15
Nov. 19	Tampa	Tuscaloosa	34-6
Nov. 26	Auburn	Birmingham	3-0
Dec. 17	Texas	Bluebonnet Bowl	3-3
Captains: Leon Fuller, Bobby Boylston			183-56

1961 (11-0, national champions, SEC champions)

Sept. 23	Georgia	Athens	32-6
Sept. 30	Tulane	Mobile	9-0
Oct. 7	Vanderbilt	Nashville	35-6
Oct. 14	North Carolina State	Tuscaloosa	26-7
Oct. 21	Tennessee	Birmingham	34-3
Oct. 28	Houston	Houston	17-0
Nov. 4	Mississippi State	Tuscaloosa	24-0
Nov. 11	Richmond	Tuscaloosa	66-0
Nov. 18	Georgia Tech	Birmingham	10-0
Dec. 2	Auburn	Birmingham	34-0
Jan. 1, 1962	Arkansas	Sugar Bowl	10-3
Captains: Pat Trammell, Billy Neighbors			297-25

1962 (10-1)

Sept. 22	Georgia	Birmingham	35-0
Sept. 28	Tulane	New Orleans	44-6
Oct. 6	Vanderbilt	Birmingham	17-7
Oct. 13	Houston	Tuscaloosa	14-3
Oct. 20	Tennessee	Knoxville	27-7
Oct. 27	Tulsa	Tuscaloosa	35-6
Nov. 3	Mississippi State	Starkville	20-0
Nov. 10	Miami (Fla.)	Tuscaloosa	36-3
Nov. 17	Georgia Tech	Atlanta	6-7
Dec. 1	Auburn	Birmingham	38-0
Jan. 1, 1963	Oklahoma	Orange Bowl	17-0
Captains: Lee Roy Jordan, Jimmy Sharpe			289-39

1963 (9-2)

Sept. 21	Georgia	Athens	32-7
Sept. 28	Tulane	Mobile	28-0
Oct. 5	Vanderbilt	Nashville	21-6
Oct. 12	Florida	Tuscaloosa	6-10
Oct. 19	Tennessee	Birmingham	35-0
Oct. 26	Houston	Tuscaloosa	21-13
Nov. 2	Mississippi State	Tuscaloosa	20-19
Nov. 16	Georgia Tech	Birmingham	27-11
Nov. 30	Auburn	Birmingham	8-10
Dec. 14	Miami (Fla.)	Miami	17-12
Jan. 1, 1964	Mississippi	Sugar Bowl	12-7
Captains: Benny Nelson, Steve Allen			227-95

1964 (10-1, national champions, SEC champions)

Sept. 19	Georgia	Tuscaloosa	31-3
Sept. 26	Tulane	Mobile	36-6
Oct. 3	Vanderbilt	Birmingham	24-0
Oct. 10	North Carolina State	Tuscaloosa	21-0
Oct. 17	Tennessee	Knoxville	19-8

Oct. 24	Florida	Tuscaloosa	17-14
Oct. 31	Mississippi State	Jackson	23-6
Nov. 7	LSU	Birmingham	17-9
Nov. 14	Georgia Tech	Atlanta	24-7
Nov. 26	Auburn	Birmingham	21-14
Jan. 1, 1965	Texas	Orange Bowl	17-21
Captains: Joe Namath, Ray Ogden			250-88

1965 (9-1-1, AP national champions, SEC champions)

Sept. 18	Georgia	Athens	17-18
Sept. 25	Tulane	Mobile	27-0
Oct. 2	Mississippi	Birmingham	17-16
Oct. 9	Vanderbilt	Nashville	22-7
Oct. 16	Tennessee	Birmingham	7-7
Oct. 23	Florida State	Tuscaloosa	21-0
Oct. 30	Mississippi State	Jackson	10-7
Nov. 6	LSU	Baton Rouge	31-7
Nov. 13	South Carolina	Tuscaloosa	35-14
Nov. 27	Auburn	Birmingham	30-3
Jan. 1, 1966	Nebraska	Orange Bowl	39-28
Captains: Steve Sloan, Paul Crane			256-107

1966 (11-0, SEC champions)

Sept. 24	Louisiana Tech	Birmingham	34-0
Oct. 1	Mississippi	Jackson	17-7
Oct. 8	Clemson	Tuscaloosa	26-0
Oct. 15	Tennessee	Knoxville	11-10
Oct. 22	Vanderbilt	Birmingham	42-6
Oct. 29	Mississippi State	Tuscaloosa	27-14
Nov. 5	LSU	Birmingham	21-0
Nov. 12	South Carolina	Tuscaloosa	24-0
Nov. 26	Southern Miss	Mobile	34-0
Dec. 3	Auburn	Birmingham	31-0
Jan. 2, 1967	Nebraska	Sugar Bowl	34-7
Captains: Ray Perkins, Richard Cole			301-44

1967 (8-2-1)

Sept. 23	Florida State	Birmingham	37-37
Sept. 30	Southern Miss	Mobile	25-3
Oct. 7	Mississippi	Birmingham	21-7
Oct. 14	Vanderbilt	Nashville	35-21
Oct. 21	Tennessee	Birmingham	13-24
Oct. 28	Clemson	Clemson	13-10
Nov. 4	Mississippi State	Tuscaloosa	13-0
Nov. 11	LSU	Baton Rouge	7-6
Nov. 18	South Carolina	Tuscaloosa	17-0
Dec. 2	Auburn	Birmingham	7-3
Jan. 1, 1968	Texas A&M	Cotton Bowl	16-20
Captains: Ken Stabler, Bobby Johns			204-131

1968 (8-3)

Sept. 21	Virginia Tech	Birmingham	14-7
Sept. 28	Southern Miss	Mobile	17-14
Oct. 5	Mississippi	Jackson	8-10
Oct. 12	Vanderbilt	Tuscaloosa	31-7
Oct. 19	Tennessee	Knoxville	9-10

Oct. 26	Clemson	Tuscaloosa	21-14
Nov. 2	Mississippi State	Tuscaloosa	20-13
Nov. 9	LSU	Birmingham	16-7
Nov. 16	Miami (Fla.)	Miami	14-6
Nov. 30	Auburn	Birmingham	24-16
Dec. 28	Missouri	Gator Bowl	10-35
Captains: Mike Hall, Donnie Sutton			184-139

1969 (6-5)

Sept. 20	Virginia Tech	Blacksburg	17-13
Sept. 27	Southern Miss	Tuscaloosa	63-14
Oct. 4	Mississippi	Birmingham	33-32
Oct. 11	Vanderbilt	Nashville	10-14
Oct. 18	Tennessee	Birmingham	14-41
Oct. 25	Clemson	Clemson	38-13
Nov. 1	Mississippi State	Jackson	23-19
Nov. 8	LSU	Baton Rouge	15-20
Nov. 15	Miami (Fla.)	Tuscaloosa	42-6
Nov. 29	Auburn	Birmingham	26-49
Dec. 13	Colorado	Liberty Bowl	33-47
Captains: Danny Ford, Alvin Samples			314-268

1970 (6-5-1)

Sept. 12	Southern Cal	Birmingham	21-42
Sept. 19	Virginia Tech	Birmingham	51-18
Sept. 26	Florida	Tuscaloosa	46-15
Oct. 3	Mississippi	Jackson	23-48
Oct. 10	Vanderbilt	Tuscaloosa	35-11
Oct. 17	Tennessee	Knoxville	0-24
Oct. 24	Houston	Houston	30-21
Oct. 31	Mississippi State	Tuscaloosa	35-6
Nov. 7	LSU	Birmingham	9-14
Nov. 14	Miami (Fla.)	Miami	32-8
Nov. 28	Auburn	Birmingham	28-33
Dec. 31	Oklahoma	Bluebonnet Bowl	24-24
Captains: Danny Gilbert, Dave Brungard			334-264

1971 (11-1, SEC champions)

Sept. 10	Southern Cal	Los Angeles	17-10
Sept. 18	Southern Miss	Tuscaloosa	42-6
Sept. 25	Florida	Gainesville	38-0
Oct. 2	Mississippi	Birmingham	40-6
Oct. 9	Vanderbilt	Nashville	42-0
Oct. 16	Tennessee	Birmingham	32-15
Oct. 23	Houston	Tuscaloosa	34-20
Oct. 30	Mississippi State	Jackson	41-10
Nov. 6	LSU	Baton Rouge	14-7
Nov. 13	Miami (Fla.)	Tuscaloosa	31-3
Nov. 27	Auburn	Birmingham	31-7
Jan. 1, 1972	Nebraska	Orange Bowl	6-38
Captains: Johnny Musso, Robin Parkhouse			368-122

1972 (10-2, SEC champions)

Sept. 9	Duke	Birmingham	35-12
Sept. 23	Kentucky	Birmingham	35-0
Sept. 30	Vanderbilt	Tuscaloosa	48-21

Oct. 7	Georgia	Athens	25-7
Oct. 14	Florida	Tuscaloosa	24-7
Oct. 21	Tennessee	Knoxville	17-10
Oct. 28	Southern Miss	Birmingham	48-11
Nov. 4	Mississippi State	Tuscaloosa	58-14
Nov. 11	LSU	Birmingham	35-21
Nov. 18	Virginia Tech	Tuscaloosa	52-13
Dec. 2	Auburn	Birmingham	16-17
Jan. 1, 1973	Texas	Cotton Bowl	13-17
Captains: Terry Davis, John Mitchell			406-150

1973 (11-1, UPI national champions, SEC champions)

Sept. 15	California	Birmingham	66-0
Sept. 22	Kentucky	Lexington	28-14
Sept. 29	Vanderbilt	Nashville	44-0
Oct. 6	Georgia	Tuscaloosa	28-14
Oct. 13	Florida	Gainesville	35-14
Oct. 20	Tennessee	Birmingham	42-21
Oct. 2	Virginia Tech	Tuscaloosa	77-6
Nov. 3	Mississippi State	Jackson	35-0
Nov. 17	Miami	Tuscaloosa	43-13
Nov. 22	LSU	Baton Rouge	21-7
Dec. 1	Auburn	Birmingham	35-0
Dec. 31	Notre Dame	Sugar Bowl	23-24
Captains: Wilbur Jackson, Chuck Strickland			477-113

1974 (11-1, SEC champions)

Sept. 14	Maryland	College Park	21-16
Sept. 21	Southern Miss	Birmingham	52-0
Sept. 28	Vanderbilt	Tuscaloosa	23-10
Oct. 5	Mississippi	Jackson	35-21
Oct. 12	Florida State	Tuscaloosa	8-7
Oct. 19	Tennessee	Knoxville	28-6
Oct. 26	Texas Christian	Birmingham	41-3
Nov. 2	Mississippi State	Tuscaloosa	35-0
Nov. 9	LSU	Birmingham	30-0
Nov. 16	Miami (Fla.)	Miami	28-7
Nov. 29	Auburn	Birmingham	17-13
Jan.1, 1974	Notre Dame	Orange Bowl	11-13
Captains: Sylvester Croom, Ricky Davis			329-96

1975 (11-1, SEC champions)

Sept. 8	Missouri	Birmingham	7-20
Sept. 20	Clemson	Tuscaloosa	56-0
Sept. 27	Vanderbilt	Nashville	40-7
Oct. 4	Mississippi	Birmingham	32-6
Oct. 11	Washington	Tuscaloosa	52-0
Oct. 18	Tennessee	Birmingham	30-7
Oct. 25	Texas Christian	Birmingham	45-0
Nov. 1	Mississippi State	Jackson	21-10
Nov. 8	LSU	Baton Rouge	23-10
Nov. 15	Southern Miss	Tuscaloosa	27-6
Nov. 29	Auburn	Birmingham	28-0
Dec. 31	Penn State	Sugar Bowl	13-6
Captains: Leroy Cook, Richard Todd			374-72

1976 (9-3)

Date	Opponent	Location	Score
Sept. 11	Mississippi	Jackson	7-10
Sept. 18	Southern Methodist	Birmingham	56-3
Sept. 25	Vanderbilt	Tuscaloosa	42-14
Oct. 2	Georgia	Athens	0-21
Oct. 9	Southern Miss	Birmingham	24-8
Oct. 16	Tennessee	Knoxville	20-13
Oct. 23	Louisville	Tuscaloosa	24-3
Oct. 30	Mississippi State	Tuscaloosa	34-17
Nov. 6	LSU	Birmingham	28-17
Nov. 13	Notre Dame	South Bend	18-21
Nov. 27	Auburn	Birmingham	38-7
Dec. 20	UCLA	Liberty Bowl	36-6
Captains: Thad Flanagan, Charles Hannah			327-140

1977 (11-1, SEC champions)

Date	Opponent	Location	Score
Sept. 10	Mississippi	Birmingham	34-13
Sept. 17	Nebraska	Lincoln	24-31
Sept. 24	Vanderbilt	Nashville	24-12
Oct. 1	Georgia	Tuscaloosa	18-10
Oct. 8	Southern Cal	Los Angeles	21-20
Oct. 15	Tennessee	Birmingham	24-10
Oct. 22	Louisville	Tuscaloosa	55-6
Oct. 29	Mississippi State	Jackson	37-7
Nov. 5	LSU	Baton Rouge	24-3
Nov. 12	Miami (Fla.)	Tuscaloosa	36-0
Nov. 26	Auburn	Birmingham	48-21
Jan. 2, 1978	Ohio State	Sugar Bowl	35-6
Captains: Ozzie Newsome, Mike Tucker			380-139

1978 (11-1, AP national champions, SEC champions)

Date	Opponent	Location	Score
Sept. 2	Nebraska	Birmingham	20-3
Sept. 16	Missouri	Columbia	38-20
Sept. 23	Southern Cal	Birmingham	14-24
Sept. 30	Vanderbilt	Tuscaloosa	51-28
Oct. 7	Washington	Seattle	20-17
Oct. 14	Florida	Tuscaloosa	23-12
Oct. 21	Tennessee	Knoxville	30-17
Oct. 28	Virginia Tech	Tuscaloosa	35-0
Nov. 4	Mississippi State	Birmingham	35-14
Nov. 11	LSU	Birmingham	31-10
Dec. 2	Auburn	Birmingham	34-16
Jan. 1, 1978	Penn State	Sugar Bowl	14-7
Captains: Marty Lyons, Jeff Rutledge, Tony Nathan			345-168

1979 (12-0, AP & UPI national champions, SEC champions)

Date	Opponent	Location	Score
Sept. 8	Georgia Tech	Atlanta	30-6
Sept. 22	Baylor	Birmingham	45-0
Sept. 29	Vanderbilt	Nashville	66-3
Oct. 6	Wichita State	Tuscaloosa	38-0
Oct. 13	Florida	Gainesville	40-0
Oct. 20	Tennessee	Birmingham	27-17
Oct. 27	Virginia Tech	Tuscaloosa	31-7
Nov. 3	Mississippi State	Tuscaloosa	24-7
Nov. 10	LSU	Baton Rouge	3-0
Nov. 17	Miami (Fla.)	Tuscaloosa	30-0
Dec. 1	Auburn	Birmingham	25-18
Jan. 1	Arkansas	Sugar Bowl	24-9
Captains: Don McNeal, Steve Whitman			383-67

1980 (10-2)

Sept. 6	Georgia Tech	Birmingham	26-3
Sept. 20	Mississippi	Jackson	59-35
Sept. 27	Vanderbilt	Tuscaloosa	41-0
Oct. 4	Kentucky	Birmingham	45-0
Oct. 11	Rutgers	East Rutherford	17-13
Oct. 18	Tennessee	Knoxville	27-0
Oct. 25	Southern Miss	Tuscaloosa	42-7
Nov. 1	Mississippi State	Jackson	3-6
Nov. 8	LSU	Tuscaloosa	28-7
Nov. 15	Notre Dame	Birmingham	0-7
Nov. 29	Auburn	Birmingham	34-18
Jan. 1, 1981	Baylor	Cotton Bowl	30-2
Captains: Major Ogilvie, Randy Scott			352-98

1981 (9-2-1 SEC champions)

Sept. 5	LSU	Baton Rouge	24-7
Sept. 12	Georgia Tech	Birmingham	21-24
Sept. 19	Kentucky	Lexington	19-10
Sept. 26	Vanderbilt	Nashville	28-7
Oct. 3	Mississippi	Tuscaloosa	38-7
Oct. 10	Southern Miss	Birmingham	13-13
Oct. 17	Tennessee	Birmingham	38-19
Oct. 24	Rutgers	Tuscaloosa	31-7
Oct. 31	Mississippi State	Tuscaloosa	13-10
Nov. 14	Penn State	State College	31-16
Nov. 28	Auburn	Birmingham	28-17
Jan. 1, 1982	Texas	Cotton Bowl	12-14
Captains: Warren Lyles, Alan Gray			296-151

1982 (8-4)

Sept. 11	Georgia Tech	Atlanta	45-7
Sept. 18	Mississippi	Jackson	42-14
Sept. 25	Vanderbilt	Tuscaloosa	24-21
Oct. 2	Arkansas State	Birmingham	34-7
Oct. 9	Penn State	Birmingham	42-21
Oct. 16	Tennessee	Knoxville	28-35
Oct. 23	Cincinnati	Tuscaloosa	21-3
Oct. 30	Mississippi State	Jackson	20-12
Nov. 6	LSU	Birmingham	10-20
Nov. 13	Southern Miss	Tuscaloosa	29-38
Nov. 27	Auburn	Birmingham	22-23
Dec. 29	Illinois	Liberty Bowl	21-15
Captains: Eddie Lowe, Steve Mott			338-216

Ray Perkins (Alabama, 32-15-1)
1983 (8-4)

Sept. 10	Georgia Tech	Birmingham	20-7
Sept. 17	Mississippi	Tuscaloosa	40-0
Sept. 24	Vanderbilt	Nashville	44-24
Oct. 1	Memphis State	Tuscaloosa	44-13
Oct. 8	Penn State	State College	28-34
Oct. 15	Tennessee	Birmingham	34-41
Oct. 29	Mississippi State	Tuscaloosa	35-18
Nov. 5	LSU	Baton Rouge	32-26
Nov. 12	Southern Miss	Birmingham	28-16
Nov. 25	Boston College	Foxboro	13-20
Dec. 3	Auburn	Birmingham	20-23
Dec. 24	Southern Methodist	Sun Bowl	28-7
Captains: Walter Lewis, Randy Edwards			366-229

1984 (5-6)

Sept. 8	Boston College	Birmingham	31-38
Sept. 15	Georgia Tech	Atlanta	6-16
Sept. 22	SW Louisiana	Tuscaloosa	37-14
Sept. 29	Vanderbilt	Tuscaloosa	21-30
Oct. 6	Georgia	Birmingham	14-24
Oct. 13	Penn State	Tuscaloosa	6-0
Oct. 20	Tennessee	Knoxville	27-28
Nov. 3	Mississippi State	Jackson	24-20
Nov. 10	LSU	Birmingham	14-16
Nov. 17	Cincinnati	Cincinnati	29-7
Dec. 1	Auburn	Birmingham	17-15
Captains: Paul Ott Carruth, Emanuel King			226-208

1985 (9-2-1)

Sept. 2	Georgia	Athens	20-16
Sept. 14	Texas A&M	Birmingham	23-10
Sept. 21	Cincinnati	Tuscaloosa	45-10
Sept. 28	Vanderbilt	Nashville	40-20
Oct. 12	Penn State	State College	17-19
Oct. 19	Tennessee	Birmingham	14-16
Oct. 26	Memphis State	Memphis	28-9
Nov. 2	Mississippi State	Tuscaloosa	44-28
Nov. 9	LSU	Baton Rouge	14-14
Nov. 16	Southern Miss	Tuscaloosa	24-13
Nov. 30	Auburn	Birmingham	25-23
Dec. 28	Southern Cal	Aloha Bowl	24-3
Captains: Jon Hand, Thornton Chandler			318-181

1986 (10-3)

Aug. 27	Ohio State	East Rutherford	16-10
Sept. 6	Vanderbilt	Tuscaloosa	42-10
Sept. 13	Southern Miss	Birmingham	31-17
Sept. 20	Florida	Gainesville	21-7
Oct. 4	Notre Dame	Birmingham	28-10
Oct. 11	Memphis State	Tuscaloosa	37-0
Oct. 18	Tennessee	Knoxville	56-28
Oct. 25	Penn State	Tuscaloosa	3-23
Nov. 1	Mississippi State	Starkville	38-3
Nov. 8	LSU	Birmingham	10-14
Nov. 15	Temple	Tuscaloosa	24-14
Nov. 29	Auburn	Birmingham	17-21
Dec. 25	Washington	Sun Bowl	28-6
Captains: Mike Shula, Cornelius Bennett			351-163

Bill Curry (Georgia Tech, 26-10)
1987 (7-5)

Sept. 5	Southern Miss	Birmingham	38-6
Sept. 12	Penn State	State College	24-13
Sept. 19	Florida	Birmingham	14-23
Sept. 26	Vanderbilt	Nashville	30-23
Oct. 3	SW Louisiana	Birmingham	38-10
Oct. 10	Memphis State	Memphis	10-13
Oct. 17	Tennessee	Birmingham	41-22
Oct. 31	Mississippi State	Birmingham	21-18
Nov. 7	LSU	Baton Rouge	22-10
Nov. 14	Notre Dame	South Bend	6-37
Nov. 27	Auburn	Birmingham	0-10
Jan. 2	Michigan	Hall of Fame	24-28
Captains: Kerry Goode, Randy Rockwell			268-213

1988 (9-3)

Sept. 10	Temple	Philadelphia	37-0
Sept. 24	Vanderbilt	Tuscaloosa	44-10
Oct. 1	Kentucky	Lexington	31-27
Oct. 8	Mississippi	Tuscaloosa	12-22
Oct. 15	Tennessee	Knoxville	28-20
Oct. 22	Penn State	Birmingham	8-3
Oct. 29	Mississippi State	Starkville	53-34
Nov. 5	LSU	Tuscaloosa	18-19
Nov. 12	SW Louisiana	Birmingham	17-0
Nov. 25	Auburn	Birmingham	10-15
Dec. 1	Texas A&M	College Station	30-10
Dec. 24	Army	Sun Bowl	29-28
Captains: David Smith, Derrick Thomas			317-188

1989 (10-2, SEC champions)

Sept. 16	Memphis State	Birmingham	35-7
Sept. 23	Kentucky	Tuscaloosa	15-3
Sept. 30	Vanderbilt	Nashville	20-14
Oct. 7	Mississippi	Jackson	62-27
Oct. 14	SW Louisiana	Tuscaloosa	24-17
Oct. 21	Tennessee	Birmingham	47-30
Oct. 28	Penn State	State College	17-16
Nov. 3	Mississippi State	Birmingham	23-10
Nov. 11	LSU	Baton Rouge	32-16
Nov. 18	Southern Miss	Tuscaloosa	37-14
Dec. 2	Auburn	Auburn	20-30
Jan. 1, 1990	Miami	Sugar Bowl	25-33
Captains: Marco Battle, Willie Wyatt			357-217

Gene Stallings (Texas A&M, 62-25)
1990 (7-5)

Sept. 8	Southern Miss	Birmingham	24-27
Sept. 15	Florida	Tuscaloosa	13-17
Sept. 22	Georgia	Athens	16-17
Sept. 29	Vanderbilt	Tuscaloosa	59-28
Oct. 6	SW Louisiana	Lafayette	25-6
Oct. 20	Tennessee	Knoxville	9-6
Oct. 27	Penn State	Tuscaloosa	0-9
Nov. 3	Mississippi State	Starkville	22-0
Nov. 10	LSU	Tuscaloosa	24-3
Nov. 17	Cincinnati	Birmingham	45-7
Dec. 1	Auburn	Birmingham	16-7
Jan. 1	Louisville	Fiesta Bowl	7-34
Captains: Gary Hollingsworth, Efrum Thomas, Philip Doyle			260-161

1991 (11-1)

Sept. 7	Temple	Birmingham	41-3
Sept. 14	Florida	Gainesville	0-35
Sept. 21	Georgia	Tuscaloosa	10-0
Sept. 28	Vanderbilt	Nashville	48-17
Oct. 5	Tennessee-Chattanooga	Birmingham	53-7
Oct, 12	Tulane	Tuscaloosa	62-0
Oct. 19	Tennessee	Birmingham	24-19
Nov. 2	Mississippi State	Tuscaloosa	13-7
Nov. 9	LSU	Baton Rouge	20-17
Nov. 16	Memphis State	Memphis	10-7
Nov. 30	Auburn	Birmingham	13-6
Dec. 28	Colorado	Blockbuster Bowl	30-25
Captains: Siran Stacy, Robert Stewart, John Sullins, Kevin Turner			324-143

1992 (13-0, national champions, SEC champions)

Sept. 5	Vanderbilt	Tuscaloosa	25-8
Sept. 12	Southern Miss	Birmingham	17-10
Sept. 19	Arkansas	Little Rock	38-11
Sept. 26	Louisiana Tech	Birmingham	13-0
Oct. 3	South Carolina	Tuscaloosa	48-7
Oct. 10	Tulane	New Orleans	37-0
Oct. 17	Tennessee	Knoxville	17-10
Oct. 24	Ole Miss	Tuscaloosa	31-10
Nov. 7	LSU	Baton Rouge	31-11
Nov. 14	Mississippi State	Starkville	30-21
Nov. 26	Auburn	Birmingham	17-0
Dec. 5	Florida	Birmingham	28-21
Jan. 1, 1993	Miami (Fla.)	Sugar Bowl	34-13
Captains: Derrick Oden, George Teague, George Wilson, Prince Wimbley			366-122

1993 (1-12, all games except LSU and the last three later forfeited by NCAA action)

Sept. 4	Tulane	Birmingham	31-17
Sept. 11	Vanderbilt	Nashville	17-6
Sept. 18	Arkansas	Tuscaloosa	43-3
Sept. 25	Louisiana Tech	Birmingham	56-3
Oct. 2	South Carolina	Columbia	17-6
Oct. 16	Tennessee	Birmingham	17-17
Oct. 23	Ole Miss	Oxford	19-14
Oct. 30	Southern Miss	Tuscaloosa	40-0
Nov. 6	LSU	Tuscaloosa	13-17
Nov. 13	Mississippi State	Tuscaloosa	36-25
Nov. 20	Auburn	Auburn	14-22
Dec. 4	Florida	Birmingham	13-28
Dec. 31	North Carolina	Gator Bowl	24-10
Captains: Chris Anderson, Lemanski Hall, Antonio Langham, Tobie Sheils			316-158

1994 (12-1)

Sept. 3	Tennessee-Chattanooga	Birmingham	42-13
Sept. 10	Vanderbilt	Tuscaloosa	17-7
Sept. 17	Arkansas	Fayetteville	13-6
Sept. 24	Tulane	Birmingham	20-10
Oct. 1	Georgia	Tuscaloosa	29-28
Oct. 8	Southern Miss	Tuscaloosa	14-6
Oct. 15	Tennessee	Knoxville	17-13
Oct. 22	Ole Miss	Tuscaloosa	21-10
Nov. 5	LSU	Baton Rouge	35-17
Nov. 12	Mississippi State	Starkville	29-25
Nov. 19	Auburn	Birmingham	21-14
Dec. 3	Florida	Atlanta	23-24
Jan. 2	Ohio State	Citrus Bowl	24-17
Captains: Jay Barker, Tommy Johnson, Tarrant Lynch, San Shade			305-190

1995 (8-3)

Sept. 2	Vanderbilt	Nashville	33-25
Sept. 9	Southern Miss	Birmingham	24-20
Sept. 16	Arkansas	Tuscaloosa	19-20
Sept. 30	Georgia	Athens	31-0
Oct. 7	North Carolina State	Tuscaloosa	27-11
Oct. 14	Tennessee	Birmingham	14-41
Oct. 21	Ole Miss	Oxford	23-9
Oct. 28	North Texas	Tuscaloosa	38-19
Nov. 4	LSU	Tuscaloosa	10-3
Nov. 11	Mississippi State	Tuscaloosa	14-9
Nov. 18	Auburn	Auburn	27-31
Captains: Shannon Brown, Brian Burgdorf, Tony Johnson, John Walters			260-188

1996 (10-3)

Aug. 31	Bowling Green	Birmingham	21-7
Sept. 7	Southern Miss	Tuscaloosa	20-10
Sept. 14	Vanderbilt	Tuscaloosa	36-26
Sept. 21	Arkansas	Little Rock	17-7
Oct. 5	Kentucky	Tuscaloosa	35-7
Oct. 12	North Carolina State	Raleigh	24-19
Oct. 19	Ole Miss	Tuscaloosa	37-0
Oct. 26	Tennessee	Knoxville	13-20
Nov. 9	LSU	Baton Rouge	26-0
Nov. 16	Mississippi State	Starkville	16-17
Nov. 23	Auburn	Birmingham	24-23
Dec. 7	Florida	Atlanta	30-45
Jan. 1, 1997	Michigan	Outback Bowl	17-14
Captains: John Causey, Fernando Davis			316-195

Mike DuBose (Alabama, 24-23)
1997 (4-7)

Aug. 30	Houston	Birmingham	42-17
Sept. 11	Vanderbilt	Nashville	20-0
Sept. 20	Arkansas	Tuscaloosa	16-17
Sept. 27	Southern Miss	Birmingham	27-14
Oct. 4	Kentucky	Lexington	34-40
Oct 18	Tennessee	Birmingham	21-38
Oct. 25	Ole Miss	Oxford	29-20
Nov. 1	Louisiana Tech	Tuscaloosa	20-26
Nov. 8	LSU	Tuscaloosa	0-27
Nov. 15	Mississippi State	Tuscaloosa	20-32
Nov. 22	Auburn	Auburn	17-18
Captains: Curtis Alexander, Paul Pickett, Rod Rutledge, Deshea Townsend			246-248

1998 (7-5)

Sept. 5	Brigham Young	Tuscaloosa	38-31
Sept. 12	Vanderbilt	Birmingham	32-7
Sept. 26	Arkansas	Fayetteville	6-42
Oct. 3	Florida	Tuscaloosa	10-16
Oct. 10	Ole Miss	Tuscaloosa	20-17
Oct. 17	East Carolina	Birmingham	23-22
Oct. 24	Tennessee	Knoxville	18-35
Oct. 31	Southern Miss	Tuscaloosa	30-20
Nov. 7	LSU	Baton Rogue	22-16
Nov. 14	Mississippi State	Starkville	14-26
Nov. 21	Auburn	Birmingham	31-17
Dec. 29	Virginia Tech	Music City Bowl	7-38
Captains: Calvin Hall, John David Phillips, Daniel Pope, Kelvin Singler, Trevis Smith			251-287

1999 (10-3, SEC champions)

Sept. 4	Vanderbilt	Nashville	28-17
Sept. 11	Houston	Birmingham	37-10
Sept. 18	Louisiana Tech	Birmingham	28-29
Sept. 25	Arkansas	Tuscaloosa	35-28
Oct. 2	Florida	Gainesville	40-39
Oct. 16	Ole Miss	Oxford	30-24
Oct. 23	Tennessee	Tuscaloosa	7-21
Oct. 30	Southern Miss	Tuscaloosa	35-14

Nov. 6	LSU	Tuscaloosa	23-17
Nov. 13	Mississippi State	Tuscaloosa	19-7
Nov. 20	Auburn	Auburn	28-17
Dec. 4	Florida	Atlanta	34-7
Jan. 1, 2000	Michigan	Orange Bowl	34-35

Captains: Shaun Alexander, Cornelius Griffin, Miguel Merritt, Ryan Pflugner, Chris Samuels   380-265

2000 (3-8)

Sept. 2	UCLA	Pasadena	24-35
Sept. 9	Vanderbilt	Birmingham	28-10
Sept. 16	Southern Miss	Birmingham	0-21
Sept. 23	Arkansas	Fayetteville	21-28
Sept. 30	South Carolina	Tuscaloosa	27-17
Oct. 14	Ole Miss	Tuscaloosa	45-7
Oct. 21	Tennessee	Knoxville	10-20
Oct. 28	Central Florida	Tuscaloosa	38-40
Nov. 4	LSU	Baton Rouge	28-30
Nov. 11	Mississippi State	Starkville	7-29
Nov. 18	Auburn	Tuscaloosa	0-9

Captains: Paul Hogan, Bradley Ledbetter, Kenny Smith   228-246

Dennis Franchione (Pittsburg State, 17-8)
2001 (7-5)

Sept. 1	UCLA	Tuscaloosa	17-20
Sept. 8	Vanderbilt	Nashville	12-9
Sept. 22	Arkansas	Tuscaloosa	31-10
Sept. 29	South Carolina	Columbia	36-37
Oct. 6	Texas-El Paso	Birmingham	56-7
Oct. 13	Ole Miss	Oxford	24-27
Oct. 20	Tennessee	Tuscaloosa	24-35
Nov. 3	LSU	Tuscaloosa	21-35
Nov. 10	Mississippi State	Tuscaloosa	24-17
Nov. 17	Auburn	Auburn	31-7
Nov. 29	Southern Miss	Birmingham	28-15
Dec. 27	Iowa State	Independence Bowl	14-13

Captains: Jarrett Johnson, Terry Jones Jr., Saleem Rasheed, Tyler Watts, Andrew Zow   304-219

2002 (10-3)

Aug. 31	Middle Tennessee State	Birmingham	39-34
Sept. 7	Oklahoma	Norman	27-37
Sept. 14	North Texas	Tuscaloosa	33-7
Sept. 21	Southern Miss	Tuscaloosa	20-7
Sept. 28	Arkansas	Fayetteville	30-12
Oct. 5	Georgia	Tuscaloosa	25-27
Oct. 19	Ole Miss	Tuscaloosa	42-7
Oct. 26	Tennessee	Knoxville	34-14
Nov. 2	Vanderbilt	Tuscaloosa	30-8
Nov. 9	Mississippi State	Tuscaloosa	28-14
Nov. 16	LSU	Baton Rouge	31-0
Nov. 23	Auburn	Tuscaloosa	7-17
Nov. 30	Hawaii	Honolulu	21-16

Captains: Lane Bearden, Ahmaad Galloway, Jarret Johnson, Kenny King, Kindal Moorehead, Tyler Watts   367-200

Mike Shula (Alabama, 10-15)
2003 (4-9)

Aug. 30	South Florida	Birmingham	40-17
Sept. 6	Oklahoma	Tuscaloosa	13-20
Sept. 13	Kentucky	Tuscaloosa	27-17
Sept. 20	Northern Illinois	Tuscaloosa	16-19
Sept. 27	Arkansas	Tuscaloosa	31-34 (2OT)
Oct. 4	Georgia	Athens	23-37
Oct. 11	Southern Miss	Tuscaloosa	17-3
Oct. 18	Ole Miss	Oxford	28-43
Oct. 25	Tennessee	Tuscaloosa	43-51 (5OT)
Nov. 8	Mississippi State	Starkville	38-0
Nov. 15	LSU	Tuscaloosa	3-27
Nov. 22	Auburn	Auburn	23-28
Nov. 29	Hawaii	Honolulu	29-37
Captains: Derrick Pope, Shaud Williams			331-333

2004 (6-6)

Sept. 4	Utah State	Tuscaloosa	48-17
Sept. 11	Ole Miss	Tuscaloosa	28-7
Sept. 18	Western Carolina	Tuscaloosa	52-0
Sept. 25	Arkansas	Fayetteville	10-27
Oct. 2	South Carolina	Tuscaloosa	3-20
Oct. 9	Kentucky	Lexington	45-17
Oct. 16	Southern Miss	Tuscaloosa	27-3
Oct. 23	Tennessee	Knoxville	13-17
Nov. 6	Mississippi State	Tuscaloosa	30-14
Nov. 13	LSU	Baton Rouge	10-26
Nov. 20	Auburn	Tuscaloosa	13-21
Dec. 31	Minnesota	Music City Bowl	16-20
Captains: Wesley Britt, Todd Bates			295-189

Appendix F: All-Time Lettermen

Abbott, Eli (T, 1892-94); Abernathy, Thad (FL, 1997); Abney, Larry (SE, 1984-87); Abrams, Jason (TE, 1992); Abrams, Charlie (TE,1986-89); Abruzzese, Raymond (HB, 1960-61); Abston, Bill (RH, 1948-49); Adams, George "Buster" (E, 1935) Adams, J.J. (P, 1993); Adcock, Mike (OT, 1981-83); Adkinson, Wayne (HB, 1970-72); Aiken, Tom (FS, 1995); Aland, Jack (T, 1942); Albright, Carl (H, 1944); Albright, George (HB, 1944); Alexander, Curtis (TB, 1994-97); Alexander, Dennis (G, 2000-03); Alexander, Shaun (TB, 1996-99); Allen, Charles G. (T, 1957-59); Allen, Doug (FB, 1985-87); Allen, John (T, 1907); Allen, Steve (G, 1961-63); Allen, Wes (SE, 1997-98); Allison, Scott (T, 1978-80); Allman, Phil (DB, 1976-78); Amelong, William (LB, 1988-89); Anderson, Andy (G, 1986); Anderson, Chris (RB, 1990-93); Anderson, Mark (DE/LB, 2002-04); Andrews, Carlos (S, 2002-04); Andrews, Mickey (HB, 1963-64); Angelich, James Dykes (HB, 1933-35); Arant, Hershel (G, 1908); Arthur, Paul (E, 1949); Atkins, Sam (T, 1988); August, Johnny (HB, 1942, 1946-47); Ausmus, Michael (CB, 1992-93); Austill, Huriescso (E, 1904); Austill, Jere (B, 1908); Avalos, Brandon (QB, 2003); Averitte, Warren (C, 1938-40); Avinger, Clarence "Butch" (QB, 1948-50); Aydelette, William Leslie "Buddy" (TE/OT, 1977-79); Ayers, Calvin (RB, 1989).

Babb, Joel (SE, 2002); Bacon, Waine (S, 2001-02); Bailey, David (SE, 1969-71); Bailey, Kecalf (CB, 1997-2000); Baker, George (T, 1921); Baker, Joseph (Mgr., 1941); Ballard, Clarence Bingham (T, 1901-02); Bankhead, M.H. (B, 1895); Bankhead, Wm. Brockman (FB, 1892-93); Banks, R.R. (G, 1901); Barger, William (G, 1990-93); Barker, Jay (QB, 1991-94); Barker, Troy (G, 1931-33); Barnes, Emile "Red" (HB, 1925-26); Barnes, Gary (S, 1999); Barnes, Ronnie Joe (DE, 1973-74); Barnes, W.A. (T, 1912); Barnes, Wiley (C, 1978-79); Barnett, Henry Herndon (C, 1911); Barron, Chad (K, 2000); Barron, David (LB, 2000); Barron, Marvin (G/T, 1970-73); Barron, Randy (DT, 1966-68); Barry, Dick (FB, 1951); Bartlett, Charles (HB, 1920-22); Baswell, Ben (T, 1935); Bates, C.F. (B, 1914); Bates, Tim (LB, 1964-65); Bates, Todd (DE, 2001-02, 2004); Batey, Joseph Dwight "Bo" (G, 1976); Battle, Bill (E, 1960-62); Battle, Marco (WR, 1987-99); Baty, William C. Jr. (HB, 1921-23); Baughman, Bill (C, 1946); Baumhower, Robert Glenn (DT, 1974-76); Baxley, Lannis (T, 2000-02); Bealle, Sherman "Bucky" (E, 1929); Bean, Dickie (HB, 1966); Beard, Brad (QB, 1999); Beard, Jeff (DT, 1969-71); Beard, Ken (T, 1963); Beard, Santonio (TB, 2001-02); Beard, Silas "Buddy" (HB, 1937-38); Bearden, Lane (P, 1999-2002); Beazley, Joe (DT, 1979-82); Beck, Ellis (HB, 1971-73); Beck, Willie (E, 1956-57); Beddingfield, David (QB, 1969); Bedwell, David (DB, 1965-67); Bell, Albert (SE, 1985-86); Bell, Stanley (E, 1959); Belser, Maurice (G, 1992-95); Bendross, Jesse (SE, 1980-83); Bennett, Cornelius (LB, 1983-86); Bentley, Edward Jr. (DB, 1970); Bentley, Jeff (G, 1986-87); Berrey, Fred Benjamin "Bucky" (K, 1974-76); Bethune, George (LB/DE, 1986-88); Bevel, John (LB, 2003); Bevelle, Willis (S/WR, 1989-90, 1992); Bible, Tom (T, 1961); Biel, Brad (LB, 2002); Billingsley, Randy (HB, 1972-74); Bird, Ron (T, 1963); Bires, Andy (E, 1942); Bisceglia, Steve (FB, 1971-72); Blackburn, Darrell (LB, 1993-96); Blackmon, Sumpter (QB, 1941); Blackwell, Gene (E, 1937-39); Blackwood, J.E. (G, 1921); Blair, Bill (DB, 1968-70); Blair, Elmer (B, 1917); Blair, J.W. (T, 1897); Blalock, Ralph (E, 1956-57); Blevins, James Allen (T, 1957-59); Blitz, Jeff (DB, 1972); Blue, Al (DB, 1981-82); Bobo, Mike (FB, 1985); Bodden, Vann (DE, 1993-95); Bohanon, Shaun (TB, 1999-2000); Bolden, Hirchel (CB/WR, 1999-2002); Bolden, Ray (DB, 1974-75); Boler, Clark (T, 1962-63); Boler, Thomas (T, 1980); Boles, John "Duffy" (HB, 1973-75); Bolt, Scott (T, 1990); Bolton, Bruce (SE, 1976-78); Boman, Atokie (FL, 1997); Boman, T.D. (T, 1914-15); Booker, David (SE, 1979); Booker, Steve (LB, 1981-83); Boone, Alfred Morgan "Dan" (E, 1917-19); Boone, Isaac "Ike" (E, 1919); Booth, Baxter (E, 1956-58); Boothe, Vince (G, 1977-79); Boozer, Young (HB, 1934-36); Borders, Tom (T, 1939); Boschung, Paul (DT, 1967-69); Bostick, Brian (K, 2002-04); Bostick, Lewis (G 1936-38); Boswell, Charley (HB, 1938-39); Bowdoin, James "Goofy" (G 1927-28); Bowdoin, Jimmy (HB, 1954-56); Bowens, Tim (FL 1996-

99); Bowman, Steve (FB, 1963-65); Box, Jimmy (E, 1960); Boyd, Thomas (LB, 1978-81); Boykin, Dave (FB, 1928-29); Boykin, Gideon Frierson (G, 1894); Boylan, Pat (G, 2000); Boyles, J.V. (E, 1904); Boyles, R.E. (G, 1892-93); Boylston, Robert W. (T, 1959-60); Bradford, James "Jim" (G, 1977); Bradford, Vic (QB, 1936-38); Bragan, Dale (LB, 1976); Braggs, Byron (DT, 1977-80); Braggs, Chester (RB, 1983-86); Bramblett, Dante (LB, 1984); Bramblett, Gary (G, 1979-82); Brannan, Troy Crampton (FB, 1914); Brannen, Jay (LB, 1993); Brannen, Jerre Lamar (E, 1957-58); Brasfield, Davis (HB, 1927); Brewer, Richard (SE, 1965-67); Britt, Gary (LB, 1977); Britt, Justin (DT, 2004); Britt, Wesley (T, 2001-04); Brock, Jim (G, 1981); Brock, Jon (K, 1996); Brock, Mike (G 1977-79); Brodie, Brooks (C 1997-98); Brooker, Johnny (K, 1982); Brooker, William T. "Tommy" (E, 1959-61); Brooks, Brandon (SE, 2003-04); Brooks, William S. "Billy" (C 1954-56); Brown, Bill (DB, 1982); Brown, Billy (HB, 1928); Brown, Carl Abercrombie (G 1898-99); Brown Connie (DB, 2000); Brown, Curtis (SE 1991-95); Brown, Dave (HB, 1940-42); Brown Elverett (NT, 1991-93, 1995); Brown, Halver "Buddy" (G, 1971-73); Brown, Jack (QB, 1948-51); Brown, Jerry (TE, 1974-75); Brown, Johnny Mack (HB 1923-25); Brown, Keith (FL, 2004); Brown, Larry (TE, 1979-82); Brown, Marshall (FB, 1955-57); Brown, Marvin (FB, 1998-99, 2001); Brown, Phillip (LB, 1983, 1986-87); Brown, Randy (T, 1968); Brown, Rick (FL, 1991-92, 1994); Brown, Robert (B, 1916-17); Brown, Shannon (DE, 1992-95); Brown, Tolbert "Red" (HB, 1926-27); Brown, Randall (B, 1908-09); Brown, T.L. (T, 1919-20); Brown, Will (LB 1991-93); Brungard, David (FB, 1970); Brunson, Jon (DE, 2003); Bryan, Corey (LB, 2000); Bryan, Richard (DT, 1972-74); Bryant, Anthony (NT, 2001-04); Bryant, Fernando (CB, 1995-98); Bryant, Paul W. "Bear" (E, 1933-35); Buchanan, Richard Woodruff "Woody" (FB, 1976); Buchanan, Shamari (SE, 1996-99); Buck, Oran (K, 1969); Buckler, Wm. E. "Bill" (G, 1923-25); Buckner, Tyrell (LB, 1993-96); Bumgardner, Robert (E, 1909-10); Bunch, Jim (G, 1976-79); Burgdorf, Brian (QB, 1992-95); Burkhart, C.T. (E, 1920); Burgett, John Irwin (T, 1893); Burkett, Jim (FB, 1949-50); Burks, Auxford (HB, 1903-05); Burks, Basil Manly (T, 1913-14); Burks, Henry Thomas (T, 1906-08); Burnett, Hunter Tennile (B, 1914-15); Burns, Harmon Theron (B, 1901-02); Burr, Borden (B, 1893-94); Burroughs, Anthony (FB, 1994); Burton, Kendrick (DE, 1993-95); Busbee, Kent (DB, 1967); Busby, Max (G, 1977); Bush, Jeff (B, 1933-34); Bush, Jim (G, 1945-46); Busky, Steve (TE, 1990-92); Butcher, C.P. (T, 1904); Butler, Clary-Webb (S, 1999); Butler, Clyde (T, 1970).

Caddell, Matt (FL, 2004); Cadenhead, Billy (RH, 1946-49); Cain, Jim (E, 1945-48); Cain, Johnny (FB, 1930-32); Caldwell, Herman "Blackie" (B, 1936); Caldwell, Herschel (HB, 1925-26); Callaway, Neil (LB/DE/T, 1975-77); Callies, Kelly (DT, 1977); Calvert, John (G, 1965-66); Calvin, Tom (FB, 1948-50); Camp, Joseph "Pete" (T, 1923-25); Campbell, John (QB, 1928-30); Campbell, Mike (DB, 1988-92); Campbell, Tiden "Happy" (QB, 1934-35); Canale, Blair (S, 1993-95); Canterbury, Frank (HB, 1964-66); Capps, Chris (T, 2004); Cargile, C.J. (B, 1914); Carrigan, Ralph (C, 1951-53); Carroll, Jimmy (C, 1965-66); Carroll, Travis (LB, 1997-98); Carruth, Paul Ott (RB, 1981-82, 1984); Carter, Antonio (FL, 1999-2001, 2004); Carter, Jamie (DT, 1996-99); Carter, Joe (RB, 1980-83); Carter, Marcus (S, 2004); Cary, Robert H. "Robin" (DB, 1972-73); Cash, Danny (T, 1987-89); Cash, Jeraull Wayne "Jerry" (E, 1970-71); Cash, Steve (LB, 1980); Cashio, Gri (G, 1947); Cassady, Michael (SE, 1996); Cassidy, Francis (T, 1944-47); Cassimus, John (DB/RB/WR, 1987-89); Casteal, David (HB, 1986-88); Castille, Jeremiah (DB, 1979-82); Castille, Simeon (CB, 2004); Castille, Tim (FB, 2003-04); Causey, Joe (HB, 1931); Causey, John (C, 1993-96); Cavan, David (TE, 2002-04); Cavan, Peter Alexander (HB, 1975-77); Cayavec, Bob (T, 1980-82); Chaffin, Phil (FB, 1968-70); Chambers, Jimmy (C, 1967); Chambers, Lee (QB, 1999); Chandler, Thornton (TE, 1983-85); Chapman, Herb (C, 1947); Chapman, Roger (K, 1977-78); Chappell, Howard (B, 1931-33); Chatman, Terrill (T, 1987-90); Chatwood, David (FB, 1965-67); Childers, Morris (B, 1960); Childress, Ahmad (DT, 2002-03); Childs, Bob (LB, 1966-68); Chiodetti, Larry (LH, 1950-51); Christensen, Jamie (K, 2004); Christian, Hunter (LB, 1995); Christian, Knute Rockne (C, 1954-55); Christian, Myles (FB, 1999); Ciemny, Richard (K, 1969-70); Clark, Brent (NT, 1991); Clark, Cotton (HB, 1961-62); Clark, Frank Barnard (B, 1903-04); Clark, Jeremy (DT, 2003-04); Clark, Phil (G, 1956); Clark, Tim (SE, 1978-81); Clarke, Donald (TE, 2002-03); Clay, Hugh Stephen (G, 1969); Clay, John (LB/OG) 1990-93; Clemens, Al (E, 1921-23); Clement, C.B. "Foots" (T, 1928-30); Clements, Mike (DB, 1978-80); Cline, Jackie (DT, 1980-82); Clonts, Steve (C, 1989); Clorefeline, Julius (G, 1911); Closner, J.B. (C, 2003-04); Cochran, Bob (LH, 1947-49); Cochran, Chris (LB, 1989-90); Cochran, Donald (G, 1957-59); Cochran, Ralph (QB, 1949); Cochrane, David (B, 1931); Cochrane, Henry (QB, 1937); Cohen, Andy (B 1923-24); Cokely, Donald (T, 1970-71); Colburn, Rocky (DB, 1982-84); Colburn, Roman (FL, 1992-94); Cole, Jason (LB, 1994); Cole, Lorenzo (FL, 1990-93); Cole, Richard (DT, 1965-66); Cole,

Steve (K, 1991-92); Cole, Tommy (NG/DT, 1985-88); Coleman, Michael (SE, 1978); Coley, Ken (DB/QB, 1979-82); Collins, Danny (DE, 1976-77); Collins, Doug (G, 1979-80); Collins, Earl (FB, 1980-81); Collins, Matt (LB, 2004); Collins, Sam (SE, 1999-2002); Compton, Ben (LG, 1923-25); Compton, Charley (T, 1942, 1946-47); Compton, Joe (FB, 1949-51); Comstock, Charles Dexter (B, 1895-96); Comstock, Donald (HB, 1956); Condon, Bill (G, 1984-87); Conn, Mickey (CB, 1992-94); Conner, Don (C, 1955); Constant, Marvin (MLB, 1999-2000); Conway, Bob (RH, 1950-52); Conway, William P. "Bill" (G, 1944); Cook, Elbert (LB, 1960-62); Cook, Jackson (C, 1994-96); Cook, Leroy (DE, 1972-75); Cook, Ted (E, 1942-46); Cook, Wayne (TE, 1964-66); Cooper, Britton (DB, 1983-86); Cooper, Ernest "Shorty" (T, 1921-23); Cope, Robert (G, 1892-93); Copeland, John (DE, 1991-92); Corbitt, James "Corky" (RH, 1945-46); Costigan, Chris (SE, 1989); Couch, L.B. (C, 1949-50); Countess, C.C. (C, 1907-08); Courtney, Earlando (DB, 1986-87); Cowell, Vince (G, 1978-80); Cox, Adam (TB/LB, 1998-01); Cox, Allen (T, 1972); Cox, Brent (LB, 1998); Cox, Carey (C, 1937-39); Cox, Nathan (FB, 2003); Cox, Tony (LB, 1988); Coyle, Dan Joseph Jr. (E, 1954-55); Craft, Russ (HB, 1940-42); Crane, Paul (C/LB, 1963-65); Crenshaw, Curtis (T, 1961); Creen, Cecil (LB, 1916); Crim, Travis (S, 1996-97); Croom, Sylvester (C, 1972-74); Cross, Andy (LB, 1972); Cross, Howard (TE, 1985-88); Crow, John David Jr. (HB, 1975-77); Crowson, Roger (FB, 1968); Croyle, Brodie (QB, 2002-04); Croyle, John (DE, 1971-73); Crumbley, Allen (DB, 1976-78); Crutchfield, Rance (LB, 1996); Crutchfield, Rhett (TE, 1997-98); Cryder, Robert (G, 1975-77); Culliver, Calvin (FB, 1973-76); Culpepper, Ed (T, 1951-54); Culwell, Ingram (HB, 1961-62); Cummings, Joe (E, 1952-53); Cunningham, Brian (K, 1996-98); Cunningham, Derek (CB, 1997); Cunningham, E.A. "Jim" (T, 1955-56); Curry, Eric (DE, 1990-92); Curtis, Joe (E, 1950-52); Curtis, Nathan Stephenson (B, 1906); Cuthbert, Will (T, 1997-2000).

Daniel, David (DT, 2000-01); Daniels, Brooks (LB, 2000-02); Danner, Tom (G, 1951-54); Darby, Kenneth (TB, 2003-04); Dare, Charlie (G, 1989-91); Dasher, Bob (G, 1981); Davidson, James Lafayette (C, 1900); Davidson, Trent (TE, 2004); Davis, Alvin "Pig" (FB, 1937-38); Davis, Bill (K, 1971-73); Davis, Charley (RH, 1948-49); Davis, Danny (S, 1992-93); Davis, Fernando (LB, 1993-96); Davis, Fred (T, 1938-40); Davis, Fred Jr. (T, 1964); Davis, Jim (G, 1951-53); Davis, John (E, 1987-89); Davis, Johnny Lee (FB, 1975-77); Davis, Mike (K, 1975); Davis, Ricky (S, 1973-74); Davis, Steve (K, 1965-67); Davis, Terry Ashley (QB, 1970-72); Davis, Terry Lane (E, 1970); Davis, Tim (K, 1961-63); Davis, Vantreise (LB, 1986-89); Davis, Wayne (LB, 1983-86); Davis, William (DT, 1978); Davis, William "Junior" (T, 1967-68); Dawson, Jimmy Dale (LB, 1973); Dean, Brandon (LB, 2003); Dean, Louis (DB, 1984); Dean, Mike (DB, 1967-69); Dean, Steve (HB, 1972-73); Deason, Dennis (C, 1992-93); DeLaurentis, Vincent (C, 1952-53); Demos, Joe (G, 1989); Dempsey, Benny (C, 1956-57); Demyanovich, Joe (FB, 1932-34); DeNiro, Gary (DE, 1978-80); DeShane, Charley (QB, 1940); Dewberry, John Robert (G, 1894-95); Dichiara, Ron (K, 1974); Diehl, Bryne (P, 1992-94); Dildy, Jim (T, 1931-33); Dildy, Joe (C, 1933-34); Dill, Jimmy (W, 1962-63); DiMario, Pete (G, 1993-96); Dismuke, Joe (T, 1982-83); Dixon, Dennis (TE, 1967-68); Dixon, Gerald (CB, 1999-2002); Dixon, Tony (S, 1997-2000); Dobbs, Edgar (E, 1928-30); Domnanovich, Joe (C, 1940-42); Donald, Joseph Glenn (C, 1905-06); Donaldson, Paul (E, 1954); Donnelly, Chris (S, 1992-93); Doran, Stephen Curtis (TE, 1969-70); Dotherow, Autrey (E, 1930-31); Dover, Don (C, 1992); Dowdell, Anthony (DE 1994-96); Dowdy, Cecil (T, 1964-66); Doyle, Philip (K, 1987-90); Draper, Shawn (TE/DE, 1997-2000); Drennen, Earl (QB, 1900-01); Drinkard, Reid (G, 1968-70); Drummond, Jeremy (TE, 2001); DuBose, Mike (DE, 1972-74); Duke, Jim (DT, 1967-69); Dukes, Jeffrey (S, 2004); Duncan, Conley (LB,1973-75); Duncan, Jerry (T, 1965-66); Dunn, Jeff (QB, 1987-89); Durby, Ron (T 1963-64); Dyar, Warren E. (TE, 1972-73); Dye, George (C, 1927); Dyess, Johnny (RB, 1981); Dyess, Marlin (HB, 1957-59).

Eberdt, Jess (C, 1929-30); Eckenrod, Michael Lee (C, 1973); Eckerly, Charles (G, 1952-54); Edwards, Bryant B. (RE, 1906-08); Edwards, Chris (LB, 1995-98); Edwards, Marion "Buddy" (T, 1944); Edwards, Randy (DT, 1980-83); Elder, Venson (LB, 1982-83); Elias, Johnny (Mgr., 1981-82); Ellard, Butch (Mgr., 1982); Ellett, Alvin (T, 1955); Ellington, Dante (T, 1999-2001); Ellis, Billy (B, 1928); Ellis, Raiford (C, 1934); Ellis, Victor (LB, 1998-2001); Elmore, Albert Sr. (E, 1929-30); Elmore, Albert Jr. (QB, 1953-55); Elmore, Grady (K/HB, 1962-64); Emerson, Ken (DB, 1969-70); Emmett, J.H. (HB, 1919-22); Emmons, James Thomas (T, 1954); Enis, Ben (E, 1926); Ephriam, Alonzo (C, 2000-02); Epps, Craig (LB, 1984-87); Etter, Scott (QB, 1990); Ewing, Von (G, 2004).

Fagan, Jeff (RB, 1979-82); Faust, Donald W. (FB, 1975-77); Faust, Douglas (DT 1972); Favors, Michael (G, 1994); Feagin, Michael (FL, 1995-98); Fedak, Frank (HB, 1945); Felder, Shannon (DB, 1985-87); Fell, Howie (LB, 1995); Ferguson, Burr (LE, 1892-93); Ferguson, Charles M. (G, 1968-69);

Ferguson, Corey (CB, 2001-02); Ferguson, Hill (B, 1895-86); Ferguson, Lee (TE, 1997); Ferguson, Mitch (RB, 1977, 1979-80); Ferguson, Richard (G, 1969); Fichman, Leon (T, 1941-42); Fields, Paul (QB, 1982-83); Fields, William H. (E, 1944); Filippini, Bruno (G, 1944-47); Finkley, Donnie (WR, 1989-90, 1992); Finlay, Louis Malone (T, 1909-10); Finnell, Edward Judson (B, 1911); Flanagan, Thad (SE, 1974-76); Fletcher, Maurice (QB, 1937); Fletcher, Zach (FL, 2002-03); Florence, Craige (DB, 1981-82); Florette, Anthony Ray (E, 1920); Flowers, Dick (T, 1946-47); Flowers, Kevin (DE, 1997); Flowers, Lee (T, 1945); Floyd, Chad (K, 1999); Floyd, Lamont (LB, 1993-96); Forbus, Roy (E, 1956); Ford, Brad (CB, 1944-45); Ford, Danny (T, 1967-69); Ford, Mike (DE, 1966-68); Ford, Steven (DB, 1973-74); Forman, James R. (T, 1901-02); Fortunato, Steve (G, 1946-48); Foshee, Jeff (LB/FB, 1991-94); Foshee, Jess (G, 1937-38); Fountain, Will (FL, 2003); Foust, Warren (QB/S, 1995-98); Fowler, Conrad (SE, 1966-68); Fowler, Les (DB, 1976); Fox, Alex (K/Holder, 2004); Fracchia, Mike (FB, 1960-63); Fraley, Robert (QB, 1974-75); Francis, Kavanaugh "Kay" (C, 1933-35); Frank, Milton (G, 1958-59); Frank, Morris (1962); Franklin, Arthur (RT, 1906); Franko, Jim (G, 1947-49); Frazer, Thomas Sydney (B, 1892-93); Freelend, Bo, (P, 2003-04); Freeman, Wayne (G, 1962-64); French, Buddy (K, 1963-64); Frey, Calvin (G, 1931-33); Friend, Will (G, 1994-97); Fruhmorgen, John (G, 1986-88); Fuhrman, Darrel (LB, 1987); Fulgham, Dre (WR, 2000-03); Fuller, Jimmy (T, 1964-66); Fuller, Leon (HB, 1959-60).

Gage, Fred Harrison (B, 1916); Galloway, Ahmaad (TB, 1999-2002); Gambrell, D. Joe (C, 1945-46); Gammon, George (HB, 1941-42); Gandy, Joseph Maury (T, 1912-13); Gandy, Ralph (E, 1932-35); Gantt, Greg (K, 1971-73); Gardner, Charles (DB, 1989-91); Garrett, Broox Cleveland (E, 1909); Garrett, Corna, Jr. (E, 1905-06); Garth, Juwan (LB, 2003-04); Gartman, John (SE, 2000); Gartman, Randy (S, 1993); Gaston, Willie (S, 1992-94); Gay, Stan (DB, 1981-83); Gellerstedt, Sam (NG, 1968); Gerasimchuk, David (G, 1975-76); Gerber, Elwood (G, 1940); Germanos, Nicholas "Nick" (E, 1954-55); Getchell, Billy (SE, 1984); Giangrosso, James (DE, 1991); Giardinia, Gabe (K, 2003); Gibbons, James Booth (T, 1914); Gibson, Richard (E, 1945); Gibson, Rondi (WR, 1994-95); Gilberry, Wallace (DE, 2004); Gilbert, Danny (DB, 1968-70); Gilbert, Darius (LB, 1998-2001); Gilbert, Greg (LB, 1985-88); Gilder, Andrew (FB, 1993); Gilliland, Rickey (LB, 1976-78); Gillis, Grant (QB, 1923-25); Gilmer, Creed (DE, 1964-65); Gilmer, David (G, 1984-85); Gilmer, Harry (HB, 1944-47); Gladden, Chad (C, 1991-93); Glover, Martin (FL, 1999); Godfree, Newton (T, 1930-32); Godwin, Joe (LB, 1984-86); Goode, Chris (DB, 1986); Goode, Clyde (CB, 1989-91); Goode, Kerry (RB, 1983, 1986-87); Goode, Pierre (WR, 1987-89); Gornto, Jack "Red" (E, 1938); Goss, Chad (FL, 1995-97); Gossett, Don Lee (Mgr., 1969); Gothard, Andrew "Andy" (DB, 1975-76); Gothard, Preston (TE, 1983-84); Graham, Glen W. (C, 1955-56); Grammer, James W. (C, 1969-71); Grammer, Richard (C, 1967-69); Granade, James Napoleon (E, 1898-99); Grant, Fred (FB, 1944-46); Grantham, Jim (E, 1945-46); Graves, Bibb (1892); Gray, Alan (QB, 1979-81); Gray, Charles (E, 1956-58); Gray, Eric (CB, 2004); Grayson, David Allison (RE, 1892-93); Green, Jack (G, 1945); Green, Louis E. (G, 1974-77); Greene, Edgar D. (RT, 1907-08); Greene, Hamp (K, 1991-92); Greenwood, Darren (CB, 1989-90); Greer, Brandon (WR, 2000, 2002-03); Greer, Charles West (B, 1910-11); Gregory, James (NG, 1990-93); Gresham, Owen Garside (T, 1908-09); Grice, Matt (S, 2004); Griffin, Cornelius (DT, 1998-99); Griffin, Rudy (DT, 2004); Grimes, Reggie (DT, 1996-99); Grissett, Mitch (SN, 2003); Grobe, Mark (S, 1995); Grogan, Jay (TE, 1981-83); Gryska, Clem (HB, 1947-48); Guillon, Marc (QB, 2004); Guinyard, Mickey (RB, 1981-82); Gunnells, Ross (LB, 1999); Gwin, James C. C. (C, 1903).

Hagan, James "Dink" (QB, 1913-17); Hagler, Ellis (C, 1927-28); Hall, Calvin (SE, 1995-98); Hall, DJ (FL, 2004); Hall, Lemanski (S/LB, 1990-93); Hall, Mike (LB, 1966-68); Hall, Randy Lee (DT, 1972-74); Hall, Wayne (LB, 1971-73); Hamer, Norris (DE, 1967-68); Hamilton, Wayne (DE, 1977-79); Hammond, Matt (T, 1990-93); Hammond, Spencer (LB, 1987-90); Hamner, Robert Lee (B, 1925-27); Hand, Jon (DT, 1982-85); Hand, Mike (LB/G, 1968-70); Handley, Chad (FL, 2000); Haney, James (RB, 1979); Hannah, Charles (DT, 1974-76); Hannah, David (T, 1975-79); Hannah, Herb (G, 1948-50); Hannah, John (G, 1970-72); Hannah, William C. (T, 1957-59); Hannon, Emile "Chick" (1907); Hanrahan, Gary (G, 1973); Hansen, Cliff (T, 1940-41); Hanson, John (FB, 1939-40); Hape, Patrick (TE, 1993-96); Haqq, Hamid (S, 2002); Harkins, Grover (G, 1937-38); Harkness, Fred (Mgr., 1980); Harper, Roman (S, 2002-04); Harpole, Allen "Bunk" (DG, 1965-67); Harrell, Billy (HB, 1940); Harris, Charles (DE, 1965-67); Harris, Craig (RB, 1989-92); Harris, Chris (DE, 2004); Harris, Don (DT, 1968-70); Harris, Hudson (HB, 1962-64); Harris, Jim Bob (DB, 1978-81); Harris, Joe Dale (SE, 1975); Harris, Paul (DE, 1974-76); Harris, Steven (LB, 1995-97); Harrison, Bill (DT, 1976); Harrison, Monroe (TE, 1990-91); Harrison, Matt (C, 1997); Harrison, Stacy (DB, 1988-91); Harsh, Griffin R. (QB,

1914); Harsh, William L. (HB, 1914-15); Harville, Joey (T, 1991-94); Hayden, Neb (QB, 1969-70); Heard, Victor John (B, 1910); Heard, Vigil Willis (B, 1910-11); Heath, Donnie (C, 1960); Hecht, George (G, 1940-42); Helms, Sandy (G, 1949-50); Helton, Rodney (LB,1989); Henderson, Josh (DB, 1982); Henderson, Wm. T. "Bill" (TE, 1975-77); Henderson, S.W. (1892); Henry, Butch (E, 1961-63); Herrion, Atlas (T, 2001-03); Hewes, Willis (C, 1931-32); Hickerson, Ed (G, 1938-40); Hicks, Billy (QB, 1928-29); Hicks, J.W. (G, 1912-13); Higginbotham, Robert (DB, 1967-68); Higginbotham, Steve (DB, 1969-71); High, Tracy (CB, 1993-95); Hill, John (RB, 1979-80); Hill, Marvin "Buster" (QB, 1952-54); Hill, Murry (RB, 1988-89); Hill Roosevelt (LB, 1982-83); Hill, Thomas (CB, 1996); Hilman, R.G. (E, 1895); Hines, Edward T. (DE, 1970-72); Hinton, Robert Poole (B, 1922-23); Hite, John H. (HB, 1944); Hobbs, Sam (G, 1907); Hobson, Clell (QB, 1950-52); Hodges, Bruce (DE/T, 1977); Hodges, Norwood (FB, 1944-47); Hogan, Paul (C, 1997-2000); Holcombe, Danny (G, 1980-82); Holdbrooks, Byron (DT, 1987-90); Holder, Harry (B, 1927); Holdnak, Ed (G, 1948-49); Holley, Hillman D. (B, 1930-32); Holliday, Joel (T, 1994-97); Hollie, Allen (NT, 2001); Hollingsworth, Gary (QB, 1989-90); Hollingsworth, Patrick (C, 2001); Hollis, William C. (HB, 1954-44); Holloway, Steven (T, 1999); Holm, Bernard "Tony" (FB, 1927-29); Holm, Charlie (FB, 1937-38); Holmes, Gordon "Sherlock" (C, 1924-26); Holoman, Desmond (LB, 1985-86); Holsomback, Roy (G, 1959-60); Holt, Darwin (LB, 1960-61); Holt, James Jay "Buddy" (P, 1977-79); Holt, Zac (S, 2002); Homan, Dennis (SE, 1965-67); Homan, Scott (DT, 1979-82); Hood, Bob (T, 1946-48); Hood, Chris (DE, 1995-97); Hood, Edwin P. (T, 1919-1920); Hood, Sammy (DB, 1982-83); Hope, Alvin (DB, 1990-92); Hopper, Mike (E, 1961-62, 1964); Horne, Chris (LB, 1997-99); Horstead, Don (HB, 1982, 1984-85); Horton, Jimmy (DE, 1971); Houston, Ellis "Red" (C, 1930-32); Houston, Martin (FB, 1990-92); Hovater, Dexter Louis (B, 1914-15); Hovater, Jack (E, 1919-21); Hovater, Walter E. (RH, 1917-19); Hoven, Michael (TB, 1993); Howard, Frank (G, 1928-30); Howard, Johnny (T, 1989-92); Howell, Millard "Dixie" (HB, 1932-34); Howle, G.D. (FB, 1907); Hubbard, Colenzo (LB, 1974-76); Hubert, Allison T.S. "Pooley" (FB, 1922-25); Hudson, Ben (E 1923-25); Hudson, H. Clayton (E, 1921-22); Hudson, Ray (TB, 2001-04); Hufstetler, Thomas R Jr. (C, 1977-78); Hughes, Hal (QB, 1937-38); Hughes, Howard (T, 1941); Hughes, Larry (B, 1931-33); Humphrey, Bobby (HB, 1985-88); Humphries, Marvin (LB, 1984); Hundertmark, John (T, 1933); Hunt, Ben (G, 1920-22); Hunt, Morris Parker (T, 1972-73); Hunt, Travis (T, 1950-52); Hunter, Antoine (CB, 1997-98); Hunter, Eddie (LB, 1995-98); Hunter, Jamie (LB, 2000); Hunter, Scott (QB, 1968-70); Hupke, Tom (G, 1931-33); Hurd, Clarence S. (E, 1908-09); Hurlbut, Jack (QB, 1962-63); Hurst, Tim (T, 1975-77); Hurt, Cecil A. (E, 1927-29); Husband, Hunter (TE, 1967-69); Husband, Woodward A. "Woodie" (LB, 1969-70); Hutson, Don (E, 1932-34); Hutt, John (LB, 1993).

Ikner, Lou (RB, 1977-78); Ingram, Cecil "Hootie" (DB, 1952-54); Irvin, Bobby Joe (LB, 1954); Israel, Jimmy Kent (QB, 1966); Israel, Thomas Murray (G, 1969); Ivy, Hyrle, Jr. (E, 1951-53); Ivy, Jim (DT, 1983-84).

Jack, Jason (QB, 1993); Jackson, Billy (RB, 1978-80); Jackson, Bobby (QB, 1957-58); Jackson, Kevin (S, 1995-96); Jackson, Mark (C, 1981-83); Jackson, Max (T, 1930-31); Jackson, Quincy (FL, 1997-98); Jackson, Wilbur (HB, 1971-73); Jacobs, Donald (QB, 1979-90); James, Chris (S, 2001-04); James, Kenneth Morris (T, 1969-70); James, Michael (SE, 2000-01); Jarvis, Curt (NG, 1983-86); Jeffries, Dameian (DE, 1991-94); Jelks, Gene (HB/DB, 1985-89); Jenkins, John Felix (E, 1894-95); Jenkins, Jug (E, 1949-51); Jenkins, Tom "Bobby" (FB, 1942); Jilleba, Pete (FB, 1967-69); Johns, Aaron (TB, 2004); Johns, Bobby (DB, 1965-67); Johnson, Billy (C, 1965-67); Johnson, Cornell (HB, 1959-60); Johnson, D.B. (1892); Johnson, Forney (QB, 1899); Johnson, Harold (C, 1951); Johnson, Hoss (T, 1984-86); Johnson, James (HB, 1924-25); Johnson, J. Goree (FB, 1915-16); Johnson, Jarrett (DT, 1999-2002); Johnson, Tommy (CB, 1991-94); Johnson, Tony (TE, 1992-95); Johnston, Clint (TE, 2002-04); Johnston, Donny (HB, 1966-69); Johnston, Sidney (G, 1919-20); Johnston, Wm. McDow (HB, 1914); Jones, Amos (RB, 1980); Jones, Brice Sidney (E, 1906-07); Jones, Bruce (G, 1923-25); Jones, Charles (S, 2001-03); Jones, H.H. (T, 1901); Jones, Howard Criner (G, 1914); Jones, Jason (S, 1997-2000); Jones, Joe (RB, 1978-80); Jones, Joey (SE, 1980-83); Jones, Kevin (QB, 1977-78); Jones, Paul B. (RHB, 1907); Jones, Ralph (E, 1944); Jones, Ralph Lee (G, 1917-19); Jones, Raymond William (E, 1912); Jones, Robbie (LB, 1979-82); Jones, Robert (RB, 1989); Jones, Terrence (LB, 2003-04); Jones, Terry, Jr. (TE, 1998-01); Jones, Terry Wayne (C/NG, 1975-77); Joplin, Charles West (QB/HB/E, 1911-12); Jordan, Alex (S, 1991-92); Jordan, Chris (T, 1995-96); Jordan, Lee Roy (LB, 1960-62); Jordan, Lint (E, 1950-51); Junior, Ester James III "E.J." (DE, 1977-80).

Kearley, Dan (DT, 1962-64); Kellen, Jason (P, 2000); Keller, Phillip Brooks (G, 1911); Keller,

Thomas B. "Red" (E, 1937); Kelley, Joe (QB, 1966-68); Kelley, Leslie (FB, 1964-66); Kelley, Max (FB, 1954-56); Kelly, William Milner (E, 1920-21); Kemp, Chris (K, 1999-2000); Kendrick, Kermit (S, 1985-88); Kennedy, President John F. (Honorary, 1961); Kent, William (RB, 1988); Kerley, Eric (DT, 1994-97); Kerr, Dudley (K, 1966-67); Key, Chad (SE, 1993-95); Kilgrow, Joe (HB, 1935-37); Killgore, Terry (C, 1965-67); Kilroy, William (FB, 1952); Kim, Peter (KS, 1980-82); Kimball, Morton (G, 1941); Kinderknecht, Donald H. (FB, 1955-56); King, Emanuel (DE, 1982-84); King, Joe (T, 1985-87); King, Juke (LB, 2004); King, Kenny (DT, 1999-2002); King, Tyrone (DB, 1972-75); Kirby, Lelias E. (HB, 1920-21); Kirkland, B'Ho (G, 1931-33); Kitchens, Freddie (QB, 1993, 1995-97); Knapp, David (HB, 1970-72); Knight, Canary (LB, 1998-99); Knight, Ezekial (SE, 2004); Knight, William (HB, 1957); Komisar, Kevin (LB, 1994); Kramer, Michael (DB, 1975-77); Krapf, James Paul (C, 1970-72); Krauss, Barry (LB, 1976-78); Krout, Bart (TE, 1978-81); Kubelius, Skip (DT, 1972-73); Kulback, Steve Joseph (DT, 1973-74); Kyser, G.H. "Hub" (E/RH, 1893).

LaBue, John (RB, 1976); LaBue, Joseph II (HB, 1970-72); Lambert, Buford (T, 1976); Lambert, Jerry (E, 1952); Lambert, Randolph (C, 1973-74); Lancaster, John (DE, 1979); Lane, Drew (SN, 2004); Laney, Greg (S, 1993); Langdale, Noah (T, 1940-41); Langham, Antonio (CB, 1990-93); Langhorne, Jack (T, 1922-24); Langston, Griff (SE, 1968-70); Lanier, M.B. (B, 1905); Lary, Al (E, 1948-50); Lary, Ed (E, 1949-51); Laslie, Carney (T, 1930-32); Lassic, Derrick (RB, 1989-92); Lauer, Larry (C, 1948-50); Law, Phil (T, 1971); Lawley, Lane (SE, 1970); Lawson, Kirk (T, 1993); Layton, Dale (E, 1962); Lazenby, K.J. (T, 1974-76); Leach, Foy (E, 1931-33); Ledbetter, Bradley (SN, 1998-2000); Lee, Dominic (DT, 2003-04); Lee, Harry C. (G/LB, 1951-54); Lee, Kevin (WR, 1990-93); Lee, Mickey (FB, 1968-69); Lee, Shon (DB, 1985-86); Leeth, Wheeler (E, 1941-42); Legg, Murray (DB, 1976-78); Leland, Billy (FB, 1996); Lenoir, David (DE/TE, 1987-89); Lenoir, E.B. "Mully" (HB, 1917-20); Leon, Tony (G, 1941-42); Letcher, Marion (C, 1893-94); Lett, Frank Montague (G, 1901-02); Lewis, Al (G, 1961-63); Lewis, Butch (C, 1985, 1987-88); Lewis, Chester (SN, 1994-96); Lewis, Milo (CB, 1999-2000); Lewis, Tommy (FB, 1951-53); Lewis, Walter (QB, 1980-83); Little, Poc (FB, 1920); Little, William (G, 1892-93); Locke, Eric (WR, 1998); Lockett, Victor (LB, 1990-92); Lockridge, Doug (C, 1948-49); Loftin, James (HB, 1956-57); Logan, Ron (FL, 2000); Lomax, Matt (C, 2003); Lombardo, John (DB, 1984); London, Antonio (LB, 1989-92); Long, Charles Allen (B, 1913-14); Long, Leon (HB, 1929-31); Lopez, Alan (K, 1987); Love, Henry Benton (G, 1912); Lowe, Donnie (LB/FB, 2000-01); Lowe, Eddie (LB, 1980-82); Lowe, Woodrow (LB, 1972-75); Lowery, Jackson (S, 1993); Lowman, Joseph Allen (E, 1916-17); Luke, Triandos (SE, 2000-03); Lumley, Wade H. (G, 1907); Lumpkin, Billy Neal (HB, 1955); Luna, Robert K. "Bobby" (HB, 1951-54); Lusk, Thomas Joseph III (DE, 1970-72); Lutz, Bill (TE, 1987); Lutz, Harold "Red" (E/K, 1949-51); Lyles, Warren (NG, 1978-81); Lynch, Curtis R. (E, 1953-55); Lynch, Tarrant (RB, 1990-94); Lyon, Samuel Hamilton (T, 1934-35); Lyons, Martin A. "Marty" (DT, 1977-78).

MacAfee, Ken (E, 1951); MacCartee, Allen Graham (HB, 1922-23); Machtolff, Jack (C, 1937); Madden, Montoya (RB, 1995-98); Maddox, Sam H. (TE, 1976-77); Madison, Anthony (CB, 2002-04); Malcolm, Charles (FB, 1952); Mallard, James (SE, 1980); Malone, Alex (FB, 1999); Malone, Toderick (SE, 1993-95); Mancha, Vaughn (C, 1944-47); Mangum, John (DB, 1986-89); Mangum, Kris (TE, 1992); Manley, Harold (E, 1950-51); Mann, Frank (K, 1968-70); Manning, Thomas (C, 1910-11); Marcello, Jerry (DB, 1973); Marcus, Van J. (T, 1950-52); Mardini, Georges (K, 1980); Marks, Keith (SE ,1979-82); Marlow, Bobby (HB, 1950-52); Marr, Charles (G, 1933-34); Marsh, Griffith (QB, 1913-15); Marsh, William "Bill" (LH, 1915-16); Marshall, Fred H. (C, 1970-71); Marshall, Jeff (1990); Martin, Darrell (T, 1987); Martin, Gary (HB, 1961-63); Martin, Kenny (FB, 1996-97); Martz, Danny (G, 2004); Mason, George L. (T, 1952-54); Mathis, Evan (C/T/G, 2001-04); Mauro, John (DR, 1978-80); Maxwell, Raymond Edward (T, 1972-75); May, Walter (B, 1949); Martz, Danny (G, 2003-04); Mayfield, Dave (T, 1949-50); Maynor, E.W. (C, 1915-16); McAddley, Jason (SE, 1998-01); McAlpine, Frank (FB, 1944); McBee, Jerry (HB, 1955); McBride, Roberto (CB, 2001, 2003); McCain, George (HB, 1950-51); McCants, A.G. (RH, 1892-94); McCants, Keith (LB, 1988-89); McClain, Le'Ron (FB, 2003-04); McClendon, Frankie (T, 1962-64); McClintock, Dustin (FB, 1997-99); McClintock, Graham (E/B, 1922-24, 1927); McCollough, Gaylon (C, 1962-64); McCombs, Eddie (T, 1978-80); McConville, John (E, 1944); McCorquodale, John C. (T, 1902); McCorvery, Gessner T. (B, 1900-01); McCrary, Tom (DT, 1982-84); McCullough, Jeff (T, 1994); McDonald, James T. (T, 1927); McDonald, Jason (T, 1996-99); McDowell, Holt Andrews (B, 1911-12); McElroy, Alan (K, 1978-79); McFadden, Chauvon (DT, 2000); McGahey, T.A. "Son" (T, 1934-35); McGee, Barry (G, 1975); McGhee, Chad (S, 1998); McGill, Larry (HB, 1962-63); McGriff, Curtis (Mgr., 1977-79);

McInnish, Carl (S, 2002); McIntosh, John (G, 1983-85); McIntosh, S.W. (T, 1894); McIntyre, David (T, 1975-76); McKay-Loescher, Nautyn (DE, 2001-03); McKewen, Jack (T, 1941-42); McKewen, Jack II (T, 1968); McKinney, Robert B. Jr. (DB, 1970-72); McKosky, Ted (G, 1941-42, 1946); McLain, Greg (FB, 2002-04); McLain, Rick (TE, 1974-75); McLeod, Ben (DE, 1965); McLeod, Ben W. (HB, 1934-36); McMakin, David (DB, 1971-73); McMillian, Mark (CB, 1990-91); McMillian, Thomas E. (E, 1933); McNatt, Drew (SN, 1998); McNeal, Don (DB, 1977-79); McNeal, Kareem (T, 1992-95); McQueen, Mike (T, 1981-83); McRae, Scott (LB, 1982-84); McRight, Ralph (HB, 1928-30); McSorley, Joey (FB, 1999); McWhorter, Jim (QB, 1942); Meadows, Brenon (G, 1996-97); Means, Albert (DT, 2000); Melton, James "Bimbo" (HB, 1949-51); Merrill, Walter (T, 1937-39); Merrill, William Hoadley (G, 1910); Merritt, Miguel (LB, 1998-99); Mikel, Bobby (DE, 1976); Miller, Andrew McMurray (C, 1914); Miller, Floyd (T, 1948-49); Miller, Hugh (G, 1929-30); Miller, John (G, 1928-30); Miller, Marc (LB/S, 2001-02); Miller, Matt (FL, 2003-04); Miller, Noah Dean (LB, 1973); Mills, Wayne (TE, 1991); Milner, Jason (DE, 1993); Milons, Freddie (SE, 1998-2001); Mims, Carl (HB, 1941); Mims, Fred (G, 1950-52); Miree, Brandon (TB, 2000); Mitchell, David Dewey (LB, 1975-77); Mitchell, John (DE, 1971-72); Mitchell, Ken "Tank" (G, 1964); Mitchell, Lydell (LB, 1985-87); Mitchell, Ripp (DB, 1989-90); Mizerany, Mike (G, 1948-50); Mohr, Chris (P, 1985-88); Mollicone, Marc (TE, 1999); Monroe, Aires (DE, 2000-01); Monsky, Leroy (G, 1936-37); Montgomery, Greg (LB, 1972-75); Montgomery, Robert M. (DE, 1970); Montgomery, William Gabriel (T, 1920-21); Moody, Farley (B, 1912); Moody, Wash (G, 1906); Mooneyham, Marlin (FB, 1962); Moore, Brett (CB, 2001); Moore, Eric (S, 2002); Moore, Harold (FB, 1965-66); Moore, Jimmy (E, 1928-30); Moore, John (HB, 1962); Moore, Kelvin (DE, 1993-96); Moore, Mal (QB, 1962); Moore, Michael (G, 1996-97); Moore, Pete (FB, 1968-69); Moore, Randy (TE, 1970-73); Moore, Ricky (FB, 1981-84); Moore, Robert "Bud" (E, 1958-60); Moore, Stephen (FL, 2001); Moorehead, Kindal (DE, 1998-99, 2001-02); Moorer, Jefferson (G, 1953-54); Morgan, Ed (FB, 1966-68); Morgan, Patrick (P, 1999); Moring, Marcus (FB, 1993); Morris, Mario (LB, 1991-93); Morrison, Duff (HB, 1958-59, 1961); Morrison, William (FB, 1926); Morrow, Bob Ed (G, 1934); Morrow, Hugh (QB, 1944-47); Morton, Farris (E, 1962); Morton, L.D. (E, 1916); Moseley, Elliott (C, 1960); Moseley, Frank "Chesty" (B, 1931-33); Mosley, Herschel "Herky" (HB, 1938-39); Mosley, John (HB, 1964-66); Mosley, Norman "Monk" (HB, 1942, 1946-47); Mosley, Russ (HB, 1941-42); Moss, Clay (SE, 1983); Moss, Stan (E, 1965-67); Moss, Stan (P, 1990-92); Mott, Steve (C, 1980-82); Moyle, Lamar (C, 1934-36); Mudd, Joseph Paul (B, 1908-09); Mullinex, Scott (G, 1993); Murphy, Phillip (HB, 1973); Musso, Johnny (HB, 1969-71); Myers, Michael (DT, 1996); Myles, Reggie (CB, 1998-2001).

Namath, Joe Willie (QB, 1962-64); Nathan, R.L. (QB, 1912-13); Nathan, Tony (HB, 1975-78); Neal, Rick (TE, 1976-78); Neighbors, Billy (T, 1959-61); Neighbors, Keith (LB, 1990); Neighbors, Sidney (T, 1956-57); Neighbors, Wes (C, 1983-86); Nelson, Benny (HB, 1961-63); Nelson, Charles (QB, 1956); Nelson, Jimmy (HB, 1939-41); Nelson, Rod (K, 1974-76); Nesbet, James "Bubber" (FB, 1934-36); Nesmith, C.C. (HB, 1892-94); Newberry, Gene (TE, 1988); Newman, Hal (E, 1938-40); Newsome, Ozzie (SE, 1974-77); Newton, Tom (E, 1920-22); Niblett, Josh (FB, 1993-95); Nichols, Mike (SE, 1988); Nix, Mark (RB, 1979-81); Noland, John Phillip (1917-18); Noojin, Augustus Young (B, 1908); Noonan, L.W. "Red" (FB, 1945, 1947-49); Norman, Haywood Eugene "Butch" (DE, 1973); Norris, Lanny S. (DB, 1970-72); Northington, Merrill P. (G, 1893); Nunley, Jeremy (DE, 1990-93).

Oates, W.C. (G, 1906); O'Conner, J.T (B, 1919-20); O'Dell, Richard (E, 1959-60, 1962); Oden, Derrick (LB, 1989-92); Odom, Antwan (DE, 2000, 2002-03); Odom, Ernest LaVont (E, 1973); Ogden, Ray (HB, 1962-64); Ogilvie, Margan Oslin "Major" (RB, 1977-80); Olenski, Mitchell (T, 1942); O'Linger, John (C, 1959-61); Oliver, William (HB, 1952-53); Oliver, William "Brother" (DB, 1960-61); Oliver, W.S. "Country" (B/T, 1922-23, 1925); Orcutt, Ben (RB, 1981); O'Rear, Jack (QB, 1974, 1976-77); Oser, Gary (C, 1976); O'Steen, Robert "Gary" (FB, 1957-59); O'Sullivan, Pat (LB, 1947-50); O'Toole, Mike (DB, 1982); Otten, Gary (T, 1983-86); Owen, Wayne (LB, 1966-68); Owens, Donald (E, 1956-57); Ozmint, Lee (DB, 1986-89).

Paget, Manchester (LG, 1920); Palmer, Dale (LB, 1978); Palmer, David (SE, 1991-93); Palmer, Thomas W. (B, 1908-09); Panks, Heath (DT, 1996-97); Papias, Julious (HB, 1941); Pappas, Peter George (SE, 1973); Parker, Calvin (DE, 1976-78); Parker, Matt (DT, 1994-95); Parkhouse, Robin (DE, 1969-71); Parsons, Don (G, 1958); Patrick, Linnie (RB, 1980-83); Patterson, Jim (G, 1971); Patterson, Roosevelt (T, 1991-93); Patterson, Steve (G, 1972-74); Patterson, Trent (G, 1987-90); Patton, David Dane (E, 1898-1900); Patton, James "Jap" (E, 1959-61); Patton, William Pratt (E, 1906-07);

Payne, Brian (LB, 1989); Payne, Greg (SE, 1984, 1987-88); Payne, Leslie (T, 1925-27); Pearce, Clarke "Babe" (T, 1926-28); Pearl, James H. (E, 1944); Peavy, John Roberts (T, 1902-04); Peebles, Emory Bush (QB, 1908-10); Pell, Charles B. (T, 1960-62); Pennington, Jeremy (G, 1993-96); Pennington, Spencer (QB, 2003-04); Pepper, Raymond W. (FB, 1926-27); Peprah, Charlie (CB, 2002-04); Perkins, Ray (E, 1964-66); Perrin, Benny (DB, 1980-81); Perry, Anthony "Lefty" (DB, 1973); Perry, Claude (T, 1925); Person, Carlton (LB, 1997); Peter, G.F. (1892); Peters, William E. (G, 1936-37); Pettee, Robert A. "Bob" (G, 1960-62); Pettus, Gordon (HB, 1945-46, 1948); Pflugner, Ryan (K, 1998-99); Pharo, Edward (FB, 1952-56); Phillips, Gary (G, 1958-60); Phillips, Greg (S, 1998); Phillips, John (NT, 1992); Phillips, John David (QB/S, 1994, 1996, 1998); Phillips, Darryl (LB, 1988-89); Pickett, Paul (LB, 1994, 1996-97); Pickhard, Frederick (T, 1926-27); Pierce, Billy (DB, 1983-84); Pine, Matthew (C, 1990-93); Piper, Billy (HB, 1960, 1962-63); Pittman, Alec Noel (DE, 1979-82); Pitts, Mike (LB, 1979-82); Piver, Mike (LB, 1989); Pizzitola, Alan (DB, 1973-75); Poe, Monte (QB, 1999); Poole, John Paul (E, 1955-58); Pope, Daniel (P, 1997-98); Pope, Derrick (LB, 2002-03); Pope, Herman "Buddy" (T, 1973-75); Pope, Myron (LB, 1992); Portis, Marico (C, 1999, 2001-02); Potts, Douglas (G, 1954-56); Powe, Frank Houston (E, 1899-1901); Powell, Harold Mustin (T, 1910-11); Powell, Ozell (DE, 1993-96); Powell, Tripp (SN, 2000); Pratt, Derrill B. (E, 1908-09); Pratt, G.W. (G, 1907, 1909); Pratt, Henry Merrill (G, 1892-94); Prestwood, Thomas A. (DE, 1975); Price, Scott (DB, 1977); Pritchett, Bart (NT, 1992); Pritchett, James P. (E, 1955); Proctor, Michael (K, 1992-95); Prom, John (G, 1951); Propst, Clyde "Shorty" (C, 1922-24); Propst, Eddie (DB, 1966-67); Prothro, Tyrone (SE, 2003-04); Prudhomme, John Mark (DB, 1973-75); Pruitt, Jeremy (S, 1995-96); Pugh, Ed (TE, 1984); Pugh, George (TE, 1972-75); Pugh, Keith Harrison (SE, 1977-79).

Quick, Cecil Van (DE, 1970).

Raburn, Gene (FB, 1965-66); Radford, James Soloman (T, 1935-36); Ragland, Matt (SE, 2004); Raines, Billy (G, 1956-57); Raines, James Patrick (C, 1970-72); Raines, Vaughn Michael (DT, 1972-73); Ramil, Mike (DT, 1988-89); Ranager, George (SE, 1968-70); Rankin, Carlton (QB, 1962); Ranson, Brad (DT, 1994); Rasheed, Saleem (LB, 1999-2001); Rast, Holt (E, 1939-41); Raulston, Bart (G, 2000-02); Rawls, Jason (LB, 2001); Ray, Chris (G, 1999); Ray, David (SE/K, 1964-65); Ray, Michael (C, 1995-97); Ray, Shontua (CB, 1999-2001); Rayam, Thomas (DT, 1987-88); Reaves, Pete (G, 1958); Redden, Guy (G, 1904-05); Redden, Jake (G, 1937-38); Redmill, Griff (DT/G, 1997-2000); Reed, Wayne (Mgr., 1981); Reese, Kenny (HB, 1942); Reidy, Thomas (LHB, 1907-08); Reier, Chris (CB, 1998); Reilly, Mike (DB, 1966-68); Reitz, John David (DE/T, 1965-67); Reyes, Marlon (CB, 1995-96); Reynolds, Mike (S, 1995); Rhoads, Wayne R. (DE, 1969-70); Rhoden, Steve (K, 1981); Rhodes, D. Wayne Jr. (DB, 1973-75); Rice, William J. "Bill" (E, 1959-61); Rich, Jerry (HB, 1959); Richard, Arvin (TB, 1997-2000); Richardson, Greg (WR, 1983-86); Richardson, Jesse (G, 1950-52); Richardson, Ron (DB, 1971); Richardson, Todd (DB/WR, 1986-88); Richardson, W.E. (HB, 1959-61); Richeson, George (T, 1942); Richeson, Ray (T, 1946-48); Richey, Jonathan (QB, 2000-01); Riddle, Charles D. (C, 1912-13); Riddle, Dennis (TB, 1994-97); Ridgeway, Danny Howard (K, 1973-75); Ridings, Nick (SN, 2000-03); Riley, Joe (HB, 1934-36); Riley, Mike (DB, 1974); Rippetoe, Benny (QB, 1971); Roach, Freddie (LB, 2002-04); Robbins, Joe (C, 1978-80); Robbins, Shelby (LB, 1994); Roberts, James "Babs" (E, 1940-42); Roberts, Johnny (FB, 1937); Roberts, Kenneth (C, 1956-58); Roberts, Larry (DT, 1982-85); Roberts, Rob (C, 1984-85); Robertson, James (HB, 1944-46); Robertson, Ronald Dale (LB, 1973-74); Robinette, Chris (G, 1988-90); Robinson, Carlos (FB, 1986-87); Robinson, Freddie (DB, 1983-86); Robinson, Kyle (K, 2003); Robinson, Ramzee (CB, 2003-04); Rockwell, Bragg (LB, 1989-91); Rockwell, Randy (LB, 1984-87); Roddam, J.D. (HB, 1949); Roddam, Ronnie (C, 1968-69); Rodriguez, Mike (Mgr., 1981-83); Rogers, Eddie Bo (LB, 1996-97); Rogers, Isaac "Ike" (T, 1916-19); Rogers, John David (G, 1972-74); Rogers, Michael (LB, 1991-94); Rogers, O'Neal (B, 1927); Rogers, Richard (G, 1973); Rohrdanz, Clarence (FB, 1935); Ronsonet, Norbie (E, 1958-60); Root, Steve (LB, 1971); Roper, Todd (LB, 1981, 1983-85); Rose, Larry (T, 1985-88); Rosenfeld, David (HB, 1925-26); Rosenfeld, Max (QB, 1920-21); Rosser, Jimmy Lynn (T, 1969-71); Rouzie, Jefferson Carr (LB, 1970-71, 1973); Rowan, Robert "Robby" (DB, 1972); Rowe, Harry (G 1919); Rowell, Jeff (S, 1998); Rowell, Terry (DT, 1969-71); Royal, Andre (LB, 1991-93); Rudd, Dwayne (LB, 1994-96); Rudolph, Jonathan (LB, 1997); Ruffin, Larry Joe (G, 1973-75); Rumbley, Roy (G, 1981-82); Rushton, Derrick (DT, 1986, 1988-89); Russell, Lamonde (TE/SE, 1987-90); Rustin, Nathan (DT, 1966-67); Rutledge, Gary (QB, 1972-74); Rutledge, Jack (G, 1959-61); Rutledge, Jeffery R. (QB, 1975-78); Rutledge, Rod (TE, 1994-97); Ryans, DeMeco (LB, 2002-04); Ryba, Jim (T, 1937); Ryles, Willie (DT, 1985).

Sabo, Al (QB, 1940-42); Sadler, David A. (G, 1975-77); Salem, Ed (HB, 1947-50); Salem, George

(HB, 1956); Salem, George (G, 1986); Salem, Jimbo (LB, 1988); Salls, Don (FB, 1940-42); Samford, Conner (G, 1916); Samples, Alvin (G, 1967-69); Samuel, Cedric (CB, 1993-96); Samuels, Chris (T, 1996-99); Sanders, Derek (DT, 2001-02); Sanders, Terry (K, 1981-84); Sanders, Theo (TE, 2001-02); Sanderson, Craig (WR, 1988-89); Sanford, Donald (G, 1930-32); Sanford, Hayward "Sandy" (E/K, 1936-37); Sansing, Walter (FB, 1958); Sartain, Harvey (T, 1904); Sasser, Mike (DB, 1966-69); Saucier, Robert (FB, 2001); Saul, Calhoun "Sunbeam" (G, 1916); Savage, Frank (T, 1892-93); Sawyer, Bubba (SE, 1969-71); Scales, Lou (FB, 1941-42, 1945); Schamun, Russ (SE, 1974-76); Schmissrauter, Kurt (T, 1981-83); Schumann, Eric (DB, 1977); Scissum, Ed (FB, 1994-97); Scissum, Willard (G, 1981-84); Scott, Arthur (T, 1957); Scott, David (CB,. 2002-03); Scott, James Alfred (E, 1910); Scott, Randy (LB, 1978-80); Scroggins, Billy (SE, 1967-68); Searcey, Bill (G, 1978-80); Seay, Buddy (HB, 1969-70); Sebastian, Mike (DT, 1978); Secrist, Troy (WR, 1988); Segrest, Rory (T, 1995); Seibert, Chris (LB, 1996); Self, Hal (QB, 1944-46); Selman, Tom (T, 1950); Sessions, Tram (C, 1917, 1919-20); Sewell, J. Luke (QB, 1919-20); Sewell, Joe (HB, 1917-19); Sewell, Junior (FB); Sewell, Ray (QB, 1976); Sewell, Toxey (1913-14); Shackelford, James (S, 1992); Shade, Sam (CB, 1991-94); Shankles, Don (E, 1967); Sharpe, Jimmy (G, 1960-62); Sharpe, Joe F. (C, 1929-31); Sharpe, Sam (E, 1940-42); Sharpless, John W. Jr. (SE, 1972-73); Shaw, Wayne (FB, 1987-89); Shealy, Steadman (QB, 1977-79); Sheils, Tobie (C, 1990-93); Shelby, Willie (HB, 1973-75); Shephard, Willie (LB, 1985-88); Shepherd, Joe Ruffus (G, 1935-36); Sherrer, Kevin (TE, 1995); Sherrill, Jackie (FB/LB, 1963-65); Sherrill, Wm. Swift (E, 1901-03); Shinn, Richard (DT, 1980-82); Shipp, Billy (T, 1949, 1952-53); Shirley, Patrick Kyle (1910); Shoemaker, Perron "Tex" (E, 1937-39); Short, Andre (S, 1994-97); Shula, Mike (QB, 1984-86); Shultz, Roger (C, 1987-90); Sides, John "Brownie" (DT, 1966-67); Sigler, Kevin (S, 1995-98); Sign, Chris (G, 1997); Simmons, David (LB, 2003); Simmons, Jim (T, 1962-64); Simmons, Jim (TE, 1969-71); Simmons, Malcolm (P, 1981-83); Simon, Kenny (RB, 1979-81); Simpson, L.W. (T, 1893); Sims, T.S. (LG, 1905-06); Sims, Wayne (G, 1958-59); Sims, Williams Corner (G, 1931-32); Sington, Dave (T, 1956-58); Sington, Fred (T, 1928-30); Sington, Fred Jr. (T, 1958-59); Sisia, Joseph (T, 1960); Skelton, Robert "Bobby" (QB, 1957-60); Skidmore, Jim (G, 1928); Slaughter, Derrick (DT, 1985-86); Slay, Marcus (CB, 1998); Slemons, Billy (HB, 1937-38); Sloan, Steve (QB, 1963-65); Slone, Samuel Byron (E, 1893-96); Smalley, Jack (T, 1951-53); Smalley, Jack Jr. (LB, 1976-77); Smalley, Roy (G, 1950); Smiley, Anthony (DE, 1981-83); Smiley, Justin (G, 2001-03); Smith, Anthony (DT, 1985-87); Smith, Barry S. (C, 1977-79); Smith, Ben (E, 1929-31); Smith, Bill (P, 1989); Smith, Bobby (DB. 1978-79); Smith, Bobby (QB, 1956-58); Smith, Dan (P, 1984); Smith, Dan H. (LH, 1892-93); Smith, Darrell (C, 1994); Smith, David (QB, 1986-88); Smith, Earl (E, 1926-28); Smith, Jack (G, 1949); Smith, James Sidney (C, 1974-76); Smith, Joe (WR, 1983-85); Smith, Josh (TB/FB, 2003-04); Smith, Kenny (DT, 1997-2000); Smith, Mike (S/SE, 1987-1990); Smith, Molton (G/T, 1928-29); Smith, Riley H. (QB, 1933-35); Smith, Sammy Wayne (G, 1957); Smith, Tito (LB, 1996-98); Smith, Trevis (FB/LB, 1995-98); Smith, Truman A. (HB, 1903-04); Sneed, Byron (DE, 1988-91); Snoderly, John M. (C, 1952-53, 1956); Somerville, Tom (G, 1965-67); Sowell, Brent (DT, 1983-85); Speed, Elliott (C, 1948-50); Spencer, Marcus (S, 1997-2000); Spencer, Paul (FB, 1939-40); Spencer, Tom (DB, 1979); Spikes, Irving (RB, 1991); Spivey, Paul Randall (FB, 1972-73); Sprayberry, Steve (T, 1972-73); Spree, Sage (T, 1995-96, 1998); Sprinkle, Jerrill (DB, 1980-82); Spruiell, Jerry (E, 1960); Stabler, Ken "Snake" (QB, 1965-67); Stacy, Siran (RB, 1989-91); Stafford, Angelo (TE, 1986-87); Stamps, Marcel (LB, 2004); Stanford, Robert "Bobby" (T, 1969-72); Stanley, Steve (S/LB, 1995-98); Staples, John (G, 1942-46); Stapp, Charlie (HB, 1935); Stapp, Laurien "Goobie" (QB/K, 1958-60); Starling, Hugh (E, 1928-29); Starr, Bryan Bartlett (QB, 1952-55); Staten, Ralph (LB, 1993-96); Steakley, Rod (SE, 1971); Steger, Brian (TB, 1993-95); Steiner, Rebel (E, 1945, 1947-49); Stennis, Carlos (NT, 1998); Stephens, Bruce (G, 1965-67); Stephens, Charles (E, 1962-64); Stephens, Gerald (C, 1962); Stephenson, Dwight (C, 1977-79); Stephenson, Lovick Leonidas (RE, 1915-16); Stephenson, Riggs (FB, 1917, 1919-20); Stevens, Wayne (E, 1966); Stevenson, Jon (T, 1991-94); Stewart, Arthur Walter (HB, 1901); Stewart, Robert (LB/FB/NG, 1987-88, 1990-91); Stewart, Vaughn (C, 1941); Stickney, Enoch Morgan (B, 1912); Stickney, Frederick Grist (E, 1901-02); Stickney, Ravis "Red" (FB, 1957-59); Stock, Mike (HB, 1973-75); Stockton, Hayden (P, 1994-96); Stokes, Ralph Anthony (HB, 1972-74); Stone, G.E. (C, 1894); Stone, Rocky (G, 1969); Stone, William J. (FB, 1953-55); Stowers, Max Frederick (QB, 1916-17); Strickland, Charles "Chuck" (LB, 1971-73); Strickland, Lynwood (DE, 1965); Strickland, Vince (T, 1989); Strickland, William Ross (T, 1970); Strum, Richard (HB, 1957); Stubbs, Jay (FL, 1999); Sturdivant, Raymond (B, 1906-07); Stutson, Brian (DB, 1988-91); Sugg, Joseph Cullen (G, 1938-39); Sullen, James Jr. (FL, 1999); Sullins,

John (LB, 1988-91); Sullivan, Johnny (DT, 1964-66); Surlas, Tom (LB, 1970-71); Suther, John Henry (HB, 1928-30); Sutton, Donnie (SE, 1966-68); Sutton, Mike (DB, 1978); Sutton, Vince (QB, 1984, 1987-88); Swafford, Bobby "Hawk" (SE, 1967-68); Swaim, M.M. (G, 1931-32); Swain, Manuel (TE, 1989); Swann, Gerald (DB, 1982); Swinney, Dabo (WR, 1990-92); Swopes, Herold (FB, 1993); Swords, Josh (G, 1997).

Tanks, John (LB, 1993-96); Tate, Patrick (TE, 2001); Tatum, Kyle (DT/T, 2003-04); Taylor, Archie (B, 1926-27); Taylor, J.K. (RH, 1914-15); Taylor, James E. (HB, 1973-75); Taylor, Lance (FL, 2001-03); Taylor, Paul (FB, 1948); Teague, George (CB, 1989-92); Teague, Matt (FB, 1998); Terlizzi, Nicholas (T, 1945); Tew, Lowell (FB, 1944-47); Tharp, Thomas "Corky" (HB, 1951-54); Theris, Bill (T, 1948-49); Thomas, Cliff (NG, 1984-86); Thomas, Daniel Martin (C, 1970); Thomas, Derrick (LB, 1985-88); Thomas Efrum (CB/S, 1989-90); Thomas, Lester (FB, 1921); Thomas, Neal (K, 2000-01); Thomas, Ricky (S, 1983-86); Thomason, Frank Boyd (E, 1919); Thompson, Louis (DT, 1965-66); Thompson, Richard "Dickey" (DHB, 1965-67); Thompson, Wesley (T, 1951, 1955-56); Thornton, Bryan (DE, 1992-95); Thornton, George (DT, 1988-90); Tidwell, Robert Earl (C, 1903-04); Tiffin, Van (K, 1983-86); Tillman, Tommy (E, 1952-54); Tillmann, Homer Newton "Chip" (T, 1976-77); Tipton, Jim (T, 1936-37); Todd, Richard (QB, 1973-75); Tolleson, Tommy (SE, 1963-65); Torrence, Jeff (LB, 1992-93, 1995); Townsend, Deshea (CB, 1994-97); Trammell, Pat (QB, 1959-61); Travis, Timothy Lee "Tim" (TE, 1976-79); Trimble, Delan (LB, 1993); Trimble, Wayne (QB, 1964-66); Tripoli, Paul (DB, 1983-84); Trodd, Paul (K, 1981-83); Tuck, Ed (SE, 1984); Tuck, Floyd (B, 1927); Tucker, John (QB, 1930-31); Tucker, Lance (QB, 1994-97); Tucker, Michael V. (DB, 1975-77); Tucker, Richard "Ricky" (DB, 1977-80); Tuley, James (K, 1992); Turner, Craig (FB, 1982-83, 1985); Turner, Eric (S, 1992-94); Turner, Kevin (FB, 1988-91); Turner, Rory (DB, 1985-85, 1987); Turner, Steve (DT, 1987-88); Turner, Tarus (FB, 1993-94); Turnipseed, Thad (LB, 1993); Turpin, John R. (FB, 1977-78); Turpin, Richard "Dick" (DE, 1973-75); Tutwiler, Edward McGruder (B, 1898); Tyson, Adrian (NG, 1983).

Umphrey, Woody (P, 1978-80).

Vagotis, Chri (G, 1966); Valletto, Carl (E, 1957-58); Valletto, David (DB, 1983-84); Vandegraaff, Adrian V. (B, 1911-12); Vandegraaff, Hargrove (LHB, 1913); Vandegraaff, W.T. "Bully" (T/FB, 1912-15); Varnado, Carey Reid (C, 1970); Vaughn, Michael (FL, 1995-96, 1998); Vaughans, Cedric (SE, 1984); Veazy, Louis (G, 1955); Versprille, Eddie (FB, 1961-63); Versprille, Steve (LB, 1991); Vickers, Doug (G, 1981-83); Vickery, Michael (FL, 1999); Vickery, Roy Leon (T, 1956); Vines, Jay (G, 1978); Vines, Melvin (1926, 1928-29).

Wade, Steve (DB, 1971-72); Wade, Tommy (DB, 1967-68, 1970); Waggoner, Clint (TE/DE, 1996-98); Wagner, Richard (LB, 1983); Wagstaff, Granison (LB, 1995-96, 1998); Waites, W.L. (HB, 1938); Waldrop, Demarcus (LB, 2004); Walker, Bland Jr. (C, 1957); Walker, Edgar (DE, 1995-97); Walker, Erskine "Bubba" (HB, 1931-33); Walker, Hardy (T, 1981, 1983, 1985); Walker, Hilmon (E, 1936); Walker, James E. (E, 1935); Walker, Jeremy (FB, 1999); Walker, M.P. (E, 1892); Walker, Noojin (FB, 1955); Walker, Wayne D. (T, 1944); Walker, William Mudd (QB, 1892-94); Wall, Jeff (H, 1989-92); Wall, Larry "Dink" (FB, 1961-62, 1964); Walls, Clay (HB, 1955-57); Walters, John (LB, 1992-95); Ward, Alan (K, 1987-90); Ward, Lorenzo (S, 1987-90); Ward, Thurman (CB, 2001, 2003); Ward, Wm. LaFayette (HB, 1904-05); Warnock, Robert (SE, 1997); Warren, Derrick (TE, 1989-91); Warren, Erin "Tut" (E, 1937-39); Warren, Jarrod (S, 1998); Washco, Gerald George (DT, 1973-75); Washington, Eric (DB, 1990-91); Washington, Mike (DB, 1972-74); Watford, Jerry (G, 1950-52); Watkins, David (DE, 1971-73); Watson, Rick (FB, 1974-76); Watson, William C. (E, 1908); Watts, Jimmy (DE, 1981-83); Watts, Tyler (QB, 1999-2001); Watts, William (K, 1993-96); Weaver, Sam (E, 1928-29); Webb, Steve (DE, 1988-91); Weeks, George (E, 1940-42); Weeks, Phillip (S, 1999); Weigand, Tommy (HB, 1968); Weist, T.J. (WR, 1987); Welsh, Clem (HB, 1948); Wert, Thomas William (T/FB, 1899); Wesley, L.O. (QB, 1922-23); Wesley, Wm. Earl "Buddy" (FB, 1958-60); West, Marcell (FL, 1993-96); Wethington, Matt (K, 1991-94); Whaley, Frank (DE, 1965-66); Whatley, James W. (T, 1933-35); Whatley, Seaborn Thronton (B, 1906); Wheeler, Wayne (SE, 1971-73); Whetstone, Darryl (DT, 1987); Whisenhunt, Tab (LB, 1992); Whitaker, Hulet (E, 1925); White, Arthur P. "Tarzan" (G, 1934-36); White, Brent (QB, 1991); White, Chris (SE, 1987); White, Darryl (SE, 1981-82); White, Ed (E, 1947-49); White, Frank S. Jr. (FB, 1897-99); White, Gus (Mgr., 1974-76); White, Jack (Gm 1971); White, Kelvis (DT, 1998-2000); White, Laron (NT/C, 1993-96); White, Mike (G, 1983-84); White, Tommy (FB, 1958-60); Whitehurst, Clay (SE, 1984-87); Whitley, Tom (T, 1944-47); Whitlock, Darin (C, 1985-86); Whitman, Steven K. (FB, 1977-79); Whitmire, Don (G, 1941-42); Whitmore, Todd

(DT, 2000); Whittlesley, C.S. (LG, 1916-17); Whitworth, J.B. "Ears" (T, 1930-31); Wicke, Dallas (QB, 1938-39); Wieseman, Bill (G, 1962-63); Wilbanks, Danny (FB, 1957); Wilcox, George Spigener (E, 1903-04); Wilcox, Tommy (DB, 1979-82); Wilder, Ken (T, 1968-69); Wilder, Roosevelt (FB, 1982); Wilga, Bob (G, 1951-53); Wilhite, Al (T, 1949-51); Wilkins, Red (E, 1961); Wilkinson, Everett (B/K, 1909-10, 1912-13); Wilkinson, Vernon (DB, 1984-85, 1987); Williams, Billy (T, 1951-52); Williams, Charlie (FB, 1980); Williams John Byrd (G, 1965-66); Williams, Kip (FL, 2002); Williams, Leslie (DE, 2002-03); Williams, Shaud (TB, 2002-03); Williams, Shaun (T, 2001); Williams, Sherman (TB, 1991-94); Williams, Steven Edward (DB, 1969-71); Williamson, Richard (SE, 1961-62); Williamson, Tank (P, 1990-91); Williamson, Temple (QB, 1935); Willis, Perry (SE, 1967); Willis, Virgil "Bud" (E, 1951-52); Wilson, Bobby (QB, 1950-52); Wilson, George (G, 1990-92); Wilson, George "Butch" (HB, 1960-62); Wilson, Jimmy (G, 1961-62); Wilson, Steve (DB, 1985-87); Wilson, Woody (LB, 1987-89); Wimbley, Prince (SE, 1988-92); Windham, Edward Price (B, 1897); Wingo, Richard "Rich" (LB, 1976-78); Winslett, Hoyt "Wu" (E, 1924-26); Winston, Owen (CB, 1995-96, 1998); Wise, Mack (HB, 1958); Wisniewski, Mark (K, 1998); Wofford, Curtis (DB, 1984); Wofford, Lloyd (DT, 1984); Wood, Bobby (DT, 1937-38); Wood, Russ (DE, 1980-82); Wood, William B, (E, 1957); Wood, William Dexter (SE, 1970-72); Woodruff, Glen (TE, 1971); Woodson, Danny (QB, 1990-91); Woody, Rock (CB, 1991); Worley, Butch (K, 1986); Wortham, Cornelius (LB, 2000-02, 2004); Wozniak, John (G, 1944-47); Wright, Bo (FB, 1985-87); Wright, Steve (T, 1962-63); Wyatt, Willie (NG, 1986-89); Wyatt, W.S. (QB, 1903-04); Wyhonic, John (G, 1939-41).

Yates, Ollie Porter (QB, 1954); Yelvington, Gary (DB, 1973-74); Young, Cecil Hugh (HB, 1902-03); Young, William A. (T, 1936); Youngleman, Sid (T, 1952-54).

Ziifle, Michael (K, 2002); Zivich, George (HB, 1937-38); Zow, Andrew (QB, 1998-2001); Zuga, Mike (C, 1987-89).

Appendix G: They Said It

25 Famous Alabama Quotes (not appearing in the rest of the book):

"A tie is like kissing your sister."

—Paul W. "Bear" Bryant

"At Alabama, our players do not win Heisman Trophies. Our teams win national championships."

—Paul W. "Bear" Bryant

"Coach Bryant always taught us we were special and never to accept being ordinary. I think that is one thing that has sustained Alabama through the years. Players with ordinary ability feeling somehow, someway they would find it within themselves to make a play to help Alabama win a football game. There is no way to describe the pride an Alabama player feels in himself and the tradition of the school."

—Kenny Stabler

"Every time a player goes out there, at least 20 people have some amount of influence on him. His mother has more influence than anyone. I know because I played, and I loved my mama."

—Paul W. "Bear" Bryant

"He literally knocked the door down. I mean right off its hinges. A policeman came in and asked who knocked the door down, and Coach Bryant said, 'I did.' The policeman just said 'Okay' and walked off."

—Jerry Duncan on Bryant after a 7-7 game with Tennessee

"How many people watch you give a final exam? [The reply is 'About 50.'] Well, I have 50,000 watch me give mine, every Sunday."

—Paul "Bear" Bryant to English professor Tommy Mayo at Texas A&M

"Here's a twenty, bury two."

—Paul W. "Bear" Bryant after being asked to chip in $10 to help cover the cost of a sports writer's funeral

"I can reach a kid who doesn't have any ability as long as he doesn't know it."

—Paul W. "Bear" Bryant

"I can't imagine being in the Hall of Fame with Coach Bryant. There ought to be two Hall of Fames, one for Coach Bryant and one for everyone else."

—Ozzie Newsome upon his induction into the Alabama Hall of Fame

"I grew up sneaking into Legion Field to see Alabama play. I vividly remember Joe Namath's first varsity game. I remember Kenny Stabler running down the sideline in the rain and mud against Auburn. I remember Lee Roy Jordan chasing down a running back and intimidating without even

245

hitting. I really appreciate the people who have contributed to this legacy and the tradition that has been passed down. And the people who have continued it—the goal-line stand and Van Tiffin's kick and all those memories of people who have carried on the tradition of Alabama football. I really feel blessed to have had the opportunity to be part of the tradition of Alabama football."

—Johnny Musso

"If anything goes bad, I did it. If anything goes semi-good, we did it. If anything goes real good, you did it. That's all it takes to get people to win football games."

—Paul W. "Bear" Bryant

"If I could reach my students like that, I'd teach for nothing."

—An Alabama professor after seeing a pre-game talk by Coach Paul "Bear" Bryant

"If you believe in yourself and have dedication and pride, and never quit, you'll be a winner. The price of victory is high, but so are the rewards."

—Paul W. "Bear" Bryant

"In life, you'll have your back up against the wall many times. You might as well get used to it."

—Paul W. "Bear" Bryant

"No man, I majored in journalism. It was easier."

—Joe Namath after being asked if he majored in basket weaving

"No one can help but be aware of the rich tradition that is associated with this team and this university. Tradition is a burden in many ways. To have a tradition like ours means that you can't lose your cool; to have tradition like ours means you always have to show class, even when you're not quite up to it; to have tradition like ours means that you have to do some things that you don't want to do and some you even think you can't do, simply because tradition demands it of you. On the other hand, tradition is that which allows us to prevail in ways that we could not otherwise."

—Former Alabama president David Matthews.

"Playing at Alabama taught me mental toughness, being a team player, being a winner."

—Cornelius Bennett

"Show class, have pride and display character. If you do, winning takes care of itself."

—Paul W. "Bear" Bryant

"The alumni are starting to grumble, and I'm the one starting it."

—Paul W. "Bear" Bryant

"The first person I would like to thank is the Lord for giving me the ability to play the game of football, because without the ability to play the game I would have been at Auburn."

—Marty Lyons

"The first thing a football coach needs when he's starting out is a wife who's willing to put up with a whole lot of neglect. The second thing is a five-year contract."

—Paul W. "Bear" Bryant

"The first time you quit, it's hard. The second time, it gets easier. The third time, you don't even have to think about it."

—Paul W. "Bear" Bryant

"This must be what God looks like."

—George Blanda, who played for Bryant at Kentucky,
upon his first meeting the coach

"What matters . . . is not the size of the dog in the fight, but of the fight in the dog."

—Paul W. "Bear" Bryant

"You don't have to flaunt your success, but you don't have to apologize for it."

—Gene Stallings

Credits

Though the Tuscaloosa News was kind enough to let me liberally steal from my own stories, the following articles appear in their entirety (except for the game story against Western Carolina). In technical- and legalize-speak, all stories appear courtesy of the Tuscaloosa News, a New York Times Publication.

"Jury Selection Starts Monday in Young Trial." January 23, 2005, Page 1A.

"Where do we go from here?" February 13, 2005, Page 1A.

"Is Tommy Gallion the Most Important Lawyer in Alabama?" June 13, 2005, Page 1A.

"Lawyer mugged; Cottrell files stolen." May 07, 2004, Page 1A.

"Congress to Hold Hearings on NCAA." May 14, 2004, Page 1A.

"Crimson Tide strong safety has rich family legacy." September 11, 2004, Gameday special section.

"Bittersweet victory." September 19, 2004, Page 1C.

"Family matters." September 18, 2004, Gameday special section.

"Why the hostility?" October 23, 2004, Gameday special section.

"College Classics: Is Alabama-Auburn the biggest rivalry in college football?" November 20, 2004, Gameday special section.

"Yanni vs. Forrest Gump? You Decide." December 31, 2004, Gameday special section (page 3).

A condensed version of "A Family Affair" (June 20, 2004, Page 1C) appears in the first chapter of Part III.

Gene Marsh's commentary, "College Athletics is not Doom and Gloom," was printed in both the March 20 edition of the Tuscaloosa News and the Vanderbilt Journal of Entertainment Law and Practice.

Many of the historical photos appear courtesy of the Paul W. Bryant Museum.

Acknowledgments

$\mathcal{Y}$ou never realize how hard it is to thank everyone until you have to do it. The last thing I wanted to do was miss someone, so if I did let me apologize beforehand.

First off, I have to thank my family for their love, help and support. I don't know how many times you all must have wanted to tell me to find a regular job, but instead bit your tongues. Thanks.

Same goes to my extended family of friends throughout the country. Many will get a second mention, but you all know who you are.

Second, I have to thank Rick Rinehart of Taylor Trade Publishing for saying yes to making me an author. Additional kudos to Brenda Hadenfeldt for pointing me in the right direction and thanks to Jehanne Schweitzer, production editor, and Barbara Jarrett, proofreader.

This book would not have been possible if it wasn't for the people at the Tuscaloosa News, primarily publisher Tim Thompson, Executive Editor Douglas Ray and Managing Editor Gregory Enns. I also can't thank Executive Sports Editor David Wasson enough for hiring me in the first place (even after he was told he would be an idiot not to) and his support. He and his wife Jo'el are special people.

Although I did the writing, a number of people contributed to the stories that made the newspaper. Special thanks to Cecil Hurt (who is a walking encyclopedia when it comes to Alabama football), Harold Stout, Andrew Carroll, Michael Lowe, Michael Southern and Tommy Deas.

A big thank you to Robert Sutton for helping with the photographs from the Tuscaloosa News. The rest are courtesy of the Paul W. Bryant Museum, where I was also able to do research. Thanks to everyone there, especially Taylor Watson, Clem Gryska, Kenneth Gaddy and Brad Green.

Although everyone at the Tuscaloosa News has my gratitude, I specifically want to mention Alisa Beckwith, Chad Berry, Dana Beyerle, Anthony Bratina, Jerry Carpenter, Mark Hughes Cobb, Tracy Cox, Gilbert Cruz, Danny DeJarnette, Anna Maria Della Costa, Robert DeWitt, Dwayne Fatherree, Shweta Gamble, Jason Getz, Carla Gillespie, Emerson Zora Hamsa, Alyda Hardy, Stephanie Hoops, Josh Jackson, Michael James, Christine Jesson, Adam Jones, Johnny Kampis, Dan Lopez, Donald Malone, Carolyn Mason, Bill Maxwell, Alison Mitchell, Jason Morton, Michael Palmer, Reggie Perkins, Steve Reeves, Markeshia Ricks, Amy Robinson, Lydia Seabol, Trent Seibert, Jane Self, Jeff Self, Ernie Shipe, Carmen Sisson, Peggy Skelton, Betty Slowe, Porfirio Solorzano, Tommy Stevenson, Janet Sudnik, Stephanie Taylor, Ben Windham and April Wortham.

250

Thanks to everyone in Alabama Athletics Media Relations, especially Larry White, Becky Hopf, Barry Allen, John Hayden, Brian Morgan, Roots Woodruff, Brenda Burnette, Michael Banks, Chris Woodfin, C.J. Guercio and Alex Greenbaum. Others with university ties include Patrick McDonald, Jana Morrison and the greatest intern of all-time, Mitch Dobbs.

Some people who have my eternal gratitude (in no particular order) include Clint Gordon and his parents Ron and Linda, Warren Flax and his entire family, Matt and Sarah Cross, Scott and Mary Noll, David and Lori Mazanec, Elise and Kurt Schreiner, Drew and Nicole Sidenar, Jim Rosendick (and Jaime Ruppert), Janet Wilson, Sue and Dave Priest, Jeff and Jen Ellsworth, Gorp, Weasel, Bob, George, Fletch, Brad and Louise Windsor, "Coach" Barb Havens, Dwight Nale, Amy Cutter, Dan Powers, Peter Madrid, Pedro Gomez, Lisa Hansen, the entire Wilson clan including Joyce, Will and Heather, Molly Jacobs, Jim Dunn, Douglas Adams, David Dorsey, Rose Tibayan, the Hedrick family, the Rioux family, Richard Benjamin, the Bacons, Bill Watterson, Irv Harrell, Denise Scott, Bob Nightengale, Wild Honey, Irv Harrell, David and Lisa Eisenstat, Brock Dethier, Ben Jones, Aaron Warford, Mr. and Mrs. Aaron Greenfield, the Sisks, Mike Purdy, Scott Bihr, Steve Bloch, Doug MacGregor, Heather Zaida and everyone else who helped me along the way.

A big shout-out to Trip, Bo and everyone at Innisfree, who helped keep me sane (or is it insane, I can't remember) during the writing process. Special thanks to Louise Snyder. If she hadn't walked into the Sheraton Harborplace in Fort Myers when she did, I never would have become a sports writer. Same goes for Sam Cook, Keith Gibson, Layton Charles and everyone else at the Fort Myers News-Press, in addition to the Tucson Citizen and Appleton Post-Crescent.

To Dan Davis, Steve Schoenfeld, Jon Quattlebaum, Dorn Martin and my father—I miss you all.

Index